# WITH THE OLD BREED

# WITH THE OLD BREED

## AT PELELIU AND OKINAWA

E. B. Sledge

OXFORD UNIVERSITY PRESS
New York    Oxford

Oxford University Press

Oxford   New York   Toronto
Delhi   Bombay   Calcutta   Madras   Karachi
Petaling Jaya   Singapore   Hong Kong   Tokyo
Nairobi   Dar es Salaam   Cape Town
Melbourne   Auckland

and associated companies in
Berlin   Ibadan

First published in 1981 by Presidio Press,
31 Pamaron Way, Novato, California 94947

First issued as an Oxford University Press paperback, 1990

Oxford is a registered trademark of Oxford University Press

Library of Congress Cataloging-in-Publication Data
Sledge, E. B. (Eugene Bondurant), 1923–
With the old breed at Peleliu and Okinawa / E.B. Sledge.
p.   cm.
Includes bibliographical references and index.
ISBN-13 978-0-19-506714-9 (PBK.)
ISBN 0-19-506714-2 (PBK.)
1. Sledge, E. B. (Eugene Bondurant), 1923–    . 2. Peleliu Island,
Battle of, 1944. 3. World War, 1939–1945—Campaigns—Japan—Okinawa
Island. 4. World War, 1939–1945—Personal narratives, American.
5. United States. Marine Corps. Regiment, 5th. Battalion, 3rd.
Company K—History. 6. United States. Marine Corps—Biography.
7. Soldiers—United States—Biography. 8. Okinawa Island (Japan)—
History. I. Title.
D767.99.P4S55   1991
940.54'26—dc20      91-36521
                 CIP
The quote from Kipling on facing pages is from "Prelude" In Departmental
Ditties and Ballads and Barrack Room Ballads, Macmillan and Co., 1915.

29 28 27 26 25

Printed in the United States of America

In memory of Capt. Andrew A. Haldane,
beloved company commander of K/3/5,
and to the Old Breed.


*The deaths ye died I have watched beside,*
*and the lives that ye led were mine.*

Kipling

Rifles were high and holy things to them, and they knew five-inch broadside guns. They talked patronizingly of the war, and were concerned about rations. They were the Leathernecks, the Old Timers. . . . They were the old breed of American regular, regarding the service as home and war as an occupation; and they transmitted their temper and character and viewpoint to the high-hearted volunteer mass which filled the ranks of the Marine Brigade. . . .

"The Leathernecks" in *Fix Bayonets*
by John W. Thomason, Jr., Charles Scribner's
Sons, Cornwall, N.Y. 1926. pp. x–xiii

# CONTENTS

# INTRODUCTION

I owe a large debt to John Keegan, the British military historian, for it was he who first told me about this book. It was in the mid-1980s and I was searching out testimonies from Second World War combatants for my book *Wartime*. "Have you read Sledge?," Keegan asked. I'd not heard of Sledge. His book had appeared a few years before with little fanfare and minimal critical notice. But Keegan, a sharp-eyed and comprehensive researcher, had found the book and was so impressed as to write later, in his book *The Second World War*, "Among the thousands of soldiers' stories, I am haunted by one from the Pacific War." Keegan found Sledge's account of his experience fighting in the South Pacific to be "one of the most arresting documents in war literature." Keegan's *haunted* is the right word. Readers of this book will find it hard to forget, and they will not easily brush away its troubling revelations about what the modern world periodically requires its boys to do and to suffer.

One cause of this book's distinction is that its author is not an "author." Sledge wrote this memoir less for strangers than to tell his own family what his war had been like; it was his wife who persuaded him to submit it to a publisher. The book is devoid of the literary expediencies and suavities that may occasion skepticism or disgust in more artistically self-conscious war memoirs. Sledge is so little an author in the pejorative sense that his eye seems never to wander from his subject to contemplate the literary effect he's creating. His style is like windowglass: you don't pause to notice it—you look through it to the actuality it discloses. It is this honesty, simplicity, and modesty that give Sledge's book its extraordinary power.

Eugene Bondurant Sledge ("Sledgehammer" to his later Marine Corps buddies and friends) was born in Mobile, Alabama, in 1923. As a child he was sickly, afflicted first with malaria and then with rheumatic fever, which weakened his heart and confined him to a wheelchair for nearly a year, during which he had to miss school. But he recovered to enter high school in 1938, where he did better in science and history than in algebra. Latin grammar bored him, but he found translating Caesar on warfare exciting. He liked classes in literature, except when the teacher left the world of solid data and began talking about "symbolism" and the like. He learned to play the snare drum and joined both the marching band and the school orchestra, and he was attracted more to informal than to organized sports. He especially liked sandlot baseball. "Discipline at home and at school was strict," he remembers, "so I stayed out of trouble."

His family lived on the edge of town, and his father, a physician, taught him to shoot and to observe things precisely and then to "describe . . . all I had seen." Sledge read a great deal and learned to revere Washington, Audubon, Daniel Boone, and of course Robert E. Lee (his grandfathers on both sides had been Confederate officers). On his father's phonograph Sledge played Bach, Haydn, Mozart, and Beethoven. He liked pretty girls a lot, but during adolescence he seemed to like riding, hunting, and fishing even more. He was a freshman at a two-year military college in Alabama when, a year after Pearl Harbor, he decided to enter the Marines, enlisting in a program that guaranteed him a further year of school before he joined. He underwent the dire passage from innocence to experience that he describes here from 1943 to 1946.

When the war was over, he found himself miraculously unwounded, at least in body. He studied business administration at Auburn University without much sense of vocation, and then worked briefly in real estate and insurance before perceiving that his interest in biology and zoology was pointing him toward a quite different career. He returned to Auburn for a master's degree, and then went to the University of Florida for a Ph.D. in zoology. Now a professor of biology specializing in ornithology at the University of Montevallo, Alabama, Sledge lives quietly near the university, which is not far from Birmingham. On the wall of his living room, reports Studs Terkel, who interviewed Sledge for his book "The Good War", there is a plaque, the gift of Sledge's buddies, honoring "one extraordinary Marine" and concluding, "God love you, Sledgehammer," a sentiment readers of this book may want to echo. Sledge still signs his letters "Semper Fidelis."

Of course it was the Marines that attracted this high-spirited, patriotic boy, unable to resist the "dress blue trousers, khaki shirt, necktie, and white barracks hat" of the recruiting sergeant. But it wasn't long before he became acquainted with the less attractive side of life in the Marines—the ritual humiliations and abuse incident to indoctrination and infantry training. Sledge rapidly toughened physically and mentally, learned to call the ground "the deck" and a wall a "bulkhead," and came to understand that if he didn't kill the Jap, the Jap would most certainly kill him. As one instructor urged, "Kick him in the balls before he kicks you in yours." He developed new self-confidence as he mastered the use of infantry weapons, with special emphasis on the Marines' favorite, the Ka-Bar knife. While Sledge and his fellow Marines grew tougher, however, they remained innocent, protected by their "naive optimism" from noticing that the destiny they were preparing for was to be destroyed or maimed. "The fact that our lives might end violently or that we might be crippled while we were still boys didn't seem to register."

Next, the crowded, smelly troop transport and the questions tugging at Sledge's mind: "Would I do my duty or be a coward? . . . Maybe I'd . . . disgrace my outfit by running away . . ." Then came more last-minute training, now on the island of New Caledonia, with ominous emphasis on bayonet and hand-to-hand techniques. Sledge and his buddies were shunted into the Fifth Regiment of the First Marine Division, replacing people killed and wounded on Guadalcanal and at Cape Gloucester, leaving Sledge proud to be a member of this distinguished unit, which fought at Belleau Wood in the First World War—and was later to fight in Korea and Vietnam. When Sledge joined, it was recuperating and training on the miserable island of Pavuvu, north of Guadalcanal. Sledge was assigned to the 60mm. mortar section of Company K, commanded by Captain Andrew A. ("Ack Ack") Haldane, remembered by Sledge as "the finest and most popular officer I ever knew." On Pavuvu rumors from the Guadalcanal campaign were numerous, and accounts of Japanese sadism and brutality fueled an attitude of murderous hatred for that enemy, hatred fully reciprocated, the Marines knew, by the Japanese. This mutual hatred, says Sledge, "resulted in savage, ferocious fighting with no holds barred. This was not the dispassionate killing seen on other fronts or in other wars. This was a brutish, primitive hatred, as characteristic of the horror of war in the Pacific as the palm trees and the islands." Once, after hearing blood-curdling screams close by at night, Sledge found the next morning that a Japanese soldier had jumped into a Marine fox-hole, where the Marine had jammed his stiff forefinger deep into the Japanese soldier's eye socket, killing him in agony. "Such," says Sledge, "was the physical horror and brutish reality of war for us." Both sides declined to take prisoners, and both sides defiled enemy corpses. Japanese skulls, thoroughly cleansed, became so popular as Marine and Army trophies that collecting them was finally officially forbidden.

The next assignment for the First Marine Division was the reduction of the Japanese-held island of Peleliu, one of the Palau island group, some 500 miles east of the Philippines. Many now believe that the invasion of this six-square-mile island was entirely unnecessary, irrelevant to the winning of the Pacific war; some believed it at the time, holding that the island could be bypassed safely without its posing any threat to the imminent invasion of the Philippines. Just to be sure, however, Admiral Nimitz decided to neutralize the threat. Sledge and his buddies did so, at a cost of 1,262 dead and 5,274 wounded Marines (and 10,000 dead Japanese). The fighting on Peleliu was supposed to last three or four days. It lasted for almost two months, from mid-September to November, 1944, and it was one of the worst slaughters of Marines in the Pacific, if one of the less well publicized. Tarawa became better known because it was virtually the first terrible island invasion, and Iwo Jima became famous in part because of Joe Rosenthal's photography; however, the conditions for fighting on Peleliu were about as bad as they could be. The weather was hot and humid, with frequent rain and temperatures rising to 115°. "On the fourth day," wrote Robert Martin, a *Time* magazine correspondent with the Marines, "there were as many casualties from heat prostration as from wounds." The island was of coral, with solid coral ridges and mesas in which the Japanese had been excavating caves and passage-ways for years. They used these for command posts and troop-assembly chambers, and they positioned mortars and artillery pieces and machine guns at the entrances, which were often protected by moveable steel doors. Although the Marines hopefully carried entrenching shovels, they found it virtually impossible to dig in through the coral, and thus they had to lie largely on the surface under deadly accurate mortar and artillery fire. To hit the jagged coral deck meant cutting and abrading yourself each time, and Marine uniforms and shoes were torn to bits. Because digging the usual toilet cat-holes was impossible, excrement was everywhere before the island was secured, its stench blending with the smells of the dead, with the whole hellish scene baked in the hot sun. As Martin reported, "Peleliu is a terrible place."

Few combat veterans have remembered as well as Sledge the effects of fear, and Sledge knows that the fear is not just of being killed or wounded, it is fear of something even worse—fear of not being able to take it and exhibiting the symptoms of cowardice to an audience of men who have trusted you. Sledge tells how when his landing craft approaches the beach, the naval gunfire deafening everyone, his fear is of something seldom mentioned in more heroic and bellicose military narratives: "I . . . felt that my bladder would surely empty itself and reveal me to be the coward I was." But once ashore under heavy fire, Sledge forgets himself in his pity for the others. As he looks around and sees Marines being slaughtered—his word for it—he feels simply sick. As he writes, "I had tasted the bitterest essence of war, the sight of helpless comrades being slaughtered, and it filled me with disgust." Disgusting as well is his first sight of a Japanese corpse, its viscera displayed and "glistening, . . . bespecked with fine coral dust." And when he sees a medical corpsman bending over a boy Marine who just died, he invokes a word that will resonate throughout this book. The word is *waste*:

> A blood-soaked battle dressing was on the side of the dead man's neck. His fine, handsome, boyish face was ashen. "What a pitiful waste," I thought. "He can't be a day over seventeen years old." I thanked God his mother couldn't see him. The corpsman held the dead Marine's chin tenderly between the thumb and fingers of his left hand and made the sign of the cross with his right hand. Tears streamed down his dusty, tanned, grief-contorted face while he sobbed quietly.

Prayer is Sledge's frequent solace, the Lord's Prayer and the 23d Psalm his favorites. It is "Yea, though I walk through the valley of the shadow of death, I will fear no evil" that he recites as his battalion attacks en masse, running across the bare airfield, and he sees Marines everywhere going down, blown up and torn apart by artillery or mangled by machine-gun bullets. Sledge can't imagine how he survived this massacre, and he concludes that this murderous dash across several hundreds yards under massed fire was his very worst combat experience. Not long after, in a moment of silence during a quiet conversation, he hears, as he says, "a loud voice say clearly and distinctly, 'You will survive the war!' " No one in the group has spoken. The voice has been heard by Sledge alone. Perhaps he has come momentarily unhinged, or perhaps the intensity of the unspoken wish to come out alive has skewed his hearing and his understanding. Normally skeptical of visions and ghost stories and the like, Sledge is persuaded that God spoke to him that night. As a result, he says, he resolved (like other infantrymen who have barely escaped death) to make his life "amount to something after the war."

Astonished and appalled by the unbelievable carnage, Sledge felt he had to make a record of it. Diaries were forbidden, but in a little rubber bag he took from a Japanese body Sledge carried his small New Testament, and into its pages he slipped tiny sheets of paper covered with notes. His frequent recourse to his Testament misled his buddies into imagining him more pious than he was. He was actually, as he says, "keepin' notes." After some patrolling and night defensive work, during which one K Company Marine goes noisily mad and becomes quiet only when hit with a shovel—in the morning he turns out to be dead—Sledge's battalion encounters the Army infantrymen of the veteran 81st Division sent to reinforce the Peleliu operation. The popular and amusing animosities between Army and Marines are suddenly laid aside. Things are now too serious for the normal Marine sport of barking at the dogfaces, and as a result of common experience, says Sledge, "We respected each other completely."

"Something in me died at Peleliu," Sledge writes. One of the many casualties there is his initial innocence about human evil. Without turning mechanically pessimistic or cynical, Sledge is obliged to complicate and deepen his under-standing of human possibility when he watches a fellow Marine use his Ka-Bar knife to extract gold teeth from a wounded but still living Japanese, who kicks and writhes as the Marine goes to work. Frustrated and impatient, the Marine finally eases his task by slicing his prisoner's cheeks ear to ear, which, if it makes him gurgle in his own blood and thrash about, exposes the teeth nicely. Watching this, Sledge learns what every generation would learn if it could see its youth engaged in infantry fighting. As a Marine sergeant told Philip Caputo during the Vietnam War, "Before you leave here, sir, you're going to learn that one of the most brutal things in the world is your average nineteen-year-old American boy."

Of nasty, sadistic episodes like this, Sledge writes: "Such was the incredible cruelty that decent men could commit when reduced to a brutish existence in their fight for survival amid the violent death, terror, tension, fatigue, and filth that was the infantryman's war." He goes on to emphasize that such an under-standing of human behavior, obvious to all on the line, was not readily available to those removed only a short distance to the rear. If you are back only a couple of hundred yards behind anger and cruelty and hysteria and fear of death, you are too far back to understand, and that is one of the reasons Sledge has written this book. It is about the mystique—that is the right word—of killing to avoid being killed, torturing to avoid being tortured. At various headquarters reason may govern, but the line is a place of passion and madness. Sledge uses the words *totally incomprehensible*, absolute as they are, responsibly when, observ-ing that "Peleliu . . . made savages of us all," he declares, "We existed in an environment totally incomprehensible to men behind the lines—service troops and civilians."

Sledge and his buddies can hardly believe it when, ragged, filthy, and hollow-eyed, they are finally relieved by Army infantry—which required six more weeks to end the battle. Sledge's Company K, formerly 235 strong, climbs aboard the departing transport with only 85 survivors, including two of the original seven officers. Back on Pavuvu, there is the shock of re-encountering people innocent of murder and cruelty and fear—a nice Red Cross girl who proffers paper cups of grapefruit juice to men coming off the ship; a new, unblooded second lieu-tenant whose uniform is too neat and clean and who offends Sledge by calling him "Sonny." Back under tents, Company K receives replacements, and before long training resumes and rumors begin to imply that there is going to be another rugged campaign soon. News about the carnage then in progress on Iwo Jima suggested that the Japanese were resisting more insanely the nearer the war came to their main islands. Okinawa was very near.

As a defensive position, Okinawa was a Peleliu ten times larger. The island was sixty miles long and eighteen miles wide at its widest point. It was defended by 110,000 Japanese who had excavated and fortified elaborate caves, tunnels, and casemates concealing a deadly accumulation of artillery. This time, Sledge's battalion was in reserve at first, but it still had to land on the beach on D-Day—April 1, 1945. Climbing down the landing net, Sledge was still frightened, although, having been through Peleliu, not as frightened as before. But this time there proved little reason for fright: the landing was virtually unopposed, and the soldiers and Marines, a force ultimately numbering half a million, waded ashore smiling and even singing. To Sledge, it was "the most pleasant surprise of the war." The weather the first few days was cool and dry, too, and the deck was not of coral but of eminently diggable dirt. The smell so far, was mainly of pine trees. The battle plan was first to attack across the island, cutting it in two, and then for the Marines to attack to the north and the Army to the south. Cutting the island in half took only four days: resistance was light and scattered. The seizing of the northern part of the island was not too bad either: the 6th Marine Division did it in seven days. In the south, however, the Army met fantastic resistance, and soon the Marines were called to assist. The 1st Marine Division relieved the badly chewed-up 27th Infantry Division, and Sledge was headed for action again, "filled with dread." This time he was on the line or mortally near it for fifty days, beginning May 1 with a failed Marine attack on one of the numerous southern ridges, in rain and mud against terrible fire. The news arriving May 8 that Germany had surrendered did little to raise Marine Corps spirits, for everyone knew that the Japanese on Okinawa would resist until all were killed and that, as Sledge says, "Japan would have to be invaded with the same gruesome prospects." But only a fatuously optimistic Marine could believe he would survive long enough for that horror.

Today, almost fifty years later, Sledge still has nightmares about "the bloody, muddy month of May on Okinawa," when the artillery fire from both sides was so heavy and unremitting that he had a constant headache. The Japanese were lodged so deeply in their caves that the American artillery hardly bothered them, and when it paused they resumed their defense with rifles, grenades, mortars, and machine guns, firing at corpsmen and litter-bearers in purposeful contempt for Western civilities. The battlefield was soon scarred, cratered, and treeless, a mess of mud and water-filled holes and slippery ridges, looking like Verdun in the Great War. A week-long stay in a muddy hole on Half Moon ridge near Shuri, the main Japanese point of resistance, almost drove Sledge insane: there he existed in an atmosphere of unburied, stinking Japanese and Marine corpses, maggots, flies, rain, dysentery, knee-deep mud, and the constant fear of death at any moment. "It was the most ghastly corner of hell I had ever witnessed," Sledge writes. Peleliu had been bad, but this was "an environment so degrading I believed we had been flung into hell's own cesspool." To slip in the mud and fall was to have one's clothing filled with wriggling maggots from the rotting corpses, and "if a Marine slipped and slid down the back slope of the muddy ridge, he was apt to reach the bottom vomiting.'' The war, for Sledge and the others fighting in conditions like this, ''was insanity.'' And some Marines went insane, reduced by the shelling to crying or mad shouting and screaming. Others were removed from the line suffering from malaria or pneumonia. Those with trench foot stayed put.

The Japanese, finally driven out of their Shuri positions, withdrew further south to a last-stand defense at Kunishi Ridge, where as usual they occupied deep caves largely resistant to artillery, aerial bombing, and naval gunfire. Despite hopes for some respite, Sledge's company had to continue with its dreadful work, and, sensing that his luck was running out—one can't expect to beat the terrible odds forever—Sledge was in a near-panic. But he did not break. When his battalion finally reached the southern shore of the island, Company K was down to fifty men. The reduction of Okinawa had taken eighty-two days. Pfc. Eugene Sledge had lost twenty-five pounds, and on his hands and arms were open sores that would not heal for months. But a final indignity: his battalion had to now move north again, burying the blackened Japanese corpses and salvaging brass shell cases. American casualties on Okinawa came to almost 40,000. There were also more than 26,000 ''neuropsychiatric'' cases—men evacuated after psychological breakdowns. In addition to the destruction of the Japanese defenders, some 42,000 Okinawan civilians were killed. Knowing all too well what the forthcoming invasion of Japan would mean for them, Sledge and the lucky survivors in his outfit heard the news of the A-bombing of Hiroshima and Nagasaki with ''an indescribable sense of relief.'' They would live, even if shaken and illuminated for a lifetime about the depth of human iniquity.

Sledge's testimony about these almost incredible events is entirely credible because of his evident decency and his remoteness from any sort of disingenuousness, actual or literary. His way with both life and language is straight, without irony, hyperbole, or the desire to show off. If another writer asserted that in the shower he had seen a long-time member of the Old Breed, Gunnery Sergeant St. Elmo M. Haney, briskly scrubbing his genital organs with a GI brush, we might disbelieve. When Sledge tells us this, we know it is true. Veterans of front lines everywhere will applaud the accuracy with which Sledge registers the sights and sounds of combat. ''Authors'' (and screenwriters) are likely to assert that bullets ''whine.'' Sledge knows that they snap. (It is artillery shells that whine, while mortar shells whisper faintly.) Also remarkably accurate is Sledge's memory of physical details. He recalls exactly what it's like to hike with a heavy pack in a long column that frequently, and inexplicably, stops. ''If a man put down his load . . . , he was sure to hear, 'Pick up your gear; we're moving out!' '' When the column paused, each man was faced with what Sledge calls, without irony, a ''big decision'': ''The big decision in every man's mind at each pause in the column's forward progress was whether to drop his load and hope for a lengthy pause or to stand there and support all the weight rather than putting it down and having to pick it up again right away.''

Sledge's precise description and honest narration accommodate without apology or ex post facto self-consciousness his boyish pride in being a Marine and helping to win the war, as well as his natural disdain for those in the rear so unimaginative as not to be able to understand what the line troops go through. He honestly hero-worships his company's skipper, Captain Haldane, and he honestly reports his sobs when he hears that Haldane has been killed—and he still mourns him after all these years. His sharp eye for evidence of nobility and courage in others prompts him to celebrate the ''selfless dedication'' of the corpsmen. Sledge's sense of honor obliges him to keep his promises, even apparently trivial ones. His book indicates the way he has been true to his wartime experience: he has not allowed the passage of time or subsequent political history to soften the cruel outlines of an experience he must not euphemize or forget.

After fifteen days of fighting on Peleliu, Sledge was finally overcome by the strain:

> I felt myself choking up. I slowly turned my back to the men facing me, as I sat on my helmet, and put my face in my hands to try to shut out reality. I began sobbing. . . . My body shuddered and shook.

But what occasioned this outburst is less Sledge's own fear than his pity for others. He has just heard of a severely wounded Marine nearby whose body, lifted onto a litter, ''came apart.'' ''I was sickened and revolted to see healthy young men get hurt and killed day after day. I felt I couldn't take any more.'' It is this extraordinary compassion that makes Sledge so unique a memoirist of war. One expects an infantryman or Marine to feel fear and pity for himself, but it is rare for a soldier to be distraught because he feels for others (total strangers, often), and to be distraught without a trace of sentimental affectation or secret self-congratulation. For this reason, Sledge doubtless suffered more than many of his fellow Marines, and he has not notably hardened since.

''I don't like to watch television shows with violence in them,'' he says today. A poem he likes to quote comes from the First World War, but he knows it will serve for the Second and subsequent wars as well. It is Wilfred Owen's ''Insensibility''—Owen's ironic celebration of men devoid of compassion and imagination, whose experiences in war are easier (and more forgettable) than those of their sensitive comrades:

> Happy are men who yet before they are killed
> Can let their veins run cold.
> Whom no compassion fleers

Or makes their feet
Sore on the alleys cobbled with their brothers.

.  .  .

Happy are those who lose imagination;
They have enough to carry with ammunition.

.  .  .

Happy the soldier home, with not a notion
How somewhere, every dawn, some men attack. . . .

.  .  .

But cursed are dullards whom no cannon stuns . . .
By choice they made themselves immune
To pity. . . .

If it was Sledge's fine sensibility that caused him to suffer more than some, it is that same sensibility that in this book has kept the distinctions firm, the compassion warm, the imagination agile, and the values admirable.

PAUL FUSSELL

# PREFACE

This book is an account of my World War II experiences in training and in combat with Company K, 3d Battalion, 5th Marine Regiment, 1st Marine Division during the Peleliu and Okinawa campaigns. It is not a history, and it is not my story alone. I have attempted, rather, to be the spokesman for my comrades, who were swept with me into the abyss of war. I hope they will approve my efforts.

I began writing this account immediately after Peleliu while we were in rest camp on Pavuvu Island. I outlined the entire story with detailed notes as soon as I returned to civilian life, and I have written down certain episodes during the years since then. Mentally, I have gone over and over the details of these events, but I haven't been able to draw them all together and write them down until now.

I have done extensive research with published and unpublished histories and documents pertaining to my division's role in the Peleliu and Okinawa campaigns. I have been amazed at the vast difference in the perception of events recounted in these narratives as contrasted to my experience on the front line.

My Pacific war experiences have haunted me, and it has been a burden to retain this story. But time heals, and the nightmares no longer wake me in a cold sweat with pounding heart and racing pulse. Now I can write this story, painful though it is to do so. In writing it I'm fulfilling an obligation I have long felt to my comrades in the 1st Marine Division, all of whom suffered so much for our country. None came out unscathed. Many gave their lives, many their health, and some their sanity. All who survived will long remember the horror they would rather forget. But they suffered and they did their duty so a sheltered homeland can enjoy the peace that was purchased at such a high cost. We owe those Marines a profound debt of gratitude.

E.B.S.

# ACKNOWLEDGMENTS

A lthough this is a personal account, which was originally written for my family, there have been numerous people who have helped shape it into book form for the general reader.

First I want to thank Jeanne, my wonderful wife. She typed the Peleliu portion of the manuscript from stacks of my handwritten pages, and was the first to suggest that this narrative might be of interest to others than our family. She has encouraged and aided me with ideas, advice, editing, and typing. That the lengthy original manuscript was completed after years of spare-time writing and research during graduate school and child rearing is due as much to her assistance as to my efforts.

Deepest appreciation is extended to my editor, Lt. Col. Robert W. Smith, USMC (Ret.). During his last year as editor of the *Marine Corps Gazette,* he became interested in seeing this complete account in book form during our work on extracts which appeared as a three-part article, "Peleliu: A Neglected Battle." His interest has been my good fortune. In addition to his vast editing skill, Bob has been an inexhaustible source of good ideas and advice. On more than one occasion he has bolstered my sagging morale when I've become weary with what is not a happy subject. His objectivity has guided me through the forest when I couldn't see the trees, and when it was painful to both of us to omit parts of the original. I am grateful for his sensitivity and impeccable professionalism.

I want to thank my publisher, Col. Robert V. Kane, USA (Ret.), and

Adele Horwitz, Editor in Chief of Presidio Press, who saw in my verbose original manuscript a story that should be told.

This book could not have been written without the benefit of Marine Corps historical material. My requests for help were rapidly and efficiently granted in every instance. For this I want to thank Brig. Gen. Edwin H. Simmons USMC (Ret.), Director of Marine Corps History and Museums, Benis Frank, Ralph Donnelly, and Henry I. Shaw.

For their help and encouragement I express my gratitude to Brig. Gen. Walter McIlhenny, USMC (Ret.), Lt. Col. John A. Crown, USMC (Ret.), Brig. Gen. Austin Shofner, USMC (Ret.), Capt. John A. Moran, USMC (Ret.), and Maj. Allan Bevilacqua, USMC (Ret.).

M. Sgt. Robert F. Fleischauer, USMC (Ret.), is due recognition and thanks for his fine work on the maps and sketches.

I thank Mrs. Hilda Van Landingham for typing the first draft of the Okinawa portion. Mary Frances Tipton, Reference Librarian at the University of Montevallo, merits my deepest appreciation for her help. Dr. Lucille Griffith, Professor Emeritus of History, University of Montevallo, was one of the first people to suggest this account be published. Her faith in it is redeemed, and I thank her.

My heartiest thanks to my old K/3/5 buddies who have assisted so much in verifying company casualty figures, countless other details, and photograph identification: Ted (Tex) Barrow, Henry A. Boyes, Valton Burgin, Jessie Crumbacker, Art Dimick, John Hedge, T. L. Hudson, William Leyden, Sterling Mace, Tom Matheny, Jim McEney, Vincent Santos, George Sarrett, Thomas (Stumpy) Stanley. If I have omitted any names, I apologize. Any errors in the manuscript are solely mine.

I appreciate the cooperation and understanding of my sons John and Henry and their patience with a father who was often preoccupied with past events.

A grant from the University of Montevallo Faculty Research Committee aided in the preparation of the manuscript.

E.B.S.

# PART I

PELELIU: A NEGLECTED BATTLE

# FOREWORD TO PART I

The 1st Marine Division's assault on the Central Pacific island of Peleliu thirty-seven years ago was, in the overall perspective of World War II, a relatively minor engagement. After a war is over, it's deceptively easy to determine which battles were essential and which could have gone unfought. Thus, in hindsight, Peleliu's contribution to total victory was dubious. Moreover, World War II itself has faded into the mists with the more immediate combat in Korea and Vietnam.

To the men of the 1st Marine Division who made the assault on Peleliu (the youngest of whom are in their fifties today), there was nothing minor about it. For those who were there, it was a bloody, wearying, painful, and interminable engagement. For a single-division operation, the losses were extraordinarily heavy.

Eugene B. Sledge served in Company K, 3d Battalion, 5th Marines throughout the battle. I had the privilege of commanding Company I of the same battalion in the same period. His account awoke vivid memories which had lain dormant for years.

Don't read this personal narrative seeking the significance of the battle or of grand strategy. Rather read it for what it is, intense combat as seen by an individual Marine rifleman. For those who have experienced battle elsewhere, the similarities will be obvious.

John A. Crown
Lieutenant Colonel
U.S. Marine Corps

Atlanta, Georgia

# CHAPTER ONE

# MAKING OF A MARINE

I enlisted in the Marine Corps on 3 December 1942 at Marion, Alabama. At the time I was a freshman at Marion Military Institute. My parents and brother Edward had urged me to stay in college as long as possible in order to qualify for a commission in some technical branch of the U.S. Army. But, prompted by a deep feeling of uneasiness that the war might end before I could get overseas into combat, I wanted to enlist in the Marine Corps as soon as possible. Ed, a Citadel graduate and a second lieutenant in the army, suggested life would be more beautiful for me as an officer. Mother and Father were mildly distraught at the thought of me in the Marines as an enlisted man—that is, "cannon fodder." So when a Marine recruiting team came to Marion Institute, I compromised and signed up for one of the Corps' new officer training programs. It was called V-12.

The recruiting sergeant wore dress blue trousers, a khaki shirt, necktie, and white barracks hat. His shoes had a shine the likes of which I'd never seen. He asked me lots of questions and filled out numerous official papers. When he asked, "Any scars, birthmarks, or other unusual features?" I described an inch-long scar on my right knee. I asked why such a question. He replied, "So they can identify you on some Pacific beach after the Japs blast off your dog tags." This was my introduction to the stark realism that characterized the Marine Corps I later came to know.

The college year ended the last week of May 1943. I had the month of

June at home in Mobile before I had to report 1 July for duty at Georgia Tech in Atlanta.

I enjoyed the train trip from Mobile to Atlanta because the train had a steam engine. The smoke smelled good, and the whistle added a plaintive note reminiscent of an unhurried life. The porters were impressed and most solicitous when I told them, with no little pride, that I was on my way to becoming a Marine. My official Marine Corps meal ticket got me a large, delicious shrimp salad in the dining car and the admiring glances of the steward in attendance.

On my arrival in Atlanta, a taxi deposited me at Georgia Tech, where the 180-man Marine detachment lived in Harrison Dormitory. Recruits were scheduled to attend classes year round (in my case, about two years), graduate, and then go to the Marine base at Quantico, Virginia, for officers' training.

A Marine regular, Capt. Donald Payzant, was in charge. He had served with the 1st Marine Division on Guadalcanal. Seeming to glory in his duty and his job as our commander, he loved the Corps and was salty and full of swagger. Looking back, I realize now that he had survived the meat grinder of combat and was simply glad to be in one piece with the good fortune of being stationed at a peaceful college campus.

Life at Georgia Tech was easy and comfortable. In short, we didn't know there was a war going on. Most of the college courses were dull and uninspiring. Many of the professors openly resented our presence. It was all but impossible to concentrate on academics. Most of us felt we had joined the Marines to fight, but here we were college boys again. The situation was more than many of us could stand. At the end of the first semester, ninety of us—half of the detachment—flunked out of school so we could go into the Corps as enlisted men.

When the navy officer in charge of academic affairs called me in to question me about my poor academic performance, I told him I hadn't joined the Marine Corps to sit out the war in college. He was sympathetic to the point of being fatherly and said he would feel the same way if he were in my place.

Captain Payzant gave the ninety of us a pep talk in front of the dormitory the morning we were to board the train for boot camp at the Marine Corps Recruit Depot, San Diego, California. He told us we were the best men and the best Marines in the detachment. He said he admired our spirit for wanting to get into the war. I think he was sincere.

After the pep talk, buses took us to the railway station. We sang and cheered the whole way. We were on our way to war at last. If we had only known what lay ahead of us!

Approximately two and a half years later, I came back through the Atlanta railway station on my way home. Shortly after I stepped off the car for a stroll, a young army infantryman walked up to me and shook hands. He said he had noticed my 1st Marine Division patch and the campaign ribbons on my chest and wondered if I had fought at Peleliu. When I said I had, he told me he just wanted to express his undying admiration for men of the 1st Marine Division.

He had fought with the 81st Infantry Division (Wildcats) which had come in to help us at Peleliu.* He was a machine gunner, had been hit by Japanese fire on Bloody Nose Ridge, and was abandoned by his army comrades. He knew he would either die of his wounds or be cut up by the Japanese when darkness fell. Risking their lives, some Marines had moved in and carried him to safety. The soldier said he was so impressed by the bravery, efficiency, and esprit of the Marines he saw on Peleliu that he swore to thank every veteran of the 1st Marine Division he ever ran across.

The "Dago people"—as those of us bound for San Diego were called—boarded a troop train in a big railroad terminal in Atlanta. Everyone was in high spirits, as though we were headed for a picnic instead of boot camp—and a war. The trip across the country took several days and was uneventful but interesting. Most of us had never been west, and we enjoyed the scenery. The monotony of the trip was broken with card games, playing jokes on each other, and waving, yelling, and whistling at any and all women visible. We ate some meals in dining cars on the train; but at certain places the train pulled onto a siding, and we ate in the restaurant in the railroad terminal.

Nearly all of the rail traffic we passed was military. We saw long trains composed almost entirely of flatcars loaded with tanks, halftracks, artillery pieces, trucks, and other military equipment. Many troop trains passed us going both ways. Most of them carried army troops. This rail traffic impressed on us the enormousness of the nation's war effort.

We arrived in San Diego early one morning. Collecting our gear, we fell into ranks outside our cars as a first sergeant came along and told the NCOs on our train which buses to get us aboard. This first sergeant looked old to us teenagers. Like ourselves, he was dressed in a green wool Marine

---

*Together with the 1st Marine Division, the U.S. Army's 81st Infantry Division comprised the III Amphibious Corps commanded by Maj. Gen. Roy S. Geiger, USMC. For the Palau operation, the 1st Marine Division assaulted Peleliu on 15 September 1944 while the 81st Division took Angaur Island and provided a regiment as corps reserve. The 81st Division relieved the 1st Marine Division on Peleliu on 20 October and secured the island on 27 November.

uniform, but he had campaign ribbons on his chest. He also wore the green French *fourragère* on his left shoulder. (Later, as a member of the 5th Marine Regiment, I would wear the braided cord around my left arm with pride.) But this man sported, in addition, two single loops outside his arm. That meant he had served with a regiment (either the 5th or 6th Marines) that had received the award from France for distinguished combat service in World War I.

The sergeant made a few brief remarks to us about the tough training we faced. He seemed friendly and compassionate, almost fatherly. His manner threw us into a false sense of well-being and left us totally unprepared for the shock that awaited us when we got off those buses.

"Fall out, and board your assigned buses!" ordered the first sergeant.

"All right, you people. Get aboard them buses!" the NCOs yelled. They seemed to have become more authoritarian as we approached San Diego.

After a ride of only a few miles, the buses rolled to a stop in the big Marine Corps Recruit Depot—boot camp. As I looked anxiously out the window, I saw many platoons of recruits marching along the streets. Each drill instructor (DI) bellowed his highly individual cadence. The recruits looked as rigid as sardines in a can. I grew nervous at seeing how serious —or rather, scared—they seemed.

"All right, you people, off them damned buses!"

We scrambled out, lined up with men from the other buses, and were counted off into groups of about sixty. Several trucks rolled by carrying work parties of men still in boot camp or who had finished recently. All looked at us with knowing grins and jeered, "You'll be sorreee." This was the standard, unofficial greeting extended to all recruits.

Shortly after we debused, a corporal walked over to my group. He yelled, "Patoon, teehut. Right hace, forwart huah. Double time, huah."

He ran us up and down the streets for what seemed hours and finally to a double line of huts that would house us for a time. We were breathless. He didn't even seem to be breathing hard.

"Patoon halt, right hace!" He put his hands on his hips and looked us over contemptuously. "You people are stupid," he bellowed. From then on he tried to prove it every moment of every day. "My name is Corporal Doherty. I'm your drill instructor. This is Platoon 984. If any of you idiots think you don't need to follow my orders, just step right out here and I'll beat your ass right now. Your soul may belong to Jesus, but your ass belongs to the Marines. You people are *recruits*. You're *not* Marines. You may not have what it takes to be Marines."

No one dared move, hardly even to breathe. We were all humbled, because there was no doubt the DI meant exactly what he said.

Corporal Doherty wasn't a large man by any standard. He stood about five feet ten inches, probably weighed around 160 pounds, and was muscular with a protruding chest and flat stomach. He had thin lips, a ruddy complexion, and was probably as Irish as his name. From his accent I judged him to be a New Englander, maybe from Boston. His eyes were the coldest, meanest green I ever saw. He glared at us like a wolf whose first and foremost desire was to tear us limb from limb. He gave me the impression that the only reason he didn't do so was that the Marine Corps wanted to use us for cannon fodder to absorb Japanese bullets and shrapnel so genuine Marines could be spared to capture Japanese positions.

That Corporal Doherty was tough and hard as nails none of us ever doubted. Most Marines recall how loudly their DIs yelled at them, but Doherty didn't yell very loudly. Instead he shouted in an icy, menacing manner that sent cold chills through us. We believed that if he didn't scare us to death, the Japs couldn't kill us. He was always immaculate, and his uniform fitted him as if the finest tailor had made it for him. His posture was erect, and his bearing reflected military precision.

The public pictures a DI wearing sergeant stripes. Doherty commanded our respect and put such fear into us that he couldn't have been more effective if he had had the six stripes of a first sergeant instead of the two of a corporal. One fact emerged immediately with stark clarity: this man would be the master of our fates in the weeks to come.

Doherty rarely drilled us on the main parade ground, but marched or double-timed us to an area near the beach of San Diego Bay. There the deep, soft sand made walking exhausting, just what he wanted. For hours on end, for days on end, we drilled back and forth across the soft sand. My legs ached terribly for the first few days, as did those of everyone else in the platoon. I found that when I concentrated on a fold of the collar or cap of the man in front of me or tried to count the ships in the bay, my muscles didn't ache as badly. To drop out of ranks because of tired legs was unthinkable. The standard remedy for such shirking was to "double time in place to get the legs in shape"—before being humiliated and berated in front of the whole platoon by the DI. I preferred the pain to the remedy.

Before heading back to the hut area at the end of each drill session, Doherty would halt us, ask a man for his rifle, and tell us he would demonstrate the proper technique for holding the rifle while creeping and crawling. First, though, he would place the butt of the rifle on the sand, release the weapon, and let it drop, saying that anyone who did that would have a miserable day of it. With so many men in the platoon, it was uncanny how often he asked to use my rifle in this demonstration. Then, after demonstrating how to cradle the rifle, he ordered us to creep and crawl. Naturally, the man in front kicked sand onto the rifle of the one behind him. With this and several other techniques, the DI made it necessary for us to clean our rifles several times each day. But we learned quickly and well an old Marine Corps truism, "The rifle is a Marine's best friend." We always treated it as just that.

During the first few days, Doherty once asked one of the recruits a question about his rifle. In answering, the hapless recruit referred to his rifle as "my gun." The DI muttered some instructions to him, and the recruit blushed. He began trotting up and down in front of the huts holding his rifle in one hand and his penis in the other, chanting, "This is my rifle," as he held up his M1, "and this is my gun," as he moved his other arm. "This is for Japs," he again held aloft his M1; "and this is for fun," he held up his other arm. Needless to say, none of us ever again used the word "gun" unless referring to a shotgun, mortar, artillery piece, or naval gun.

A typical day in boot camp began with reveille at 0400 hours. We tumbled out of our sacks in the chilly dark and hurried through shaves, dressing, and chow. The grueling day ended with taps at 2200. At any time between taps and reveille, however, the DI might break us out for rifle inspection, close-order drill, or for a run around the parade ground or over the sand by the bay. This seemingly cruel and senseless harassment stood me in good stead later when I found that war allowed sleep to no man, particularly the infantryman. Combat guaranteed sleep of the permanent type only.

We moved to two or three different hut areas during the first few weeks, each time on a moment's notice. The order was, "Platoon 984, fall out on the double with rifles, full individual equipment, and seabags with all gear properly stowed, and prepare to move out in ten minutes." A mad scramble would follow as men gathered up and packed their equipment. Each man had one or two close buddies who pitched in to help each other don packs and hoist heavy seabags onto sagging shoulders. Several men from each hut would stay behind to clean up the huts and surrounding area as the other men of the platoon struggled under their heavy loads to the new hut area.

Upon arrival at the new area, the platoon halted, received hut assignments, fell out, and stowed gear. Just as we got into the huts we would get orders to fall in for drill with rifles, cartridge belts, and bayonets. The sense of urgency and hurry never abated. Our DI was ingenious in finding ways to harass us.

One of the hut areas we were in was across a high fence from an aircraft factory where big B-24 Liberator bombers were made. There was an airstrip, too, and the big four-engine planes came and went low over the tops of the huts. Once one belly-landed, going through the fence near our huts. No one was hurt, but several of us ran down to see the crash. When we got back to our area, Corporal Doherty delivered one of his finest orations on the subject of recruits never leaving their assigned area without the permission of their DI. We were all impressed, particularly with the tremendous number of push-ups and other exercises we performed instead of going to noon chow.

During close-order drill, the short men had the toughest time staying in step. Every platoon had its "feather merchants"—short men struggling along with giant strides at the tail end of the formation. At five feet nine inches, I was about two-thirds of the way back from the front guide of Platoon 984. One day while returning from the bayonet course, I got out of step and couldn't pick up the cadence. Corporal Doherty marched along beside me. In his icy tone, he said, "Boy, if you don't get in step and stay in step, I'm gonna kick you so hard in the behind that they're gonna have to take both of us to sick bay. It'll take a major operation to get my foot outa your ass." With those inspiring words ringing in my ears, I picked up the cadence and never ever lost it again.

The weather became quite chilly, particularly at night. I had to cover up with blankets and overcoat. Many of us slept in dungaree trousers and sweat shirts in addition to our skivvies. When reveille sounded well before daylight, we only had to pull on our boondockers [field shoes] before falling in for roll call.

Each morning after roll call, we ran in the foggy darkness to a large asphalt parade ground for rifle calisthenics. Atop a wooden platform, a muscular physical training instructor led several platoons in a long series of tiring exercises. A public address system played a scratchy recording of "Three O'Clock in the Morning." We were supposed to keep time with the music. The monotony was broken only by frequent whispered curses and insults directed at our enthusiastic instructor, and by the too frequent appearance of various DIs who stalked the extended ranks making sure all hands exercised vigorously. Not only did the exercises harden our bodies, but our hearing became superkeen from listening for the DIs as we skipped a beat or two for a moment of rest in the inky darkness.

At the time, we didn't realize or appreciate the fact that the discipline we were learning in responding to orders under stress often would mean the difference later in combat—between success or failure, even living or dying. The ear training also proved to be an unscheduled dividend when Japanese infiltrators slipped around at night.

Shortly we received word that we were going to move out to the rifle range. We greeted the announcement enthusiastically. Rumor had it that we would receive the traditional broad-brimmed campaign hats. But the supply ran out when our turn came. We felt envious and cheated every time we saw those salty-looking "Smokey Bear" hats on the range.

Early on the first morning at the rifle range, we began what was probably the most thorough and the most effective rifle marksmanship training given to any troops of any nation during World War II. We were divided into two-man teams the first week for dry firing, or "snapping-in." We concentrated on proper sight setting, trigger squeeze, calling of shots, use of the leather sling as a shooting aid, and other fundamentals.

It soon became obvious why we all received thick pads to be sewn onto the elbows and right shoulders of our dungaree jackets: during this snapping-in, each man and his buddy practiced together, one in the proper position (standing, kneeling, sitting, or prone) and squeezing the trigger, and the other pushing back the rifle bolt lever with the heel of his hand, padded by an empty cloth bandolier wrapped around the palm. This procedure cocked the rifle and simulated recoil.

The DIs and rifle coaches checked every man continuously. Everything had to be just so. Our arms became sore from being contorted into various positions and having the leather sling straining our joints and biting into our muscles. Most of us had problems perfecting the sitting position (which I never saw used in combat). But the coach helped everyone the way he did me—simply by plopping his weight on my shoulders until I was able to "assume the correct position." Those familiar with firearms quickly forgot what they knew and learned the Marine Corps' way.

Second only to accuracy was safety. Its principles were pounded into us mercilessly. *"Keep* the piece pointed toward the target. *Never* point a rifle at anything you don't intend to shoot. *Check* your rifle *each* time you pick it up to be sure it isn't loaded. Many *accidents* have occurred with 'unloaded' rifles."

We went onto the firing line and received live ammunition the next week. At first, the sound of rifles firing was disconcerting. But not for long. Our snapping-in had been so thorough, we went through our paces automatically. We fired at round black bull's-eye targets from 100, 300, and 500 yards. Other platoons worked the "butts."* When the range officer ordered, "Ready on the right, ready on the left, all ready on the firing line,

---

*"Butts" refers to the impact area on a rifle range. It consists of the targets mounted on a vertical track system above a sheltered dugout, usually made of concrete, in which other shooters operate, mark, and score the targets for those on the firing line.

commence firing," I felt as though the rifle was part of me and vice versa. My concentration was complete.

Discipline was ever present, but the harassment that had been our daily diet gave way to deadly serious, businesslike instruction in marksmanship. Punishment for infractions of the rules came swiftly and severely, however. One man next to me turned around slightly to speak to a buddy after "cease firing" was given; the action caused his rifle muzzle to angle away from the targets. The sharp-eyed captain in charge of the range rushed up from behind and booted the man in the rear so hard that he fell flat on his face. The captain then jerked him up off the deck and bawled him out loudly and thoroughly. We got his message.

Platoon 984 took its turn in the butts. As we sat safely in the dugouts and waited for each series of firing to be completed, I had somber thoughts about the crack and snap of bullets passing overhead.

Qualification day dawned clearly and brightly. We were apprehensive, having been told that anyone who didn't shoot high enough to qualify as "marksman" wouldn't go overseas. When the final scores were totaled, I was disappointed. I fell short of "expert rifleman" by only two points. However, I proudly wore the Maltese Cross–shaped sharpshooter's badge. And I didn't neglect to point out to my Yankee buddies that most of the high shooters in our platoon were Southern boys.

Feeling like old salts, we returned to the recruit depot for the final phases of recruit training. The DIs didn't treat us as veterans, though; harassment picked up quickly to its previous intensity.

By the end of eight grueling weeks, it had become apparent that Corporal Doherty and the other DIs had done their jobs well. We were hard physically, had developed endurance, and had learned our lessons. Perhaps more importantly, we were tough mentally. One of our assistant drill instructors even allowed himself to mumble that we might become Marines after all.

Finally, late in the afternoon of 24 December 1943, we fell in without rifles and cartridge belts. Dressed in service greens, each man received three bronze Marine Corps globe-and-anchor emblems, which we put into our pockets. We marched to an amphitheater where we sat with several other platoons.

This was our graduation from boot camp. A short, affable-looking major standing on the stage said, "Men, you have successfully completed your recruit training and are now United States Marines. Put on your Marine Corps emblems and wear them with pride. You have a great and proud tradition to uphold. You are members of the world's finest fighting outfit, so be worthy of it." We took out our emblems and put one on each lapel of our green wool coats and one on the left side of the overseas caps. The major told several dirty jokes. Everyone laughed and whistled. Then he said, "Good luck, men." That was the first time we had been addressed as men during our entire time in boot camp.

Before dawn the next day, Platoon 984 assembled in front of the huts for the last time. We shouldered our seabags, slung our rifles, and struggled down to a warehouse where a line of trucks was parked. Corporal Doherty told us that each man was to report to the designated truck as his name and destination was called out. The few men selected to train as specialists (radar technicians, aircraft mechanics, etc.) were to turn in their rifles, bayonets, and cartridge belts.

As the men moved out of ranks, there were quiet remarks of, "So long, see you, take it easy." We knew that many friendships were ending right there. Doherty called out, "Eugene B. Sledge, 534559, full individual equipment and M1 rifle, infantry, Camp Elliott."

Most of us were designated for infantry, and we went to Camp Elliott or to Camp Pendleton.* As we helped each other aboard the trucks, it never occurred to us why so many were being assigned to infantry. We were destined to take the places of the ever mounting numbers of casualties in the rifle or line companies in the Pacific. We were fated to fight the war first hand. We were cannon fodder.

After all assignments had been made, the trucks rolled out, and I looked at Doherty watching us leave. I disliked him, but I respected him. He had made us Marines, and I wondered what he thought as we rolled by.

---

*Camp Elliott was a small installation located on the northern outskirts of San Diego. It has been used rarely since World War II. Thirty-five miles north of San Diego lies Camp Joseph H. Pendleton. Home today of the 1st Marine Division, it is the Marine Corps' major west coast amphibious base.

# CHAPTER TWO

# PREPARATION FOR COMBAT

## Infantry Training

**M**ost of the buildings at Camp Elliott were neat wooden barracks painted cream with dark roofs. The typical two-story barracks was shaped like an H, with the squad bays in the upright parts of the letter. The many-windowed squad bays held about twenty-five double-decker metal bunks. The room was big, roomy, and well lighted. The ensuing two months were the only period during my entire service in World War II that I lived in a barracks. The remaining time I slept under canvas or the open sky.

No one yelled at us or screamed orders to hurry up. The NCOs seemed relaxed to the point of being lethargic. We had the free run of the camp except for certain restricted areas. Taps and lights out were at 2200. We were like birds out of a cage after the confinement and harassment of boot camp. With several boys who bunked near me, I sampled the draught beer at the slop chute (enlisted men's club), bought candy and ice cream at the PX (post exchange), and explored the area. Our newly found freedom was heady stuff.

We spent the first few days at Camp Elliott at lectures and demonstrations dealing with the various weapons in a Marine infantry regiment. We received an introduction to the 37mm antitank gun, 81mm mortar, 60mm mortar, .50 caliber machine gun, .30 caliber heavy and light machine guns, and the Browning Automatic Rifle (BAR). We also ran through combat tactics for the rifle squad. Most of our conversation around the barracks concerned the various weapons and whether or not it would be "good duty" to be on a 37mm gun crew, light machine gun or 81mm mortar. There was always one man, frequently—in fact, usually—a New Englander who knew it all and claimed to have the latest hot dope on everything.

"I talked to a guy over at the PX who had been through 81mm mortar school, and he said them damn mortars are so heavy he wished to hell he had gotten into 37mm guns so he could ride in a jeep while it pulled the gun."

"I talked to a guy over at Camp Pendleton, and he said a mortar shell blew up over there just as it was fired and killed the instructor and all the crew. I'm getting into light machine guns; they say that's a good deal."

"Like hell. My uncle was in France in World War I, and he said the average life of a machine gunner was about two minutes. I'm gonna be a rifleman, so I won't have to tote all that weight around."

So it went. None of us had the slightest idea what he was talking about.

One day we fell in and were told to separate into groups according to which weapon we wanted to train with. If our first choice was filled, we made a second selection. The mere fact that we had a choice amazed me. Apparently the idea was that a man would be more effective on a weapon he had picked rather than one to which he had been assigned. I chose 60mm mortars.

The first morning, those in 60mm mortars marched behind a warehouse where several light tanks were parked. Our mortar instructor, a sergeant, told us to sit down and listen to what he had to say. He was a clean-cut, handsome blond man wearing neat khakis faded to just that right shade that indicated a "salty" uniform. His bearing oozed calm self-confidence. There was no arrogance or bluster about him, yet he was obviously a man who knew himself and his job and would put up with no nonsense from anybody. He had an intangible air of subdued, quiet detachment, a quality possessed by so many of the combat veterans of the Pacific campaigns whom I met at that time. Sometimes his mind seemed a million miles away, as though lost in some sort of melancholy reverie. It was a genuine attribute, unrehearsed and spontaneous. In short, it couldn't be imitated consciously. I noted this carefully in my early days in the Marine Corps but never understood it until I observed the same thing in my buddies after Peleliu.

One man raised his hand, and the sergeant said, "OK, what's your question?"

The man began with, "Sir." The sergeant laughed and said, "Address me as sergeant, not sir."

"Yes, sir."

"Look, you guys are U.S. Marines now. You are not in boot camp anymore. Just relax, work hard, and do your job right, and you won't have any trouble. You'll have a better chance of getting through the war." He won our respect and admiration instantly.

"My job is to train you people to be 60mm mortarmen. The 60mm mortar is an effective and important infantry weapon. You can break up enemy attacks on your company's front with this weapon, and you can soften enemy defenses wth it. You will be firing over the heads of your own buddies at the enemy a short distance away, so you've got to know exactly what you're doing. Otherwise there'll be short rounds and you'll kill and wound your own men. I was a 60mm mortarman on Guadalcanal and saw how effective this weapon was against the Japs there. Any questions?"

On the chilly January morning of our first lesson in mortars, we sat on the deck under a bright sky and listened attentively to our instructor.

"The 60mm mortar is a smoothbore, muzzle-loaded, high-angle-fire weapon. The assembled gun weighs approximately forty-five pounds and consists of the tube—or barrel—bipod, and base plate. Two or sometimes three 60mm mortars are in each rifle company. Mortars have a high angle of fire and are particularly effective against enemy troops taking cover in defilades or behind ridges where they are protected from our artillery. The Japs have mortars and know how to use 'em, too. They will be particularly anxious to knock out our mortars and machine guns because of the damage these weapons can inflict on their troops."

The sergeant then went over the nomenclature of the gun. He demonstrated the movements of gun drill, during which the bipod was unstrapped and unfolded from carrying position, the base plate set firmly on the deck, the bipod leg spikes pressed into the deck, and the sight snapped into place on the gun. We were divided into five-man squads and practiced these evolutions until each man could perform them smoothly. During subsequent lessons he instructed us in the intricacies of the sight with its cross-level and longitudinal-level bubbles and on how to lay the gun and sight it on an aiming stake lined up with a target. We spent hours learning how to take a compass reading on a target area, then place a stake in front of the gun to correspond to that reading.

Each squad competed fiercely to be the fastest and most precise in gun drill. When my turn came to act as number one gunner, I would race to the position, unsling the mortar from my right shoulder, set it up, sight in on the base stake, remove my hands from it and yell, "Ready." The sergeant would check his stopwatch and give the time. Many shouts of encouragement came from a gunner's squad urging each man on. Each of us rotated as number one gunner, as number two gunner (who dropped the shells into the tube at number one's command), and as ammo carriers.

We were drilled thoroughly but were quite nervous about handling live ammunition for the first time. We fired at empty oil drums set on a dry hillside. There were no mishaps. When I saw the first shell burst with a dull *bang* about two hundred yards out on the range, I suddenly realized what a deadly weapon we were dealing with. A cloud of black smoke appeared at the point of impact. Flying steel fragments kicked up little puffs of dust all around an area about nine by eighteen yards. When three shells were fired from one weapon, the bursts covered an area about thirty-five by thirty-five yards with flying fragments.

"Boy, I'd pity any Jap that had all that shrapnel flying around him," murmured one of my more thoughtful buddies.

"Yeah, it'll tear their asses up all right. But don't forget they're gonna be throwing stuff at you just as fast as they can," said the mortar sergeant.

This, I realized, was the difference between war and hunting. When I survived the former, I gave up the latter.

We also received training in hand-to-hand combat. This consisted mostly of judo and knife fighting. To impress us with the effectiveness of his subject, the judo instructor methodically slammed each of us to the ground as we tried to rush him.

"What good is this kind of fighting gonna do us if the Japs can pick us off with machine guns and artillery at five hundred yards?" someone asked.

"When dark comes in the Pacific," the instructor replied, "the Japs always send men into our positions to try to infiltrate the lines or just to see how many American throats they can slit. They are tough and they like close-in fighting. You can handle them, but you've got to know how." Needless to say, we paid close attention from then on.

"Don't hesitate to fight the Japs dirty. Most Americans, from the time they are kids, are taught not to hit below the belt. It's not sportsmanlike. Well, nobody has taught the Japs that, and war ain't sport. Kick him in the balls before he kicks you in yours," growled our instructor.

We were introduced to the Marine's foxhole companion, the Ka-Bar knife. This deadly piece of cutlery was manufactured by the company bearing its name. The knife was a foot long with a seven-inch-long by one-and-a-half-inch-wide blade. The five-inch handle was made of leather washers packed together and had "USMC" stamped on the blade side of the upper hand guard. Light for its size, the knife was beautifully balanced.

"Everybody has heard a lot about all those kinds of fancy fighting knives that are, or should be, carried by infantry troops: throwing knives, stilettos, daggers, and all that stuff. Most of it is nothing but bull. Sure, you'll probably open more cans of C rations than Japs with this knife, but if a Jap ever jumps in your hole, you're better off with a Ka-Bar than any other knife. It's the very best and it's rugged, too. If you guys were gonna fight Germans, I'd guess you'd never need a fighting knife, but with the Japs it's different. I guarantee that you or the man in the next foxhole will use a Ka-Bar on a Jap infiltrator before the war is over." He was right.*

All of our instructors at Camp Elliott did a professional job. They presented us with the material and made it clear that our chances of surviving the war depended to a great extent on how well we learned. As teachers they had no problem with student motivation.

But I don't recall that anyone really comprehended what was happening outside our own training routine. Maybe it was the naive optimism of youth, but the awesome reality that we were training to be cannon fodder in a global war that had already snuffed out millions of lives never seemed to occur to us. The fact that our lives might end violently or that we might be crippled while we were still boys didn't seem to register. The only thing that we seemed to be truly concerned about was that we might be too afraid to do our jobs under fire. An apprehension nagged at each of us that he might appear to be "yellow" if he were afraid.

One afternoon two veterans of the Bougainville campaign dropped into my barracks to chat with some of us. They had been members of the Marine raider battalion that had fought so well along with the 3d Marine Division on Bougainville. They were the first veterans we had met other than our instructors. We swamped them with questions.

"Were you scared?" asked one of my buddies.

"Scared! Are you kiddin? I was so goddamn scared the first time I heard slugs coming at me I could hardly hold onto my rifle," came the reply.

The other veteran said, "Listen, mate, everybody gets scared, and anybody says he don't is a damn liar." We felt better.

The mortar school continued during my entire stay at Camp Elliott. Swimming tests were the last phase of special training we received before embarking for the Pacific. Mercifully, in January 1944 we couldn't foresee the events of autumn. We trained with enthusiasm and the faith that the battles we were destined to fight would be necessary to win the war.

*Earlier, on 20–23 November 1943, the 2d Marine Division carried out its memorable assault on the coral atoll of Tarawa in the Gilbert Islands. Many military historians and others consider the battle for Tarawa as the first modern head-on amphibious assault.*

*A coral reef extended out about five hundred yards and surrounded the atoll. Tarawa was subject to unpredictable dodging tides that sometimes*

---

*The U.S. Marine Corps still uses Ka-Bar's fine fighting knife. The manufacturer's name now has become to Marines a noun *(kabar)* meaning their fighting knife.

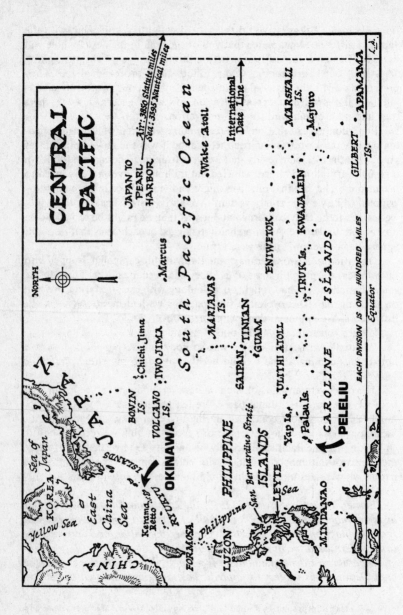

*lowered water levels and caused Higgins boats (LCVP: Landing Craft, Vehicle and Personnel) to strand on the reef.*

*Plans called for the use of amphibian tractors (LVTs: Landing Vehicles, Tracked; now called assault amphibians) to carry the troops across the reef. But only enough amtracs existed to take in the first three waves. After the first three assault waves got ashore in amtracs, the supporting waves had to wade across the reef through murderous Japanese fire, because their Higgins boats hung up at the reef's edge.*

*The 2d Division suffered terrible losses—3,381 dead and wounded. Its Marines killed all but seventeen of the 4,836 Japanese defenders of the tiny atoll.*

*There was loud and severe criticism of the Marine Corps by the American public and some military leaders because of the number of casualties. Tarawa became a household word in the United States. It took its rightful place with Valley Forge, the Alamo, Belleau Wood, and Guadalcanal as a symbol of American courage and sacrifice.*

*The young Marines at Camp Elliott didn't have the remotest idea that in about nine months they would participate as part of the 1st Marine Division in the assault on Peleliu. That battle would prove to be so vicious and costly that the division's losses would just about double those of the 2d Marine Division at Tarawa. To add tragedy to its horror, hindsight would show that the seizure of Peleliu was of questionable necessity. As more than one Marine historian has said, it's unfortunate to the memory of the men who fought and died on Peleliu that it remains one of the lesser known and poorly understood battles of World War II.*

## Overseas at Last

Early on the morning of 28 February 1944, the men of the 46th Replacement Battalion got off trucks at dockside in San Diego Harbor and lined up to board a troopship that would take us to the Pacific. The *President Polk* had been a luxury liner of the President Line during peacetime. Painted battleship gray, the ship now looked gloomy and ominous with its antiaircraft guns and life rafts. I had the uneasy feeling that this was going to be a one-way trip for some of us.

Loaded down with full transport pack, bed roll (mattress with canvas cover), M1 carbine, and helmet, I struggled up a steep gangplank. Once on deck we went into our troop compartment one deck below. A blast of hot, foul air hit me as I entered the hatch and started down the ladder. About halfway down, the man in front of me slipped and clattered to the bottom.

We were all concerned about his fall and helped him up and into his gear again. Later such an incident would elicit almost nothing but a casual glance and a quick helping hand.

We stood crowded in the compartment and waited for what seemed like hours for an officer to check the muster roll and assign each of us to a sack or rack (bunk). Each sack consisted of canvas laced onto a pipe frame hinged to metal uprights, head and foot, extending from deck to the overhead. Chains held each rack onto the ones above and below.

When I crawled onto mine, I realized the rack above was only about two feet away. With mattress unrolled and gear laid out, a man barely had room to stretch out. I had to climb up about four racks to get to mine, which was almost at the highest level.

Dim electric bulbs overhead gave us barely enough light to see. As soon as I could, I went topside searching for relief from the foul, crowded compartment. The deck was jammed, too, but the air was fresh.

Many of us were too excited to sleep, so we explored the ship for hours, talked to the crewmen, or watched the completion of loading. Finally, around midnight, I went below and climbed into my rack. Several hours later I awoke to the vibration of the ship's engine. I pulled on my boondockers and dungaree pants and jacket and raced topside, filled with apprehension and excitement. It was about 0500. The deck was crowded with other Marines subdued by the realization that each turn of the ship's screws would take us farther from home and closer to the unknown.

Harsh questions raced through my mind. Would I ever see my family again? Would I do my duty or be a coward? Could I kill? Fantasy captivated me in the brief period. Maybe I'd be put into a rear-echelon outfit and never see a Japanese. Maybe I'd be an infantryman and disgrace my outfit by running away from the enemy. Or, maybe I'd kill dozens of Japanese and win a Navy Cross or Silver Star and be a national hero.

The tension finally broke as we watched the sailors rushing about casting off hawsers and lines, preparing the ship for the open sea.

The *President Polk* moved on a zigzag course toward a destination unknown to those of us sweltering in her bowels. Our daily routine was dull, even for those like myself who rather enjoyed being aboard a ship. We rolled out of our racks each morning about sunrise. Brushing my teeth and shaving with nonlathering shaving cream was my morning toilet. Each day an officer or NCO led us through an exercise period of calisthenics. And we could always count on a rifle inspection. Other than that, we had practically no duties.

Every few days we had abandon-ship drills, which helped offset the boredom. And the ship's crew conducted gun drills frequently. The first time they held target practice with live ammunition was exciting to watch. Yellow balloons were released from the bridge. As they were caught by the wind, the gunners opened fire upon order from the fire control officer. The rapid-fire 20mm and 40mm antiaircraft guns seemed to do an effective job. But to some of us Marines, the 3-inch and 5-inch cannons didn't accomplish much other than hurt our ears. Considering the number of balloons that escaped, we felt the gun crews should have practiced more. This was probably because none of us had ever had any experience with antiaircraft guns and didn't realize what a difficult type of gunnery was involved.

Beyond some letter writing and a lot of conversation—so-called bull sessions—we spent much of our time waiting in chow lines strung along gangways and passages leading to the ship's galley. Chow was an unforgettable experience. After the inevitable wait in line, I entered the hatch leading to the galley and was met with a blast of hot air laden with a new set of odors differing only slightly from the typical troop compartment aroma. To the same basic ingredients (paint, grease, tobacco, and sweat) were added the smells of rancid cooking and something of a bakery. It was enough to turn a civilian's stomach inside out, but we rapidly and necessarily adjusted.

We moved along the cafeteria-style line and indicated to sweating navy messmen what foods we wanted served onto shining compartmentalized steel trays. The messmen wore skivvy shirts and were tattooed profusely on their arms. They all mopped the sweat from their faces constantly. Amid the roar of ventilators, we ate standing at long folding tables. Everything was hot to the touch but quite clean. A sailor told me that the tables had been used as operating tables for Marine casualties that the ship took on during one of the earlier Pacific campaigns. That gave me a strange feeling in the pit of my stomach every time I went to chow on the *President Polk*.

The heat was intense—at least 100 degrees—but I gulped down a cup of hot "joe" (black coffee), the stuff that replaced bread as the staff of life for Marines and sailors. I grimaced as the dehydrated potatoes battered my taste buds with an unsavory aftertaste characteristic of all World War II–vintage dehydrated foods. The bread was a shock—heavy, and with a flavor that was a combination of bitterness, sweetness, and uncooked flour. No wonder hot joe had replaced it as the staff of life!

After chow in the steaming galley, we went topside to cool off. Everyone was soaked with sweat. It would have been a relief to eat on deck, but we were forbidden to take chow out of the galley.

One day, as we moved along some nameless companionway in a chow line, I passed a porthole that gave me a view into the officers' mess. There I saw Navy and Marine officers clad neatly in starched khakis sitting at tables in a well-ventilated room. White-coated waiters served them pie and ice cream. As we inched along the hot companionway to our steaming joe and dehydrated fare, I wondered if my haste to leave the V-12 college life hadn't been a mistake. After all, it would have been nice to have been declared a gentleman by Congress and to have lived like a human being aboard ship. To my immense satisfaction, however, I discovered later that such niceties and privileges of rank were few on the front lines.

During the morning of 17 March we looked out across the bow and saw a line of white breakers on the horizon. The Great Barrier Reef extends for thousands of miles, and we were to pass through it to New Caledonia. As we neared the reef, we saw several hulks of wooden ships stranded high and dry, apparently blown there years ago by some storm.

As we closed on the harbor of Noumea, we saw a small motor launch head our way. The *Polk* signaled with flags and blinker lights to this pilot boat, which soon pulled alongside. The pilot climbed a ladder and boarded the ship. All sorts of nautical protocol and mutual greetings between him and the ship's officers ensued as he went to the bridge to guide us in. This man was a middle-aged, pleasant-looking civilian dressed in a neat white Panama suit, straw hat, and black tie. Surrounded by sailors in blue denim and ship's officers in khaki, he looked like a fictional character out of some long-forgotten era.

The blue water of the Pacific turned to green as we passed into the channel leading into the harbor of Noumea. There was a pretty white lighthouse near the harbor. White houses with tile roofs nestled around it and up the base of slopes of high mountains. The scene reminded me of a photo of some picturesque little Mediterranean seaport.

The *President Polk* moved slowly through the harbor as the speaker system ordered a special sea detail to stand by. We tied up to a dock with long warehouses where United States military personnel were moving crates and equipment. Most of the shipping I saw was U.S. Navy, but there also were some American and foreign merchant freighters along with a few quaint-looking civilian fishing boats.

The first Pacific native I saw wasn't dressed in a hula skirt or waving a spear but nonchalantly driving a freight-moving tractor on the dock. He was a short muscular man—black as ink—clad only in a loin cloth with a bone in his nose and a bushy head of kinky hair like a Fuzzy Wuzzy out of a Kipling story. The incredible thing about this hair was its color, beautiful amber. A sailor explained that the natives were fond of bleaching their hair with blueing they got from Americans in exchange for seashells. Bone in the nose notwithstanding, the man was an admirable tractor driver.

## New Caledonia

After weeks at sea, cramped into a troopship, we were relieved to move onto land again. We piled into Marine Corps trucks and drove through the main section of Noumea. I was delighted to see the old French architecture, which reminded me of the older sections of Mobile and New Orleans.

The trucks sped along a winding road with mountains on each side. We saw small farms and a large nickel mine in the valley. Some of the land was cleared, but thick jungle covered much of the low areas. Although the weather was pleasant and cool, the palms and other growth attested to the tropical climate. After several miles we turned into Camp Saint Louis, where we would undergo further training before being sent "up north" to the combat zone as replacements.

Camp Saint Louis was a tent camp comprised of rows of tents and dirt streets. We were assigned to tents, stowed our gear, and fell in for chow. The galley rested on a hill just past the camp's brig. In full view were two wire cages about the size of phone booths. We were told that those who caused trouble were locked in there, and a high-pressure fire hose was turned on them periodically. The strictness of discipline at Camp Saint Louis caused me to assume the explanation of the cages was true. In any event, I resolved to stay out of trouble.

Our training consisted of lectures and field exercises. Combat veteran officers and NCOs lectured on Japanese weapons, tactics, and combat methods. Most of the training was thorough and emphasized individual attention. We worked in groups of ten or twelve.

I usually was placed in a squad instructed by a big redheaded corporal who had been in a Marine raider battalion during the fighting in the Solomon Islands. Big Red was good-natured but tough as nails. He worked us hard. One day he took us to a small rifle range and taught us how to fire a Japanese pistol, rifle, and heavy and light machine guns. After firing a few rounds from each, Red put about five of us into a pit about five feet deep with a one-foot embankment in front and the steep slope of a ridge behind as a backstop.

"One important thing you must learn fast to survive is exactly what enemy fire sounds like coming at you and what kind of weapon it is. Now when I blow this whistle, get down and stay down until you hear the whistle again. If you get up before the signal, you'll get your head blowed off, and the folks back home will get your insurance.''

Red blew the whistle and we got down. He announced each type of Japanese weapon and fired several rounds from it over our hole into the bank. Then he and his assistants fired them all together for about fifteen seconds. It seemed a lot longer. The bullets popped and snapped as they went over. Several machine-gun tracers didn't embed in the bank but bounced off and rolled—white-hot, sizzling, and sputtering—into the hole. We cringed and shifted about, but no one got burned.

This was one of the most valuable training exercises we underwent. There were instances later on Peleliu and Okinawa which it prepared me to come through unscathed.

A salty sergeant conducted bayonet training. He had been written about in a national magazine because he was so outstanding. On the cinder-covered street of an old raider camp, I witnessed some amazing feats by him. He instructed us in how to defend ourselves barehanded against an opponent's bayonet thrust.

"Here's how it's done," he said.

He picked me out of the squad and told me to charge him and thrust the point of my bayonet at his chest when I thought I could stick him. I got a mental image of myself behind bars at Mare Island Naval Prison for bayoneting an instructor, so I veered off just before making my thrust.

"What the hell's the matter with you? Don't you know how to use a bayonet?"

"But, Sarge, if I stick you, they'll put me in Mare Island."

"There's less chance of you bayoneting me than of me whipping your ass for not following my orders."

"OK," I thought to myself, "if that's the way you feel about it, we have witnesses."

So I headed for him on the double and thrust at his chest. He sidestepped neatly, grabbed my rifle behind the front sight, and jerked it in the direction I was running. I held onto the rifle and tumbled onto the cinders. The squad roared with laughter. Someone yelled, "Did you bayonet him, Sledgehammer?" I got up looking sheepish.

"Knock it off, wise guy," said the instructor. "You step up here, and let's see what you can do, big mouth."

My buddy lifted his rifle confidently, charged, and ended up on the cinders, too. The instructor made each man charge him in turn. He threw them all.

He then took up a Japanese Arisaka rifle with fixed bayonet and showed us how the Japanese soldiers used the hooked hand guard to lock onto the U.S. blade. Then, with a slight twist of his wrist, he could wrench the M1 rifle out of the opponent's hands and disarm him. He coached us carefully to hold the M1 on its side with the left side of the blade toward the deck instead of the cutting edge, as we had been taught in the States. This way, as we parried a Japanese's blade, he couldn't lock ours.

We went on long hikes and forced marches through the jungles, swamps, and over endless steep hills. We made countless practice landings from Higgins boats on small islets off the coast. Each morning after chow we marched out of camp equipped with rifles, cartridge belts, two canteens of water, combat pack, helmet, and K rations. Our usual pace was a rapid route step for fifty minutes with a ten-minute rest. But the officers and NCOs always hurried us and frequently deleted the ten-minute rest.

When trucks drove along the road, we moved onto the sides, as columns of infantry have done since early times. The trucks frequently carried army troops, and we barked and yapped like dogs and kidded them about being dogfaces. During one of these encounters, a soldier hanging out of a truck just ahead of me shouted, "Hey, soldier. You look tired and hot, soldier. Why don't you make the army issue you a truck like me?"

I grinned and yelled, "Go to hell."

His buddy grabbed him by the shoulder and yelled, "Stop calling that guy soldier. He's a Marine. Can't you see his emblem? He's not in the army. Don't insult him."

"Thanks," I yelled. That was my first encounter with men who had no esprit. We might grumble to each other about our officers or the chow or the Marine Corps in general, but it was rather like grumbling about one's own family—always with another member. If an outsider tried to get into the discussion, a fight resulted.

One night during exercises in defense against enemy infiltration, some of the boys located the bivouac of Big Red and the other instructors who were supposed to be the infiltrators and stole their boondockers. When the time came for their offense to commence, they threw a few concussion grenades around and yelled like Japanese but didn't slip out and capture any of us. When the officers realized what had happened, they reamed out the instructors for being too sure of themselves. The instructors had a big fire built in a ravine. We sat around it, drank coffee, ate K rations, and sang some songs. It didn't seem like such a bad war so far.

All of our training was in rifle tactics. We spent no time on heavy weapons (mortars and machine guns), because when we went "up north" our unit commander would assign us where needed. That might not be in our specialties. As a result of the field exercises and obstacle course work, we reached a high level of physical fitness and endurance.

During the last week of May we learned that the 46th Replacement Battalion would go north in a few days. We packed our gear and boarded the USS *General Howze* on 28 May 1944. This ship was quite different from the *President Polk*. It was much newer and apparently had been constructed as a troopship. It was freshly painted throughout and spic and span. With only about a dozen other men, I was assigned to a small, well-ventilated compartment on the main deck, a far cry from the cavernous, stinking hole I bunked in on the *Polk*. The *General Howze* had a library from which troop passengers could get books and magazines. We also received our first atabrine tablets. These small, bitter, bright yellow pills prevented malaria. We took one a day.

On 2 June the *General Howze* approached the Russell Islands and moved into an inlet bordered by large groves of coconut palms. The symmetrical groves and clear water were beautiful. From the ship we could see coral-covered roadways and groups of pyramidal tents among the coconut palms. This was Pavuvu, home of the 1st Marine Division.

We learned we would debark the next morning, so we spent our time hanging over the rail, talking to a few Marines on the pier. Their friendliness and unassuming manner struck me. Although clad neatly in khakis or dungarees, they appeared hollow-eyed and tired. They made no attempt to impress us green replacements, yet they were members of an elite division known to nearly everybody back home because of its conquest of Guadalcanal and more recent campaign at Cape Gloucester on New Britain. They had left Gloucester about 1 May. Thus, they had been on Pavuvu about a month.

Many of us slept little during the night. We checked and rechecked our gear, making sure everything was squared away. The weather was hot, much more so than at New Caledonia. I went out on deck and slept in the open air. With a mandolin and an old violin, two of our Marines struck up some of the finest mountain music I'd ever heard. They played and sang folk songs and ballads most of the night. We thought it was mighty wonderful music.

## With the Old Breed

About 0900 the morning of 3 June 1944, carrying the usual mountain of gear, I trudged down the gangplank of the *General Howze*. As we moved to waiting trucks, we passed a line of veterans waiting to go aboard for the voyage home. They carried only packs and personal gear, no weapons. Some said they were glad to see us, because we were their replacements.

They looked tanned and tired but relieved to be headed home. For them the war was over. For us, it was just beginning.

In a large parking area paved with crushed coral, a lieutenant called out our names and counted us off into groups. To my group of a hundred or more he said, "Third Battalion, Fifth Marines."

*If I had had an option—and there was none, of course—as to which of the five Marine divisions I served with, it would have been the 1st Marine Division. Ultimately, the Marine Corps had six divisions that fought with distinction in the Pacific. But the 1st Marine Division was, in many ways, unique. It had participated in the opening American offensive against the Japanese at Guadalcanal and already had fought a second major battle at Cape Gloucester, north of the Solomon Islands. Now its troops were resting, preparing for a third campaign in the Palau Islands.*

*Of regiments, I would have chosen the 5th Marines. I knew about its impressive history as a part of the 1st Marine Division, but I also knew that its record went back to France in World War I. Other Marines I knew in other divisions were proud of their units and of being Marines, as well they should have been. But the 5th Marines and the 1st Marine Division carried not only the traditions of the Corps but had traditions and a heritage of their own, a link through time with the "Old Corps."*

*The fact that I was assigned to the very regiment and division I would have chosen was a matter of pure chance. I felt as though I had rolled the dice and won.\**

The trucks drove along winding coral roads by the bay and through coconut groves. We stopped and unloaded our gear near a sign that said "3rd Bn., 5th Marines." An NCO assigned me to Company K. Soon a lieutenant came along and took aside the fifteen or so men who had received crew-served weapons training (mortars and machine guns) in the States. He asked each of us which weapon he wanted to be assigned to in the company.

---

*The history of the 5th Marines continued after World War II. The regiment fought in the Korean War and again in Vietnam. Thus it is the only Marine regiment to have fought in all of the nation's major wars in this century.

No Marine division fought in World War I. [The 5th and 6th Marine Regiments fought in France as part of the 2d Division (Regular) American Expeditionary Force (AEF), a mixed unit of Marine and Army brigades.] But the 1st Marine Division was the only Marine division to fight in Korea. Along with the 3d Marine Division, it also fought in Vietnam. It is, therefore, the sole Marine division to have fought in all of our major wars during the past sixty years.

Today the 5th Marines still forms a part of the 1st Marine Division. Stationed on the west coast, the division can deploy units for duty in the western Pacific.

*Major McIlhenny and his company commanders; 3d Bn, 5th Marines, 1st Marine Division. Pavuvu, June 1944. (L to R: Capt. Bishop, Capt. Neville, Capt. McAuliffe, McIlhenny, Capt. Haldane, Capt. Crown).*

I asked for 60mm mortars and tried to look too small to carry a seventy-pound flamethrower. He assigned me to mortars, and I moved my gear into a tent that housed the second squad of the 60mm mortar section.

For the next several weeks I spent most of my time during the day on work parties building up the camp. The top sergeant of Company K, 1st Sergeant Malone, would come down the company street shouting, "All new men outside for a work party, on the double." Most of the time the company's veterans weren't included. Pavuvu was supposed to be a rest camp for them after the long, wet, debilitating jungle campaign on Cape Gloucester. When Malone needed a large work party he would call out, "I need every available man." So we referred to him as "Available" Malone.

None of us, old hands or replacements, could fathom why the division command chose Pavuvu. Only after the war did I find out that the leaders were trying to avoid the kind of situation the 3d Marine Division endured when it went into camp on Guadalcanal after its campaign on Bougainville. Facilities on Guadalcanal, by then a large rear-area base, were reasonably good, but the high command ordered the 3d Division to furnish about a thousand men each day for working parties all over the island. Not only did the Bougainville veterans get little or no rest, but when replacements came, the division had difficulty carrying out its training schedule in preparation for the next campaign, Guam.

If Pavuvu seemed something less than a tropical paradise to us replacements fresh from the States and New Caledonia, it was a bitter shock to the Gloucester veterans.* When ships entered Macquitti Bay, as the *General Howze* had, Pavuvu looked picturesque. But once ashore, one found the extensive coconut groves choked with rotting coconuts. The apparently solid ground was soft and turned quickly to mud when subjected to foot or vehicular traffic.

Pavuvu was the classical embodiment of the Marine term "boondocks." It was impossible to explain after the war what life on Pavuvu was like. Most of the griping about being "rock happy" and bored in the Pacific came from men stationed at the big rear-echelon bases like Hawaii or New Caledonia. Among their main complaints were that the ice cream wasn't good, the beer not cold enough, or the USO shows too infrequent. But on Pavuvu, simply living was difficult.

For example, most of the work parties I went on in June and July were pick-and-shovel details to improve drainage or pave walkways with crushed coral, just to get us out of the water. Regulations called for wooden decks in all tents, but I never saw one on Pavuvu.

Of all the work parties, the one we hated most was collecting rotten coconuts. We loaded them onto trucks to be dumped into a swamp. If we were lucky, the coconut sprout served as a handle. But more often, the thing fell apart, spilling stinking coconut milk over us.

We made sardonic, absurd jokes about the vital, essential, classified work we were doing for the war effort and about the profundity and wisdom of the orders we received. In short, we were becoming "Asiatic," a Marine Corps term denoting a singular type of eccentric behavior characteristic of men who had served too long in the Far East. I had done a good deal of complaining about Pavuvu's chow and general conditions during my first week there; one of the veterans in our company, who later became a close friend, told me in a restrained but matter-of-fact way that, until I had been in combat, there was really nothing to complain about. Things could be a good deal worse, he said, and advised me to shut up and quit whining. He shamed me thoroughly. But for the first weeks on Pavuvu, the stench of rotting coconuts permeated the air. We could even taste it in the drinking water. I'm still repulsed even today by the smell of fresh coconut.

---

*After Guadalcanal, the 1st Marine Division went to Melbourne, Australia, for rest and refitting for the New Britain campaign. When Cape Gloucester ended, the men assumed they were headed back to Australia. Instead they were dumped on a deserted island in the Russell Islands group, sixty miles from Guadalcanal.

The most loathsome vermin on Pavuvu were the land crabs. Their blue-black bodies were about the size of the palm of a man's hand, and bristles and spines covered their legs. These ugly creatures hid by day and roamed at night. Before putting on his boondockers each morning, every man in the 1st Marine Division shook his shoes to roust the land crabs. Many mornings I had one in each shoe and sometimes two. Periodically we reached the point of rage over these filthy things and chased them out from under boxes, seabags, and cots. We killed them with sticks, bayonets, and entrenching tools. After the action was over, we had to shovel them up and bury them, or a nauseating stench developed rapidly in the hot, humid air.

Each battalion had its own galley, but chow on Pavuvu consisted mainly of heated C rations: dehydrated eggs, dehydrated potatoes, and that detestable canned meat called Spam. The synthetic lemonade, so-called battery acid, that remained after chow was poured on the concrete slab deck of the galley to clean and bleach it. It did a nice job. As if hot C rations didn't get tedious week in and week out, we experienced a period of about four days when we were served oatmeal morning, noon, and night. Scuttlebutt was that the ship carrying our supplies had been sunk. Whatever the cause, our only relief from monotonous chow was tidbits in packages from home. The bread made by our bakers was so heavy that when you held a slice by one side, the rest of the slice broke away of its own weight. The flour was so massively infested with weevils that each slice of bread had more of the little beetles than there are seeds in a slice of rye bread. We became so inured to this sort of thing, however, that we ate the bread anyway; the wits said, "It's a good deal. Them beetles give you more meat in your diet."

We had no bathing facilities at first. Shaving each morning with a helmet full of water was simple enough, but a bath was another matter. Each afternoon when the inevitable tropical downpour commenced, we stripped and dashed into the company street, soap in hand. The trick was to lather, scrub, and rinse before the rain stopped. The weather was so capricious that the duration of a shower was impossible to estimate. Each downpour ended as abruptly as it had begun and never failed to leave at least one or more fully lathered, cursing Marines with no rinse water.

Morning sick call was another bizarre sight during the early days on Pavuvu. The Gloucester veterans were in poor physical condition after the wettest campaign in World War II, during which men endured soakings for weeks on end. When I first joined the company, I was appalled at their condition: most were thin, some emaciated, with jungle rot in their armpits and on their ankles and wrists. At sick call they paired off with a bottle of gentian violet and cotton swabs, stood naked in the grove, and painted each other's sores. So many of them needed attention that they had to treat each other under a doctor's supervision. Some had to cut their boondockers into sandals, because their feet were so infected with rot they could hardly walk. Needless to say, Pavuvu's hot, humid climate prolonged the healing process.

"I think the Marine Corps has forgotten where Pavuvu is," one man said.

"I think God has forgotten where Pavuvu is," came a reply.

"God couldn't forget because he made everything."

"Then I bet he wishes he could forget he made Pavuvu."

This exchange indicates the feeling of remoteness and desolation we felt on Pavuvu. On the big island bases, men had the feeling of activity around their units and contact through air and sea traffic with other bases and with the States. On Pavuvu we felt as though we were a million miles from not only home but from anything else that bespoke of civilization.

I believe we took in stride all of Pavuvu's discomforts and frustrations for two reasons. First, the division was an elite combat unit. Discipline was stern. Our esprit de corps ran high. Each man knew what to do and what was expected of him. All did their duty well, even while grumbling.

NCOs answered our complaining with, "Beat your gums. It's healthy." Or, "Whatta ya griping for? You volunteered for the Marine Corps, didn't ya? You're just gettin' what ya asked for."

No matter how irritating or uncomfortable things were on Pavuvu, things could always be worse. After all, there were no Japanese, no bursting shells, no snapping and whining bullets. And we slept on cots. Second, make-up of the division was young: about 80 percent were between the ages of eighteen and twenty-five; about half were under twenty-one when they came overseas. Well-disciplined young men can put up with a lot even though they don't like it; and we were a bunch of high-spirited boys proud of our unit.

But we had another motivating factor, as well: a passionate hatred for the Japanese burned through all Marines I knew. The fate of the Goettge patrol was the sort of thing that spawned such hatred.* One day as we piled stinking coconuts, a veteran Marine walked past and exchanged greetings with a couple of our "old men." One of our group asked us if we knew who he was.

---

*During the first week of the Guadalcanal campaign, the Marines captured a Japanese soldier who claimed some of his starving comrades west of the Matanikau River would surrender if the Marines would "liberate" them. With twenty-five picked men (scouts, intelligence specialists, a surgeon, and a linguist) from the division's headquarters and the 5th Marines, Col. Frank Goettge—the division's intelligence officer—went on a mission more humanitarian than military. The Japanese ambushed the patrol as it debarked from landing craft in the darkness. Only three Marines escaped.

"No, I never saw him," someone said.

"He's one of the three guys who escaped when the Goettge patrol got wiped out on Guadalcanal. He was lucky as hell."

"Why did the Japs ambush that patrol?" I asked naively.

A veteran looked at me with unbelief and said slowly and emphatically, "Because they're the meanest sonsabitches that ever lived."

*The Goettge patrol incident plus such Japanese tactics as playing dead and then throwing a grenade—or playing wounded, calling for a corpsman, and then knifing the medic when he came—plus the sneak attack on Pearl Harbor, caused Marines to hate the Japanese intensely and to be reluctant to take prisoners.*

*The attitudes held toward the Japanese by noncombatants or even sailors or airmen often did not reflect the deep personal resentment felt by Marine infantrymen. Official histories and memoirs of Marine infantrymen written after the war rarely reflect that hatred. But at the time of battle, Marines felt it deeply, bitterly, and as certainly as danger itself. To deny this hatred or make light of it would be as much a lie as to deny or make light of the esprit de corps or the intense patriotism felt by the Marines with whom I served in the Pacific.*

*My experiences on Peleliu and Okinawa made me believe that the Japanese held mutual feelings for us. They were a fanatical enemy; that is to say, they believed in their cause with an intensity little understood by many postwar Americans—and possibly many Japanese, as well.*

*This collective attitude, Marine and Japanese, resulted in savage, ferocious fighting with no holds barred. This was not the dispassionate killing seen on other fronts or in other wars. This was a brutish, primitive hatred, as characteristic of the horror of war in the Pacific as the palm trees and the islands. To comprehend what the troops endured then and there, one must take into full account this aspect of the nature of the Marines' war.*

Probably the biggest boost to our morale about this time on Pavuvu was the announcement that Bob Hope would come over from Banika and put on a show for us. Most of the men in the division crowded a big open area and cheered as a Piper Cub circled over us. The pilot switched off the engine briefly, while Jerry Colonna poked his head out of the plane and gave his famous yell, "Ye ow ow ow ow ow." We went wild with applause.

Bob Hope, Colonna, Frances Langford, and Patti Thomas put on a show on a little stage by the pier. Bob asked Jerry how he liked the trip over from Banika, and Jerry answered that it was "tough sledding." When asked why, he replied, "No snow." We thought it was the funniest thing we had ever heard. Patti gave several boys from the audience dancing lessons

*Pavuvu. Bob Hope and 1st Marine Division officers during his show before Peleliu.*

amid much grinning, cheering, and applause. Bob told many jokes and really boosted our spirits. It was the finest entertainment I ever saw overseas.*

Bob Hope's show remained the main topic of conversation as we got down to training in earnest for the coming campaign. Pavuvu was so small that most of our field exercises were of company size rather than battalion or regimental. Even so, we frequently got in the way of other units involved in their training exercises. It was funny to see a company move forward in combat formation through the groves and become intermingled with the rigid ranks of another company standing weapons inspection, the officers shouting orders to straighten things out.

We held numerous landing exercises—several times a week, it seemed—on the beaches and inlets around the island away from camp. We usually practiced from amtracs. The newest model had a tailgate that dropped as soon as the tractor was on the beach, allowing us to run out and deploy.

"Get off the beach fast. Get off the damned beach as fast as you can

*I renewed my acquaintance with Bob Hope last spring when he played in a charity golf tournament in Birmingham, Alabama. Earlier I had sent him copies of the *Marine Corps Gazette* (November and December 1979 and January 1980) that had serialized portions of my Peleliu story. He was enthusiastic about the account and remembered well the young Marines of the 1st Marine Division on Pavuvu. Despite a clamoring public on a hectic day in Birmingham, this most gracious man took the time to reminisce with me about the old breed.

and move inland. The Nips are going to plaster it with everything they've got, so your chances are better the sooner you move inland,'' shouted our officers and NCOs. We heard this over and over day after day. During each landing exercise, we would scramble out of our tractors, move inland about twenty-five yards, and then await orders to deploy and push forward.

The first wave of tractors landed rifle squads. The second wave landed more riflemen, machine gunners, bazooka gunners, flamethrowers, and 60mm mortar squads. Our second wave typically trailed about twenty-five yards behind the first as the machines churned through the water toward the beach. As soon as the first wave unloaded, its amtracs backed off, turned around, and headed past us out to sea to pick up supporting waves of infantry from Higgins boats circling offshore. It all worked nicely on Pavuvu. But there were no Japanese there.

In addition to landing exercises and field problems before Peleliu, we received refresher instructions and practice firing all small arms assigned to the company: M1 rifle, BAR, carbine, .45 caliber pistol, and Thompson submachine gun. We also learned how to operate a flamethrower.

During instruction with the flamethrower, we used a palm stump for a target. When my turn came, I shouldered the heavy tanks, held the nozzle in both hands, pointed at the stump about twenty-five yards away, and pressed the trigger. With a whoosh, a stream of red flame squirted out, and the nozzle bucked. The napalm hit the stump with a loud splattering noise. I felt the heat on my face. A cloud of black smoke rushed upward. The thought of turning loose hellfire from a hose nozzle as easily as I'd water a lawn back home sobered me. To shoot the enemy with bullets or kill him with shrapnel was one of the grim necessities of war, but to fry him to death was too gruesome to contemplate. I was to learn soon, however, that the Japanese couldn't be routed from their island defenses without it.

About this time I began to feel a deeper appreciation for the influence of the old breed on us newer Marines. Gunnery Sergeant Haney* provided a vivid example of their impact.

*Gunnery Sgt. Elmo M. Haney served with Company K, 3d Battalion, 5th Marines in France during World War I. Between the two world wars, he taught school in Arkansas for about four years, then rejoined the Marine Corps where he was assigned to his old unit. He fought on Guadalcanal and at Cape Gloucester with Company K. In the latter action he won a Silver Star for heroism when he "took care of some Japs by himself with a few hand grenades," as one Marine described the scene.

Haney was more than fifty years old when the 1st Marine Division assaulted Peleliu. Although a gunnery sergeant by rank, he held no official position in Company K's chain of command. In the field he seemed to be everywhere at once, correcting mistakes and helping out. He withdrew himself from the front lines on the second day of Peleliu, admitting sadly that he could no longer take the heat and the battle.

I had seen Haney around the company area but first noticed him in the shower one day because of the way he bathed. About a dozen naked, soapy replacements, including myself, stared in wide-eyed amazement and shuddered as Haney held his genitals in his left hand while scrubbing them with a GI brush the way one buffs a shoe. When you consider that the GI brush had stiff, tough, split-fiber bristles embedded in a stout wooden handle and was designed to scrub heavy canvas 782 (web) gear, dungarees, and even floors, Haney's method of bathing becomes truly impressive.

1 first saw him exert his authority one day on a pistol range where he was in charge of safety. A new second lieutenant, a replacement like myself, was firing from the position I was to assume. As he fired his last round, another new officer behind me called to him. The lieutenant turned to answer with his pistol in his hand. Haney was sitting next to me on a coconut-log bench and hadn't uttered a word except for the usual firing range commands. When the lieutenant turned the pistol's muzzle away from the target, Haney reacted like a cat leaping on its prey. He scooped up a large handful of coral gravel and flung it squarely into the lieutenant's face. He shook his fist at the bewildered officer and gave him the worst bawling out I ever heard. Everyone along the firing line froze, officers as well as enlisted men. The offending officer, with his gold bars shining brightly on his collar, cleared his weapon, holstered it, and took off rubbing his eyes and blushing visibly. Haney returned to his seat as though nothing had happened. Along the firing line, we thawed. Thereafter we were much more conscious of safety regulations.

Haney was about my size, at 135 pounds, with sandy crew-cut hair and a deep tan. He was lean, hard, and muscular. Although not broad-shouldered or well-proportioned, his torso reminded me of some anatomy sketch by Michelangelo: every muscle stood out in stark definition. He was slightly barrel-chested with muscles heaped up on the back of his shoulders so that he almost had a hump. Neither his arms nor his legs were large, but the muscles in them reminded me of steel bands. His face was small-featured with squinting eyes and looked as though it was covered with deeply tanned, wrinkled leather.

Haney was the only man I ever knew in the outfit who didn't seem to have a buddy. He wasn't a loner in the sense that he was sullen or unfriendly. He simply lived in a world all his own. I often felt that he didn't even see his surroundings; all he seemed to be aware of was his rifle, his bayonet, and his leggings. He was absolutely obsessed with wanting to bayonet the enemy.

We all cleaned our weapons daily, but Haney cleaned his M1 before muster, at noon chow, and after dismissal in the afternoon. It was a ritual. He would sit by himself, light a cigarette, field strip his rifle, and meticulously clean every inch of it. Then he cleaned his bayonet. All the while he talked to himself quietly, grinned frequently, and puffed his cigarette down to a stump. When his rifle was cleaned he reassembled it, fixed his bayonet, and went through a few minutes of thrust, parry, and butt-stroke movements at thin air. Then Haney would light up another cigarette and sit quietly, talking to himself and grinning while awaiting orders. He carried out these proceedings as though totally unaware of the presence of the other 235 men of the company. He was like Robinson Crusoe on an island by himself.

To say that he was "Asiatic" would be to miss the point entirely. Haney transcended that condition. The company had many rugged individualists, characters, old salts, and men who were "Asiatic," but Haney was in a category by himself. I felt that he was not a man born of woman, but that God had issued him to the Marine Corps.

Despite his personal idiosyncracies, Haney inspired us youngsters in Company K. He provided us with a direct link to the "Old Corps." To us he *was* the old breed. We admired him—and we loved him.

Then there was Company K's commanding officer, Capt. "Ack Ack" Haldane.* Late one afternoon as we left the rifle range, a heavy rain set in. As we plodded along Pavuvu's muddy roads, slipping and sliding under the downpour, we began to feel that whoever was leading the column had taken a wrong turn and that we were lost. At dusk in the heavy rain, every road looked alike: a flooded trail cut deeply with ruts, bordered by towering palms, winding aimlessly through the gloom. As I struggled along feeling chilled and forlorn and trying to keep my balance in the mud, a big man came striding from the rear of the column. He walked with the ease of a pedestrian on a city sidewalk. As he pulled abreast of me, the man looked at me and said, "Lovely weather, isn't it, son?"

*Capt. Andrew Allison Haldane, USMCR, was born 22 August 1917 in Lawrence, Massachusetts. He graduated from Bowdoin College, Brunswick, Maine, in 1941.

Captain Haldane served with the 1st Marine Division on Guadalcanal and was commanding officer of Company K at Cape Gloucester, where he won the Silver Star. During a five-day battle, he and his Marines repulsed five Japanese bayonet charges within one hour in the predawn darkness. He led Company K through most of the fight for Peleliu. On 12 October 1944, three days before the Marines came off the lines, he died in action. The Marines of Company K, and the rest of the division who knew him, suffered no greater loss during the entire war.

Bowdoin College annually honors the memory of Captain Haldane by presenting the Haldane Cup to the graduating senior who has displayed outstanding qualities of leadership and character. The cup was a gift from officers who had served with Captain Haldane in the Pacific. Among them was the late senator from Illinois, Paul Douglas, himself a member of the 5th Marines on Peleliu and Okinawa.

*Capt. Andrew A. Haldane. Photo by Lt. Col. John A. Crown.*

I grinned at Haldane and said, "Not exactly, sir." He recognized me as a replacement and asked how I liked the company. I told him I thought it was a fine outfit.

"You're a Southerner, aren't you?" he asked. I told him I was from Alabama. He wanted to know all about my family, home, and education. As we talked the gloom seemed to disappear, and I felt warm inside. Finally he told me it wouldn't rain forever, and we could get dry soon. He moved along the column talking to other men as he had to me. His sincere interest in each of us as a human being helped to dispel the feeling that we were just animals training to fight.

Acclaimed by superiors and subordinates alike for his leadership abilities, Captain Haldane was the finest and most popular officer I ever knew. All of the Marines in Company K shared my feelings. Called the "skipper," he had a strong face full of character, a large, prominent jaw, and the kindest eyes I ever saw. No matter how often he shaved or how hard he tried, he always had a five o'clock shadow. He was so large that the combat pack on his back reminded me of the bulge of his wallet, while mine covered me from neck to waist.

Although he insisted on strict discipline, the captain was a quiet man who gave orders without shouting. He had a rare combination of intelligence, courage, self-confidence, and compassion that commanded our respect and admiration. We were thankful that Ack Ack was our skipper, felt more secure in it, and felt sorry for other companies not so fortunate. While some officers on Pavuvu thought it necessary to strut or order us around to impress us with their status, Haldane quietly told us what to do. We loved him for it and did the best job we knew how.

Our level of training rose in August and so did the intensity of "chicken" discipline. We suffered through an increasing number of weapons and equipment inspections, work parties, and petty clean-up details around the camp. The step-up in harassment, coupled with the constant discomforts and harsh living conditions of Pavuvu, drove us all into a state of intense exasperation and disgust with our existence before we embarked for Peleliu.

"I used to think the lieutenant was a pretty good joe, but damned if I ain't about decided he ain't nothin' but a hosse's ass," grumbled one Marine.

"You said that right, ole buddy," came back another.

"Hell, he ain't the only one that's gone crazy over insisting that every-thing be just so, and then bawlin' us out if it ain't. The gunny's mean as hell, and nothin' suits him anymore," responded yet another man.

"Don't let it get you down, boys. It's just part of the USMC plan for keeping the troops in fighting shape," calmly remarked a philosophical old salt of prewar service.

"What the hell you talking about?" snapped an irritated listener.

"Well, it's this way," answered the philosopher. "If they get us mad enough, they figure we'll take it out on the Nips when we hit this beach coming up. I saw it happen before Guadalcanal and Gloucester. They don't pull this kind of stuff on rear-echelon boys. They want us to be mean, mad, and malicious. That's straight dope, I'm telling you. I've seen it happen every time before we go on a campaign."

"Sounds logical. You may be right. But what's malicious?" someone said.

"Forget it, you nitwit," the philosopher growled.

"Right or not, I'm sure tired of Pavuvu," I said.

"That's the plan, Sledgehammer. Get you fed up with Pavuvu, or wherever the hell you happen to be, and you'll be hot to go anywhere else even if the Nips are there waiting for you," the philosopher said.

We fell silent, thinking about that and finally concluded he was right. Many of the more thoughtful men I knew shared his view.

I griped as loudly as anyone about our living conditions and discipline. In retrospect, however, I doubt seriously whether I could have coped with the psychological and physical shock and stress encountered on Peleliu and Okinawa had it been otherwise. The Japanese fought to win. It was a savage, brutal, inhumane, exhausting, and dirty business. Our commanders knew that if we were to win and survive, we must be trained realistically for it whether we liked it or not.*

---

*In the postwar years, the Marine Corps came in for a great deal of undeserved criticism, in my opinion, from well-meaning persons who did not comprehend the magnitude of stress and horror that combat can be. The technology that developed the rifled barrel, the machine gun, and high-explosive shells has turned war into prolonged, subhuman slaughter. Men must be trained realistically if they are to survive it without breaking mentally and physically.

# CHAPTER THREE

# ON TO PELELIU

I n late August we completed our training. About the 26th, Company K boarded LST (landing ship, tank) 661* for a voyage that would end three weeks later on the beach at Peleliu.

Each rifle company assigned to the assault waves against Peleliu made the trip in an LST carrying the amtracs that would take the men ashore. Our LST lacked sufficient troop compartment space to accommodate all of the men of the company, so the platoon leaders drew straws for the available space. The mortar section got lucky. We were assigned to a troop compartment in the forecastle with an entrance on the main deck. Some of the other platoons had to make themselves as comfortable as possible on the main deck under and around landing boats and gear secured there.

Once loaded, we weighed anchor and headed straight for Guadalcanal, where the division held maneuvers in the Tassafaronga area. This area bore little resemblance to the beaches we would have to hit on Peleliu, but we spent several days in large- and small-unit amphibious landing exercises.

Some of our Guadalcanal veterans wanted to visit the island's cemetery to pay their respects to buddies killed during the division's first campaign. The veterans I knew were not allowed to make the trip to the cemetery, and

---

*LSTs were a class of shallow-draft amphibious ships developed just before World War II. An LST could drive its front end directly onto a beach and then unload its cargo of vehicles through the large clamshell doors that formed the ship's bow when closed. Or as in the case at Peleliu, LSTs could debark troop-carrying assault amphibians (amtracs) at sea. Advanced models of the LST serve the American fleet today.

there was a great deal of understandable bitterness and resentment on their part because of this.

Between training exercises, some of us explored the beach area and looked over the stranded wrecks of Japanese landing barges, the troopship *Yamazuki Maru*, and a two-man submarine. One of the Guadalcanal veterans told us what a helpless feeling it had been to sit back in the hills and watch Japanese reinforcements come ashore unopposed during the dark days of the campaign when the Japanese navy was so powerful in the Solomon Islands. Evidence of earlier fighting remained in the goodly number of shattered trees and several human skeletons we found in the jungle growth.

We also had our lighter moments. When the amtracs returned us to the LST each afternoon, we hurried to our quarters, stowed our gear, stripped, and went below to the tank deck. After all the amtracs were aboard, the ship's CO (commanding officer) obligingly left the bow doors open and the ramp down so we could swim in the blue waters of Sealark Channel (called more appropriately Iron Bottom Bay because of all the ships that had been sunk there during the Guadalcanal campaign). We dove, swam, and splashed in the beautiful water like a bunch of little boys, and for a few fleeting hours forgot why we were there.

The thirty LSTs carrying the 1st Marine Division's assault companies finally weighed anchor early on the morning of 4 September to make the approximately 2,100-mile voyage to Peleliu. The trip proved to be uneventful. The sea was smooth, and we ran into rain squalls only once or twice.

After chow each morning, several of us went aft to the ship's fantail to watch Gunnery Sergeant Haney's show. Dressed in khaki shorts, boondockers, and leggings, Haney went through his ritual of bayonet drill and rifle cleaning. He kept the scabbard on his bayonet and used a canvas-covered stanchion running down from the ship's superstructure as his target. It was a poor substitute for a moving parry stick, but Haney didn't let that stop him. For about an hour he went through his routine, complete with monologue, while dozens of Company K men lounged around on coils of rope and other gear, smoking and talking. Sometimes a spirited game of pinochle went on almost under his feet. He was as oblivious of the players as they were of him. Occasionally a sailor would come by and stare in disbelief at Haney. Several asked me if he were Asiatic. Not being able to overcome the temptation to kid them a bit, I told them no, he was just typical of our outfit. Then they would stare at me as they had at Haney.

I always had the feeling that sailors looked on Marine infantrymen as though we were a bit crazy, wild, or reckless. Maybe we were. But maybe we had to develop a don't-give-a-damn attitude to keep our sanity in the face of what we were about to endure.

In the ranks, we knew little about the nature of the island that was our objective. During a training lecture on Pavuvu we learned that Peleliu must be taken to secure Gen. Douglas MacArthur's right flank for his invasion of the Philippines, and that it had a good airfield that could support MacArthur. I don't recall when we heard the name of the island, although we viewed relief maps and models during lectures. (It had a nice sounding name, Pel' e loo.) Although our letters from Pavuvu were carefully censored, our officers apparently feared taking a chance on some character writing in code to someone back home that we were to hit an island named Peleliu. As a buddy said to me later, however, no one back home would have known where to look for it on a map anyway.

*The Palaus, the westernmost part of the Caroline Islands chain, consist of several large islands and more than a hundred smaller ones. Except for Angaur in the south and a couple of small atolls in the north, the whole group lies within an encircling coral reef. About five hundred miles to the west lie the southern Philippines. To the south at about the same distance is New Guinea.*

*Peleliu, just inside the Palau reef, is shaped like a lobster's claw, extending two arms of land. The southern arm reaches northeastward from flat ground to form a jumble of coral islets and tidal flats overgrown thickly with mangroves. The longer northern arm is dominated by the parallel coral ridges of Umurbrogol Mountain.*

*North to south, the island is about six miles long, with a width of approximately two miles. On the wide, largely flat southern section, the Japanese had constructed an airfield shaped roughly like the numeral 4. The ridges and most of the island outside the airfield were thickly wooded; there were only occasional patches of wild palms and open grass areas. The thick scrub so completely masked the true nature of the terrain that aerial photographs and pre–D day photos taken by United States submarines gave intelligence officers no hint of its ruggedness.*

*The treacherous reef along the landing beaches and the heavily defended coral ridges inland made the invasion of Peleliu a combination of the problems of Tarawa and of Saipan. The reef, over six hundred yards long, was the most formidable natural obstacle: Because of it, troops and equipment making the assault had to be transported in amtracs; Higgins boats could not negotiate across the rough coral and the varying depths of water.*

Before leaving Pavuvu, we had been told that the 1st Marine Division would be reinforced to about 28,000 men for the assault on Peleliu. As every man in the ranks knew, however, a lot of those people included in the term *reinforced* were neither trained nor equipped as combat troops. They were specialists attached to the division to implement the landing and supply by working on ships and later on the beaches. They would not be doing the fighting.

Upon sailing for Peleliu, the 1st Marine Division numbered 16,459 officers and men. A rear echelon of 1,771 remained on Pavuvu. Of these, only about 9,000 were infantrymen in the three infantry regiments. Intelligence sources estimated that we would face more than 10,000 Japanese defenders on Peleliu. The big topic of conversation among us troops had to do with those comparative strengths.

"Hey, you guys, the lieutenant just told me that the 1st Division is gonna be the biggest Marine division to ever make a landing. He says we got reinforcements we never had before."

A veteran looked up from cleaning his .45 automatic and said, "Boy, has that shavetail lieutenant been smoke-stacking you!"

"Why?"

"Use your head, buddy. Sure we got the 1st Marines, the 5th Marines, and the 7th Marines; them's infantry. The 11th Marines is our division artillery. Where the hell's all them people who is supposed to 'reinforce' the division? Have you seen 'em? Who the hell are they, and where the hell are they?"

"I don't know, I'm just telling you what the lieutenant said."

"Well, I'll tell you who them 'reinforcements' is. They's all what they call specialists, and they ain't line company Marines. Remember this, buster. When the stuff hits the fan, and you and me are trying to live through that shootin' and the shellin', them damned specialists'll be settin' on they cans back at division CP [command post] on the beach, writin' home about how war is hell. And who is gonna have all the casualties and lose all the men fightin' the Nips? The 1st Marines, the 5th Marines, and the 7th Marines'll all catch hell, and the 11th Marines'll lose some men too. Wake up, boy, them shavetail lieutenants is as useless as tits on a boar hog. The NCOs run things when the shootin' starts."*

---

*During World War II, amphibious planners considered the safe ratio of attackers to defenders in an amphibious assault to be three to one. To the leaders at Peleliu, the total Marine force of 30,000 provided a safe margin over the Japanese. Although at least one regimental commander—the redoubtable Col. Lewis B. ("Chesty") Puller—pointed out the disparity in actual combat forces, the division's commander, Maj. Gen. William H. Rupertus, and his staff believed his fears were groundless.

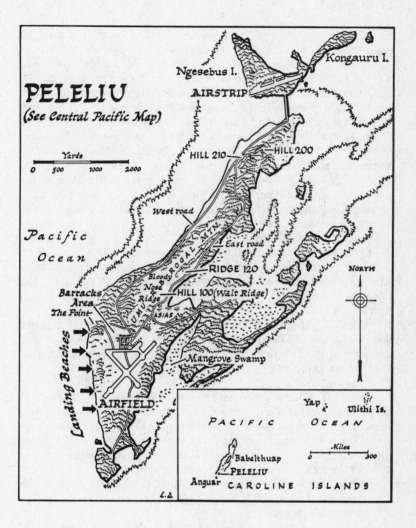

PELELIU
(See Central Pacific Map)

# D Minus 1

After evening chow on 14 September 1944, a buddy and I leaned against the rail of LST 661 and talked about what we would do after the war. I tried to appear unconcerned about the next day, and he did too. We may have fooled each other and ourselves a little, but not much. As the sun disappeared below the horizon and its glare no longer reflected off a glassy sea, I thought of how beautiful the sunsets always were in the Pacific. They were even more beautiful than over Mobile Bay. Suddenly a thought hit me like a thunderbolt. Would I live to see the sunset tomorrow? My knees nearly buckled as panic swept over me. I squeezed the railing and tried to appear interested in our conversation.

The ships in the convoy turned into dark hulks gliding along as the squawk box interrupted our conversation, "Now hear this. Now hear this." Talking quietly in pairs and small groups, the men around us seemed to pay more than the usual attention to the command. "All troops lay below to quarters. All troops lay below to quarters."

My buddy and I went to our forecastle compartment. One of our NCOs sent a work party to another compartment to draw rations and ammunition. After it returned, our lieutenant came in, gave us "at ease," and said he had some things to say. His brow was knit, his face drawn, and he looked worried.

"Men, as you probably know, tomorrow is D day. General Rupertus says the fighting will be extremely tough but short. It will be over in four days, maybe three. A fight like Tarawa. It's going to be rough but fast. Then we can return to a rest area.

"Remember what you've been taught. Keep your heads down going in on the amtrac. A lot of unnecessary casualties at Saipan were the result of men looking over the side to see what was happening. As soon as the amtrac stops on the beach, get out on the double, and get off the beach fast. Keep out of the way of amtracs on their way back out to pick up more troops from the supporting waves. Our tanks will be coming in behind us, too. The drivers have their hands full and can't dodge around the infantry, so you keep out of their way. Get off the beach fast! The Japs will plaster it with everything they've got, and if we get pinned down on the beach, artillery and mortars will ruin us.

"Have your weapons ready because the Japs always try to stop us at the beach line. They may meet us at the beach with bayonets as soon as our naval gunfire barrage lifts and moves inland. So come out of the amtracs ready for anything. Have a round in the chamber of your small arms and lock your pieces [snap on the safety]. Have the canister containers of your high-explosive mortar rounds untaped and stowed in your ammo bags ready for immediate use as soon as we are called on to deliver fire on the company front. Fill your canteens, draw rations and salt tablets, and clean your weapons. Reveille will be before daylight, and H hour will be at 0830. Hit the sack early. You will need the rest. Good luck and carry on.''

He left the compartment and the NCOs issued us ammo, K rations, and salt tablets.

"Well," said one man, "that scuttlebutt we heard during maneuvers on Guadalcanal about how this blitz gonna be rough but fast must be true if the division CG says so."

"San Antone," muttered a Texan. "Imagine, only four, maybe three days for a battle star. Hell, I can put up with anything for no longer than that."

He reflected the feelings of most of us, and we were encouraged by the commanding general's announcement confirming the oft-repeated "rough but fast" rumors we had been hearing.* We kept trying to convince ourselves that the CG knew what he was talking about. We all dreaded a long, protracted campaign that would drag on beyond endurance like Guadalcanal and Cape Gloucester. Our morale was excellent, and we were trained for anything no matter how rough. But we prayed that we could get it over with in a hurry.

We sat on our sacks, cleaned our weapons, packed our combat packs, and squared away our gear. Throughout history, combat troops of various armies have carried packs weighing many pounds into action; but we traveled light, carrying only absolute necessities—the way fast-moving Confederate infantry did during the Civil War.

My combat pack contained a folded poncho, one pair of socks, a couple of boxes of K rations, salt tablets, extra carbine ammo (twenty rounds), two hand grenades, a fountain pen, a small bottle of ink, writing paper in a waterproof wrapper, a toothbrush, a small tube of toothpaste, some photos of my folks along with some letters (in a waterproof wrapper), and a dungaree cap.

My other equipment and clothing were a steel helmet covered with camouflaged-cloth covering, heavy green dungaree jacket with a Marine

---

*In a sealed letter opened D day minus 1 by civilian news correspondents assigned to cover the battle, Maj. Gen. William H. Rupertus predicted that Peleliu would fall in four days after a short, tough fight. His forecast colored the tactical thinking ashore for much of the next month. Because of his optimism, many of the thirty-six newsmen never went ashore; of those who did, only six stayed through the critical early stages of the battle. Thus, the medium's eyes saw little of what actually happened.

emblem and *USMC* dyed above it on the left breast pocket, trousers of the same material, an old toothbrush for cleaning my carbine, thin cotton socks, ankle-high boondockers, and light tan canvas leggings (into which I tucked my trouser legs). Because of the heat, I wore no skivvy drawers or shirt. Like many men, I fastened a bronze Marine emblem to one collar for good luck.

Attached to my web pistol belt, I carried a pouch containing a combat dressing, two canteens, a pouch with two fifteen-round carbine magazines —clips, we called them, and a fine brass compass in a waterproof case. My kabar hung in its leather sheath on my right side. Hooked over the belt by its spoon (handle), I carried a grenade. I also had a heavy-bladed knife similar to a meat cleaver that my dad had sent me; I used this to chop through the wire braces wrapped around the stout crates of 60mm mortar shells.

On the stock of my carbine I fastened an ammo pouch with two extra clips. I carried no bayonet, because the model carbine I had lacked a bayonet lug. Onto the outside of my pack, I hooked my entrenching tool in its canvas cover. (The tool proved useless on Peleliu, because of the hard coral.)

All officers and men dressed much the same. The main differences among us were in the type of web belt worn and the individual weapon carried.

We tried to appear unconcerned and talked about anything but the war. Some wrote last latters.

"What are you going to do after the war, Sledgehammer?" asked a buddy sitting across from me. He was an extremely intelligent and intellectually active young man.

"I don't know, Oswalt. What are you planning to do?"

"I want to be a brain surgeon. The human brain is an incredible thing; it fascinates me," he replied.

But he didn't survive Peleliu to realize his ambition.

Slowly the conversations trailed off, and the men hit the sack. It was hard to sleep that night. I thought of home, my parents, my friends—and whether I would do my duty, be wounded and disabled, or be killed. I concluded that it was impossible for me to be killed, because God loved me. Then I told myself that God loved us all and that many would die or be ruined physically or mentally or both by the next morning and in the days following. My heart pounded, and I broke out in a cold sweat. Finally, I called myself a damned coward and eventually fell asleep saying the Lord's Prayer to myself.

# D Day, 15 September 1944

I seemed to have slept only a short time when an NCO came into the compartment saying, "OK, you guys, hit the deck." I felt the ship had slowed and almost stopped. If only I could hold back the hands of the clock, I thought. It was pitch dark with no lights topside. We tumbled out, dressed and shaved, and got ready for chow—steak and eggs, a 1st Marine Division tradition honoring a culinary combination learned from the Australians. Neither the steak nor the eggs was very palatable, though; my stomach was tied in knots.

Back in my compartment, a peculiar problem had developed. Haney, who had been one of the first to return from chow about forty-five minutes earlier, had ensconced himself on the seat of one of the two toilets in the small head on our side of the compartment. There he sat, dungaree trousers down to his knees, his beloved leggings laced neatly over his boondockers, grinning and talking calmly to himself while smoking a cigarette. Nervous Marines lined up using the other toilet one after another. Some men had been to the head on the other side of the compartment while others, in desperation, dashed off to the heads in other troop compartments. The facilities in our compartment normally were adequate, but D day morning found us all nervous, tense, and afraid. The veterans already knew what I was to find out: during periods of intense fighting, a man might not have the opportunity to eat or sleep, much less move his bowels. All the men grumbled and scowled at Haney, but because he was a gunnery sergeant, no one dared suggest he hurry. With his characteristic detachment, Haney ignored us, remained unhurried, and left when he pleased.

The first light of dawn was just appearing as I left my gear on my bunk, all squared away and ready to put on, and went out onto the main deck. All the men were talking quietly, smoking, and looking toward the island. I found Snafu* and stayed close by him; he was the gunner on our mortar, so we stuck together. He was also a Gloucester veteran, and I felt more secure around veterans. They knew what to expect.

He pulled out a pack of cigarettes and drawled, "Have a smoke, Sledgehammer."

"No thanks, Snafu. I've told you a million times I don't smoke."

"I'll bet you two bits, Sledgehammer, that before this day is over you'll be smokin' the hell outa every cigarette you can get your hands on."

I just gave him a sickly grin, and we looked toward the island. The sun

---

*Cpl. Merriell A. ("Snafu") Shelton came from Louisiana.

was just coming up, and there wasn't a cloud in the sky. The sea was calm. A gentle breeze blew.

A ship's bell rang, and over the squawk box came, "Get your gear on and stand by." Snafu and I hurried to our bunks, nodding and speaking to other grim-faced buddies who were rushing to get their gear. In the crowded compartment we helped each other with packs, straightened shoulder straps, and buckled on cartridge belts. Generals and admirals might worry about maps and tons of supplies, but my main concern at the moment was how my pack straps felt and whether my boondockers were comfortable.

The next bell rang. Snafu picked up the forty-five pounds of mortar and slung the carrying strap over his shoulder. I slung my carbine over one shoulder and the heavy ammo bag over the other. We filed down a ladder to the tank deck where an NCO directed us to climb aboard an amtrac. My knees got weak when I saw that it wasn't the newer model with the tailgate ramp for troop exit in which we had practiced. This meant that once the amtrac was on the beach, we'd have to jump over the high sides, exposed much more to enemy fire. I was too scared and excited to say much, but some of the guys grumbled about it.

The ship's bow doors opened and the ramp went down. All the tractors' engines roared and spewed out fumes. Exhaust fans whirred above us. Glaring daylight streamed into the tank deck through the opened bow of the ship as the first amtrac started out and clattered down the sloping ramp.

Our machine started with a jerk, and we held on to the sides and to each other. The amtrac's treads ground and scraped against the iron ridges on the ramp, then it floated freely and settled onto the water like a big duck. Around us roared the voices of the ships' guns engaged in the preassault bombardment of Peleliu's beaches and defensive positions.

The Marine Corps had trained us new men until we were welded with the veterans into a thoroughly disciplined combat division. Now the force of events unleashed on that two-mile by six-mile piece of unfriendly coral rock would carry us forward unrelentingly, each to his individual fate.

Everything my life had been before and has been after pales in the light of that awesome moment when my amtrac started in amid a thunderous bombardment toward the flaming, smoke-shrouded beach for the assault on Peleliu.

*Since the end of World War II, historians and military analysts have argued inconclusively about the necessity of the Palau Islands campaign. Many believed after the battle—and still believe today—that the United States didn't need to fight it as a prerequisite to General MacArthur's return to the Philippines.*

Adm. William F. ("Bull") Halsey suggested calling off the Palau operation after high-level planners learned that Japanese air power in the Philippines wasn't as strong as intelligence originally had presumed it to be. But MacArthur believed the operation should proceed, and Adm. Chester W. Nimitz said it was too late to cancel the operation, because the convoy was already underway.

Because of important events in Europe at the time and the lack of immediate, apparent benefits from the seizure of Peleliu, the battle remains one of the lesser known or understood of the Pacific war. Nonetheless, for many it ranks as the roughest fight the Marines had in World War II.

Maj. Gen. (later Lt. Gen.) Roy S. Geiger, the rugged commander of the III Amphibious Corps, said repeatedly that Peleliu was the toughest battle of the entire Pacific war. A former commandant of the Marine Corps, Gen. Clifton B. Cates, said Peleliu was one of the most vicious and stubbornly contested battles of the war, and that nowhere was the fighting efficiency of the U.S. Marine demonstrated more convincingly.

Peleliu also was important to the remainder of the Marines' war in the Pacific because of the changes in Japanese tactics encountered there. The Japanese abandoned their conventional all-out effort at defending the beach in favor of a complex defense based upon mutually supporting, fortified positions in caves and pillboxes extending deeply into the interior of the island, particularly in the ridges of Umurbrogol Mountain.

In earlier battles, the Japanese had exhausted their forces in banzai charges against the Marines once the latter had firmly established a beachhead. The Marines slaughtered the wildly charging Japanese by the thousands. Not a single banzai charge had been successful for the Japanese in previous campaigns.

But on Peleliu the Japanese commander, Col. Kunio Nakagawa, let the Marines come to him and the approximately 10,000 troops of his proud 14th Infantry Division. From mutually supporting positions, the Japanese covered nearly every yard of Peleliu from the beach inland to the center of Nakagawa's command post, deep beneath the coral rock in the center of the ridge system. Some positions were large enough to hold only one man. Some caves held hundreds. Thus the Marines encountered no one main defense line. The Japanese had constructed the perfect defense-in-depth with the whole island as a front line. They fought until the last position was knocked out.

Aided by the incredibly rugged terrain, the new Japanese tactics proved so successful that the 1st Marine Division suffered more than twice as many casualties on Peleliu as the 2d Marine Division had on Tarawa. Proportionately, United States casualties on Peleliu closely approximated those *suffered later on Iwo Jima where the Japanese again employed an intricate defense-in-depth, conserved forces, and fought a battle of attrition. On an even greater scale, the skillful, tenacious defense of the southern portion of Okinawa used the same sophisticated, in-depth defensive system first tested on Peleliu.*

# CHAPTER FOUR

# ASSAULT INTO HELL

H-hour, 0800. Long jets of red flame mixed with thick black smoke rushed out of the muzzles of the huge battleships' 16-inch guns with a noise like a thunderclap. The giant shells tore through the air toward the island, roaring like locomotives.

"Boy, it must cost a fortune to fire them 16-inch babies," said a buddy near me.

"Screw the expense," growled another.

Only less impressive were the cruisers firing 8-inch salvos and the host of smaller ships firing rapid fire. The usually clean salty air was strong with the odors of explosives and diesel fuel. While the assault waves formed up and my amphibious tractor lay still in the water with engines idling, the tempo of the bombardment increased to such intensity that I couldn't distinguish the reports of the various types of weapons through the thunderous noise. We had to shout at each other to be heard. The big ships increased their fire and moved off to the flanks of the amtrac formations when we started in so as not to fire over us at the risk of short rounds.

We waited a seeming eternity for the signal to start toward the beach. The suspense was almost more than I could bear. Waiting is a major part of war, but I never experienced any more supremely agonizing suspense than the excruciating torture of those moments before we received the signal to begin the assault on Peleliu. I broke out in a cold sweat as the tension mounted with the intensity of the bombardment. My stomach was tied in knots. I had a lump in my throat and swallowed only with great difficulty.

*D day, Peleliu. Smoke from naval and aerial bombardment hiding the beach. USMC photo.*

My knees nearly buckled, so I clung weakly to the side of the tractor. I felt nauseated ánd feared that my bladder would surely empty itself and reveal me to be the coward I was. But the men around me looked just about the way I felt. Finally, with a sense of fatalistic relief mixed with a flash of anger at the navy officer who was our wave commander, I saw him wave his flag toward the beach. Our driver revved the engine. The treads churned up the water, and we started in—the second wave ashore.

We moved ahead, watching the frightful spectacle. Huge geysers of water rose around the amtracs ahead of us as they approached the reef. The beach was now marked along its length by a continuous sheet of flame backed by a thick wall of smoke. It seemed as though a huge volcano had erupted from the sea, and rather than heading for an island, we were being drawn into the vortex of a flaming abyss. For many it was to be oblivion.

The lieutenant braced himself and pulled out a half-pint whiskey bottle.

"This is it, boys," he yelled.

Just like they do in the movies! It seemed unreal.

He held the bottle out to me, but I refused. Just sniffing the cork under those conditions might have made me pass out. He took a long pull on the bottle, and a couple of the men did the same. Suddenly a large shell exploded with a terrific concussion, and a huge geyser rose up just to our right front. It barely missed us. The engine stalled. The front of the tractor lurched to the left and bumped hard against the rear of another amtrac that was either stalled or hit. I never knew which.

We sat stalled, floating in the water for some terrifying moments. We

*Platoon Sgt. John Marmet, returning from Peleliu. Private photo.*

*D day, Peleliu. The inferno on the beach before we started in. National Archives photo.*

were sitting ducks for the enemy gunners. I looked forward through the hatch behind the driver. He was wrestling frantically with the control levers. Japanese shells were screaming into the area and exploding all around us. Sgt. Johnny Marmet leaned toward the driver and yelled something. Whatever it was, it seemed to calm the driver, because he got the engine started. We moved forward again amid the geysers of exploding shells.

Our bombardment began to lift off the beach and move inland. Our dive bombers also moved inland with their strafing and bombing. The Japanese increased the volume of their fire against the waves of amtracs. Above the din I could hear the ominous sound of shell fragments humming and growling through the air.

"Stand by," someone yelled.

I picked up my mortar ammo bag and slung it over my left shoulder, buckled my helmet chin strap, adjusted my carbine sling over my right shoulder, and tried to keep my balance. My heart pounded. Our amtrac came out of the water and moved a few yards up the gently sloping sand.

"Hit the beach!" yelled an NCO moments before the machine lurched to a stop.

The men piled over the sides as fast as they could. I followed Snafu, climbed up, and planted both feet firmly on the left side so as to leap as far away from it as possible. At that instant a burst of machine-gun fire with white-hot tracers snapped through the air at eye level, almost grazing my face. I pulled my head back like a turtle, lost my balance, and fell awkwardly forward down onto the sand in a tangle of ammo bag, pack, helmet, carbine, gas mask, cartridge belt, and flopping canteens. "Get off the beach! Get off the beach!" raced through my mind.

Once I felt land under my feet, I wasn't as scared as I had been coming across the reef. My legs dug up the sand as I tried to rise. A firm hand gripped my shoulder. "Oh god, I thought, it's a Nip who's come out of a pillbox!" I couldn't reach my kabar—fortunately, because as I got my face out of the sand and looked up, there was the worried face of a Marine bending over me. He thought the machine-gun burst had hit me, and he had crawled over to help. When he saw I was unhurt, he spun around and started crawling rapidly off the beach. I scuttled after him.

Shells crashed all around. Fragments tore and whirred, slapping on the sand and splashing into the water a few yards behind us. The Japanese were recovering from the shock of our prelanding bombardment. Their machine gun and rifle fire got thicker, snapping viciously overhead in increasing volume.

Our amtrac spun around and headed back out as I reached the edge of the beach and flattened on the deck. The world was a nightmare of flashes, violent explosions, and snapping bullets. Most of what I saw blurred. My mind was benumbed by the shock of it.

I glanced back across the beach and saw a DUKW (rubber-tired amphibious truck) roll up on the sand at a point near where we had just landed. The instant the DUKW stopped, it was engulfed in thick, dirty black smoke as a shell scored a direct hit on it. Bits of debris flew into the air. I watched with that odd, detached fascination peculiar to men under fire, as a flat metal panel about two feet square spun high into the air then splashed into shallow water like a big pancake. I didn't see any men get out of the DUKW.

Up and down the beach and out on the reef, a number of amtracs and DUKWs were burning. Japanese machine-gun bursts made long splashes on the water as though flaying it with some giant whip. The geysers belched up relentlessly where the mortar and artillery shells hit. I caught a fleeting glimpse of a group of Marines leaving a smoking amtrac on the reef. Some

*An amphibious tractor burns on the beach as Marines take shelter under a DUKW.
D day, Peleliu. Private photo (Pfc. John J. Smith).*

fell as bullets and fragments splashed among them. Their buddies tried to
help them as they struggled in the knee-deep water.

I shuddered and choked. A wild desperate feeling of anger, frustration,
and pity gripped me. It was an emotion that always would torture my mind
when I saw men trapped and was unable to do anything but watch as they
were hit. My own plight forgotten momentarily, I felt sickened to the depths
of my soul. I asked God, "Why, why, why?" I turned my face away and
wished that I were imagining it all. I had tasted the bitterest essence of war,
the sight of helpless comrades being slaughtered, and it filled me with
disgust.

I got up. Crouching low, I raced up the sloping beach into a defilade.
Reaching the inland edge of the sand just beyond the high-water mark, I
glanced down and saw the nose of a huge black and yellow bomb protruding from the sand. A metal plate attached to the top served as a pressure
trigger. My foot had missed it by only inches.

I hit the deck again just inside the defilade. On the sand immediately in front of me was a dead snake about eighteen inches long. It was colorful, somewhat like American species I had kept as pets when a boy. It was the only snake I saw on Peleliu.

Momentarily I was out of the heavy fire hitting on the beach. A strong smell of chemicals and exploding shells filled the air. Patches of coral and sand around me were yellowed from the powder from shell blasts. A large white post about four feet high stood at the edge of the defilade. Japanese writing was painted on the side facing the beach. To me, it appeared as though a chicken with muddy feet had walked up and down the post. I felt a sense of pride that this was enemy territory and that we were capturing it for our country to help win the war.

One of our NCOs signaled us to move to our right, out of the shallow defilade. I was glad, because the Japanese probably would pour mortar fire into it to prevent it being used for shelter. At the moment, however, the gunners seemed to be concentrating on the beach and the incoming waves of Marines.

I ran over to where one of our veterans stood looking to our front and flopped down at his feet. "You'd better get down," I yelled as bullets snapped and cracked all around.

"Them slugs are high, they're hittin' in the leaves, Sledgehammer," he said nonchalantly without looking at me.

"Leaves, hell! Where are the trees?" I yelled back at him.

Startled, he looked right and left. Down the beach, barely visible, was a shattered palm. Nothing near us stood over knee high. He hit the deck.

"I must be crackin' up, Sledgehammer. Them slugs sound just like they did in the jungle at Gloucester, and I figured they were hittin' leaves," he said with chagrin.

"Somebody gimme a cigarette," I yelled to my squad mates nearby.

Snafu was jubilant. "I toldja you'd start smokin', didn't I, Sledgehammer?"

A buddy handed me a smoke, and with trembling hands we got it lit. They really kidded me about going back on all my previous refusals to smoke.

I kept looking to our right, expecting to see men from the 3d Battalion, 7th Marines (3/7), which was supposed to be there. But I saw only the familiar faces of Marines from my own company as we moved off the beach. Marines began to come in behind us in increasing numbers, but none were visible on our right flank.

Unfamiliar officers and NCOs yelled and shouted orders, "K Company, first platoon, move over here," or "K Company, mortar

*Orange Beach 3 on D day, Peleliu, to the right of where K/3/5 had landed earlier. USMC photo.*

section, over here.'' Considerable confusion prevailed for about fifteen minutes as our officers and the leaders from our namesake company in the 7th Marines straightened out the two units.

*From left to right along the 2,200-yard beach front, the 1st Marines, the 5th Marines and the 7th Marines landed abreast. The 1st Marines landed one battalion on each of the two northern White beaches. In the division's center, the 5th Marines landed its 1st Battalion (1/5) over Orange Beach One and its 3d Battalion (3/5) over Orange Beach Two. Forming the right flank of the division, the 7th Marines was to land one battalion (3/7) in the assault over Orange Beach Three, the southernmost of five designated beaches.*

*In the confusion of the landing's first few minutes, K/3/5 actually got in ahead of the assault companies of 3/7 and slightly farther to the right than intended. As luck would have it, the two companies got mixed together as the right flank of the division. For about fifteen minutes we were the exposed right flank of the entire beachhead.*

We started to move inland. We had gone only a few yards when an enemy machine gun opened up from a scrub thicket to our right. Japanese 81mm and 90mm mortars then opened up on us. Everyone hit the deck; I dove into a shallow crater. The company was completely pinned down. All movement ceased. The shells fell faster, until I couldn't make out individual explosions, just continuous, crashing rumbles with an occasional ripping sound of shrapnel tearing low through the air overhead amid the roar. The air was murky with smoke and dust. Every muscle in my body was as tight as a piano wire. I shuddered and shook as though I were having a mild convulsion. Sweat flowed profusely. I prayed, clenched my teeth, squeezed my carbine stock, and cursed the Japanese. Our lieutenant, a Cape Gloucester veteran who was nearby, seemed to be in about the same shape. From the meager protection of my shallow crater I pitied him, or anyone, out on that flat coral.

The heavy mortar barrage went on without slackening. I thought it would never stop. I was terrified by the big shells arching down all around us. One was bound to fall directly into my hole, I thought.

If any orders were passed along, or if anyone yelled for a corpsman, I never heard it in all the noise. It was as though I was out there on the battlefield all by myself, utterly forlorn and helpless in a tempest of violent explosions. All any man could do was sweat it out and pray for survival. It would have been sure suicide to stand up in that fire storm.

Under my first barrage since the fast-moving events of hitting the beach, I learned a new sensation: utter and absolute helplessness. The shelling lifted in about half an hour, although it seemed to me to have crashed on for hours. Time had no meaning to me. (This was particularly true when under a heavy shelling. I never could judge how long it lasted.) Orders then came to move out and I got up, covered by a layer of coral dust. I felt like jelly and couldn't believe any of us had survived that barrage.

The walking wounded began coming past us on their way to the beach where they would board amtracs to be taken out to one of the ships. An NCO who was a particular friend of mine hurried by, holding a bloody battle dressing over his upper left arm.

"Hit bad?" I yelled.

His face lit up in a broad grin, and he said jauntily, "Don't feel sorry for me, Sledgehammer. I got the million-dollar wound. It's all over for me."

We waved as he hurried on out of the war.

We had to be alert constantly as we moved through the thick sniper-infested scrub. We received orders to halt in an open area as I came upon the first enemy dead I had ever seen, a dead Japanese medical corpsman and two riflemen. The medic apparently had been trying to administer aid when he was killed by one of our shells. His medical chest lay open beside him, and the various bandages and medicines were arranged neatly in compartments. The corpsman was on his back, his abdominal cavity laid bare. I stared in horror, shocked at the glistening viscera bespecked with fine coral dust. This can't have been a human being, I agonized. It looked more like the guts of one of the many rabbits or squirrels I had cleaned on hunting trips as a boy. I felt sick as I stared at the corpses.

A sweating, dusty Company K veteran came up, looked first at the dead, and then at me. He slung his M1 rifle over his shoulder and leaned over the bodies. With the thumb and forefinger of one hand, he deftly plucked a pair of hornrimmed glasses from the face of the corpsman. This was done as casually as a guest plucking an hors d'oeuvre from a tray at a cocktail party.

"Sledgehammer," he said reproachfully, "don't stand there with your mouth open when there's all these good souvenirs laying around." He held the glasses for me to see and added, "Look how thick that glass is. These sonsabitches must be half blind, but it don't seem to mess up their marksmanship any."

He then removed a Nambu pistol, slipped the belt off the corpse, and took the leather holster. He pulled off the steel helmet, reached inside, and took out a neatly folded Japanese flag covered with writing. The veteran pitched the helmet on the coral where it clanked and rattled, rolled the corpse over, and started pawing through the combat pack.

The veteran's buddy came up and started stripping the other Japanese corpses. His take was a flag and other items. He then removed the bolts from the Japanese rifles and broke the stocks against the coral to render them useless to infiltrators. The first veteran said, "See you, Sledgehammer. Don't take any wooden nickels." He and his buddy moved on.

I hadn't budged an inch or said a word, just stood glued to the spot almost in a trance. The corpses were sprawled where the veterans had dragged them around to get into their packs and pockets. Would I become this casual and calloused about enemy dead? I wondered. Would the war dehumanize me so that I, too, could "field strip" enemy dead with such nonchalance? The time soon came when it didn't bother me a bit.

Within a few yards of this scene, one of our hospital corpsmen worked in a small, shallow defile treating Marine wounded. I went over and sat on the hot coral by him. The corpsman was on his knees bending over a young Marine who had just died on a stretcher. A blood-soaked battle dressing was on the side of the dead man's neck. His fine, handsome, boyish face was ashen. "What a pitiful waste," I thought. "He can't be a day over seventeen years old." I thanked God his mother couldn't see him. The corpsman held the dead Marine's chin tenderly between the thumb and fingers of his left hand and made the sign of the cross with his right hand.

Tears streamed down his dusty, tanned, grief-contorted face while he sobbed quietly.

The wounded who had received morphine sat or lay around like zombies and patiently awaited the "doc's" attention. Shells roared overhead in both directions, an occasional one falling nearby, and machine guns rattled incessantly like chattering demons.

We moved inland. The scrub may have slowed the company, but it concealed us from the heavy enemy shelling that was holding up other companies facing the open airfield. I could hear the deep rumble of the shelling and dreaded that we might move into it.

That our battalion executive officer had been killed a few moments after hitting the beach and that the amtrac carrying most of our battalion's field telephone equipment and operators had been destroyed on the reef made control difficult. The companies of 3/5 lost contact with each other and with 3/7 on our right flank.*

As I passed the different units and exchanged greetings with friends, I was astonished at their faces. When I tried to smile at a comment a buddy made, my face felt as tight as a drumhead. My facial muscles were so tensed from the strain that I actually felt it was impossible to smile. With a shock I realized that the faces of my squad mates and everyone around me looked masklike and unfamiliar.

As we pushed eastward, we halted briefly along a North-South trail. Word was passed that we had to move forward faster to a trail where we would come up abreast of 3/7.

We continued through the thick scrub and heavy sniper fire until we came out into a clearing overlooking the ocean. Company K had reached the eastern shore. We had reached our objective. To our front was a shallow bay with barbed wire entanglements, iron tetrahedrons and other obstacles against landing craft. I was glad we hadn't tried to invade this coast.

About a dozen Company K riflemen commenced firing at Japanese soldiers wading along the reef several hundred yards away at the mouth of the bay. Other Marines joined us. The enemy were moving out from a narrow extension of the mangrove swamp on the left toward the southeastern promontory on our right. About a dozen enemy soldiers were alternately swimming and running along the reef. Some of the time only their heads were above the water as my buddies sent rifle fire into their midst. Most of the running enemy went down with a splash.

---

*Historical accounts of battles often leave a reader with the impression that the individual participants had a panoramic view of events. Such is not the case, however. Even the historians have never been able to piece together completely what happened to 3/5 on D day at Peleliu.

We were elated over reaching the eastern shore, and at being able to fire on the enemy in the open. A few Japanese escaped and scrambled among the rocks on the promontory.

"OK, you guys, line 'em up and squeeze 'em off," said a sergeant. "You don't kill 'em with the noise. It's the slugs that do it. You guys couldn't hit a bull in the ass with a bass fiddle," he roared.

Several more Japanese ran out from the cover of the mangroves. A burst of rifle fire sent every one of them splashing. "That's better," growled the sergeant.

The mortarmen put down our loads and stood by to set up the guns. We didn't fire at the enemy with our carbines. Rifles were more effective than carbines at that range. So we just watched.

Firing increased from our rear. We had no contact with Marine units on our right or left. But the veterans weren't concerned wth anything but the enemy on the reef.

"Stand by to move out!" came the order.

"What the hell," grumbled a veteran as we headed back into the scrub. "We fight like hell and reach our objective, and they order us to fall back." Others joined in the grumbling.

"Aw, knock it off. We gotta gain contact with the 7th Marines," an NCO said.

We headed back into the thick scrub. For some time I completely lost my bearings and had no idea where we were going.

*Unknown to the Marines, there were two parallel North-South trails about two hundred yards apart winding through the thick scrub. Poor maps, poor visibility, and numerous snipers made it difficult to distinguish the two trails.*

*When 3/5, with Company K on its right flank, reached the first (westernmost) trail, it was then actually abreast of 3/7. However, due to poor visibility, contact couldn't be made between the two battalions. It was thought 3/5 was too far to the rear. So, 3/5 was ordered to move forward to come abreast of 3/7. By the time this error was realized, 3/5 had pushed 300–400 yards ahead of the 7th Marine's flank. For the second time on D day, K-3-5 was the forward-most exposed right flank element of the division. The entire 3d Battalion 5th Marines formed a deep salient reaching into enemy territory to the east coast. To make matters worse, the battalion's three companies had lost contact with each other. These isolated units were in critical danger of being cut off and surrounded by the Japanese.*

*Caliber .30 aircooled machine gun in action. Peleliu. USMC photo.*

The weather was getting increasingly hot, and I was soaked with sweat. I began eating salt tablets and taking frequent drinks of tepid water from my canteens. We were warned to save our water as long as possible, because no one knew when we would get any more.

A sweating runner with a worried face came up from the rear. "Hey, you guys, where's K Company's CO?" he asked. We told him where we thought Ack Ack could be located.

"What's the hot dope?" someone asked, with that same anxious question always put to runners.

"Battalion CP says we just gotta establish contact with the 7th Marines, 'cause if the Nips counterattack they'll come right through the gap," he said as he hurried on.

"Jesus!" said a man near me.

We moved forward and came up with the rest of the company in a clearing. The platoons formed up and took casualty reports. Japanese mortar and artillery fire increased. The shelling became heavy, indicating

*D day afternoon after Marines smashed Japanese tank attack. Peleliu. USMC photo.*

the probability of a counterattack. Most of their fire whistled over us and fell to our rear. This seemed strange although fortunate to me at the time. The order came for us to move out a short distance to the edge of the scrub. At approximately 1650 I looked out across the open airfield toward the southern extremities of the coral ridges—collectively called Bloody Nose Ridge—and saw vehicles of some sort moving amid swirling clouds of dust.

"Hey," I said to a veteran next to me, "what are those amtracs doing all the way across the airfield toward the Jap lines?"

"Them ain't amtracs; they're Nip tanks!" he said.

Shell bursts appeared among the enemy tanks. Some of our Sherman tanks had arrived at the edge of the airfield on our left and opened fire. Because of the clouds of dust and the shellfire, I couldn't see much and didn't see any enemy infantry, but the firing on our left was heavy.

Word came for us to deploy on the double. The riflemen formed a line at the edge of the scrub along a trail and lay prone, trying to take what cover they could. From the beginning to the end on Peleliu, it was all but impossible to dig into the hard coral rock, so the men piled rocks around themselves or got behind logs and debris.

Snafu and I set up our 60mm mortar a few yards behind them, across the trail in a shallow crater. Everyone got edgy as the order came, "Stand by to repel counterattack. Counterattack hitting I Company's front."

I didn't know where Company I was, but I thought it was on our left—somewhere. Although I had great confidence in our officers and NCOs, it seemed to me that we were alone and confused in the middle of a rumbling chaos with snipers everywhere and with no contact with any other units. I thought all of us would be lost.

"They needta get some more damned troops up here," growled Snafu, his standard remark in a tight spot.

Snafu set up the gun, and I removed an HE (high explosive) shell from a canister in my ammo bag. At last we could return fire!

Snafu yelled, "Fire!"

Just then a Marine tank to our rear mistook us for enemy troops. As soon as my hand went up to drop the round down the tube, a machine gun cut loose. It sounded like one of ours—and from the rear of all places! As I peeped over the edge of the crater through the dust and smoke and saw a Sherman tank in a clearing behind us, the tank fired its 75mm gun off to our right rear. The shell exploded nearby, around a bend in the same trail we were on. I then heard the report of a Japanese field gun located there as it returned fire on the tank. Again I tried to fire, but the machine gun opened up as before.

"Sledgehammer, don't let him hit that shell. We'll all be blown to hell," said a worried ammo carrier crouched in the crater near me.

"Don't worry, that's my hand he just about hit," I snapped.

Our tank and the Japanese field gun kept up their duel.

"By god, when that tank knocks out that Nip gun he'll swing his 75 over thisaway, and it'll be our ass. He thinks we're Nips," said a veteran in the crater.

"Oh, Jesus!" someone moaned.

A surge of panic rose within me. In a brief moment our tank had reduced me from a well-trained, determined assistant mortar gunner to a quivering mass of terror. It was not just that I was being fired at by a machine gun that unnerved me so terribly, but that it was one of ours. To be killed by the enemy was bad enough; that was a real possibility I had prepared myself for. But to be killed by mistake by my own comrades was something I found hard to accept. It was just too much.

An authoritative voice across the trail yelled, "Secure the mortar."

A volunteer crawled off to the left, and soon the tank ceased firing on us. We learned later that our tankers were firing on us because we had moved too far ahead. They thought we were enemy support for the field gun. This also explained why the enemy shelling was passing over and exploding behind us. Tragically, the marine who saved us by identifying us to the tanker was shot off the tank and killed by a sniper.

The heavy firing on our left had about subsided, so the Japanese counterattack had been broken. Regrettably, I hadn't helped at all, because we were pinned down by one of our own tanks.

Some of us went along the trail and looked at the Japanese field gun. It was a well-made, formidable-looking piece of artillery, but I was surprised that the wheels were the heavy wooden kind typical of field guns of the nineteenth century. The Japanese gun crew was sprawled around the piece.

"Them's the biggest Nips I ever saw," one veteran said.

"Look at them sonsabitches; they's all over six foot tall," said another.

"That must be some of that 'Flower of the Kwantung Army' we've been hearing about," put in a corporal.

The Japanese counterattack was no wild, suicidal *banzai* charge such as Marine experience in the past would have led us to expect. Numerous times during D day I heard the dogmatic claim by experienced veterans that the enemy would *banzai*.

"They'll pull a *banzai,* and we'll tear their ass up. Then we can get the hell offa this hot rock, and maybe the CG will send the division back to Melbourne."

Rather than a *banzai,* the Japanese counterthrust turned out to be a well-coordinated tank-infantry attack. Approximately one company of Japanese infantry, together with about thirteen tanks, had moved carefully across the airfield until annihilated by the Marines on our left. This was our first warning that the Japanese might fight differently on Peleliu than they had elsewhere.

Just before dusk, a Japanese mortar concentration hit 3/5's command post. Our CO, Lt. Col. Austin C. Shofner,* was hit while trying to establish contact among the companies of our battalion. He was evacuated and put aboard a hospital ship.

Companies I, K, and L couldn't regain contact before nightfall. Each dug in in a circular defense for the night. The situation was precarious. We were isolated, nearly out of water in the terrible heat, and ammunition was low. Lt. Col. Lewis Walt, accompanied by only a runner, came out into that

---

*Shofner had assumed command of 3/5 before the Peleliu campaign. Not only was he highly respected, but his men considered him someone special. As a captain, he had survived the fighting on Corregidor, been captured by the Japanese, escaped, and had returned to combat. He came back to the division later, and commanded the 1st Battalion, 1st Marines on Okinawa. He retired from the Corps as a brigadier general.

*Japanese soldier killed alongside his field piece. Note Jap grenade in center foreground. Peleliu. USMC photo.*

pitch dark, enemy-infested scrub, located all the companies, and directed us into the division's line on the airfield. He should have won a Medal of Honor for that feat!*

Rumor had it, as we dug in, that the division had suffered heavy casualties in the landing and subsequent fighting. The veterans I knew said it had been about the worst day of fighting they had ever seen.†

---

*Walt was the executive officer of the 5th Marines when the battle for Peleliu began. He remained with 3/5 for a few days as its commanding officer until a replacement was named. A combat Marine in the truest sense, Walt had served with the 1st Marine Division on Guadalcanal and at Cape Gloucester. He had won the Navy Cross for heroism. He went on to serve in the Korean War and later in Vietnam where, as a lieutenant general, he commanded the III Marine Amphibious Corps for nearly two years. He retired as a general after serving as assistant commandant of the Marine Corps.

† Casualty figures for the 1st Marine Division on D day reflected the severity of the fighting and the ferocity of the Japanese defense. The division staff had predicted D day losses of 500 casualties, but the total figure was 1,111 killed and wounded, not including heat prostration cases.

It was an immense relief to me when we got our gun pit completed and had registered in our gun by firing two or three rounds of HE into an area out in front of Company K. My thirst was almost unbearable, my stomach was tied in knots, and sweat soaked me. Dissolving some K ration dextrose tablets in my mouth helped, and I took the last sip of my dwindling water supply. We had no idea when relief would get through with additional water. Artillery shells shrieked and whistled back and forth overhead with increasing frequency, and small-arms fire rattled everywhere.

In the eerie green light of star shells swinging pendulumlike on their parachutes so that shadows danced and swayed around crazily, I started taking off my right shoe.

"Sledgehammer, what the hell are you doin'?" Snafu asked in an exasperated tone.

"Taking off my boondockers; my feet hurt," I replied.

"Have you gone Asiatic?" he asked excitedly. "What the hell are you gonna do in your stockin' feet if the Nips come bustin' outa that jungle, or across this field? We may have to get outa this hole and haul tail if we're ordered to. They're probably gonna pull a *banzai* before daybreak, and how do you reckon you'll move around on this coral in your stockin's?"

I said that I just wasn't thinking. He reamed me out good and told me we would be lucky to get our shoes off before the island was secured. I thanked God my foxhole buddy was a combat veteran.

Snafu then nonchalantly drew his kabar and stuck it in the coral gravel near his right hand. My stomach tightened and gooseflesh chilled my back and shoulders at the sight of the long blade in the greenish light and the realization of why he placed it within such easy reach. He then checked his .45 automatic pistol. I followed his example with my kabar as I crouched on the other side of the mortar, checked my carbine, and looked over the mortar shells (HE and flares) stacked up within reach. We settled down for the long night.

"Is that theirs or ours, Snafu?" I asked each time a shell went over.

There was nothing subtle or intimate about the approach and explosion of an artillery shell. When I heard the whistle of an approaching one in the distance, every muscle in my body contracted. I braced myself in a puny effort to keep from being swept away. I felt utterly helpless.

As the fiendish whistle grew louder, my teeth ground against each other, my heart pounded, my mouth dried, my eyes narrowed, sweat poured over me, my breath came in short irregular gasps, and I was afraid to swallow lest I choke. I always prayed, sometimes out loud.

Under certain conditions of range and terrain, I could hear the shell approaching from a considerable distance, thus prolonging the suspense

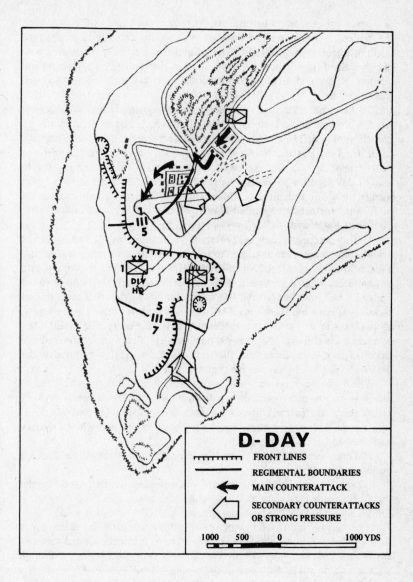

## D-DAY

┉┉┉┉┉┉  FRONT LINES

──────────  REGIMENTAL BOUNDARIES

◀━━━━  MAIN COUNTERATTACK

⬅  SECONDARY COUNTERATTACKS
OR STRONG PRESSURE

1000    500    0         1000 YDS

into seemingly unending torture. At the instant the voice of the shell grew the loudest, it terminated in a flash and a deafening explosion similar to the crash of a loud clap of thunder. The ground shook and the concussion hurt my ears. Shell fragments tore the air apart as they rushed out, whirring and ripping. Rocks and dirt clattered onto the deck as smoke of the exploded shell dissipated.

To be under a barrage or prolonged shelling simply magnified all the terrible physical and emotional effects of one shell. To me, artillery was an invention of hell. The onrushing whistle and scream of the big steel package of destruction was the pinnacle of violent fury and the embodiment of pent-up evil. It was the essence of violence and of man's inhumanity to man. I developed a passionate hatred for shells. To be killed by a bullet seemed so clean and surgical. But shells would not only tear and rip the body, they tortured one's mind almost beyond the brink of sanity. After each shell I was wrung out, limp and exhausted.

During prolonged shelling, I often had to restrain myself and fight back a wild, inexorable urge to scream, to sob, and to cry. As Peleliu dragged on, I feared that if I ever lost control of myself under shell fire my mind would be shattered. I hated shells as much for their damage to the mind as to the body. To be under heavy shell fire was to me by far the most terrifying of combat experiences. Each time it left me feeling more forlorn and helpless, more fatalistic, and with less confidence that I could escape the dreadful law of averages that inexorably reduced our numbers. Fear is many-faceted and has many subtle nuances, but the terror and desperation endured under heavy shelling are by far the most unbearable.

The night wore on endlessly, and I was hardly able to catch even so much as a catnap. Toward the predawn hours, numerous enemy artillery pieces concentrated their fire on the area of scrub jungle from which Lt. Col. Lewis Walt had brought us. The shells screeched and whined over us and crashed beyond in the scrub.

"Whoo, boy, listen to them Nip gunners plaster that area," said a buddy in the next hole.

"Yeah," Snafu said, "they must think we're still out there and I betcha they'll counterattack right across through that place, too."

"Thank God we are here and not out there," our buddy said.

The barrage increased in tempo as the Japanese gave the vacant scrub jungle a real pounding. When the barrage finally subsided, I heard someone say with a chuckle, "Aw, don't knock it off now, you bastards. Fire all your goddamn shells out there in the wrong place."

"Don't worry, knucklehead, they'll have plenty left to fire in the right place, which is going to be where they see us when daylight comes," another voice said.

Supplies had been slow in keeping up with the needs of the 5th Marines' infantry companies on D day. The Japanese kept heavy artillery, mortar, and machine-gun fire on the entire regimental beach throughout the day; enemy artillery and mortar observers called down their fire on amphibian vehicles as soon as they reached the beach. This made it difficult to get the critical supplies ashore and the wounded evacuated. All of Peleliu was a front line on D day. No one but the dead was out of reach of enemy fire. The shore party people* did their best, but they couldn't make up for the heavy losses of amtracs needed to bring the supplies to us.

We weren't aware of the problems on the beach, being too occupied with our own. We griped, cursed, and prayed that water would get to us. I had used mine more sparingly than some men had, but I finally emptied both of my canteens by the time we finished the gun pit. Dissolving dextrose tablets in my mouth helped a little, but my thirst grew worse through the night. For the first time in my life, I appreciated fully the motion picture cliche of a man on a desert crying, "Water, water."

Artillery shells still passed back and forth overhead just before dawn, but there wasn't much small-arms fire in our area. Abruptly, there swept over us some of the most intense Japanese machine-gun fire I ever saw concentrated in such a small area. Tracers streaked and bullets cracked not more than a foot over the top of our gun pit. We lay flat on our backs and waited as the burst ended.

The gun cut loose again, joined by a second and possibly a third. Streams of bluish white tracers (American tracers were red) poured thickly overhead, apparently coming from somewhere near the airfield. The cross fire kept up for at least a quarter of an hour. They really poured it on.

Shortly before the machine guns opened fire, we had received word to move out at daylight with the entire 5th Marine regiment in an attack across the airfield. I prayed the machine-gun fire would subside before we had to move out. We were pinned down tightly. To raise anything above the edge of the gun pit would have resulted in its being cut off as though by a giant scythe. After about fifteen minutes, firing ceased abruptly. We sighed in relief.

# D Plus 1

Dawn finally came, and with it the temperature rose rapidly.

"Where the hell is our water?" growled men around me. We had suffered many cases of heat prostration the day before and needed water or we'd all pass out during the attack, I thought.

*The shore party battalion consisted of Marines assigned the mission of unloading and handling supplies and of directing logistics traffic on the beach during an amphibious assault.

"Stand by to move out!" came the order. We squared away all of our personal gear. Snafu secured the gun, took it down by folding the bipod and strapping it, while I packed my remaining shells in my ammo bag.

"I've got to get some water or I'm gonna crack up," I said.

At that moment, a buddy nearby yelled and beckoned to us, "Come on, we've found a well."

I snatched up my carbine and took off, empty canteens bouncing on my cartridge belt. About twenty-five yards away, a group of Company K men gathered at a hole about fifteen feet in diameter and ten feet deep. I peered over the edge. At the bottom and to one side was a small pool of milky-looking water. Japanese shells were beginning to fall on the airfield, but I was too thirsty to care. One of the men was already in the hole filling canteens and passing them up. The buddy who had called me was drinking from a helmet with its liner removed. He gulped down the milky stuff and said, "It isn't beer, but it's wet." Helmets and canteens were passed up to those of us waiting.

"Don't bunch up, you guys. We'll draw Jap fire sure as hell," shouted one man.

The first man who drank the water looked at me and said, "I feel sick."

A company corpsman came up yelling, "Don't drink that water, you guys. It may be poisoned." I had just lifted a full helmet to my lips when the man next to me fell, holding his sides and retching violently. I threw down my water, milky with coral dust, and started assisting the corpsman with the man who was ill. He went to the rear, where he recovered. Whether it was poison or pollution we never knew.

"Get your gear on and stand by," someone yelled.

Frustrated and angry, I headed back to the gun pit. A detail came up about that time with water cans, ammo, and rations. A friend and I helped each other pour water out of a five-gallon can into our canteen cups. Our hands shook, we were so eager to quench our thirst. I was amazed that the water looked brown in my aluminum canteen cup. No matter, I took a big gulp—and almost spit it out despite my terrible thirst. It was awful. Full of rust and oil, it stunk. I looked into the cup in disbelief as a blue film of oil floated lazily on the surface of the smelly brown liquid. Cramps gripped the pit of my stomach.

My friend looked up from his cup and groaned, "Sledgehammer, are you thinking what I'm thinking?"

"I sure am, that oil drum steam-cleaning detail on Pavuvu," I said wearily. (We had been together on a detail assigned to clean out the drums.)

"I'm a sonofabitch," he growled. "I'll never goof off on another work party as long as I live."

*75mm howitzer of the 11th Marines fires close support for frontline troops. Peleliu. USMC photo.*

I told him I didn't think it was our fault. We weren't the only ones assigned to the detail, and it was obvious to us from the start (if not to some supply officer) that the method we had been ordered to use didn't really clean the drums. But that knowledge was slight consolation out there on the Peleliu airfield in the increasing heat. As awful as the stuff was, we had to drink it or suffer heat exhaustion. After I drained my cup, a residue of rust resembling coffee grounds remained, and my stomach ached.

We picked up our gear and prepared to move out in preparation for the attack across the airfield. Because 3/5's line during the night faced south and was back-to-back with that of 2/5, we had to move to the right and prepare to attack northward across the airfield with the other battalions of the regiment. The Japanese shelling of our lines began at daylight, so we had to move out fast and in dispersed formation. We finally got into position for the attack and were told to hit the deck until ordered to move again. This suited me fine, because the Japanese shelling was getting worse. Our

*Men of the 5th Marines attack across the open fireswept airfield on 16 September. Peleliu. USMC photo.*

artillery, ships, and planes were laying down a terrific amount of fire in front on the airfield and ridges beyond in preparation for our attack. Our preattack barrage lasted about half an hour. I knew we would move out when it ended.

As I lay on the blistering hot coral and looked across the open airfield, heat waves shimmered and danced, distorting the view of Bloody Nose Ridge. A hot wind blew in our faces.

An NCO hurried by, crouching low and yelling, "Keep moving out there, you guys. There's less chance you'll be hit if you go across fast and don't stop."

"Let's go," shouted an officer who waved toward the airfield. We moved at a walk, then a trot, in widely dispersed waves. Four infantry battalions—from left to right 2/1, 1/5, 2/5, and 3/5 (this put us on the edge of the airfield)—moved across the open, fire-swept airfield. My only concern then was my duty and survival, not panoramic combat scenes. But I often wondered later what that attack looked like to aerial observers and to those not immersed in the fire storms. All I was aware of were the small area immediately around me and the deafening noise.

Bloody Nose Ridge dominated the entire airfield. The Japanese had concentrated their heavy weapons on high ground; these were directed from observation posts at elevations as high as three hundred feet from which they could look down on us as we advanced. I could see men moving ahead of my squad, but I didn't know whether our battalion, 3/5, was moving across behind 2/5 and then wheeling to the right. There were also men about twenty yards to our rear.

We moved rapidly in the open, amid craters and coral rubble, through ever increasing enemy fire. I saw men to my right and left running bent as low as possible. The shells screeched and whistled, exploding all around us. In many respects it was more terrifying than the landing, because there were no vehicles to carry us along, not even the thin steel sides of an amtrac for protection. We were exposed, running on our own power through a veritable shower of deadly metal and the constant crash of explosions.

For me the attack resembled World War I movies I had seen of suicidal Allied infantry attacks through shell fire on the Western Front. I clenched my teeth, squeezed my carbine stock, and recited over and over to myself, "The Lord is my shepherd; I shall not want. Yea, though I walk through the valley of the shadow of death, I will fear no evil, for Thou art with me; Thy rod and Thy staff comfort me. . . ."

The sun bore down unmercifully, and the heat was exhausting. Smoke and dust from the barrage limited my vision. The ground seemed to sway back and forth under the concussions. I felt as though I were floating along in the vortex of some unreal thunderstorm. Japanese bullets snapped and cracked, and tracers went by me on both sides at waist height. This deadly small-arms fire seemed almost insignificant amid the erupting shells. Explosions and the hum and the growl of shell fragments shredded the air. Chunks of blasted coral stung my face and hands while steel fragments spattered down on the hard rock like hail on a city street. Everywhere shells flashed like giant firecrackers.

Through the haze I saw Marines stumble and pitch forward as they got hit. I then looked neither right nor left but just straight to my front. The farther we went, the worse it got. The noise and concussion pressed in on my ears like a vise. I gritted my teeth and braced myself in anticipation of the shock of being struck down at any moment. It seemed impossible that any of us could make it across. We passed several craters that offered shelter, but I remembered the order to keep moving. Because of the superb discipline and excellent esprit of the Marines, it had never occurred to us that the attack might fail.

About halfway across, I stumbled and fell forward. At that instant a large shell exploded to my left with a flash and a roar. A fragment ricocheted off the deck and growled over my head as I went down. On my right, Snafu let out a grunt and fell as the fragment struck him. As he went down, he grabbed his left side. I crawled quickly to him. Fortunately the fragment had spent much of its force, and luckily hit against Snafu's heavy web pistol belt. The threads on the broad belt were frayed in about an inch-square area.

I knelt beside him, and we checked his side. He had only a bruise to show for his incredible luck. On the deck I saw the chunk of steel that had hit him. It was about an inch square and a half inch thick. I picked up the fragment and showed it to him. Snafu motioned toward his pack. Terrified though I was amid the hellish chaos, I calmly juggled the fragment around in my hands—it was still hot—and dropped it into his pack. He yelled something that sounded dimly like, "Let's go." I reached for the carrying strap of the mortar, but he pushed my hand away and lifted the gun to his shoulder. We got up and moved on as fast as we could. Finally we got across and caught up with other members of our company who lay panting and sweating amid low bushes on the northeastern side of the airfield.

How far we had come in the open I never knew, but it must have been several hundred yards. Everyone was visibly shaken by the thunderous barrage we had just come through. When I looked into the eyes of those fine Guadalcanal and Cape Gloucester veterans, some of America's best, I no longer felt ashamed of my trembling hands and almost laughed at myself with relief.

To be shelled by massed artillery and mortars is absolutely terrifying, but to be shelled in the open is terror compounded beyond the belief of anyone who hasn't experienced it. The attack across Peleliu's airfield was the worst combat experience I had during the entire war. It surpassed, by the intensity of the blast and shock of the bursting shells, all the subsequent horrifying ordeals on Peleliu and Okinawa.

The heat was incredibly intense. The temperature that day reached 105 degrees in the shade (we were *not* in the shade) and would soar to 115 degrees on subsequent days. Corpsmen tagged numerous Marines with heat prostration as being too weak to continue. We evacuated them. My boondockers were so full of sweat that my feet felt squishy when I walked. Lying on my back, I held up first one foot and then the other. Water literally poured out of each shoe.

"Hey, Sledgehammer," chuckled a man sprawled next to me, "you been walking on water."

"Maybe that's why he didn't get hit coming across that airfield," laughed another.

*The wounded could not survive long without water in the 115° F heat. Peleliu. USMC photo.*

I tried to grin and was glad the inevitable wisecracks had started up again.

Because of the shape of the airfield, 3/5 was pinched out of the line by 2/5 on our left and 3/7 on our right after our crossing. We swung eastward and Company K tied in with 3/7, which was attacking in the swampy areas on the eastern side of the airfield.

As we picked up our gear, a veteran remarked to me with a jerk of his head toward the airfield where the shelling continued, "That was rough duty; hate to have to do that every day."

We moved through the swamps amid sniper fire and dug in for the night with our backs to the sea. I positioned my mortar in a meager gun pit on a slight rise of ground about fifteen feet from a sheer rock bluff that dropped about ten feet to the ocean. The jungle growth was extremely thick, but we had a clear hole in the jungle canopy above the gun pit through which we could fire the mortar without having shells hit the foliage and explode.

Most of the men in the company were out of sight through the thick mangroves. Still short of water, everyone was weakened by the heat and the exertions of the day. I had used my water as sparingly as possible and had to eat twelve salt tablets that day. (We kept close count of these tablets. They caused retching if we took more than necessary.)

The enemy infiltration that followed was a nightmare. Illumination fired above the airfield the previous night (D day) had discouraged infiltration in my sector, but others had experienced plenty of the hellish sort of thing we now faced and would suffer every night for the remainder of our time on Peleliu. The Japanese were noted for their infiltration tactics. On Peleliu they refined them and practiced them at a level of intensity not seen in the past.

After we had dug in late that afternoon we followed a procedure used nearly every night. Using directions from our observer, we registered in the mortar by firing a couple of HE shells into a defilade or some similar avenue of approach in front of the company not covered by our machine-gun or rifle fire where the enemy might advance. We then set up alternate aiming stakes to mark other terrain features on which we could fire. Everyone lighted up a smoke, and the password for the night was whispered along the line, passed from foxhole to foxhole. The password always contained the letter *L,* which the Japanese had difficulty pronouncing the way an American would.

Word came along as to the disposition of the platoons of the company and of the units on our flanks. We checked our weapons and placed equipment for quick access in the coming night. As darkness fell, the order was passed, "The smoking lamp is out." All talking ceased. One man in each foxhole settled down as comfortably as he could to sleep on the jagged rock while his buddy strained eyes and ears to detect any movement or sound in the darkness.

An occasional Japanese mortar shell came into the area, but things were pretty quiet for a couple of hours. We threw up a few HE shells as harassing fire to discourage movement in front of the company. I could hear the sea lapping gently against the base of the rocks behind us.

The Japanese soon began trying to infiltrate all over the company front and along the shore to our rear. We heard sporadic bursts of small-arms fire and the bang of grenades. Our fire discipline had to be strict in such situations so as not to mistakenly shoot a fellow Marine. The loose accusation was often made during the war that Americans were "trigger happy" at night and shot at anything that moved. This accusation was often correct when referring to rear-area or inexperienced troops; but in the rifle companies, it was also accepted as gospel that anybody who moved out of his hole at night without first informing the men around him, and who

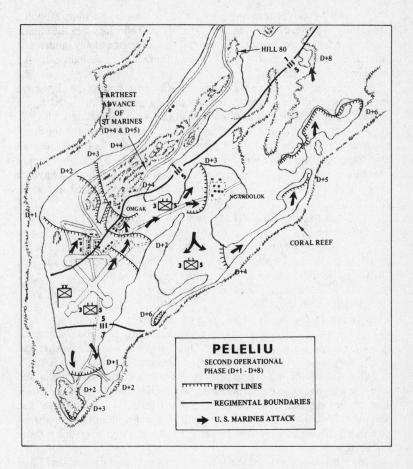

**PELELIU**

SECOND OPERATIONAL
PHASE (D+1 - D+8)

⊢⊢⊢⊢⊢  FRONT LINES

⟶  REGIMENTAL BOUNDARIES

➤  U. S. MARINES ATTACK

didn't reply immediately with the password upon being challenged, could expect to get shot.

Suddenly movement in the dried vegetation toward the front of the gun pit got my attention. I turned cautiously around and waited, holding Snafu's cocked .45 automatic pistol at the ready. The rustling movements drew closer. My heart pounded. It was definitely not one of Peleliu's numerous land crabs that scuttled over the ground all night, every night. Someone was slowly crawling toward the gun pit. Then silence. More noise, then silence. Rustling noises, then silence—the typical pattern.

It must be a Japanese trying to slip in as close as possible, stopping frequently to prevent detection, I thought. He probably had seen the muzzle flash when I fired the mortar. He would throw a grenade at any moment or jump me with his bayonet. I couldn't see a thing in the pale light and inky blackness of the shadows.

Crouching low so as to see better any silhouette against the sky above me, I flipped off the thumb safety on the big pistol. A helmeted figure loomed up against the night sky in front of the gun pit. I couldn't tell from the silhouette whether the helmet was U.S. or Japanese. Aiming the automatic at the center of the head, I pressed the grip safety as I also squeezed the trigger slightly to take up the slack. The thought raced through my mind that he was too close to use his grenade so he would probably use a bayonet or knife on me. My hand was steady even though I was scared. It was he or I.

"What's the password?" I said in a low voice.

No answer.

"Password!" I demanded as my finger tightened on the trigger. The big pistol would fire and buck with recoil in a moment, but to hurry and jerk the trigger would mean a miss for sure. Then he'd be on me.

"Sle-Sledgehammer!" stammered the figure.

I eased up on the trigger.

"It's de l'Eau, Jay de l'Eau. You got any water?"

"Jay, why didn't you give the password? I nearly shot you!" I gasped.

He saw the pistol and moaned, "Oh, Jesus," as he realized what had nearly happened. "I thought you knew it was me," he said weakly.

Jay was one of my closest friends. He was a Gloucester veteran and knew better than to prowl around the way he had just done. If my finger had applied the last bit of pressure to that trigger, Jay would have died instantly. It would have been his own fault, but that wouldn't have mattered to me. My life would have been ruined if I had killed him, even under those circumstances.

My right hand trembled violently as I lowered the big automatic. I had to flip on the thumb safety with my left hand; my right thumb was too weak. I felt nauseated and weak and wanted to cry. Jay crept over and sat on the edge of the gun pit.

"I'm sorry, Sledgehammer. I thought you knew it was me," he said.

After handing him a canteen, I shuddered violently and thanked God that Jay was still alive. "Just how in the hell could I tell it was you in the dark with Nips all over the place?" I snarled. Then I reamed out one of the best friends I ever had.

# Heading North

"Get your gear on and stand by to move out."

We shouldered our loads and began moving slowly out of the thick swamp. As I passed a shallow foxhole where Robert B. Oswalt had been dug in, I asked a man nearby if the word were true about Oswalt being killed. Sadly, he said yes. Oswalt had been fatally wounded in the head. A bright young mind that aspired to delve into the mysteries of the human brain to alleviate human suffering had itself been destroyed by a tiny chunk of metal. What a waste, I thought. War is such self-defeating, organized madness the way it destroys a nation's best.

I wondered also about the hopes and aspirations of a dead Japanese we had just dragged out of the water. But those of us caught up in the maelstrom of combat had little compassion for the enemy. As a wise, salty NCO had put it one day on Pavuvu when asked by a replacement if he ever felt sorry for the Japanese when they got hit, "Hell no! It's them or us!"

We moved out, keeping our five-pace interval, through the thick swamp toward the sound of heavy firing. The heat was almost unbearable, and we were halted frequently to prevent heat prostration in the 115-degree temperature.

We came to the eastern edge of the airfield and halted in the shade of a scrub thicket. Throwing down our gear, we fell on the deck, sweating, panting, exhausted. I had no more than reached for a canteen when a rifle bullet snapped overhead.

"He's close. Get down," said an officer. The rifle cracked again. "Sounds like he's right through there a little way," the officer said.

"I'll get him," said Howard Nease.

"OK, go ahead, but watch yourself."

Nease, a Gloucester veteran, grabbed his rifle and took off into the scrub with the nonchalance of a hunter going after a rabbit in a bush. He angled to one side so as to steal up on the sniper from the rear. We waited a few anxious moments, then heard two M1 shots.

"Ole Howard got him," confidently remarked one of the men.

Soon Howard reappeared wearing a triumphant grin and carrying a Japanese rifle and some personal effects. Everyone congratulated him on his skill, and he reacted with his usual modesty.

"Rack 'em up, boys," he laughed.

We moved out in a few minutes through some knee-high bushes onto the open area at the edge of the airfield. The heat was terrific. When we halted again, we lay under the meager shade of the bushes. I held up each foot and let the sweat pour out of my boondockers. A man on the crew of the other weapon in our mortar section passed out. He was a Gloucester veteran, but Peleliu's heat proved too much for him. We evacuated him, but unlike some heat prostration cases, he never returned to the company.

Some men pulled the rear border of their camouflaged helmet cover out from between the steel and the liner so the cloth hung down over the backs of the necks. This gave them some protection against the blistering sun, but they looked like the French foreign legion in a desert.

After a brief rest, we continued in dispersed order. We could see Bloody Nose Ridge to our left front. Northward from that particular area, 2d Battalion, 1st Marines (2/1) was fighting desperately against Japanese hidden in well-protected caves. We were moving up to relieve 1st Battalion, 5th Marines (1/5) and would tie in with the 1st Marines. Then we were to attack northward along the eastern side of the ridges.

On this particular day, 17 September, the relief was slow and difficult. As 3/5 moved in and the men of 1/5 moved out, the Japanese in the ridges on our left front poured on the artillery and mortar fire. I pitied those tired men in 1/5 as they tried to extricate themselves without casualties. Their battalion, as with the others in the 5th Marines, had had a rough time crossing the airfield through the heavy fire the previous day. But once they got across they met heavy resistance from pillboxes on the eastern side. We had been more fortunate: after getting across the airfield, 3/5 moved into the swamp, which wasn't defended as heavily.

With the relief of 1/5 finally completed, we tied in with the 1st Marines on our left and 2/5 on our right. Our battalion was to attack during the afternoon through the low ground along the eastern side of Bloody Nose, while 2/5 was to clean out the jungle between our right flank and the eastern shore.

As soon as we moved forward, we came under heavy flanking fire from Bloody Nose Ridge on our left. Snafu delivered his latest communiqué on the tactical situation to me as we hugged the deck for protection: "They need to git some more damn troops up here," he growled.

Our artillery was called in, but our mortars could fire only to the front of the company and not on the left flank area, because that was in the area of the 1st Marines. The Japanese observers on the ridge had a clear, unobstructed view of us. Their artillery shells whined and shrieked, accompanied by the deadly whispering of the mortar shells. Enemy fire grew more intense, until we were pinned down. We were getting the first bitter taste of Bloody Nose Ridge, and we had increasing compassion for the 1st Marines on our left who were battering squarely into it.

The Japanese ceased firing when our movement stopped. Yet as surely

*Dead Marines lying on the north end of Airfield D-4. Peleliu. USMC photo.*

as three men grouped together, or anyone started moving, enemy mortars opened up on us. If a general movement occurred, their artillery joined in. The Japanese began to demonstrate the excellent fire discipline that was to characterize their use of all weapons on Peleliu. They fired only when they could expect to inflict maximum casualties and stopped firing as soon as the opportunity passed. Thus our observers and planes had difficulty finding their well-camouflaged positions in the ridges.

When the enemy ceased firing artillery and mortars from caves, they shut protective steel doors and waited while our artillery, naval guns, and 81mm mortars blasted away at the rock. If we moved ahead under our protective fire support, the Japanese pinned us down and inflicted serious losses on us, because it was almost impossible to dig a protective foxhole in the rock. No individual events of the attack stuck in my mind, just the severe fire from our left and the feeling that any time the Japanese decided to do so, they could have blown us sky high.

Our attack was called off late in the afternoon, and we were ordered to set up our mortar for the night. An NCO came by and told me to go with him and about four others from other platoons to unload an amtrac bringing up supplies for Company K. We arrived at the designated place, dispersed a little so as not to draw fire, and waited for the amtrac. In a few minutes it came clanking up in a swirl of white dust.

"You guys from K Company, 5th Marines?" asked the driver.

"Yeah, you got chow and ammo for us?" asked our NCO.

"Yeah, sure have. Got a unit of fire,* water, and rations. Better get it unloaded as soon as you can, or we'll draw fire," the driver said as his machine lurched to a halt and he climbed down.

The tractor was an older model such as I had landed from on D day. It didn't have a drop tailgate; so we climbed aboard and hefted the heavy ammo boxes over the side and down onto the deck.

"Let's go, boys," our NCO said as he and a couple of us climbed onto the tractor.

I saw him gaze in amazement down into the cargo area of the tractor. At the bottom, wedged under a pile of ammo boxes, we saw one of those infernal fifty-five-gallon oil drums of water. Filled, they weighed several hundred pounds. Our NCO rested his arms on the side of the tractor and remarked in an exasperated tone, "It took a bloody genius of a supply officer to do that. How in the hell are we supposed to get that drum outa there?"

"I don't know," said the driver. "I just bring it up."

We cursed and began unloading the ammo as fast as possible. We had expected the water to be in several five-gallon cans, each of which weighed a little more than forty pounds. We worked as rapidly as possible, but then we heard that inevitable and deadly *whisshh-shh-shh*. Three big mortar shells exploded, one after the other, not far from us.

"Uh oh, the stuff's hit the fan now," groaned one of my buddies.

"Bear a hand, you guys. On the double," said our NCO.

"Look, you guys, I'm gonna hafta get this tractor the hell outa here. If it gets knocked out and it's my fault, the lieutenant'll have my can in a crack," groaned the driver.

We had no gripe with the driver, and we didn't blame him. The amtrac drivers on Peleliu were praised by everyone for doing such a fine job. Their

---

*Determined from experience, a unit of fire was the amount of ammunition that would last, on average, for one day of heavy fighting. A unit of fire for the M1 rifle was 100 rounds; for the carbine, 45 rounds; for the .45 caliber pistol, 14 rounds; for the light machine gun, 1,500 rounds; and for the 60mm mortar, 100 rounds.

bravery and sense of responsibility were above question. We worked like beavers as our NCO said to him, "I'm sorry, ole buddy, but if we don't get these supplies unloaded, it's *our* ass!"

More mortar shells fell out to one side, and the fragments swished through the air. It was apparent that the Japanese mortar crew was trying to bracket us, but was afraid to fire too much for fear of being seen by our observers. We sweated and panted to get the ammo unloaded. We unloaded the water drum with a rope sling.

"You fellows need any help?" asked a Marine who appeared from the rear.

We hadn't noticed him before he spoke. He wore green dungarees, leggings, and a cloth-covered helmet like ourselves and carried a .45 caliber automatic pistol like any mortar gunner, machine gunner, or one of our officers. Of course, he wore no rank insignia, being in combat. What astonished us was that he looked to be more than fifty years old and wore glasses —a rarity (for example, only two men in Company K wore them). When he took off his helmet to mop his brow, we saw his gray hair. (Most men forward of division and regimental CPs were in their late teens or early twenties. Many officers were in their mid-twenties.)

When asked who he was and what unit he was in, he replied, "Capt. Paul Douglas. I was division adjutant until that barrage hit the 5th Marines' CP yesterday, then I was assigned as R-1 [personnel officer] in the 5th Regiment. I am very proud to be with the 5th Marines," he said.

"Gosh, Cap'n! You don't have to be up here at all, do you?" asked one of our detail in disbelief as he passed ammo boxes to the fatherly officer.

"No," Douglas said, "but I always want to know how you boys up here are making out and want to help if I can. What company are you fellows from?"

"From K Company, sir," I answered.

His face lit up, and he said, "Ah, you're in Andy Haldane's company."

We asked Douglas if he knew Ack Ack. He said, yes, that they were old friends. As we finished unloading, we all agreed that there wasn't a finer company commander than Captain Haldane.

A couple more mortar shells crashed nearby. Our luck would run out soon. Japanese gunners usually got right on target. So we yelled, "Shove off," to the driver. He waved and clanked away in his unloaded amtrac. Captain Douglas helped us stack some of the ammo and told us we had better disperse.

I heard a buddy ask, "What's that crazy old gray-headed guy doing up here if he could be back at regiment?"

Our NCO growled, "Shut up! Knock it off, you eightball! He's trying to help knuckleheads like you, and he's a damned good man."*

Each man in our detail took up a load of supplies, bade Captain Douglas "so long," and started back to the company lines. Other men went back to bring up the rest of the supplies before dark. We ate chow and finished preparations for the night. That was the first night on Peleliu that I was able to make up a cup of hot bouillon from the dehydrated tablets in my K rations and a canteen cup of heated, polluted, oily water. Hot as the weather was, it was the most nourishing and refreshing food I had eaten in three days. The next day we got fresh water. It was a great relief after that polluted stuff.

Dug in next to our gun pit were 1st Lt. Edward A. ("Hillbilly") Jones, Company K's machine-gun platoon leader, and a salty sergeant, John A. Teskevich. Things were quiet in our area except for our artillery's harassing fire pouring over; so after dark obscured us from Japanese observers, the two of them slipped over and sat at the edge of our gun pit. We shared rations and talked. The conversation turned out to be one of the most memorable of my life.†

Hillbilly was second only to Ack Ack in popularity among the enlisted men in Company K. He was a clean-cut, handsome, light-complexioned man—not large, but well built. Hillbilly told me he had been an enlisted man for several prewar years, had gone to the Pacific with the company, and had been commissioned following Guadalcanal. He didn't say why he was made an officer, but the word among the men was that he had been outstanding on Guadalcanal.

It was a widespread joke among men in the ranks during the war that an officer was made an officer and a gentleman by an act of Congress when he was commissioned. An act of Congress may have made Hillbilly an officer, but he was born a gentleman. No matter how filthy and dirty everyone was on the battlefield, Hillbilly's face always had a clean, fresh appearance. He was physically tough and hard and obviously morally strong. He sweated as much as any man but somehow seemed to stand above our foul and repul-

---

*Paul Douglas became a legend in the 1st Marine Division. This remarkable man was fifty-three years old, had been an economics professor at the University of Chicago, and had enlisted in the Marine Corps as a private. In the Peleliu battle he was slightly wounded carrying flamethrower ammunition up to the lines. At Okinawa he was wounded seriously by a bullet in the arm while carrying wounded for 3/5. Even after months of therapy, he didn't regain complete use of the limb.

Years after the war, I had the great pleasure of meeting and visiting with Senator Paul Douglas. I told him about the remark referring to him as the "crazy old gray-headed guy." He laughed heartily and expressed great pride in having served with the 1st Marine Division.

†Both Hillbilly and Teskevich were later killed.

sive living conditions in the field. Hillbilly had a quiet and pleasant voice even in command. His accent was soft, more that of the deep South, which was familiar to me, than that of the hill country.

Between this man and all the Marines I knew there existed a deep mutual respect and warm friendliness. He had that rare ability to be friendly yet not familiar with enlisted men. He possessed a unique combination of those qualities of bravery, leadership, ability, integrity, dignity, straightforwardness, and compassion. The only other officer I ever knew who was his equal in all these qualities was Captain Haldane.

That night Hillbilly talked about his boyhood and his home in West Virginia. He asked me about mine. He also talked about his prewar years in the Marine Corps. Later I remembered little of what he said, but the quiet way he talked calmed me. He was optimistic about the battle in progress and seemed to understand and appreciate all my fears and apprehensions. I confided in him that many times I had been so terrified that I felt ashamed, and that some men didn't seem to be so afraid. He scoffed at my mention of being ashamed, and said that my fear had been no greater than anyone else's but that I was just honest enough to admit its magnitude. He told me that he was afraid, too, and that the first battle was the hardest because a man didn't know what to expect. Fear dwelled in everyone, Hillbilly said. Courage meant overcoming fear and doing one's duty in the presence of danger, not being unafraid.

The conversation with Hillbilly reassured me. When the sergeant came over and joined in after getting coffee, I felt almost lighthearted. As conversation trailed off, we sipped our joe in silence.

Suddenly, I heard a loud voice say clearly and distinctly, "You will survive the war!"

I looked first at Hillbilly and then at the sergeant. Each returned my glance with a quizzical expression on his face in the gathering darkness. Obviously they hadn't said anything.

"Did y'all hear that?" I asked.

"Hear what?" they both inquired.

"Someone said something," I said.

"I didn't hear anything. How about you?" said Hillbilly, turning to the sergeant.

"No, just that machine gun off to the left."

Shortly the word was passed to get settled for the night. Hillbilly and the sergeant crawled back to their hole as Snafu returned to the gun pit. Like most persons, I had always been skeptical about people seeing visions and hearing voices. So I didn't mention my experience to anyone. But I believed God spoke to me that night on that Peleliu battlefield, and I resolved to make my life amount to something after the war.

That night—the third since landing—as I settled back in the gun pit, I realized I needed a bath. In short, I stunk! My mouth felt, as the saying went, like I had gremlins walking around in it with muddy boots on. Short as it was, my hair was matted with dust and rifle oil. My scalp itched, and my stubble beard was becoming an increasing source of irritation in the heat. Drinking water was far too precious in those early days to use in brushing one's teeth or in shaving, even if the opportunity had arisen.

The personal bodily filth imposed upon the combat infantryman by living conditions on the battlefield was difficult for me to tolerate. It bothered almost everyone I knew. Even the hardiest Marine typically kept his rifle and his person clean. His language and his mind might need a good bit of cleaning up but not his weapon, his uniform, or his person. We had this philosophy drilled into us in boot camp, and many times at Camp Elliott I had to pass personal inspection, to the point of clean fingernails, before being passed as fit to go on liberty. To be anything less than neat and sharp was considered a negative reflection on the Marine Corps and wasn't tolerated.

It was tradition and folklore of the 1st Marine Division that the troops routinely referred to themselves when in the field as "the raggedy-ass Marines." The emphasis during maneuvers and field problems was on combat readiness. Once back in camp, however, no matter where in the boondocks it was situated, the troops cleaned up before anything else.

In combat, cleanliness for the infantryman was all but impossible. Our filth added to our general misery. Fear and filth went hand in hand. It has always puzzled me that this important factor in our daily lives has received so little attention from historians and often is omitted from otherwise excellent personal memoirs by infantrymen. It is, of course, a vile subject, but it was as important to us then as being wet or dry, hot or cold, in the shade or exposed to the blistering sun, hungry, tired, or sick.


Early the next morning, 18 September, our artillery and 81mm mortars shelled Japanese positions to our front as we prepared to continue the previous day's attack northward on the eastern side of Bloody Nose Ridge. A typical pattern of attack in our company, or any other rifle company, went something like this. Our two mortars would fire on certain targets or areas known or thought to harbor the enemy. Our light machine-gun squads fired on areas in front of the rifle platoons they were attached to support. Then two of the three rifle platoons moved out in dispersed order. The remaining platoon was held in company reserve.

Just before the riflemen moved out, we ceased fire with the mortars.

*81mm mortar in action. Peleliu. USMC photo.*

The machine guns stopped also unless they were situated where they could fire over the heads of the advancing riflemen. The latter moved out at a walk to conserve energy. If they received enemy fire, they moved from place to place in short rushes. Thus they advanced until they reached the objective. The mortars stood by to fire if the riflemen ran into strong opposition, and the machine-gun squads moved forward to add their fire support.

The riflemen were the spearhead of any attack. Consequently they caught more hell than anybody else. The machine gunners had a tough job, because the Japanese concentrated on trying to knock them out. The flame-thrower gunner had it rough and so did the rocket launcher gunners and the demolitions men. The 60mm mortarmen caught it from Japanese counter-battery fire of mortars and artillery, snipers (who were numerous), and bypassed Japanese machine guns (which were common). The tankers caught hell from mortar and artillery fire and mines. But it was always the riflemen who had the worst job. The rest of us only supported them.

*Typical 60mm mortar section emplacement in a bomb crater blasted out of solid corai. Peleliu. USMC photo.*

*Marine Corps tactics called for bypassing single snipers or machine guns in order to keep forward momentum. Bypassed Japanese were knocked out by a platoon or company of infantry in reserve. Thus mortars fired furiously on the enemy to the front while a small battle raged behind between bypassed, entrenched Japanese and Marines in reserve. These Japanese frequently fired from the rear, pinning down the advance and causing casualties. Troops had to be well disciplined to function this way, and leadership had to be the best to coordinate things under such chaotic conditions. Marine tactics resembled those developed by the Germans under Gen. Erich Ludendorff which proved so successful against the Allies in the spring of 1918.*

If the riflemen hit heavy opposition, our 81mm mortars, artillery, tanks, ships, and planes were called on for support. These tactics worked well on Peleliu until the Marines hit the mutually supporting complex of caves and pillboxes in the maze of coral ridges. As heavy casualties mounted, the reserve rifle platoon, mortarmen, company officers, and anybody else available acted as stretcher bearers to get the wounded out from under fire as fast as possible. Every man in Company K, no matter what his rank or job, did duty as a rifleman and stretcher bearer on numerous occasions on Peleliu and later on Okinawa.

Shelling from the ridge positions on our left slowed us down. Our planes made air strikes and our ships and artillery attacked the ridges, but Japanese shells kept coming in. The company had an increasing number of casualties. We moved our mortar several times to avoid the shelling, but the Japanese artillery and mortar fire got so heavy and caused such losses to the battalion that our attack was finally called off about noon.

On our right 2/5 made better progress. That battalion moved forward through thick jungle shielded from enemy observers, then turned east and moved out onto the smaller prong of Peleliu's "lobster claw." We moved behind 2/5 eastward across the causeway road to exploit their gain. Again shielded by thick woods, we moved away from Bloody Nose.

We pitied the 1st Marines attacking the ridges. They were suffering heavy casualties.

"The word is the 1st Marines catchin' hell," said Snafu.

"Poor guys, I pity 'em," another man said.

"Yeah, me too, but I hope like hell they take that damn ridge, and we don't have to go up there," said another.

"That shelling coming from up there was hell, and you couldn't even locate the guns with field glasses," added someone else.

From what we had seen thrown at us from the left flank during the past two days, and what I saw of the ridges then, I felt sure that sooner or later every battalion of every regiment in the division would get thrown against Bloody Nose. I was right.

The 1st Marines' predicament at the time was worse than ours in 3/5. They were attacking the end of the ridge itself, and not only received heavy shelling from enemy caves there but deadly accurate small-arms fire as well. Being tied in with the 1st Marines at the time, we got "the word" straight from the troops themselves and not from some overly optimistic officer in a CP putting pins on a map.

The word passed along the line to us told that when the men of 2/1 moved up toward the Japanese positions following preassault artillery fire, the enemy fired on them from mutually supporting positions, pinning them down and inflicting heavy losses. If they managed to get onto the slopes, the Japanese opened fire point blank from caves as soon as our artillery lifted. The enemy then moved back into their caves. If Marines got close enough to an enemy position to attack it with flamethrowers and demolition charges, Japanese in mutually supporting positions raked them with cross fire. Each slight gain by the 1st Marines on the ridges came at almost prohibitive cost in casualties. From what little we could see of the terrain and from the great deal we heard firsthand of the desperate struggle on our left, some of us suspected that Bloody Nose was going to drag on and on in a long battle with many casualties.

The troops got paid to do the fighting (I made sixty dollars a month), and the high command the thinking; but the big brass were predicting optimistically that the Japanese defenses in the ridges would be "breached any day" and Peleliu would be secured in a few days.*

As 3/5 moved eastward on 18 September, a buddy commented sadly, "You know, Sledgehammer, a guy from the 1st Marines told me they got them poor boys makin' frontal attacks with fixed bayonets on that damn ridge, and they can't even see the Nips that are shootin' at 'em. That poor kid was really depressed; don't see no way he can come out alive. There just ain't no sense in that. They can't get nowhere like that. It's slaughter."

"Yeah, some goddamn glory-happy officer wants another medal, I guess, and the guys get shot up for it. The officer gets the medal and goes back to the States, and he's a big hero. Hero, my ass; gettin' troops slaughtered ain't being no hero," said a veteran bitterly.

And bitterness it was. Even the most optimistic man I knew believed our battalion must take its turn against those incredible ridges—and dreaded it.

## Death Patrol

As we moved toward the smaller "lobster claw," Snafu chanted, "Oh, them mortar shells are bustin' up that ole gang of mine," to the tune of "Those Wedding Bells Are Breaking Up That Old Gang of Mine." We halted frequently to rest briefly and to keep down the number of cases of heat prostration.

Although not heavy, my pack felt like a steaming hot wet compress on my shoulders and upper back. We were sopping wet with sweat, and at night or during a halt in the shade our dungarees dried out a bit. When they

---

*For nearly a week of bitter combat, Maj. Gen. William H. Rupertus insisted that the 1st Marine Division could handle the job on Peleliu alone. Only after the 1st Marine Regiment was ground down to a nub—suffering 56 percent casualties—did Maj. Gen. Roy Geiger, commander of the III Marine Amphibious Corps, overrule Rupertus and order in the U.S. Army's 321st Infantry Regiment to help the Marines.

did, heavy white lines of fine, powdery salt formed, as though drawn by chalk, along the shoulders, waist, and so on. Later, as the campaign dragged on and our dungarees caked wth coral dust, they felt like canvas instead of soft cotton.

I carried a little Gideon's New Testament in my breast pocket, and it stayed soaked with sweat during the early days. The Japanese carried their personal photos and other papers in waterproof green rubber pocket-sized folding bags. I "liberated" one such bag from a corpse and used it as a covering for my New Testament. The little Bible went all the way through Okinawa's rains and mud with me, snug in its captured cover.

During one halt along a sandy road in the woods, we heard the words "hot chow" passed.

"The hell you say," someone said in disbelief.

"Straight dope; pork chops."

We couldn't believe it, but it was true. We filed past a cylindrical metal container, and each of us received a hot, delicious pork chop. The chow had been sent ashore for Company K by the crew of LST 661. I vowed if the chance ever came I would express my thanks to those sailors for that chow.*

As we sat along the road eating pork chops with our fingers, a friend sitting on his helmet next to me began to examine a Japanese pistol he had captured. Suddenly the pistol fired. He toppled over on his back but sprang up immediately, holding his hand to his forehead. Several men hit the deck, and we all ducked at the sound of the shot. I had seen what happened but ducked instinctively with an already well-developed conditioned reflex. I stood up and looked at the man's face. The bullet merely had creased his forehead. He was lucky. When the other men realized he wasn't hurt, they really began to kid him unmercifully. Typical comments went something like:

"Hey, ole buddy, I always knew you had a hard head, but I didn't know slugs would bounce off of it."

"You don't need a helmet except to sit on when we take ten."

"You're too young to handle dangerous weapons."

"Some people will do anything to get a Purple Heart."

"Is this the sort of thing you used to do to attract your mother's attention?"

He rubbed his forehead, embarrassed, and mumbled, "Aw, knock it off."

We moved along a causeway and finally halted on the edge of a swamp where the company deployed and dug in for the night. Things were fairly

---

*I fulfilled that vow in July 1945 after the battle for Okinawa ended.

quiet. The next morning the company swung south, pushing through the heavy growth behind a mortar and artillery barrage. We killed a few Japanese throughout the area. Late in the day Company K deployed again for the night.

The following day, Company K received a mission to push a strong combat patrol to the east coast of the island. Our orders were to move through the thick growth onto the peninsula that formed the smaller "claw" and set up a defensive position at the northern tip of the land mass on the edge of a mangrove swamp. Our orders didn't specify the number of days we were to remain there.

First Lt. Hillbilly Jones commanded the patrol consisting of about forty Marines plus a war dog, a Doberman pinscher. Sgt. Henry ("Hank") Boyes was the senior NCO. As with all combat patrols, we were heavily armed with rifles and BARs. We also had a couple of machine-gun squads and the mortar squad with us. Never missing an opportunity to get into the action with his cold steel, Sgt. Haney volunteered to go along.

"G-2 [division intelligence] reports there are a couple thousand Japs somewhere on the other side of that swamp, and if they try to move across it to get back to the defensive positions in Bloody Nose, we're to hold them up until artillery, air strikes, and reinforcements can join us," a veteran NCO said in a terse voice. Our mission was to make contact with the enemy, test his strength, or occupy and hold a strategic position against enemy attack. I wasn't enthusiastic about it.

We picked up extra rations and ammunition as we filed through the company lines exchanging parting remarks with friends. Heading into the thick scrub brush, I felt pretty lonesome, like a little boy going to spend his first night away from home. I realized that Company K had become my home. No matter how bad a situation was in the company, it was still home to me. It was not just a lettered company in a numbered battalion in a numbered regiment in a numbered division. It meant far more than that. It was home; it was "my" company. I belonged in it and nowhere else.

Most Marines I knew felt the same way about "their" companies in whatever battalion, regiment, or Marine division they happened to be. This was the result of, or maybe a cause for, our strong esprit de corps. The Marine Corps wisely acknowledged this unit attachment. Men who recovered from wounds and returned to duty nearly always came home to their old company. This was not misplaced sentimentality but a strong contributor to high morale. A man felt that he belonged to his unit and had a niche among buddies whom he knew and with whom he shared a mutual respect welded in combat. This sense of family was particularly important in the infantry, where survival and combat efficiency often hinged on how well men could depend on one another.*

We moved through the thick growth quietly in extended formation, with scouts out looking for snipers. Things in our area were quiet, but the battle rumbled on Bloody Nose. Thick jungle growth clogged the swamp, which also contained numerous shallow tidal inlets and pools choked with mangroves and bordered by more mangroves and low pandanus trees. If a plant were designed especially to trip a man carrying a heavy load, it would be a mangrove with its tangle of roots.

I walked under a low tree that had a pair of man-o-war birds nesting in its top. They showed no fear as they cocked their heads and looked down from their bulky stick nest. The male saw little of interest about me and began inflating his large red throat pouch to impress his mate. He slowly extended his huge seven-foot wingspan and clicked his long hooked beak. As a boy, I had seen similar man-o-war birds sailing high over Gulf Shores near Mobile, but never had I seen them this close. Several large white birds similar to egrets also perched nearby, but I couldn't identify them.

My brief escape from reality ended abruptly when a buddy scolded in a low voice, "Sledgehammer, what the hell you staring at them birds for? You gonna get separated from the patrol," as he motioned vigorously for me to hurry. He thought I'd lost my senses, and he was right. That was neither the time nor the place for something as utterly peaceful and ethereal as bird watching. But I had had a few delightful and refreshing moments of fantasy and escape from the horror of human activities on Peleliu.

We moved on and finally halted near an abandoned Japanese machine-gun bunker built of coconut logs and coral rock. This bunker served as our patrol's CP. We deployed around it and dug in. The area was just a few feet above the water level, and the coral was fairly loose. We dug the mortar gun pit within a few feet of the swamp water, about thirty feet from the bunker. Visibility through the swamp was limited to a few feet by the dense tangle of mangrove roots on three sides of the patrol's defense perimeter. We didn't register in the gun, because we had to maintain absolute quiet at all times. If we made noise, we would lose the element of surprise should the Japanese try to come across the area. We simply aimed the mortar in the direction we would be most likely to fire. We ate our rations, checked our weapons, and prepared for a long night.

*During and after the war, army men told me that if a soldier got wounded and later returned to infantry duty, there was little chance it would be to his old company. They all agreed that was regrettable. They didn't like the practice, because a recuperated veteran became just another replacement in a strange outfit.

We received the password as darkness settled on us, and a drizzling rain began. We felt isolated listening to moisture dripping from the trees and splashing softly into the swamp. It was the darkest night I ever saw. The overcast sky was as black as the dripping mangroves that walled us in. I had the sensation of being in a great black hole and reached out to touch the sides of the gun pit to orient myself. Slowly the reality of it all formed in my mind: we were expendable!

It was difficult to accept. We come from a nation and a culture that values life and the individual. To find oneself in a situation where your life seems of little value is the ultimate in loneliness. It is a humbling experience. Most of the combat veterans had already grappled with this realization on Guadalcanal or Gloucester, but it struck me out in that swamp.

George Sarrett, a Gloucester veteran, was in the gun pit with me, and we tried to cheer each other up. In low tones he talked of his boyhood in Texas and about Gloucester.

Word came that Haney was crawling along checking positions.

"What's the password?" whispered Haney as he crawled up to us. George and I both whispered the password. "Good," said Haney. "You guys be on the alert, you hear?"

"OK, Haney," we said. He crawled over to the CP where I assumed he settled down.

"I guess he'll be still for a while now," I said.

"Hope the hell you're right," answered George.

Well, I wasn't, because in less than an hour Haney made the rounds again.

"What's the password?" he whispered as he poked his head up to the edge of our hole.

We told him. "Good," he said. "You guys check your weapons. Got a round in the chamber?" he asked each of us.

We answered yes. "OK, stand by with that mortar. If the Nips come through this swamp at high port with fixed bayonets, you'll need to fire HE and flares as fast as you can." He crawled off.

"Wish that Asiatic old boy would settle down. He makes me nervous. He acts like we are a bunch of green boots," my companion growled. George was a cool-headed, self-possessed veteran, and he spoke my sentiments. Haney was making me jittery, too.

Weary hours dragged on. We strained our eyes and ears in the dripping blackness for indications of enemy movement. We heard the usual jungle sounds caused by animals. A splash, as something fell into the water, made my heart pound and caused every muscle to tighten. Haney's inspection tours got worse. He obviously was getting more nervous with each hour.

"I wish to hell Hillbilly would grab him by the stackin' swivel and anchor him in the CP," George mumbled.

The luminous dial of my wristwatch showed the time was after midnight. In the CP a low voice sounded, "Oh, ah, oh" and trailed off, only to repeat the sound louder.

"What's that?" I asked George anxiously.

"Sounds like some guy havin' a nightmare," he replied nervously. "They sure as hell better shut him up before every Nip in this damned swamp knows our position." We heard someone moving and thrashing around in the CP.

"Knock it off," several men whispered near us.

"Quiet that man down!" Hillbilly ordered in a stern low voice.

"Help! help! Oh God, help me!" shouted the wild voice. The poor Marine had cracked up completely. The stress of combat had finally shattered his mind. They were trying to calm him down, but he kept thrashing around. In a firm voice filled with compassion, Hillbilly was trying to reassure the man that he was going to be all right. The effort failed. Our comrade's tragically tortured mind had slipped over the brink. He screamed more loudly. Someone pinioned the man's arms to his sides, and he screamed to the Doberman pinscher, "Help me, dog; the Japs have got me! The Japs have got me and they're gonna throw me in the ocean." I heard the sickening crunch of a fist against a jaw as someone tried to knock the man unconscious. It didn't faze him. He fought like a wildcat, yelling and screaming at the top of his voice.

Our corpsman then gave him an injection of morphine in the hope of sedating him. It had no effect. More morphine; it had no effect either. Veterans though they were, the men were all getting jittery over the noise they believed would announce our exact location to any enemy in the vicinity.

"Hit him with the flat of that entrenching shovel!" a voice commanded in the CP. A horrid *thud* announced that the command was obeyed. The poor man finally became silent.

"Christ a'mighty, what a pity," said a Marine in a neighboring foxhole.

"You said that right, but if the goddamn Nips don't know we're here, after all that yellin', they'll never know," his buddy said.

A tense silence settled over the patrol. The horror of the whole affair stimulated Haney to check our positions frequently. He acted like some hyperactive demon and cautioned us endlessly to be on the alert.

When welcome dawn finally came after a seemingly endless blackness, we all had frayed nerves. I walked the few paces over to the CP to find out what I could. The man was dead. Covered with his poncho, his body lay next to the bunker. The agony and distress etched on the strong faces of Hillbilly, Hank, and the others in the CP revealed the personal horror of the night. Several of these men had received or would receive decorations for bravery in combat, but I never saw such agonized expressions on their faces as that morning in the swamp. They had done what any of us would have had to do under similar circumstances. Cruel chance had thrust the deed upon them.

Hillbilly looked at the radioman and said, "I'm taking this patrol in. Get battalion for me."

The radioman tuned his big pack-sized radio and got the battalion CP. Hillbilly told the battalion CO, Major Gustafson, that he wanted to bring in the patrol. We could hear the major tell Hillbilly he thought we should stay put for a couple of days until G-2 could determine the disposition of the Japanese. Hillbilly, a first lieutenant, calmly disagreed, saying we hadn't fired a shot, but because of circumstances we all had a pretty bad case of nerves. He felt strongly that we should come in. I saw several old salts raise their eyebrows and smile as Hillbilly stated his opinion. To our relief, Gus agreed with him; I have always thought it was probably because of his respect for Hillbilly's judgment.

"I'll send a relief column with a tank so you won't have any trouble coming in," said the major's voice. We all felt comforted. The word went rapidly through the patrol that we were going in. Everyone breathed easier. In about an hour we heard a tank coming. As it forced its way through the thick growth, we saw familiar faces of Company K men with it. We placed the body on the tank, and we returned to the company's lines. I never heard an official word about the death thereafter.

## Relief for the 1st Marines

Over the next few days, the 5th Marines patrolled most of the southern "claw." We had set up defensive positions to prevent any possible counterlanding by the Japanese along the exposed southern beaches.

On about 25 September (D + 10) the battered 1st Marine Regiment was relieved by the U.S. Army's 321st Infantry Regiment of the 81st Infantry Division. The 1st Marines moved into our area where they were to await a ship to return them to Pavuvu. We picked up our gear and moved out from the relative quiet of the beach to board trucks that would speed our regiment to a position straddling the west road. From there we would attack northward along the western side of the ridges.

As we walked along one side of a narrow road, the 1st Marines filed along the other side to take over our area. I saw some familiar faces as the three decimated battalions trudged past us, but I was shocked at the absence of so many others whom I knew in that regiment. During the frequent halts typical to the movement of one unit into the position of another, we exchanged greetings with buddies and asked about the fate of mutual friends. We in the 5th Marines had many a dead or wounded friend to report about from our ranks, but the men in the 1st Marines had so many it was appalling.

"How many men left in your company?" I asked an old Camp Elliott buddy in the 1st Marines.

He looked at me wearily with bloodshot eyes and choked as he said, "Twenty is all that's left in the whole company, Sledgehammer. They nearly wiped us out. I'm the only one left out of the old bunch in my company that was with us in mortar school at Elliott."

I could only shake my head and bite my lip to keep from getting choked up. "See you on Pavuvu," I said.

"Good luck," he said in a dull resigned tone that sounded as though he thought I might not make it.

What once had been companies in the 1st Marines looked like platoons; platoons looked like squads. I saw few officers. I couldn't help wondering if the same fate awaited the 5th Marines on those dreadful ridges. Twenty bloody, grueling, terrible days and nights later, on 15 October (D + 30) my regiment would be relieved. Its ranks would be just about as decimated as those we were filing past.

We boarded trucks that carried us southward along the east road then some distance northward along the west road. As we bumped and jolted past the airfield, we were amazed at all the work the Seabees (naval construction battalions) had accomplished on the field. Heavy construction equipment was everywhere, and we saw hundreds of service troops living in tents and going about their duties as though they were in Hawaii or Australia. Several groups of men, Army and Marine service troops, watched our dusty truck convoy go by. They wore neat caps and dungarees, were clean-shaven, and seemed relaxed. They eyed us curiously, as though we were wild animals in a circus parade. I looked at my buddies in the truck and saw why. The contrast between us and the onlookers was striking. We were armed, helmeted, unshaven, filthy, tired, and haggard. The sight of clean comfortable noncombatants was depressing, and we tried to keep up our morale by discussing the show of U.S. material power and technology we saw.

We got off the trucks somewhere up the west road parallel to the section of the ridges on our right that was in American hands. We heard firing on the closest ridge. The troops I saw along the road as we unloaded were army infantrymen from the 321st Infantry Regiment, veterans of Angaur.

As I exchanged a few remarks with some of these men, I felt a deep comradeship and respect for them. Reporters and historians like to write about interservice rivalry among military men; it certainly exists, but I found that front-line combatants in all branches of the services showed a sincere mutual respect when they faced the same danger and misery. Combat soldiers and sailors might call us "gyrenes," and we called them "dogfaces" and "swabbies," but we respected each other completely.

*After the relief of 1st Marines, a new phase of the fight for Peleliu began. No longer would the Marines suffer prohibitive casualties in fruitless frontal assaults from the south against the ridges. Rather they would sweep up the western coast around the enemy's last-ditch defenses in search of a better route into the final pocket of resistance.*

*Although the bitter battle for Peleliu would drag on for another two months, the 1st Marine Division seized all of the terrain of strategic value in the first week of bitter fighting. In a series of exhausting assaults, the division had taken the vital airfield, the commanding terrain above it, and all of the island south and east of Umurbrogol Mountain. Yet the cost had been high: 3,946 casualties. The division had lost one regiment as an effective fighting unit, and had severely depleted the strength of its other two.*

# CHAPTER FIVE

# ANOTHER AMPHIBIOUS ASSAULT

The 5th Marines now had the mission to secure the northern part of the island—that is, the upper part of the larger "lobster claw." Following that chore the regiment was to move south again on the eastern side of the Umurbrogol ridges to complete the isolation and encirclement. Most of us in the ranks never saw a map of Peleliu except during training on Pavuvu, and had never heard the ridge system referred to by its correct name, Umurbrogol Mountain. We usually referred to the whole ridge system as "Bloody Nose," "Bloody Nose Ridge," or simply "the ridges."

As we moved through the army lines, Japanese machine guns were raking the crest of the ridge on our right. The slugs and bluish white tracers pinned down the American troops on the ridge but passed high above us on the road. The terrain was flat and sparsely wooded. Tanks supported us, and we were fired on by small arms, artillery, and mortars from the high coral ridges to our right and from Ngesebus Island a few hundred yards north of Peleliu.

Our battalion turned right at the junction of West Road and East Road, headed south along the latter, and stopped at dusk. As usual, there wasn't much digging in as such, mostly finding some crater or depression and piling rocks around it for what protection we could get.

I was ordered to carry a five-gallon can of water over to the company CP. When I got there, Ack Ack was studying a map by the light of a tiny flashlight that his runner shielded with another folded map. The company's radioman was sitting with him, quietly tuning his radio and calling an artillery battery of the 11th Marines.

Putting the water can down, I sat on it and watched my skipper with admiration. Never before had I regretted so profoundly my lack of artistic talent and inability to draw the scene before me. The tiny flashlight faintly illuminated Captain Haldane's face as he studied the map. His big jaw, covered with a charcoal stubble of beard, jutted out. His heavy brow wrinkled with concentration just below the rim of his helmet.

The radioman handed the phone to Ack Ack. He requested a certain number of rounds of 75mm HE to be fired out to Company K's front. A Marine on the other end of the radio questioned the need for the request. Haldane answered pleasantly and firmly, "Maybe so, but I want my boys to feel secure." Shortly the 75s came whining overhead and started bursting in the dark thick growth across the road.

Next day I told several men what Ack Ack had said. "That's the skipper for you, always thinking of the troops' feelings," was the way one man summed it up.

Several hours passed. It was my turn to be on watch in our hole. Snafu slept fitfully and ground his teeth audibly, which he usually did during sleep in combat. The white coral road shone brightly in the pale moonlight as I strained my eyes looking across into the wall of dark growth on the other side.

Suddenly two figures sprang up from a shallow ditch directly across the road from me. With arms waving wildly, yelling and babbling hoarsely in Japanese, they came. My heart skipped a beat, then began pounding like a drum as I flipped off the safety of my carbine. One enemy soldier angled to my right, raced down the road a short distance, crossed over, and disappeared into a foxhole in the line of the company on our right flank. I focused on the other. Swinging a bayonet over his head, he headed at me.

I dared not fire at him yet, because directly between us was a foxhole with two Marines in it. If I fired just as the Marine on watch rose up to meet the Japanese intruder, my bullet would surely hit a comrade in the back. The thought flashed through my mind, "Why doesn't Sam or Bill fire at him?"

With a wild yell the Japanese jumped into the hole with the two Marines. A frantic, desperate, hand-to-hand struggle ensued, accompanied by the most gruesome combination of curses, wild babbling, animalistic guttural noises, and grunts. Sounds of men hitting each other and thrashing around came from the foxhole.

I saw a figure pop out of the hole and run a few steps toward the CP. In the pale moonlight, I then saw a Marine nearest the running man jump up.

Holding his rifle by the muzzle and swinging it like a baseball bat, he blasted the infiltrator with a smashing blow.

From our right, where the Japanese had gone into the company on our flank, came hideous, agonized, and prolonged screams that defied description. Those wild, primitive, brutish yellings unnerved me more than what was happening within my own field of vision.

Finally a rifle shot rang out from the foxhole in front of me, and I heard Sam say, "I got him."

The figure that had been clubbed by the rifle lay groaning on the deck about twenty feet to the left of my hole. The yelling over to our right ceased abruptly. By this time, of course, everyone was on the alert.

"How many Nips were there?" asked a sergeant near me.

"I saw two," I answered.

"There must'a been more," someone else put in.

"No," I insisted, "only two came across the road here. One of them ran to the right where all that yelling was, and the other jumped into the hole where Sam shot him."

"Well, then, if there were just those two Nips, what's all that groanin' over here then?" he asked, indicating the man felled by the rifle butt.

"I don't know, but I didn't see but two Nips, and I'm sure of it," I said adamantly—with an insistence that has given me peace of mind ever since.

A man in a nearby hole said, "I'll check it out." Everyone sat still as he crawled to the groaning man in the shadows. A .45 pistol shot rang out. The moaning stopped, and the Marine returned to his hole.

A few hours later as objects around me became faintly visible with the dawn, I noticed that the still form lying to my left didn't appear Japanese. It was either an enemy in Marine dungarees and leggings, or it was a Marine. I went over to find out which.

Before I got to the prone body, its identity was obvious to me. "My God!" I said in horror.

Several men looked at me and asked what was the matter.

"It's Bill," I said.

An officer and an NCO came over from the CP.

"Did he get shot by one of those Japs?" asked the sergeant.

I didn't answer, just looked at him with a blank stare and felt sick. I looked at the man who had crawled past me to check on the groaning man in the dark. He had shot Bill through the temple, mistakenly assuming him to be a Japanese. Bill hadn't told any of us he was leaving his foxhole.

As the realization of his fatal mistake hit him, the man's face turned ashen, his jaw trembled, and he looked as though he were going to cry. Man that he was, though, he went straight over and reported to the CP. Ack Ack sent for and questioned several men who were dug in nearby, including myself, to ascertain exactly what had happened.

Ack Ack was seated off to himself. "At ease, Sledge," he said. "Do you know what happened last night?"

I told him I had a pretty good idea.

"Tell me exactly what you saw."

I told him, making clear I had seen two, and only two, Japanese and had said so at the time. I also told him where I saw those enemy soldiers go.

"Do you know who killed Bill?" the captain asked.

"Yes," I said.

Then he told me it had been a tragic mistake that anyone could have made under the circumstances and never to discuss it or mention the man's name. He dismissed me.

As far as the men were concerned, the villain in the tragedy was Sam. At the time of the incident Sam was supposed to be on watch while Bill was taking his turn at getting much-needed sleep. It was routine that at a preagreed time, the man on watch woke his buddy and, after reporting anything he had seen or heard, took his turn at sleep.

This standard procedure in combat on the front line was based on a fundamental creed of faith and trust. You could depend on your buddy; he could depend on you. It extended beyond your foxhole, too. We felt secure, knowing that one man in each hole was on watch through the night.

Sam had betrayed that basic trust and had committed an unforgivable breach of faith. He went to sleep on watch while on the line. As a result his buddy died and another man would bear the heavy burden of knowing that, accident though it was, he had pulled the trigger.

Sam admitted that he might have dozed off. The men were extremely hard on him for what had happened. He was visibly remorseful, but it made no difference to the others who openly blamed him. He whined and said he was too tired to stay awake on watch, but he only got sworn at by men who were equally tired yet reliable.

We all liked Bill a great deal. He was a nice young guy, probably in his teens. On the neatly typewritten muster roll for the 3d Battalion, 5th Marines on 25 September 1944, one reads these stark words: "_____, William S., killed in action against the enemy (wound, gunshot, head)— remains interred in grave #3/M." So simply stated. Such an economy of words. But to someone who was there, they convey a tragic story. What a waste.

The Japanese who had come across the road in front of me were probably members of what the enemy called a "close-quarter combat unit."

The enemy soldier shot by Sam was not dressed or equipped like their typical infantryman. Rather he wore only tropical khaki shorts, short-sleeved shirt, and *tabi* footwear (split-toed, rubber-soled canvas shoes). He carried only his bayonet. Why he entered our line where he did may have been pure accident, or he may have had an eye on our mortar. His comrade angled off toward the right near a machine gun on our flank. Mortars and machine guns were favorite targets for infiltrators on the front lines. To the rear, they went after heavy mortars, communications, and artillery.

Before Company K moved out, I went down the road to the next company to see what had happened during the night. I learned that those blood-chilling screams had come from the Japanese I had seen run to the right. He had jumped into a foxhole where he met an alert Marine. In the ensuing struggle each had lost his weapon. The desperate Marine had jammed his forefinger into his enemy's eye socket and killed him. Such was the physical horror and brutish reality of war for us.

## Ngesebus Island

Early the next morning our battalion made a successful assault on a small hill on the narrow neck of northern Peleliu. Because of its isolated position, it lacked the mutual support from surrounding caves that made most of the ridges on the island impregnable.

At this time the rest of the regiment was getting a lot of enemy fire from Ngesebus Island. The word was that several days earlier the Japanese had slipped reinforcements by barge down to Peleliu from the larger islands to the north; some of the barges had been shot up and sunk by the navy, but several hundred enemy troops got ashore. It was a real blow to our morale to hear this.*

"Sounds just like Guadalcanal," said a veteran. "About the time we think we got the bastards boxed in, the damn Nips bring in reinforcements, and it'll go on and on."

"Yeah," said another, "and once them slant-eyed bastards get in these caves around here, it'll be hell to pay."

On 27 September army troops took over our positions. We moved northward.

*On the night of 22–23 September about six hundred Japanese of the 2d Battalion, 15th Regiment came down from Babelthuap and got ashore on Peleliu as reinforcements.

"Our battalion is ordered to hit the beach on Ngesebus Island tomorrow," an officer told us.*

I shuddered as I recalled the beachhead we had made on 15 September. The battalion moved into an area near the northern peninsula and dug in for the night in a quiet area. It was sandy, open, and had some shattered, drooping palms. We didn't know what to expect on Ngesebus. I prayed the landing wouldn't be a repeat of the holocaust of D day.

Early in the morning of 28 September (D + 3) we squared away our gear and stood by to board the amtracs that would take us across the 500–700 yards of shallow reef to Ngesebus.

"We'll probably get another battle star for this beachhead," said a man enthusiastically.

"No we won't," answered another. "It's still just part of the Peleliu operation."

"The hell you say; it's still another beachhead," the first man responded.

"I don't make the regulation, ole buddy, but you check with the gunny, and I'll betcha I'm right." Several mumbled comments came out about how stingy the high command was in authorizing battle stars, which were little enough compensation for combat duty.

We boarded the tractors and tried to suppress our fear. Ships were firing on Ngesebus, and we saw Marine F4U Corsair fighter planes approaching from the Peleliu airfield to the south. "We gonna have lots of support for this one," an NCO said.

Our amtracs moved to the water's edge and waited for H hour as the thunderous prelanding naval gunfire bombardment covered the little island in smoke, flame, and dust. The Corsairs from Marine Fighter Squadron (VMF) 114 peeled off and began bombing and strafing the beach. The engines of the beautiful blue gull-winged planes roared, whined, and strained as they dove and pulled out. They plastered the beach with machine guns, bombs, and rockets. The effect was awesome as dirt, sand, and debris spewed into the air.†

Our Marine pilots outdid themselves, and we cheered, yelled, waved,

---

*Ngesebus had to be captured to silence the enemy fire coming into the 5th Marines' flank and to prevent its use as a landing place for Japanese reinforcements from the north. There was also an airfield on Ngesebus—a fighter strip—that was supposed to be useful for American planes.

†Ngesebus was one of the first American amphibious assaults where air support for the landing force came exclusively from Marine aircraft. In earlier landings, air support came from navy and sometimes army planes.

and raised our clenched fists to indicate our approval. Never during the war did I see fighter pilots take such risks by not pulling out of their dives until the very last instant. We were certain, more than once, that a pilot was pulling out too late and would crash. But, expert flyers that they were, they gave that beach a brutal pounding without mishap to plane or pilot. We talked about their spectacular flying even after the war ended.

Out to sea on our left, with a cruiser, destroyers, and other ships firing support, was a huge battleship. Someone said it was the USS *Mississippi,* but I never knew for sure. She ranked with the Corsairs in the mass of destruction she hurled at Ngesebus. The huge shells rumbled like freight cars—as the men always used to describe the sound of projectiles from full-sized battleships' 16-inch guns.

At H hour our tractor driver revved up his engine. We moved into the water and started the assault. My heart pounded in my throat. Would my luck hold out? "The Lord is my shepherd," I prayed quietly and squeezed my carbine stock.

To our relief we received no fire as we approached the island. When my amtrac lurched to a stop well up on the beach, the tailgate went down with a bump, and we scrambled out. With its usual din and thunder the bombardment moved inland ahead of us. Some Company K Marines on the beach were already firing into pillboxes and bunkers and dropping in grenades. With several other men, I headed inland a short distance. But as we got to the edge of the airstrip, we had to dive for cover. A Nambu (Japanese light machine gun) had cut loose on us.

A buddy and I huddled behind a coral rock as the machine-gun slugs zipped viciously overhead. He was on my right. Because the rock was small, we pressed shoulder to shoulder, hugging it for protection. Suddenly there was a sickening crack like someone snapping a large stick.

My friend screamed, "Oh God, I'm hit!" and lurched over onto his right side. He grabbed his left elbow with his right hand, groaning and grimacing with pain as he thrashed around kicking up dust.

A bypassed sniper had seen us behind the rock and shot him. The bullet hit him in the left arm, which was pressed tightly against my right arm as we sought cover from the machine gun out front. The Nambu was firing a bit high, but there was no doubt the sniper had his sights right on us. We were between a rock and a hard place. I dragged him around the rock out of sight of the sniper as the Nambu bullets whizzed overhead.

I yelled, "Corpsman!" and Ken (Doc) Caswell,* the mortar section

---

*Habitually and affectionately, Marines call all U.S. Navy corpsmen who serve with them "Doc."

*Assault on Ngesebus. View from amphibious amtrac while crossing in third wave from Peleliu. USMC photo.*

*Ngesebus: Assault troops (K/3/5) move inland. USMC photo.*

corpsman, crawled over, opening his pouch to get at his first aid supplies as he came. Another man also came over to see if he could help. While I cut away the bloody dungaree sleeve from the injured arm with my kabar, Doc began to tend the wound. As he knelt over his patient, the other Marine placed his kabar under the injured man's pack strap and gave a violent upward jerk to cut away the shoulder pack. The razor-sharp blade sliced through the thick web pack strap as though it were a piece of string. But before the Marine could arrest its upward motion, the knife cut Doc in the face to the bone.

Doc recoiled in pain from the impact of the knife thrust. Blood flowed down his face from the nasty gash to the left of his nose. He regained his balance immediately and returned to his work on the smashed arm as though nothing had happened. The clumsy Marine cursed himself for his blunder as I asked Doc what I could do to help him. Despite considerable pain, Doc kept at his work. In a quiet, calm voice he told me to get a battle dressing out of his pouch and press if firmly against his face to stop the bleeding while he finished work on the wounded arm. Such was the selfless dedication of the navy hospital corpsmen who served in Marine infantry units. It was little wonder that we held them in such high esteem. (Doc later got his face tended and was back with the mortar section in a matter of a few hours.)

While I did as Doc directed, I yelled at two Marines coming our way and pointed toward the sniper. They took off quickly toward the beach and hailed a tank. By the time a stretcher team came up and took my wounded friend, the two men trotted by, waved, and one said, "We got the bastard; he ain't gonna shoot nobody else."

The Nambu had ceased firing, and an NCO signaled us forward. Before moving out, I looked toward the beach and saw the walking wounded wading back toward Peleliu.

After we moved farther inland, we received orders to set up the mortars on the inland side of a Japanese pillbox and prepare to fire on the enemy to our company's front. We asked Company K's gunnery sergeant, Gy. Sgt. W. R. Saunders, if he knew of any enemy troops in the bunker. It appeared undamaged. He said some of the men had thrown grenades through the ventilators, and he was sure there were no live enemy inside.

Snafu and I began to set up our mortar about five feet from the bunker. Number One mortar was about five yards to our left. Cpl. R. V. Burgin was getting the sound-powered phone hooked up to receive fire orders from Sgt. Johnny Marmet, who was observing.

I heard something behind me in the pillbox. Japanese were talking in low, excited voices. Metal rattled against an iron grating. I grabbed my carbine and yelled, "Burgin, there're Nips in that pillbox."

All the men readied their weapons as Burgin came over to have a look, kidding me with, "Shucks, Sledgehammer, you're crackin' up." He looked into the ventilator port directly behind me. It was rather small, approximately six inches by eight inches, and covered with iron bars about a half inch apart. What he saw brought forth a stream of curses in his best Texas style against all Nippon. He stuck his carbine muzzle through the bars, fired two quick shots, and yelled, "I got 'em right in the face."

The Japanese inside the pillbox began jabbering loudly. Burgin was gritting his teeth and calling the enemy SOBs while he fired more shots through the opening.

Every man in the mortar section was ready for trouble as soon as Burgin fired the first shot. It came in the form of a grenade tossed out of the end entrance to my left. It looked as big as a football to me. I yelled "Grenade!" and dove behind the sand breastwork protecting the entrance at the end of the pillbox. The sand bank was about four feet high and L-shaped to protect the entrance from fire from the front and flanks. The grenade exploded, but no one was hit.

The Japanese tossed out several more grenades without causing us injury, because we were hugging the deck. Most of the men crawled around to the front of the pillbox and crouched close to it between the firing ports, so the enemy inside couldn't fire at them. John Redifer and Vincent Santos jumped on top. Things got quiet.

I was nearest the door, and Burgin yelled to me, "Look in and see what's in there, Sledgehammer."

Being trained to take orders without question, I raised my head above the sand bank and peered into the door of the bunker. It nearly cost me my life. Not more than six feet from me crouched a Japanese machine gunner. His eyes were black dots in a tan, impassive face topped with the familiar mushroom helmet. The muzzle of his light machine gun stared at me like a gigantic third eye.

Fortunately for me, I reacted first. Not having time to get my carbine into firing position, I jerked my head down so fast my helmet almost flew off. A split second later he fired a burst of six or eight rounds. The bullets tore a furrow through the bank just above my head and showered sand on me. My ears rang from the muzzle blast and my heart seemed to be in my throat choking me. I knew damned well I had to be dead! He just couldn't have missed me at that range.

A million thoughts raced through my terrified mind: of how my folks had nearly lost their youngest, of what a stupid thing I had done to look directly into a pillbox full of Japanese without even having my carbine at the ready, and of just how much I hated the enemy anyway. Many a Marine veteran had already lost his life on Peleliu for making less of a mistake than I had just made.

Burgin yelled and asked if I were all right. A hoarse squawk was all the answer I could muster, but his voice brought me to my senses. I crawled around to the front, then up on top of the bunker before the enemy machine gunner could have another try at me.

Redifer yelled, "They've got an automatic weapon in there." Snafu disagreed, and a spirited argument ensued. Redifer pointed out that there surely was an automatic weapon in there and that I should know, because it came close to blowing off my head. But Snafu was adamant. Like much of what I experienced in combat, this exchange was unreal. Here we were: twelve Marines with a bull by the tail in the form of a well-built concrete pillbox containing an unknown number of Japanese with no friendly troops near us and Snafu and Redifer—veterans—in a violent argument.

Burgin shouted, "Knock it off," and they shut up.

Redifer and I lay prone on top of the bunker, just above the door. We knew we had to get the Japanese while they were bottled up, or they would come out at us with knives and bayonets, a thought none of us relished. Redifer and I were close enough to the door to place grenades down the opening and move back before they exploded. But the Japanese invariably tossed them back at us before the explosion. I had an irrepressible urge to do just that. Brief as our face-to-face meeting had been, I had quickly developed a feeling of strong personal hate for that machine gunner who had nearly blasted my head off my shoulders. My terror subsided into a cold, homicidal rage and a vengeful desire to get even.

Redifer and I gingerly peeped down over the door. The machine gunner wasn't visible, but we looked at three long Arisaka rifle barrels with bayonets fixed. Those bayonets seemed ten feet long to me. Their owners were jabbering excitedly, apparently planning to rush out. Redifer acted quickly. He held his carbine by the barrel and used the butt to knock down the rifles. The Japanese jerked their weapons back into the bunker with much chattering.

Behind us, Santos yelled that he had located a ventilator pipe without a cover. He began dropping grenades into it. Each one exploded in the pillbox beneath us with a muffled *bam*. When he had used all of his, Redifer and I handed him our grenades while we kept watch at the door.

After Santos had dropped in several, we stood up and began to discuss with Burgin and the others the possibility that anyone could still be alive inside. (We didn't know at the time that the inside was subdivided by concrete baffles for extra protection.) We got our answer when two grenades were tossed out. Luckily for the men with Burgin, the grenades were thrown out the back. Santos and I shouted a warning and hit the deck on the sand on top of the pillbox, but Redifer merely raised his arm over his face. He took several fragments in the forearm but wasn't wounded seriously.

Burgin yelled, "Let's get the hell outa here and get a tank to help us knock this damn thing out." He ordered us to pull back to some craters about forty yards from the pillbox. We sent a runner to the beach to bring up a flamethrower and an amtrac armed with a 75mm gun.

As we jumped into the crater, three Japanese soldiers ran out of the pillbox door past the sand bank and headed for a thicket. Each carried his bayoneted rifle in his right hand and held up his pants with his left hand. This action so amazed me that I stared in disbelief and didn't fire my carbine. I wasn't afraid, as I had been under shell fire, just filled with wild excitement. My buddies were more effective than I and cut down the enemy with a hail of bullets. They congratulated each other while I chided myself for being more curious about strange Japanese customs than with being combat effective.

The amtrac rattling toward us by this time was certainly a welcome sight. As it pulled into position, several more Japanese raced from the pillbox in a tight group. Some held their bayoneted rifles in both hands, but some of them carried their rifles in one hand and held up their pants with the other. I had overcome my initial surprise and joined the others and the amtrac machine gun in firing away at them. They tumbled onto the hot coral in a forlorn tangle of bare legs, falling rifles, and rolling helmets. We felt no pity for them but exulted over their fate. We had been shot at and shelled too much and had lost too many friends to have compassion for the enemy when we had him cornered.

The amtrac took up a position on a line even with us. Its commander, a sergeant, consulted Burgin. Then the turret gunner fired three armor-piercing 75mm shells at the side of the pillbox. Each time our ears rang with the familiar *wham—bam* as the report of the gun was followed quickly by the explosion of the shell on a target at close range. The third shell tore a hole entirely through the pillbox. Fragments kicked up dust around our abandoned packs and mortars on the other side. On the side nearest us, the hole was about four feet in diameter. Burgin yelled to the tankers to cease firing lest our equipment be damaged.

Someone remarked that if fragments hadn't killed those inside, the concussion surely had. But even before the dust settled, I saw a Japanese soldier appear at the blasted opening. He was grim determination personified as he drew back his arm to throw a grenade at us.

My carbine was already up. When he appeared, I lined up my sights on

*Flamethrower gunner with supporting rifle fire team burns out enemy emplacement.
Peleliu. USMC photo.*

his chest and began squeezing off shots. As the first bullet hit him, his face
contorted in agony. His knees buckled. The grenade slipped from his grasp.
All the men near me, including the amtrac machine gunner, had seen him
and began firing. The soldier collapsed in the fusilade, and the grenade went
off at his feet.

Even in the midst of these fast-moving events, I looked down at my
carbine with sober reflection. I had just killed a man at close range. That I
had seen clearly the pain on his face when my bullets hit him came as a jolt.
It suddenly made the war a very personal affair. The expression on that
man's face filled me with shame and then disgust for the war and all the
misery it was causing.

My combat experience thus far made me realize that such sentiments
for an enemy soldier were the maudlin meditations of a fool. Look at me, a
member of the 5th Marine Regiment—one of the oldest, finest, and
toughest regiments in the Marine Corps—feeling ashamed because I had
shot a damned foe before he could throw a grenade at me! I felt like a fool
and was thankful my buddies couldn't read my thoughts.

Burgin's order to us to continue firing into the opening interrupted my
musings. We kept up a steady fire into the pillbox to keep the Japanese
pinned down while the flamethrower came up, carried by Corporal
Womack from Mississippi. He was a brave, good-natured guy and popular

with the troops, but he was one of the fiercest looking Marines I ever saw. He was big and husky with a fiery red beard well powdered with white coral dust. He reminded me of some wild Viking. I was glad we were on the same side.

Stooped under the heavy tanks on his back, Womack approached the pillbox with his assistant just out of the line of our fire. When they got about fifteen yards from the target, we ceased firing. The assistant reached up and turned a valve on the flamethrower. Womack then aimed the nozzle at the opening made by the 75mm gun. He pressed the trigger. With a *whoooooooosh* the flame leaped at the opening. Some muffled screams, then all quiet.

Even the stoic Japanese couldn't suppress the agony of death by fire and suffocation. But they were no more likely to surrender to us than we would have been to them had we ever been confronted with the possibility of surrender. In fighting the Japanese, surrender was not one of our options.

Amid our shouts of appreciation, Womack and his buddy started back to battalion headquarters to await the summons to break another deadlock somewhere on the battlefield—or lose their lives trying. The job of flamethrower gunner was probably the least desirable of any open to a Marine infantryman. Carrying tanks with about seventy pounds of flammable jellied gasoline through enemy fire over rugged terrain in hot weather to squirt flames into the mouth of a cave or pillbox was an assignment that few survived but all carried out with magnificent courage.

We left the craters and approached the pillbox cautiously. Burgin ordered some of the men to cover it while the rest of us looked over the fallen Japanese to be sure none was still alive; wounded Japanese invariably exploded grenades when approached, if possible, killing their enemies along with themselves. All of them were dead. The pillbox was out of action thanks to the flamethrower and the amtrac. There were seven enemy dead inside and ten outside. Our packs and mortars were only slightly damaged by the fire from the amtrac's 75mm gun.

Of the twelve Marine mortarmen, our only casualties were Redifer and Leslie Porter, who had taken some grenade fragments. They weren't hurt seriously. Our luck in the whole affair had been incredible. If the enemy had surprised us and rushed us, we might have been in a bad fix.

During this lull the men stripped the packs and pockets of the enemy dead for souvenirs. This was a gruesome business, but Marines executed it in a most methodical manner. Helmet headbands were checked for flags, packs and pockets were emptied, and gold teeth were extracted. Sabers, pistols, and *hari-kari* knives were highly prized and carefully cared for until

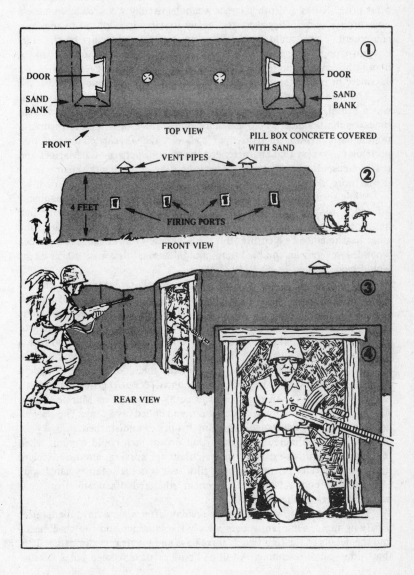

DOOR

SAND
BANK

FRONT

TOP VIEW

PILL BOX CONCRETE COVERED
WITH SAND

DOOR

SAND
BANK

VENT PIPES

4 FEET

FIRING PORTS

FRONT VIEW

REAR VIEW

they could be sent to the folks back home or sold to some pilot or sailor for a fat price. Rifles and other larger weapons usually were rendered useless and thrown aside. They were too heavy to carry in addition to our own equipment. They would be picked up later as fine souvenirs by the rear-echelon troops. The men in the rifle companies had a lot of fun joking about the hair-raising stories these people, who had never seen a live Japanese or been shot at, would probably tell after the war.

The men gloated over, compared, and often swapped their prizes. It was a brutal, ghastly ritual the likes of which have occurred since ancient times on battlefields where the antagonists have possessed a profound mutual hatred. It was uncivilized, as is all war, and was carried out with that particular savagery that characterized the struggle between the Marines and the Japanese. It wasn't simply souvenir hunting or looting the enemy dead; it was more like Indian warriors taking scalps.

While I was removing a bayonet and scabbard from a dead Japanese, I noticed a Marine near me. He wasn't in our mortar section but had happened by and wanted to get in on the spoils. He came up to me dragging what I assumed to be a corpse. But the Japanese wasn't dead. He had been wounded severely in the back and couldn't move his arms; otherwise he would have resisted to his last breath.

The Japanese's mouth glowed with huge gold-crowned teeth, and his captor wanted them. He put the point of his kabar on the base of a tooth and hit the handle with the palm of his hand. Because the Japanese was kicking his feet and thrashing about, the knife point glanced off the tooth and sank deeply into the victim's mouth. The Marine cursed him and with a slash cut his cheeks open to each ear. He put his foot on the sufferer's lower jaw and tried again. Blood poured out of the soldier's mouth. He made a gurgling noise and thrashed wildly. I shouted, "Put the man out of his misery." All I got for an answer was a cussing out. Another Marine ran up, put a bullet in the enemy soldier's brain, and ended his agony. The scavenger grumbled and continued extracting his prizes undisturbed.

Such was the incredible cruelty that decent men could commit when reduced to a brutish existence in their fight for survival amid the violent death, terror, tension, fatigue, and filth that was the infantryman's war. Our code of conduct toward the enemy differed drastically from that prevailing back at the division CP.

The struggle for survival went on day after weary day, night after terrifying night. One remembers vividly the landings and the beachheads and the details of the first two or three days and nights of a campaign; after that, time lost all meaning. A lull of hours or days seemed but a fleeting instant of heaven-sent tranquility. Lying in a foxhole sweating out an enemy artillery or mortar barrage or waiting to dash across open ground under machine-gun or artillery fire defied any concept of time.

To the noncombatants and those on the periphery of action, the war meant only boredom or occasional excitement; but to those who entered the meat grinder itself, the war was a nether world of horror from which escape seemed less and less likely as casualties mounted and the fighting dragged on and on. Time had no meaning; life had no meaning. The fierce struggle for survival in the abyss of Peleliu eroded the veneer of civilization and made savages of us all. We existed in an environment totally incomprehensible to men behind the lines—service troops and civilians.

A trip inside the pillbox by Redifer and Burgin solved the mystery of how some of the occupants had survived the grenades and shell bursts. (Burgin shot a soldier inside who was feigning death.) Concrete walls partitioned the bunker into compartments connected by small openings. Three or four enemy soldiers occupied each compartment which had its own firing ports to the outside. Each would have had to be put out of action individually had we not had the help of Womack and his flamethrower.

When our gunny came by and saw the results of our encounter with the pillbox he had thought was empty, he looked sheepish. He gazed in amazement at the enemy dead scattered around. We really razzed him about it— or rather, we gave him the nearest thing approaching the razz that we Marine privates dared hand out to the austere personage of Gy. Sergeant Saunders. I have thought often that Burgin should have been decorated for the fine leadership he exhibited in coordinating and directing the knockout of the pillbox. I'm sure men have been decorated for less.

We set up our two mortars in a large crater near the now knocked-out pillbox and registered in the guns for the night. The ammo carriers dug into the softer coral around the edge of the crater. An amtrac brought up rations and a unit of fire for the company. The wind began to blow briskly, and it got cloudy and heavily overcast. As darkness settled, heavy clouds scudded across the sky. The scene reminded me of hurricane weather on the Gulf Coast back home.

Not far behind us, the heat of the fire burning in the pillbox exploded Japanese grenades and small-arms ammunition. All night occasional shifts of wind blew the nauseating smell of burning flesh our way. The rain fell in torrents, and the wind blew hard. Ships fired star shells to illuminate the battlefield for our battalion. But as soon as the parachute of a star shell opened, the wind swept it swiftly along like some invisible hand snatching away a candle. In the few hundred yards they still held at the northern end of the island, the enemy was fairly quiet.

The next morning, again with the help of tanks and amtracs, our battalion took most of the remainder of Ngesebus. Our casualties were remarkably low for the number of Japanese we killed.* In midafternoon we learned that an army unit would relieve us shortly and complete the job on the northern end of Ngesebus.

Our mortar section halted to await orders and dispersed among some open bushes. In our midst was the wreckage of a Japanese heavy machine gun and the remains of the squad that had been wiped out by Company K. The squad members had been killed in the exact positions to be occupied by such a squad "according to the book."

At first glance the dead gunner appeared about to fire his deadly weapon. He still sat bolt upright in the proper firing position behind the breech of his machine gun. Even in death his eyes stared widely along the gun sights. Despite the vacant look of his dilated pupils, I couldn't believe he was dead. Cold chills ran along my spine. Gooseflesh tickled my back. It seemed as though he was looking through me into all eternity, that at any instant he would raise his hands—which rested in a relaxed manner on his thighs—grip the handles on the breech, and press the thumb trigger. The bright shiny brass slugs in the strip clip appeared as ready as the gunner, anxious to speed out, to kill, and to maim more of the "American devils." But he would rot, and they would corrode. Neither he nor his ammo could do any more for the emperor.

The crown of the gunner's skull had been blasted off, probably by one of our automatic weapons. His riddled steel helmet lay on the deck like a punctured tin can. The assistant gunner lay beside the gun. Apparently, he had just opened a small green wooden chest filled with strip clips of machine-gun cartridges when he was killed. Several other Japanese soldiers, ammo carriers, lay strung out at intervals behind the gun.

A Company K rifleman who had been in the fight that knocked out the machine-gun crew sat on his helmet nearby and told us the story. The action had taken place the day before while the mortar section was fighting at the pillbox. The rifleman said, "The thing that I just couldn't believe was the

*Official accounts vary somewhat as to the actual casualty figures for Ngesebus. However the Marines suffered about 15 killed and 33 wounded, while the Japanese lost 470 killed and captured. Company K suffered the largest portion of the casualties in 3/5 by losing 8 killed and 24 wounded. This undoubtedly resulted from the presence of a ridge and caves on Ngesebus in our sector.

way those Nip ammo carriers could chop chop around here on the double with those heavy boxes of ammo on their backs.''

Each ammo box had two leather straps, and each ammo carrier had a heavy box on his back with the straps around his shoulders. I lifted one of the ammo chests. It weighed more than our mortar. What the Japanese lacked in height, they certainly compensated for in muscle.

"I'd sure hate to hafta lug that thing around, wouldn't you?" asked the Marine. "When they got hit," he continued, "they fell to the deck like a brick because of all that weight."

As we talked, I noticed a fellow mortarman sitting next to me. He held a handful of coral pebbles in his left hand. With his right hand he idly tossed them into the open skull of the Japanese machine gunner. Each time his pitch was true I heard a little splash of rainwater in the ghastly receptacle. My buddy tossed the coral chunks as casually as a boy casting pebbles into a puddle on some muddy road back home; there was nothing malicious in his action. The war had so brutalized us that it was beyond belief.

I noticed gold teeth glistening brightly between the lips of several of the dead Japanese lying around us. Harvesting gold teeth was one facet of stripping enemy dead that I hadn't practiced so far. But stopping beside a corpse with a particularly tempting number of shining crowns, I took out my kabar and bent over to make the extractions.

A hand grasped me by the shoulder, and I straightened up to see who it was. "What are you gonna do, Sledgehammer?" asked Doc Caswell. His expression was a mix of sadness and reproach as he looked intently at me.

"Just thought I'd collect some gold teeth," I replied.

"Don't do it."

"Why not, Doc?"

"You don't want to do that sort of thing. What would your folks think if they knew?"

"Well, my dad's a doctor, and I bet he'd think it was kinda interesting," I replied, bending down to resume my task.

"No! The germs, Sledgehammer! You might get germs from them."

I stopped and looked inquiringly at Doc and said, "Germs? Gosh, I never thought of that."

"Yeah, you got to be careful about germs around all these dead Nips, you know," he said vehemently.

"Well, then, I guess I'd better just cut off the insignia on his collar and leave his nasty teeth alone. You think that's safe, Doc?"

"I guess so," he replied with an approving nod.

Reflecting on the episode after the war, I realized that Doc Caswell didn't really have germs in mind. He was a good friend and a fine, genuine person whose sensitivity hadn't been crushed out by the war. He was merely trying to help me retain some of mine and not become completely callous and harsh.

There was little firing going on now because 3/5 was preparing to pull back as it was relieved by an army battalion. Our tanks, two of which had been parked near us, started toward the beach. As they rattled and clanked away, I hoped they weren't leaving prematurely.

Suddenly we were jolted by the terrific blast of a Japanese 75mm artillery piece slightly to our right. We flung ourselves flat on the deck. The shriek and explosion of the shell followed instantly. Fragments tore through the air. The gun fired again rapidly.

"Jesus, what's that?" gasped a man near me.

"It's a Nip 75, and God is he close," another said.

Each time the gun fired I felt the shock and pressure waves from the muzzle blast. I was terror stricken. We began to hear shouts of "Corpsman" on our right.

"For chrissake, get them tanks back up here," someone yelled. I looked toward the tanks just in time to see several wheel around and come speeding back to help the pinned-down infantrymen.

"Mortar section, stand by," someone yelled. We might be called to fire on the enemy gun, but as yet we didn't know its location.

The tanks went into action and almost immediately knocked out the weapon. Calls came from our right for corpsmen and stretcher bearers. Several of our ammo carriers went with the corpsmen to act as stretcher bearers. Word filtered along to us that quite a number of casualties had been caused by the terrible point-blank fire of the enemy cannon. Most of those hit were members of the company that was tied in with us on our right.

Our ammo carriers and corpsmen returned shortly with a distressing account of the men next to us caught directly in front of the Japanese gun when it opened fire from a camouflaged position. When I saw one of our men's face, I knew how bad it had been. He appeared absolutely stricken with horror. I often had seen him laugh and curse the Japanese when we were under heavy shelling or scrambling out of the way of machine-gun or sniper fire. Never during the entire Peleliu campaign, or later during the bloody fighting on Okinawa, did I see such an expression on his face.

He grimaced as he described how he and the man with him put one of the casualties, someone we all knew, on a stretcher. "We knew he was hit bad, and he had passed out. I tried to lift the poor guy under his shoulders, and he [pointing to the other mortarman] lifted his knees. Just as we almost got him on the stretcher, the poor guy's body came apart. God! It was awful!''

He and the man with him looked away as everyone groaned and slowly shook their heads. We had been terrified by the enemy gun firing point-blank like that. It was an awful experience. It had been bad enough on us, but it was unbearable for those unfortunates who were in the direct line of fire.

Our company had been off to one side and had suffered no casualties during the ordeal, but it was one of the more shocking experiences I endured during the war. As I have said earlier, to be shelled was terrifying, and to be shelled in the open on your feet was horrible; but to be shelled point-blank was so shocking that it almost drove the most resilient and toughest among us to panic. Words can't convey the awesome sensation of actually feeling the muzzle blasts that accompanied the shrieks and concussions of those artillery shells fired from a gun so close by. We felt profound pity for our fellow Marines who had caught its full destructive force.

During mid-afternoon as we waited for the army infantry, we sat numbly looking at nothing with the "bulkhead stare." The shock, horror, fear, and fatigue of fifteen days of combat were wearing us down physically and emotionally. I could see it in the dirty, bearded faces of my remaining comrades: they had a hollow-eyed vacant look peculiar to men under extreme stress for days and nights on end.

"Short but rough. Three days, maybe four," the division CG had said before Peleliu. Now we had been at it fifteen terrible days with no end in sight.

I felt myself choking up. I slowly turned my back to the men facing me, as I sat on my helmet, and put my face in my hands to try to shut out reality. I began sobbing. The harder I tried to stop the worse it got. My body shuddered and shook. Tears flowed out of my scratchy eyes. I was sickened and revolted to see healthy young men get hurt and killed day after day. I felt I couldn't take any more. I was so terribly tired and so emotionally wrung out from being afraid for days on end that I seemed to have no reserve strength left.

The dead were safe. Those who had gotten a million-dollar wound were lucky. None of us left had any idea that we were just midway through what was to be a month-long ordeal for the 5th Marines and the 7th Marines.

I felt a hand on my shoulder and looked up at the tired, bloodshot eyes of Duke, our lieutenant. "What's the matter, Sledgehammer?" he asked in a sympathetic voice. After I told him how I felt, he said, "I know what you mean. I feel the same way. But take it easy. We've got to keep going. It'll be over soon, and we'll be back on Pavuvu.'' His understanding gave me the strength I needed, enough strength to endure fifteen more terrible days and nights.

When long files of soldiers accompanied by amtracs loaded with barbed wire and other supplies came by, we received orders to move out. We were glad to see those army men. As we shouldered our weapons and loads, a buddy said to me, ''Sure wish we could dig in behind barbed wire at night. Makes a fella' feel more secure.'' I agreed as we walked wearily toward the beach.

After crossing back to northern Peleliu on 29 September, 3/5 bivouacked east of Umurbrogol Mountain in the Ngardololok area. We were familiar with this area from the first week of the campaign. It was fairly quiet and had been the bivouac area of the shattered 1st Marines for about a week after they came off the line and awaited ships to take them to Pavuvu.

We were able to rest, but we were uneasy. As usual we asked about the fate of friends in other units, more often than not with depressing results. Rumor had the 5th Marines slated to join the 7th Marines already fighting on those dreaded coral ridges that had been the near destruction of the 1st Marines. The men tried not to think about it as they sat around in the muggy shade, brewed hot coffee in their canteen cups, and swapped souvenirs and small talk. From the north came the constant rattle of machine guns and the rumble of shells.

# CHAPTER SIX

# BRAVE MEN LOST

"**OK,** you people, stand by to draw rations and ammo. The battalion is going to reinforce the 7th Marines in the ridges."

We received the unwelcome but inevitable news with fatalistic resignation as we squared away our weapons and gear. Our information had the casualty figure of the 7th Marines rapidly approaching that of the 1st Marines. And our own regimental strength wasn't much better than that of the 7th. All of Peleliu except the central ridges was now in our hands. The enemy held out in the Umurbrogol Pocket, an area about 400 yards by 1,200 yards in the ruggedest, worst part of the ridges.*

The terrain was so unbelievably rugged, jumbled, and confusing, that I rarely knew where we were located. Only the officers had maps, so locations meant nothing in my mind. One ridge looked about like another, was about as rugged, and was defended as heavily as any other. We were usually told the name of this or that coral height or ridge when we attacked. To me it meant only that we were attacking the same objective where other Marine battalions had been shot up previously.

---

*My memory of the remaining events of horror and death and violence amid the Peleliu ridges is as clear and distinct as a long nightmare where specific events are recalled vividly the next day. I remember clearly the details of certain episodes that occurred before or after certain others and can verify these with my notes and the historical references. But time and duration have absolutely no meaning in relation to those events from one date to the next. I was well aware of this sensation then.

We were resigned to the dismal conclusion that our battalion wasn't going to leave the island until all the Japanese were killed, or we had all been hit. We merely existed from hour to hour, from day to day. Numbed by fear and fatigue, our minds thought only of personal survival. The only glimmer of hope was a million-dollar wound or for the battle to end soon. As it dragged on and on and casualties mounted, a sense of despair pervaded us. It seemed that the only escape was to be killed or wounded. The will for self-preservation weakened. Many men I knew became intensely fatalistic. Somehow, though, one never could quite visualize his own death. It was always the next man. But getting wounded did seem inevitable. In a rifle company it just seemed to be a matter of time. One couldn't hope to continue to escape the law of averages forever.

On 3 October our battalion made an attack on the Five Sisters, a rugged coral hill mass with five sheer-walled peaks. Before the attack the 11th Marines covered the area with artillery fire. We fired a heavy mortar barrage on the company front, and the machine guns laid down covering fire.

As we ceased firing briefly, we watched the riflemen of 3/5 move forward onto the slopes before Japanese fire stopped them. We fired the mortars rapidly to give our men cover as they pulled back. The same fruitless attack was repeated the next day with the same dismal results.* Each time we got orders to secure the guns after the riflemen stopped advancing, the mortar section stood by to go up as stretcher bearers. (We always left a couple of men on each gun in case mortar fire was needed.) We usually threw phosphorous and smoke grenades as a screen, and the riflemen covered us, but enemy snipers fired as rapidly as possible at stretcher bearers. The Japanese were merciless in this, as in everything else in combat.

Because of the rugged, rock-strewn terrain and intense heat on Peleliu, four men were needed to carry one casualty on a stretcher. Everyone in the company took his turn as a stretcher bearer nearly every day. All hands agreed it was back-breaking, perilous work.

My heart pounded from fear and fatigue each time we lifted a wounded man onto a stretcher, raised it, then stumbled and struggled across the rough ground and up and down steep inclines while enemy bullets snapped through the air and ricochets whined and pinged off the rocks. The snipers hit a stretcher bearer on more than one occasion. But luckily, we always managed to drag everybody behind rocks until help came. Frequently enemy mortars added their shells in an effort to stop us.

Each time I panted and struggled with a stretcher under fire, I marveled

---

*K/3/5 lost eight killed and twenty-two wounded at the Five Sisters.

*Corsair drops napalm on Five Sisters. Peleliu. USMC photo.*

at the attitude of the casualty. When conscious, the wounded Marine seemed at ease and supremely confident we would get him out alive. With bullets and shells coming in thick and fast, I sometimes doubted any of us could make it. Even discounting the effects of shock and the morphine administered by the corpsmen, the attitude of the wounded Marine seemed serene. When we reached a place out of the line of fire, the man usually would encourage us to put him down so we could rest. If he wasn't wounded severely, we stopped and all had a smoke. We would cheer him up by asking him to think of us when he got on board the hospital ship.

Invariably the not-so-seriously hurt were in high spirits and relieved. They were on their way out of hell, and they expressed pity for those of us left behind. With the more seriously wounded and the dying, we carried the stretcher as fast as possible to an amtrac or ambulance Jeep which then rushed them to the battalion aid station. After getting them into a vehicle, we would throw ourselves down and pant for breath.

When acting as a stretcher bearer—struggling, running, crawling over terrain so rugged that sometimes the carriers on one end held the stretcher handles above their heads while those on the other end held their handles almost on the rocks to keep the stretcher level—I was terrified that the helpless casualty might fall off onto the hard, sharp coral. I never saw this happen, but we all dreaded it.

The apparent calmness of our wounded under fire stemmed in part from the confidence we shared in each other. None of us could bear the thought of leaving wounded behind. We never did, because the Japanese certainly would have tortured them to death.

During the period between attacks by our battalion on the Five Sisters, our front line was formed on fairly level ground. The mortars were dug in some yards behind the line. The entire company was out in the open, and we knew the Japanese were watching us at all times from their lairs in the Five Sisters. We came under sniper and mortar fire only when the Japanese were sure of inflicting maximum casualties. Their fire discipline was superb. When they shot, someone usually got hit.

When night came it was like another world. Then the enemy came out of their caves, infiltrating or creeping up on our lines to raid all night, every night. Raids by individual enemy soldiers or small groups began as soon as darkness fell. Typically, one or more raiders slipped up close to Marine positions by moving during dark periods between mortar flares or star shells. They wore *tabi,* and their ability to creep in silently over rough rocks strewn with pulverized vegetation was incredible. They knew the terrain perfectly. Suddenly they rushed in jabbering or babbling incoherent sounds, sometimes throwing a grenade, but always swinging a saber, bayonet, or knife.

Their skill and daring were amazing, matched only by the cool-headed, disciplined manner in which Marines met their attacks. Strict fire discipline on our part was required to avoid shooting friends if the enemy got into a position before he was shot. All we could do was listen in the dark to the

*View showing the removal of a wounded Marine. Peleliu. USMC photo.*

*Wounded Marines being removed from the shell-blasted terrain. Peleliu. USMC photo.*

desperate animalistic sounds and the thrashing around when a hand-to-hand fight occurred.

No one was allowed out of his position after dark. Each Marine maintained a keen watch while his buddy tried to sleep. Mutual trust was essential. Frequently our men were killed or wounded in these nightly fights, but we invariably killed the foe.

One night so many Japanese crept around in front of the company and slipped in among the rocks and ground litter between some of the forward positions that much of the following morning was occupied with trying to kill them all. This was difficult, because in any direction one fired one might hit a Marine. The excellent discipline and control exhibited by the Marines finally got all the Japanese without any Company K casualties.

The only "injury" that occurred was to my friend Jay's dungaree trousers. Jay walked past my foxhole with a deliberate, stiff-kneed gait and wearing a wry expression on his face.

"What happened to you?" I asked.

"Aw hell, I'll tell you later," he grinned sheepishly.

"Go on, tell him, Jay," another man near him yelled teasingly.

Several men laughed. Jay grinned and told them to shut up. He waddled on back to battalion like a tiny child who had soiled his pants, which was just what he had done. We all had severe cases of diarrhea by this time, and it had gotten the best of Jay. Considering what had happened, the incident really wasn't funny, but it was understandable.

At daylight Jay had slung his carbine over his shoulder and walked a short distance from his foxhole to relieve himself. As he stepped over a log, his foot came down squarely on the back of a Japanese lying in hiding. Jay reacted instantaneously and so did the enemy soldier. Jay brought his carbine to bear on the Japanese's chest as the latter sprang to his feet. Jay pulled the trigger. "Click." The firing pin was broken, and the carbine didn't fire. As the enemy soldier pulled the pin from a hand grenade, Jay threw the carbine at him. It was more an act of desperation than anything else.

As Jay spun around and ran back toward us yelling, "shoot him," the Japanese threw his grenade, striking my friend in the middle of the back. It fell to the deck and lay there, a dud. The Japanese then drew his bayonet. Waving it like a sword, he took off after Jay at a dead run.

Jay had spotted a BARman and fled in his direction, yelling for him to shoot the enemy. The BARman stood up but didn't fire. The Japanese came on. Jay was running and yelling as hard as he could. After agonizing moments, the BARman took deliberate aim at the enemy soldier's belt buckle and fired most of a twenty-round magazine into him. The soldier

*Death Valley, looking north. Five Sisters on the right. Peleliu. USMC photo.*

collapsed in a heap. The blast of automatic rifle fire had cut his body nearly in two.

Terrified and winded, Jay had had a close call. When he asked the BARman why in the hell he had waited so long to fire, that character grinned. I heard him reply something to the effect that he thought he'd just let the Japanese get a little closer to see if he could cut him into two pieces with his BAR.

Jay obviously didn't appreciate his close call being used as the subject of an experiment. As all the men laughed, Jay received permission to go back to battalion headquarters to draw a clean pair of trousers. The men kidded him a great deal about the episode, and he took it all with his usual good nature.

*During the entire period among the Umurbrogol ridges, a nuisance Marine infantrymen had to contend with was the rear-echelon souvenir hunters. These characters came up to the rifle companies during lulls in the fighting and poked around for any Japanese equipment they could carry off. They were easy to spot because of the striking difference between their appearance and that of the infantry.*

*During the latter phase of the campaign the typical infantryman wore a worried, haggard expression on his filthy, unshaven face. His bloodshot eyes were hollow and vacant from too much horror and too little sleep. His camouflaged helmet cover (if it hadn't been torn off against the rocks) was gray with coral dust and had a tear or two in it. His cotton dungaree jacket (originally green) was discolored with coral dust, filthy, greasy with rifle oil, and as stiff as canvas from being soaked alternately with rain and sweat and then drying. His elbows might be out, and his knees frequently were, from much "hitting the deck" on the coral rock. His boondockers were coated with gray coral dust, and his heels were worn off completely by the sharp coral.*

*The infantryman's calloused hands were nearly blackened by weeks of accumulation of rifle oil, mosquito repellant (an oily liquid called Skat), dirt, dust, and general filth. Overall he was stooped and bent by general fatigue and excessive physical exertion. If approached closely enough for conversation, he smelled bad.*

*The front-line infantry bitterly resented the souvenir hunters. One major in the 7th Marines made it a practice of putting them into the line if they came into his area. His infantrymen saw to it that the "visitors" stayed put until released to return to their respective units in the rear areas.*

During a lull in our attacks on the Five Sisters, I was on an ammo-carrying detail and talking with a rifleman friend after handing him some bandoliers. It was quiet, and we were sitting on the sides of his shallow foxhole as his buddy was bringing up K rations. (By quiet I mean we weren't being fired on. But there was always the sound of firing somewhere on the island.) Two neat, clean, fresh-looking souvenir hunters wearing green cloth fatigue caps instead of helmets and carrying no weapons walked past us headed in the direction of the Five Sisters, several hundred yards away. When they got a few paces in front of us, one of them stopped and turned around, just as I was on the verge of calling to them to be careful where they went.

The man called back to us asking, "Hey, you guys, where's the front line?"

"You just passed through it," I answered serenely. The second souvenir hunter spun around. They looked at each other and then at us in astonishment. Then, grabbing the bills of their caps, they took off on the double back past us toward the rear. They kicked up dust and never looked back.

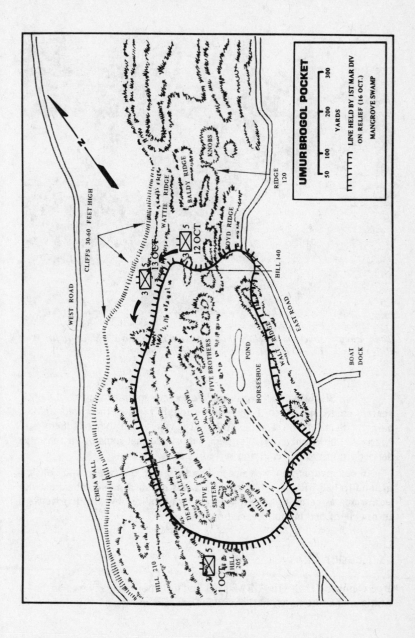

*Tank infantry attack in the Horseshoe. Looking north: Five Brothers (left), Walt Ridge (right), Hill 140 (center background). USMC photo.*

"Hell, Sledgehammer, you should'a let 'em go on so they'd get a good scare," chided my friend. I told him we couldn't just let them walk up on a sniper. "Serve them rear-echelon bastards right. And they call them guys Marines," he grumbled. (In fairness, I must add that some of the rear-area service troops volunteered and served as stretcher bearers.)

In our myopic view we respected and admired only those who got shot at, and to hell with everyone else. This was unfair to noncombatants who performed essential tasks, but we were so brutalized by war that we were incapable of making fair evaluations.

## A Leader Dies

By 5 October (D + 20) the 7th Marines had lost about as many men as the 1st Marines had lost earlier in the battle. The regiment was now finished as an assault force on the regimental level. The 5th Marines, the last of the 1st Marine Division's infantry regiments, began to relieve the 7th Marines that day. Some of the men of the battered regiment would be killed or wounded in subsequent actions in the draws and valleys among the ridges of Peleliu, but the 7th Marines were through as a fighting force for the campaign.

On 7 October 3/5 made an assault up a large draw called Horseshoe Valley, known commonly as "the Horseshoe." There were numerous enemy heavy guns in caves and emplacements in the ridges bordering the Horseshoe to the west, north, and east. Our battalion was supposed to knock out as many of them as possible. We were supported by six army tanks, because the Marine 1st Tank Battalion had been relieved on 1 October to be sent back to Pavuvu. Somebody erroneously assumed there would be no further need for tanks on Peleliu.

My guess is that the 1st Tank Battalion was relieved not because the men were "badly depleted and debilitated"—the official reason given—but because the machines were. Machines wore out or needed overhauling and maintenance, but men were expected to keep going. Tanks, amtracs, trucks, aircraft, and ships were considered valuable and difficult to replace way out in the Pacific. They were maintained carefully and not exposed needlessly to wear or destruction. Men, infantrymen in particular, were simply expected to keep going beyond the limits of human endurance until they got killed or wounded or dropped from exhaustion.

Our attack on the Horseshoe was preceded by terrific artillery fire from our big guns. The shells swished and whined toward the ridges for two and a half hours. The mortars added their bit, too. The attack was surprisingly successful. The Horseshoe wasn't secured, but many Japanese were killed. We also knocked out many caves containing heavy guns, but only after several of the tanks took hits from them.

In the estimation of the Marines, the army tankers did a good job. Here the tanks operated with our riflemen attached. It was a case of mutual support. The tanks pulled up to the caves and fired into them point-blank with their 75mm cannon—*wham bam.* Their machine guns never seemed to stop. A tank unattended by riflemen was doomed to certain destruction from enemy suicide crews carrying mines. And the riflemen got a lot of protection from the tanks.

About the only instance I know of where tanks tried to operate without riflemen in the Pacific was a case of army tanks on Okinawa. Predictably, the Japanese knocked out most of those tanks. Marine tanks always operated with riflemen, like a dog with his fleas. But with tanks and riflemen, it was mutually beneficial.

After the attack of 7 October on the Horseshoe, 3/5 pulled back some

*Col. Harold "Bucky" Harris, 5th Marines, discusses air support with some of his officers: (L to R, Lt. Col. J. R. Bailey, Harris, Maj. John "Gus" Gustafson, Lt. Col. Lewis Walt, Maj. Gordon Gayle). Peleliu. USMC photo.*

distance from the ridges. Shortly thereafter we again went up toward the northern part of the island.

Between 8 and 11 October we emplaced our 60mm mortars between the West Road and the narrow beach. We were only a few yards from the water. Thus set up, we fired over the West Road, our front line beyond, and onto the ridges. We had an observer somewhere across the road who sent us orders by the sound-powered phone.

We kept up a brisk rate of fire because Japanese had infiltrated into positions on the ridge next to the road and were sniping at vehicles and troops with deadly effect. Our mortar fire helped pin them down and clean them out. We had good gun emplacements among some rocks and were screened by a narrow strip of thick foliage between us and the road and, therefore, from the enemy in the ridge beyond.

I was extremely confused as to where we had left our company. An NCO told me our mortars were detached temporarily from Company K and were supporting another unit hard pressed by snipers. The enemy were firing from positions that were almost impossible to locate and they shot any and everybody they could—even casualties being evacuated by amtracs. More than one desperate amtrac driver, as he raced down the West Road toward the Regimental Aid Station, arrived only to find his helpless cargo slaughtered where they lay.

While we were in this position we were particularly vulnerable to infiltrators who might slip in along the beach as well as from the water to our rear. We kept watch in all directions at night; in this place, there were no friendly troops to our rear, just the water's edge about ten feet away and then the ocean-covered reef. The water was only about knee deep for quite a distance out. The Japanese would wade out, slip along the reef, and come in behind us.

One night while I was firing flare shells, James T. (Jim) Burke, a Marine we called the Fatalist, was manning Number One gun. Between firing missions, I could see him sitting on his helmet next to his gun, keeping watch to our left and rear.

"Hey, Sledgehammer, let me see your carbine a minute," he whispered nonchalantly in his usual laconic manner. He had a .45 pistol which was of little use at much distance. I handed him my carbine. I didn't know what he saw, so I followed his gaze as he pointed my carbine toward the sea. In the pale light a shadowy figure was moving slowly and silently along the reef parallel to the shoreline in the shallow water. The man couldn't have been more than thirty yards away or we couldn't have seen him in the dim moonlight. There was no doubt that he was a Japanese trying to get farther along to where he could slip ashore and creep up on our mortars.

No challenge or demand for password was even considered in a situation like that. No Marine would be creeping along the reef at night. The Fatalist rested his elbows on his knees and took careful aim as the figure moved slowly through the glassy-smooth water. Two quick shots; the figure disappeared.

The Fatalist flipped the safety back on, handed me my carbine, and said, "Thanks, Sledgehammer." He appeared as unconcerned as ever.

During the morning of 12 October, an NCO brought word that we were to take up our guns. The mortar section was to rejoin Company K. We gathered our gear and mortar. Snafu, George Sarrett, and I got into a jeep parked along a sheltered part of the road. We had to hang on because the driver took off with a lurch in a cloud of dust and drove like hell down the West Road bordered by the sniper-infested ridge. It was my first—and only—jeep ride during my entire enlistment. It was an eventful day because of that.

Shortly the driver stopped and let us off in a supply area where we waited for an NCO who was to guide us up into the ridges. Directly the rest of the Company K mortarmen arrived with directions to reach the company. We hoisted our mortar and other weapons and gear and headed across the road. We picked our way around the end of the ridge, then headed up a narrow valley filled with skeletons of shattered trees jutting up here and there on the slopes amid crazy-angled coral masses.

Johnny Marmet came striding down the incline of the valley to meet us as we started up. Even before I could see his face clearly, I knew from the way he was walking that something was dreadfully amiss. He lurched up to us, nervously clutching the web strap of the submachine gun slung over his shoulder. I had never seen Johnny nervous before, even under the thickest fire, which he seemed to regard as a nuisance that interfered with his carrying out his job.

His tired face was contorted with emotion, his brow was knitted tightly, and his bloodshot eyes appeared moist. It was obvious he had something fearful to tell us. We shuffled to a halt.

My first thought was that the Japanese had slipped in thousands of troops from the northern Palaus and that we would never get off the island. No, maybe the enemy had bombed some American city or chased off the navy as they had done at Guadalcanal. My imagination went wild, but none of us was prepared for what we were about to hear.

"Howdy, Johnny," someone said as he came up to us.

"All right, you guys, let's get squared away here," he said looking in every direction but at us. (This was strange, because Johnny wasn't the least reluctant to make eye contact with death, destiny, or the general himself.) "OK, you guys, OK, you guys," he repeated, obviously flustered. A couple of men exchanged quizzical glances. "The skipper is dead. Ack Ack has been killed," Johnny finally blurted out, then looked quickly away from us.

I was stunned and sickened. Throwing my ammo bag down, I turned away from the others, sat on my helmet, and sobbed quietly.

"Those goddamn slant-eyed sonsabitches," someone behind me groaned.

Never in my wildest imagination had I contemplated Captain Haldane's death. We had a steady stream of killed and wounded leaving us, but somehow I assumed Ack Ack was immortal. Our company commander represented stability and direction in a world of violence, death, and destruction. Now his life had been snuffed out. We felt forlorn and lost. It was the worst grief I endured during the entire war. The intervening years have not lessened it any.

Capt. Andy Haldane wasn't an idol. He was human. But he commanded our individual destinies under the most trying conditions with the utmost compassion. We knew he could never be replaced. He was the finest Marine officer I ever knew. The loss of many close friends grieved me deeply on Peleliu and Okinawa. But to all of us the loss of our company commander at Peleliu was like losing a parent we depended upon for security—not our physical security, because we knew that was a commodity beyond our reach in combat, but our mental security.

Some of the men threw their gear violently to the deck. Everybody was cursing and rubbing his eyes.

Finally Johnny pulled himself together and said, "OK, you guys, let's move out." We picked up mortars and ammo bags. Feeling as though our crazy world had fallen apart completely, we trudged slowly and silently in single file up the rubble-strewn valley to rejoin Company K.*

So ended the outstanding combat career of a fine officer who had distinguished himself at Guadalcanal, Cape Gloucester, and Peleliu. We had lost our leader and our friend. Our lives would never be the same. But we turned back to the ugly business at hand.

# The Stench of Battle

Johnny led us on up through a jumble of rocks on Hill 140. Company K's line was emplaced along a rock rim, and we set up the mortars in a shallow depression about twenty yards behind it. The riflemen and machine gunners in front of us were in among rocks along the rim of Hill 140 facing east toward Walt Ridge and the northern end of the infamous Horseshoe. We had previously attacked that valley from its southern end. From the rim of Hill 140 the rock contours dropped away in a sheer cliff to a canyon below. No one could raise his head above the rim rock without immediately drawing heavy rifle and machine-gun fire.

The fighting around the pocket was as deadly as ever, but of a different type from the early days of the campaign. The Japanese fired few artillery or mortar barrages, just a few rounds at a time when assured of inflicting maximum casualties. That they usually did, and then secured the guns to escape detection. Sometimes there was an eerie quiet. We knew they were

---

*At the time of Captain Haldane's death, the bulk of Company K was operating with its parent battalion (3/5) on Hill 140 within the Umurbrogol Pocket. In an attempt to orient himself to the strange terrain his company was occupying, Haldane raised his head and looked over a ridge. A sniper's bullet killed him instantly. First Lt. Thomas J. ("Stumpy") Stanley succeeded him as commander of K/3/5. Stanley led Company K through the remainder of the Peleliu campaign and on to Okinawa the following spring.

everywhere in the caves and pillboxes. But there was no firing in our area, only the sound of firing elsewhere. The silence added an element of unreality to the valleys.

If we moved past a certain point, the Japanese opened up suddenly with rifle, machine-gun, mortar, and artillery fire. It was like a sudden storm breaking. More often than not we had to pull back, and not a man in the company had seen a live enemy anywhere.

They couldn't hope to drive us off by then or to be reinforced themselves. From that point onward, they killed solely for the sake of killing, without hope and without higher purpose. We were fighting in Peleliu's ridges and valleys, in terrain the likes of which most Americans could not even visualize, against an enemy unlike anything most Americans could imagine.

The sun bore down on us like a giant heat lamp. Once I saw a misplaced phosphorous grenade explode on the coral from the sun's intense heat. We always shaded our stacked mortar shells with a piece of ammo box to prevent this.

Occasional rains that fell on the hot coral merely evaporated like steam off hot pavement. The air hung heavy and muggy. Everywhere we went on the ridges the hot humid air reeked with the stench of death. A strong wind was no relief; it simply brought the horrid odor from an adjacent area. Japanese corpses lay where they fell among the rocks and on the slopes. It was impossible to cover them. Usually there was no soil that could be spaded over them, just the hard, jagged coral. The enemy dead simply rotted where they had fallen. They lay all over the place in grotesque positions with puffy faces and grinning buck-toothed expressions.

It is difficult to convey to anyone who has not experienced it the ghastly horror of having your sense of smell saturated constantly with the putrid odor of rotting human flesh day after day, night after night. This was something the men of an infantry battalion got a horrifying dose of during a long, protracted battle such as Peleliu. In the tropics the dead became bloated and gave off a terrific stench within a few hours after death.

Whenever possible we removed Marine dead to the rear of the company's position. There they were usually laid on stretchers and covered with ponchos which stretched over the head of the corpse down to the ankles. I rarely saw a dead Marine left uncovered with his face exposed to sun, rain, and flies. Somehow it seemed indecent not to cover our dead. Often, though, the dead might lie on the stretchers for some time and decompose badly before the busy graves registration crews could take them for burial in the division cemetery near the airfield.

During the fighting around the Umurbrogol Pocket, there was a constant movement of one weary, depleted Marine company being relieved by another slightly less weary, depleted company. We seemed to rotate from one particularly dangerous part of the line to one slightly less so and back again continuously.

There were certain areas we moved into and out of several times as the campaign dragged along its weary, bloody course. In many such areas I became quite familiar with the sight of some particular enemy corpse, as if it were a landmark. It was gruesome to see the stages of decay proceed from just killed, to bloated, to maggot-infested rotting, to partially exposed bones—like some biological clock marking the inexorable passage of time. On each occasion my company passed such a landmark we were fewer in number.

Each time we moved into a different position I could determine the areas occupied by each rifle company as we went into that sector of the line. Behind each company position lay a pile of ammo and supplies and the inevitable rows of dead under their ponchos. We could determine how bad that sector of the line was by the number of dead. To see them so always filled me with anger at the war and the realization of the senseless waste. It depressed me far more than my own fear.

Added to the awful stench of the dead of both sides was the repulsive odor of human excrement everywhere. It was all but impossible to practice simple, elemental field sanitation on most areas of Peleliu because of the rocky surface. Field sanitation during maneuvers and combat was the responsibility of each man. In short, under normal conditions, he covered his own waste with a scoop of soil. At night when he didn't dare venture out of his foxhole, he simply used an empty grenade canister or ration can, threw it out of his hole, and scooped dirt over it next day if he wasn't under heavy enemy fire.

But on Peleliu, except along the beach areas and in the swamps, digging into the coral rock was nearly impossible. Consequently, thousands of men —most of them around the Umurbrogol Pocket in the ridges, many suffering with severe diarrhea, fighting for weeks on an island two miles by six miles—couldn't practice basic field sanitation. This fundamental neglect caused an already putrid tropical atmosphere to become inconceivably vile.

Added to this was the odor of thousands of rotting, discarded Japanese and American rations. At every breath one inhaled hot, humid air heavy with countless repulsive odors. I felt as though my lungs would never be cleansed of all those foul vapors. It may not have been that way down on the airfield and in other areas where the service troops were encamped, but around the infantry in the Umurbrogol Pocket, the stench varied only from foul to unbearable.

In this garbage-filled environment the flies, always numerous in the tropics anyway, underwent a population explosion. This species was not the unimposing common housefly (the presence of one of which in a restaurant is enough to cause most Americans today to declare the place unfit to serve food to the public). Peleliu's most common fly was the huge blowfly or bluebottle fly. This creature has a plump, metallic, greenish-blue body, and its wings often make a humming sound during flight.

The then new insecticide DDT was sprayed over the combat areas on Peleliu for the first time anywhere. It supposedly reduced the adult fly population while Marines were still fighting on the ridges, but I never noticed that the flies became fewer in number.

With human corpses, human excrement, and rotting rations scattered across Peleliu's ridges, those nasty insects were so large, so glutted, and so lazy that some could scarcely fly. They could not be waved away or frightened off a can of rations or a chocolate bar. Frequently they tumbled off the side of my canteen cup into my coffee. We actually had to shake the food to dislodge the flies, and even then they sometimes refused to move. I usually had to balance my can of stew on my knee, spooning it up with my right hand while I picked the sluggish creatures off the stew with my left. They refused to move or to be intimidated. It was revolting, to say the least, to watch big fat blowflies leave a corpse and swarm into our C rations.

Even though none of us had much appetite, we still had to eat. A way to solve the fly problem was to eat after sunset or before sunrise when the insects were inactive. Chow had to be unheated then, because no sterno tablets or other form of light could be used after dark. It was sure to draw enemy sniper fire.

Each morning just before sunrise, when things were fairly quiet, I could hear a steady humming sound like bees in a hive as the flies became active with the onset of daylight. They rose up off the corpses, refuse, rocks, brush, and wherever else they had settled for the night like a swarm of bees. Their numbers were incredible.

Large land crabs crawled all over the ridges at night, attracted by corpses. Their rustling through dry debris often was indistinguishable from prowling enemy soldiers. We responded by tossing a grenade at the sound.

In addition to rotting corpses and organic waste, the litter of smashed and worn out equipment of every type became more abundant as the battle dragged on and the size of the Umurbrogol Pocket shrank slowly. The ridges and ravines were littered with the flotsam of fierce combat. Debris of battle was everywhere and became more noticeable as the weeks dragged on.

I still see clearly the landscape around one particular position we occupied for several days. It was a scene of destruction and desolation that no fiction could invent. The area was along the southwestern border of the pocket where ferocious fighting had gone on since the second day of battle (16 September). The 1st Marines, the 7th Marines, and now the 5th Marines, all in their turn, had fought against this same section of ridges. Our exhausted battalion, 3/5, moved into the line to relieve another slightly more exhausted battalion. It was the same old weary shuffling of one tired, depleted outfit into the line to relieve another whose sweating men trudged out of their positions, hollow-eyed, stooped, grimy, bearded zombies.

The Company K riflemen and machine gunners climbed up the steep ridge and into the crevices and holes of the company we relieved. Orders were given that no one must look over the crest of the ridge, because enemy rifle and machine-gun fire would kill instantly anyone who did.

As usual the troops pulling out gave our men "the dope" on the local conditions: what type fire to expect, particular danger spots and possible infiltration routes at night.

My mortar went into a gun pit occupied by one of the 60mm mortars of the company we were relieving. The gun pit was among coral rocks about twenty yards from the foot of the ridge. An extremely youthful Marine was just buckling the leather strap around the bipod and tube of his 60mm mortar as I walked up near the position and put down my heavy ammo bag. I sat on my helmet and started talking to him as the rest of our squad moved into their positions. As the young man looked up, I was struck by the agonized expression on his face. He didn't seem happy, the way he should have, about being relieved.

"You guys watch out for the Japs at night. Two of the bastards got into this gun pit last night and cut up our gunner and assistant gunner," he said.

He told me in a strained voice that the crew was so occupied firing the mortar during the previous night that two Japanese who slipped through the line on the ridge managed to creep up close to the pit without detection. They jumped in and cut up the two men working the mortar before nearby mortar ammo carriers killed them. The wounded Marines had been evacuated, but one of them had died, and the other was in poor condition. The bodies of the Japanese had been thrown into some nearby bushes.

The man telling me of the tragedy and another crouching beside the gun pit had been ammo carriers but had now assumed new duties as gunner and assistant. I noticed that as the new gunner folded and strapped his gun to leave, he seemed reluctant to touch the bottom or sides of the emplacement. When he left and we came closer to the gun pit to set up our mortar, I saw why. The white coral sides and bottom were spattered and smeared with the dark red blood of his two comrades.

After we got our gun emplaced, I collected up some large scraps of cardboard from ration and ammo boxes and used them to cover the bottom of the pit as well as I could. Fat, lazy blowflies were reluctant to leave the blood-smeared rock.

I had long since become used to the sight of blood, but the idea of sitting in that bloodstained gun pit was a bit too much for me. It seemed almost like leaving our dead unburied to sit on the blood of a fellow Marine spilled out on the coral. I noticed that my buddy looked approvingly at my efforts as he came back from getting orders for our gun. Although we never discussed the subject, he apparently felt as I did. As I looked at the stains on the coral, I recalled some of the eloquent phrases of politicians and newsmen about how "gallant" it is for a man to "shed his blood for his country," and "to give his life's blood as a sacrifice," and so on. The words seemed so ridiculous. Only the flies benefited.

The wind blew hard. A drizzling rain fell out of a leaden sky that seemed to hang just above the ridge crest. Shattered trees and jagged rocks along the crest looked like stubble on a dirty chin. Most green trees and bushes had long since been shattered and pulverized by shell fire. Only the grotesque stumps and branches remained. A film of fine coral dust covered everything. It had been dust before the rain, but afterward it was a grimy coating of thin plaster.

The overwhelming grayness of everything in sight caused sky, ridge, rocks, stumps, men, and equipment to blend into a grimy oneness. Weird, jagged contours of Peleliu's ridges and canyons gave the area an unearthly alien appearance. The shattered vegetation and the dirty-white splotches peppering the rocks where countless bullets and shell fragments had struck off the weathered gray surfaces contributed to the unreality of the harsh landscape.

Rain added the final touch. On a battlefield rain made the living more miserable and forlorn and the dead more pathetic. To my left lay a couple of bloated Japanese corpses teaming with maggots and inactive flies who seemed to object to the rain as much as I did. Each dead man still wore the two leather cartridge boxes, one on either side of his belt buckle, neat wrap leggings, *tabi* shoes, helmets, and packs. Beside each corpse lay a shattered and rusting Arisaka rifle, smashed against a rock by some Marine to be certain it wasn't used again.

Cans of C rations and K ration boxes, opened and unopened, lay around our gun pit along with discarded grenade and mortar shell canisters. Scattered about the area were discarded U.S. helmets, packs, ponchos, dungaree jackets, web cartridge belts, leggings, boondockers, ammo boxes of every type, and crates. The discarded articles of clothing and the inevitable bottle of blood plasma bore mute testimony that a Marine had been hit there.

Many tree stumps had a machine-gun ammo belt draped over them. Some of these belts were partially filled with live cartridges. Amid all this evidence of violent combat, past and continuing, I was interested in the fact that spent, or partially so, machine-gun ammo belts so often seemed to be draped across a shattered stump or bush rather than lying on the ground. In combat, I often experienced fascination over such trivia, particularly when exhausted physically and strained emotionally. Many combat veterans told me they also were affected the same way.

All around us lay the destruction and waste of violent combat. Later, on the muddy clay fields and ridges of Okinawa, I would witness similar scenes on an even vaster scale. There the battlefield would bear some resemblance to others described in World War II. During the muddy stalemate before Shuri, the area would resemble descriptions I had read of the ghastly corpse-strewn morass of Flanders during World War I.

These, though, were typical modern battlefields. They were nothing like the crazy-contoured coral ridges and rubble-filled canyons of the Umurbrogol Pocket on Peleliu. Particularly at night by the light of flares or on a cloudy day, it was like no other battlefield described on earth. It was an alien, unearthly, surrealistic nightmare like the surface of another planet.

I have already mentioned several times the exhaustion of the Marines as the campaign wore on. Our extreme fatigue was no secret to the Japanese either. As early as 6 October, nine days before we were relieved, a captured document reported that we appeared worn out and were fighting less aggressively.

The grinding stress of prolonged heavy combat, the loss of sleep because of nightly infiltration and raids, the vigorous physical demands forced on us by the rugged terrain, and the unrelenting, suffocating heat were enough to make us drop in our tracks. How we kept going and continued fighting I'll never know. I was so indescribably weary physically and emotionally that I became fatalistic, praying only for my fate to be painless. The million-dollar wound seemed more of a blessing with every weary hour that dragged by. It seemed the only escape other than death or maiming.

In addition to the terror and hardships of combat, each day brought some new dimension of dread for me: I witnessed some new, ghastly, macabre facet in the kaleidoscope of the unreal, as though designed by some fiendish ghoul to cause even the most hardened and calloused observer among us to recoil in horror and disbelief.

Late one afternoon a buddy and I returned to the gun pit in the fading light. We passed a shallow defilade we hadn't noticed previously. In it were three Marine dead. They were lying on stretchers where they had died before their comrades had been forced to withdraw sometime earlier. (I usually avoided confronting such pitiful remains. I never could bear the sight of American dead neglected on the battlefield. In contrast, the sight of Japanese corpses bothered me little aside from the stench and the flies they nourished.)

As we moved past the defilade, my buddy groaned, "Jesus!" I took a quick glance into the depression and recoiled in revulsion and pity at what I saw. The bodies were badly decomposed and nearly blackened by exposure. This was to be expected of the dead in the tropics, but these Marines had been mutilated hideously by the enemy. One man had been decapitated. His head lay on his chest; his hands had been severed from his wrists and also lay on his chest near his chin. In disbelief I stared at the face as I realized that the Japanese had cut off the dead Marine's penis and stuffed it into his mouth. The corpse next to him had been treated similarly. The third had been butchered, chopped up like a carcass torn by some predatory animal.

My emotions solidified into rage and a hatred for the Japanese beyond anything I ever had experienced. From that moment on I never felt the least pity or compassion for them no matter what the circumstances. My comrades would field strip their packs and pockets for souvenirs and take gold teeth, but I never saw a Marine commit the kind of barbaric mutilation the Japanese committed if they had access to our dead.

When we got back to the gun pit, my buddy said, "Sledgehammer, did you see what the Nips did to them bodies? Did you see what them poor guys had in their mouths?" I nodded as he continued, "Christ, I hate them slant-eyed bastards!"

"Me too. They're mean as hell," was all I could say.

## Victory at High Cost

Twelve October continued to be an eventful day for us on Hill 140. Following Captain Haldane's death in the morning, we set up our mortars below and behind a 75mm pack howitzer tied down within Company K's lines. We were to fire our usual support for the company, but we also were to provide covering fire for the artillery piece.

Johnny Marmet was observing for us through a crack in the coral rock up near the howitzer when he suddenly called down to us that he saw some Japanese officers just outside the mouth of a cave. Apparently confident they were sheltered from American fire, they were just sitting down to eat at a table on a ledge beneath a thatched canopy.

Johnny called the range to us and the order to fire five rounds. Snafu sighted in on the proper aiming stake, repeated Johnny's range, and yelled, "Fire one." I grabbed a shell, repeated the range and charge, pulled off the proper number of powder increments from between the tail fins, put my right thumb over the safety pin, pulled the safety wire, and dropped the shell into the muzzle. Snafu realigned the sight after the recoil, grabbed the bipod feet and yelled, "Fire two." I prepared the second shell and dropped it into the tube. It went smoothly and we got all the rounds off in short order. We listened tensely for them to explode on target. My heart pounded away the seconds. It was a rare occasion to get Japanese officers bunched up and rarer indeed on Peleliu for them to expose themselves.

After seemingly endless seconds of suspense we heard the dull boom as each shell exploded over the ridge and across the valley. Something was wrong though. I heard one less explosion than the number of shells we had fired. We looked anxiously up at Johnny who had his eyes glued to the target. Suddenly he spun around, snapped his finger, and stamped his foot. Scowling down at us he yelled, "Right on target, zeroed in! But the first damned round was a *dud!* What the hell happened?" We groaned and cursed with frustration. The first shell had gone right through the thatched roof and the Japanese officers dove for the cave. But the shell didn't explode. Our remaining shells were right on target, too, smashing up and blowing apart the thatched canopy and the table. But the enemy officers were safe inside the cave. Our pinpoint accuracy had been remarkable for a 60mm mortar that normally functioned to neutralize an area with fragments from its bursting shells. Our golden opportunity had vanished because of a dud shell. We set about trying to figure out what had gone wrong.

Everybody in the mortar section was cursing and groaning. Suddenly Snafu accused me of forgetting to pull the safety wire to arm that first shell. I was confident that I had pulled the pin. Some defense worker in an ammunition plant back in the States had made a mistake in the manufacture of the shell, I contended. Snafu wouldn't accept that, and we got into a hot argument. I was angry and frustrated enough myself. We had missed our one chance in a million to avenge the death of our CO. But Snafu was in a rage. It was a matter of pride with him, because he was the gunner and, therefore, in command of our mortar crew.

Snafu was a good Marine and an expert mortarman. His performance of his duties bore absolutely no resemblance to his nickname, "Situation Normal All Fouled Up." He felt it was a reflection on him that a chance to clobber several Japanese officers had failed because his assistant gunner hadn't pulled the safety wire on a shell. He was proud of a newspaper clipping from his hometown paper in Louisiana describing the effective fire his "mortar gun" had poured on the Japs during the bloody fighting for Hill 660 on Cape Gloucester. Snafu was a unique character known and respected by everybody. The guys loved to kid him about his intrepid "mortar gun" on Hill 660, and he thrived on it. But this foul-up and escape of those enemy officers because of a dud shell was another matter.

As we argued, I knew that unless I could prove the dud wasn't my fault, I'd never hear the end of it from Snafu and the other Company K survivors of Peleliu. Fortunately, luck was on my side. We had fired only a couple of shells to register the gun before Johnny called on us to fire on the Japanese. Consequently I had an accurate count of the number of rounds we had fired from this position. While Snafu ranted and raved I crawled around on all fours a few feet in front of the gun. With incredible good luck I found what I was seeking amid the coral gravel and pulverized plant material. I retrieved the safety wire from each shell we had fired.

I held them out to Snafu and said, "OK, count them and then tell me I didn't pull the wires on all those rounds."

He counted them. We knew that no other 60mm mortar had occupied this newly captured position, so all the wires were ours. I was angry the shell had been a dud and the Japanese had escaped, but I was delighted that it wasn't due to my carelessness. I heard no more about the dud. We all wanted to forget it.

Word also came that day that the high command had declared the "assault phase" of the Palau Islands operation at an end. Many profane and irreverent remarks were made by my buddies to the effect that our leaders were as crazy as hell if they thought that held true on Peleliu. "Somebody from the division CP needs to come up here and tell them damned Nips the 'assault phase' is over," grumbled one man.

After dark the Japanese reinfiltrated some of the positions they had been driven out of around Hill 140. It was the usual hellish night in the ridges, exhausted Marines trying to fight off incredibly aggressive Japanese slipping all around. It was mortar flares, HE shells, grenades, and small-arms fire. I was so tired I held one eye open with the fingers of one hand to stay awake while clutching a grenade or other weapon with the other hand.

The next day, 13 October, 3/5 was ordered to renew the offensive and to straighten our lines, forming a salient on Hill 140. Our battalion was the only unit of the 5th Marines still on the lines and ordered to attack. Snipers raised hell all over the place. It seemed to me the fighting would never end, as we fired covering fire for our weary riflemen. Our artillery fired heavy support. The next morning, 14 October, Corsairs made a napalm strike against the Japanese on our right. Company I made a probing attack after a mortar barrage was halted by heavy sniper fire. Companies K and L improved their positions and put out more sandbags and concertina wire.

The battalion's efforts at attacking seemed like the gasping of a tired steam engine struggling to pull its string of cars up a steep grade. We were barely making it. Rumors flew that army troops would relieve us the next day, but my cynicism kept me from believing them.

We found some Japanese rifles and ammunition in our area. Hidden under pieces of corrugated iron, I discovered two boxes containing about a dozen Japanese grenades. I suggested to an NCO that we take them in case we needed them during the coming night, but he said we could get them later if necessary. We got busy on firing missions with our mortar, and the first time I glanced back toward the boxes, the souvenir hunters had moved in and were emptying them. Another mortarman and I yelled at the scavenging pests. They left, but all the Japanese grenades were gone.

A wave of hope and excitement spread through the ranks that evening when we got solid information that we would be relieved by the army the next morning. I got less sleep that night than ever. With the end in sight, I didn't want to get my throat slit at the last moment before escaping from the meat grinder.

During the morning of 15 October soldiers of the 2d Battalion, 321st Infantry Regiment, 81st Infantry Division (Wildcats) began moving single-file into our area. I couldn't believe it! We were being relieved at last!

As the soldiers filed by us into position, a grizzled buddy squatting on his battered helmet eyed them critically and remarked, "Sledgehammer, I don't know about them dogfaces. Look how many of 'em wearin' glasses, and they look old enough to be my daddy. Besides, them pockets on their dungaree pants sure do look baggy."

"They look fine to me. They're our replacements," I answered.

"I guess you're right. Thank God they're here," he said reflectively.

His observations were correct though, because most of our fellow Marines hadn't reached the age of twenty-one yet, and army dungarees did have large side pockets.

"We sure are glad to see you guys," I said to one of the soldiers.

He just grinned and said, "Thanks." I knew he wasn't happy to be there.*

The relief, which had gone smoothly, was completed by 1100, and we were on our way to the northern defense zone of Peleliu. Our battalion

---

*By 15 October, the Marines had compressed the Umurbrogol Pocket to an area of about 400 to 500 yards. Yet the soldiers of the 81st Infantry Division faced six more weeks of fighting before the process of constant pressure and attrition wiped out the final vestiges of Japanese opposition.

deployed along the East Road facing seaward, where we were to stop any counterlanding the Japanese might try.

My mortar was emplaced near the road so we could fire on the strip of mangrove swamp between the narrow beach and the sea as well as up the road toward the Umurbrogol Pocket if necessary. There was a sloping ridge to our rear along which the rest of the company dug in defensively. We stayed there from the time we came off the line until the last week of the month.

The area was quiet. We relaxed as much as we could with the nagging fear that we might get thrown into the line again if an emergency developed.

We learned that our battalion would leave Peleliu as soon as a ship was available to transport us back to Pavuvu. By day we rested and swapped souvenirs, but we had to be on the alert at night for possible Japanese movement. To the south we could hear the constant rattle of machine guns and the thud of mortars and artillery as the 81st Infantry Division kept up the pressure around the Umurbrogol Pocket.

One day a buddy told me he had a unique souvenir to show me. We sat on a rock as he carefully removed a package from his combat pack. He unwrapped layers of waxed paper that had originally covered rations and proudly held out his prize for me to see.

"Have you gone Asiatic?" I gasped. "You know you can't keep that thing. Some officer'll put you on report sure as hell," I remonstrated as I stared in horror at the shriveled human hand he had unwrapped.

"Aw, Sledgehammer, nobody'll say anything. I've got to dry it in the sun a little more so it won't stink," he said as he carefully laid it out on the rock in the hot sun. He explained that he thought a dried Japanese hand would be a more interesting souvenir than gold teeth. So when he found a corpse that was drying in the sun and not rotting, he simply took out his kabar and severed the hand from the corpse, and here it was, and what did I think?

"I think you're nuts," I said. "You know the CO will raise hell if he sees that."

"Hell no, Sledgehammer, nobody says anything about the guys collecting gold teeth, do they?" he argued.

"Maybe so," I said, "but it's just the idea of a human hand. Bury it."

He looked grimly at me, which was totally out of character for his amiable good nature. "How many Marines you reckon that hand pulled the trigger on?" he asked in an icy voice.

I stared at the blackened, shriveled hand and wondered about what he said. I thought how I valued my own hands and what a miracle to do good or evil the human hand is. Although I didn't collect gold teeth, I had gotten used to the idea, but somehow a hand seemed to be going too far. The war had gotten to my friend; he had lost (briefly, I hoped) all his sensitivity. He was a twentieth-century savage now, mild mannered though he still was. I shuddered to think that I might do the same thing if the war went on and on.

Several of our Marines came over to see what my buddy had. "You dumb jerk, throw that thing away before it begins to stink," growled an NCO.

"Hell yes," added another man, "I don't want you going aboard ship with me if you got that thing. It gives me the creeps," he said as he looked disgustedly at the souvenir.

After several other men chimed in with their disapproval, my friend reluctantly flung his unique souvenir among the rocks.

We had good rations and began to eat heartily and enjoy being out of the line as we relaxed more each day. Good water came up by jeep with the rations, and I never brushed my teeth so many times a day. It was a luxury. Rumors began to spread that we would soon board ship and leave Peleliu.

Toward the end of October, we moved to another part of the island. Our spirits soared. We bivouacked in a sandy, flat area near the beach. Jeeps brought in our jungle hammocks and our knapsacks.* We received orders to shave and to put on the clean dungarees we all carried in our knapsacks.

Some men complained that it would be easier to clean up aboard ship. But one NCO laughed and said that if our scroungy, stinking bunch of Marines climbed a cargo net aboard ship, the sailors would jump over the other side as soon as they saw us.

My hair, though it had been short on D day, had grown into a thick matted mass plastered together with rifle oil and coral dust. Long ago I had thrown away my pocket comb, because most of the teeth had broken out when I tried to comb my hair. I managed now to clean up my head with soap and water, and it took both edges of two razor blades and a complete tube of shaving soap to shave off the itching, greasy tangle of coral-encrusted beard. I felt like a man freed of a hair shirt.

My dungaree jacket wasn't torn, and I felt I must keep it as a souvenir of good luck. I rinsed it in the ocean, dried it in the sun, and put it into my pack.†

*A knapsack was the lower half of the two-part World War II Marine combat pack. The upper part was called the haversack. The latter half was the part a Marine normally carried with him into a fight.

†I later wore this same lucky jacket through the long, muddy Okinawa campaign. Faded now, it hangs peacefully in my closet, one of my most prized possessions.

My filthy dungaree trousers were ragged and torn in the knees so I threw them into a campfire along with my stinking socks. The jagged coral had worn away the tough, inch-thick cord soles of my new boondockers of 15 September to the thin innersoles. I had to keep these until we returned to Pavuvu, because my replacement shoes were back there in my seabag.

That afternoon, 29 October, we learned that we would board ship the next day. With a feeling of intense relief, I climbed into my hammock at dusk and zipped up the mosquito netting along the side. I was delighted at how comfortable it was to lie on something other than hard, rocky ground. I lay back, sighed, and thought of the good sleep I should get until my turn for sentry duty came around. I could look inland and see the ragged crest of those terrible ridges against the skyline. Thank goodness that section was in U.S. hands, I thought.

Suddenly, *zip, zip, zip, zip,* a burst of Japanese machine-gun fire (blue-white tracers) slashed through the air *under* my hammock! The bullets kicked up sand on the other side of a crater beneath me. I jerked open the hammock zipper. Carbine in hand, I tumbled out into the crater. After all I had been through, I wasn't taking any chances on getting my rear end shot off in a hammock.

Judging from the sound made by the bullets, the machine gun was a long way off. The gunner was probably firing a burst toward the army lines over on some ridge between him and me. But a man could get killed just as dead by a stray bullet as an aimed one. So after my brief moments of comfort in the hammock, I slept the rest of the night in the crater.

Next morning, 30 October, we squared away our packs, picked up our gear, and moved out to board ship. Even though we were leaving bloody Peleliu at last, my mind was distracted by an oppressive feeling that Bloody Nose Ridge was pulling us back like some giant, inexorable magnet. It had soaked up the blood of our division like a great sponge. I believed that it would get us yet. Even if we boarded ship, we would get jerked off and thrown into the line to help stop a counterattack or some threat to the airfield. I suppose I had become completely fatalistic; our casualties had been so heavy that it was impossible for me to believe we were actually leaving Peleliu. The sea was quite rough, and I looked back at the island with great relief as we put out for the ship.

We pulled alongside a big merchant troopship, the *Sea Runner,* and prepared to climb a cargo net to get aboard. We had done this sort of thing countless times in our training but never when we were so terribly exhausted. We had a hard time even getting started up the net because we kept bobbing up and down in the heavy sea. Several men stopped to rest on the way, but no one fell. As I struggled upward with my load of equipment,

*K/3/5 survivors before boarding ship for Pavuvu.*

I felt like a weary insect climbing a vine. But at last I was crawling up out of the abyss of Peleliu!

We were assigned to quarters in troop compartments below decks. I stowed my gear on my rack and went topside. The salt air was delicious to breathe. What a luxury to inhale long deep breaths of fresh clean air, air that wasn't heavy with the fetid stench of death.

*The cost in casualties for a tiny island was terrible. The fine 1st Marine Division was shattered. It suffered a total loss of 6,526 men (1,252 dead and 5,274 wounded). The casualties in the division's infantry regiments were: 1st Marines, 1,749; 5th Marines, 1,378; 7th Marines, 1,497. These were severe losses considering that each infantry regiment started with about 3,000 men. The army's 81st Infantry Division would lose another 3,278 men (542 dead and 2,736 wounded) before it secured the island.*

*Most of the enemy garrison on Peleliu died. Only a few were captured. Estimates as to the exact losses by the Japanese vary somewhat, but conservatively, 10,900 Japanese soldiers died and 302 became prisoners. Of the prisoners only 7 were soldiers and 12 sailors. The remainder were labor-ers of other oriental extractions.*

*Company K, 3d Battalion, 5th Marines went into Peleliu with approxi-mately 235 men, the normal size of a World War II Marine rifle company. It left with only 85 unhurt. It suffered 64 percent casualties. Of its original seven officers, two remained for the return to Pavuvu.*

*For its actions on Peleliu and Ngesebus, the 1st Marine Division received the Presidential Unit Citation.*

Even at a distance Peleliu was ugly with the jagged ridges and shattered trees. Haney came up alongside me and leaned on the rail. He looked gloomily at the island and puffed a cigarette.

"Well, Haney, what did you think of Peleliu?" I asked. I really was curious what a veteran with a combat record that included some of the big battles of the Western Front during World War I thought of the first battle in which I had participated. I had nothing in my experience to make a comparison with Peleliu.

Instead of the usual old salt comment—something like, "You think that was bad, you oughta been in the old Corps,"—Haney answered with an unexpected, "Boy, that was terrible! I ain't never seen nothin' like it. I'm ready to go back to the States. I've had enough after that."

A common perception has it that the "worst battle" to any man is the one he had been in himself. In view of Haney's comments, I concluded that Peleliu must have been as bad as I thought it was even though it was my first battle. Haney's long Marine Corps career as a combat infantryman certain-ly qualified him as a good judge of how bad a battle had been. His simple words were enough to convince me about the severity of the fight we had just been through.

None of us would ever be the same after what we had endured. To some degree that is true, of course, of all human experience. But something in me died at Peleliu. Perhaps it was a childish innocence that accepted as faith the claim that man is basically good. Possibly I lost faith that politicians in high places who do not have to endure war's savagery will ever stop blundering and sending others to endure it.

But I also learned important things on Peleliu. A man's ability to depend on his comrades and immediate leadership is absolutely necessary. I'm convinced that our discipline, esprit de corps, and tough training were the ingredients that equipped me to survive the ordeal physically and mentally—given a lot of good luck, of course. I learned realism, too. To defeat an enemy as tough and dedicated as the Japanese, we had to be just as tough. We had to be just as dedicated to America as they were to their emperor. I think this was the essence of Marine Corps doctrine in World War II, and that history vindicates this doctrine.

To this private first class, Peleliu was also a vindication of Marine Corps training, particularly of boot camp. I speak only from a personal viewpoint and make no generalizations, but for me, in the final analysis, Peleliu was:

- thirty days of severe, unrelenting inhuman emotional and physical stress;
- proof that I could trust and depend completely on the Marine on each side of me and on our leadership;
- proof that I could use my weapons and equipment efficiently under severe stress; and
- proof that the critical factor in combat stress is duration of the combat rather than the severity.

Boot camp taught me that I was expected to excel, or try to, even under stress. My drill instructor was a small man. He didn't have a big mouth. He was neither cruel nor sadistic. He wasn't a bully. But he was a strict disciplinarian, a total realist about our future, and an absolute perfectionist dedicated to excellence. To him more than to my disciplined home life, a year of college ROTC before boot camp, and months of infantry training afterward I attribute my ability to have withstood the stress of Peleliu.

The Japanese were as dedicated to military excellence as U.S. Marines. Consequently, on Peleliu the opposing forces were like two scorpions in a bottle. One was annihilated, the other nearly so. Only Americans who excelled could have defeated them.

Okinawa would be the longest and largest battle of the Pacific war. There my division would suffer about as many casualties as it did on Peleliu. Again the enemy garrison would fight to the death. On Okinawa I would be shelled and shot at more, see more enemy soldiers, and fire at more of them with my mortar and with small arms than on Peleliu. But there was a ferocious, vicious nature to the fighting on Peleliu that made it unique for me. Many of my veteran comrades agreed.

Perhaps we can say of Peleliu as the Englishman, Robert Graves, said of World War I, that it:

. . . gave us infantrymen so convenient a measuring-stick for discomfort, grief, pain, fear, and horror, that nothing since has greatly daunted us. But it also brought new meanings of courage, patience, loyalty, and greatness of spirit; incommunicable, we found to later times.*

As I crawled out of the abyss of combat and over the rail of the *Sea Runner,* I realized that compassion for the sufferings of others is a burden to those who have it. As Wilfred Owen's poem "Insensibility" puts it so well, those who feel most for others suffer most in war.

---

*Graves, Robert, "Introduction" in *Old Soldiers Never Die* by Frank Richards, Berkley Publishing Corp., N.Y. 1966.

# PART II

OKINAWA: THE FINAL TRIUMPH

# FOREWORD TO PART II

Peleliu took its toll. As the executive officer and then commander of Company K, 3d Battalion, 5th Marines, I saw in the eyes of each survivor the price he paid for thirty days of unrelenting close combat on that hunk of blasted coral.

For those weary men returning to Pavuvu in November 1944, the war was far from over. Pavuvu was a better place the second time around than when we had left it. But it wasn't a rest haven. The survivors of Peleliu weren't allowed such a luxury. There was little time for licking wounds. We had to absorb a lot of new men as replacements for those lost on Peleliu and for the rotation home of the Guadalcanal veterans who by then had fought three campaigns.

Peleliu was something special for the Marines of K/3/5—for all of the 1st Marine Division. It has remained so down through the years. Yet Okinawa had its own character, more forbidding in many ways than its predecessor. There the 1st Marine Division fought a different war under a new set of rules where tactics and movement were used in a fashion previously unknown to the island-fighting Marines.

Okinawa is a large island, more than sixty miles long and from two to eighteen miles wide. It introduced the Marines to "land" warfare for the first time. Even in 1945 it had a city, towns and villages, several large airfields, an intricate road network, and a good-sized civilian population. Most important, the Japanese defended it with more than 100,000 of their best troops. Okinawa was Japanese territory. They knew it was our final stepping-stone to the home islands of Japan.

The Marines had learned a lot on the way to Okinawa. We had improved our force structure, tactics, and techniques for combat along the way. The Japanese had learned, too. On Okinawa we faced a set of defenses and defensive tactics made sophisticated by the Japanese through application of lessons learned from all of their previous losses. They also fought with an intensity born of a certain knowledge that if they failed, nothing remained to prevent our direct assault into their homeland.

Irrespective of the new elements, the battle for Okinawa was fought and ultimately decided the way all battles have been fought and won or lost. The men on both sides, facing each other day after day across the sights of a rifle, determined the outcome. Pfc. Eugene B. Sledge was one of those men. In this book he gives us a unique experience of seeing and feeling war at its most important level, that of the enlisted fighting man. His words ring true, clean of analysis and reaction to past events. They simply reflect what happened to him and, therefore, to all of the Marines who fought there. I know, because I fought with them.

For the men of the "old breed" who struggled, bled, died, and eventually won on Peleliu and Okinawa, Sledgehammer is their most eloquent spokesman. I'm proud to have served with them—and with him.

Capt. Thomas J. Stanley
U.S. Marine Corps Reserve (Ret.)

Houston, Texas

# CHAPTER SEVEN

# REST AND REHABILITATION

Early next morning the *Sea Runner,* in convoy with other ships including those carrying the survivors of the 7th Marines, put out for Pavuvu. I was glad to be aboard ship again, even a troopship. I drank gallons of ice cold water from the electrically cooled "scuttlebutts."*

Most of my old friends in rifle companies had been wounded or killed. It was terribly depressing, and the full realization of our losses bore down heavily on me as we made inquiries. The survivors on board gave us all the details regarding our friends who hadn't made it through Peleliu. We thanked them and moved on. After a few of the visits and bad news about lost friends, I began to feel that I hadn't been just lucky but was a survivor of a major tragedy.

One day after noon chow a friend and I were sitting on our racks discussing things in general. The conversation drifted off, and we fell silent. Suddenly he looked at me with an intense, pained expression on his face and said, "Sledgehammer, why the hell did we have to take Peleliu?" I must have looked at him blankly, because he began to argue that our losses on Peleliu had been useless and hadn't helped the war effort at all, and that the island could have been bypassed. "Hell, the army landed troops on Morotai [Netherlands East Indies] with light opposition the same day we landed on

---

*This is a naval slang word referring either to water coolers aboard ship or to rumors. Perhaps the double meaning derived from a habit of sailors and Marines of swapping rumors when gathered around a water cooler for a drink.

Peleliu, and we caught hell, and the damn place still ain't secured. And while we were still on Peleliu, MacArthur hit Leyte [in the Philippines, 20 October] and walked ashore standing up. I just don't see where we did any good," he continued.

I replied gloomily, "I don't know." He just stared at the bulkhead and sadly shook his head. He was the same friend who had been with me the time we saw the three terribly mutilated Marine dead. I could imagine what he was thinking.

Despite these momentary lapses, the veterans of Peleliu knew they had accomplished something special. That these Marines had been able to survive the intense physical exertion of weeks of combat on Peleliu in that incredibly muggy heat gave ample evidence of their physical toughness. That we had survived emotionally—at least for the moment—was, and is, ample evidence to me that our training and discipline were the best. They prepared us for the worst, which is what we experienced on Peleliu.

On 7 November 1944, (three days after my twenty-first birthday) the *Sea Runner* entered Macquitti Bay. After passing familiar islets, she dropped anchor off Pavuvu's steel pier. I was surprised at how good Pavuvu looked after the desolation of Peleliu.

We picked up our gear and debarked shortly. On the beach we walked over to one of several tables set up nearby. There I saw—of all things—an American Red Cross girl. She was serving grapefruit juice in small paper cups. Some of my buddies looked at the Red Cross woman sullenly, sat on their helmets, and waited for orders. But together with several other men, I went over to the table where the young lady handed me a cup of juice, smiled, and said she hoped I liked it. I looked at her with confusion as I took the cup and thanked her. My mind was so benumbed by the shock and violence of Peleliu that the presence of an American girl on Pavuvu seemed totally out of context. I was bewildered. "What the hell is she doing here?" I thought. "She's got no more business here than some damn politician." As we filed past to board trucks, I resented her deeply.

Next to a table counting off the men to board the trucks stood a brand-spanking-new boot second lieutenant. He was so obviously fresh from the States and officers' candidate school that his khakis were new, and he wasn't even suntanned. As I moved slowly by the table he said, "OK, sonny, move out." Since my enlistment in the Marine Corps, I had been called about everything imaginable—printable and unprintable. But fresh off of Peleliu I was unprepared for "sonny." I turned to the officer and stared at him blankly. He returned my gaze and seemed to realize his mistake. He looked hurriedly away. My buddies' eyes still carried that vacant hollow look typical of men recently out of the shock of battle. Maybe that's what the young lieutenant saw in mine, and it made him uncomfortable.

The trucks sped past neat tent areas, much improved since we had last seen Pavuvu. We arrived at our familiar camp area to find numerous self-conscious replacements sitting and standing in and around the tents. We were the "old men" now. They appeared so relaxed and innocent of what lay ahead of us that I felt sorry for them. We took off our packs and settled into our tents. In the best way we could, we tried to unwind and relax.

Shortly after we arrived back at Pavuvu and on an occasion when all the replacements were out of the company area on work parties, 1st Sgt. David P. Bailey yelled "K Company, fall in." As the survivors of Peleliu straggled out of their tents into the company street, I thought about how few remained out of the 235 men we started with.

Dressed in clean khakis and with his bald head shining, Bailey walked up to us and said, "At ease, men." He was a real old-time salty Marine and a stern disciplinarian, but a mild-mannered man whom we highly respected. Bailey had something to say, and it wasn't merely a pep talk. Unfortunately, I don't remember his exact words, so I won't attempt to quote him, but he told us we should be proud. He said we had fought well in as tough a battle as the Marine Corps had ever been in, and we had upheld the honor of the Corps. He finished by saying, "You people have proved you are good Marines." Then he dismissed us.

We returned silently and thoughtfully to our tents. I heard no cynical comments about Bailey's brief remarks. Words of praise were rare from the heart of such a stern old salt who expected every man to do his best and tolerated nothing less. His straightforward, sincere praise and statement of respect and admiration for what our outfit had done made me feel like I had won a medal. His talk was not the loud harangue of a politician or the cliché-studded speech of some rear-echelon officer or journalist. It was a quiet statement of praise from one who had endured the trials of Peleliu with us. As far as being a competent judge of us, there was nobody better qualified than an old combat Marine and a senior NCO like Bailey, who had observed us and endured the fight himself. His words meant a lot to me, and they apparently did to my comrades, too.

One of our first activities after getting settled in our Pavuvu tents was to renew our old feud with the rats and land crabs. Our seabags, cots, and other gear had been stacked around the center tent pole while we were gone. The land crabs had moved in and made themselves at home. When several of my tent mates and I started unstacking the items around the tent pole, the crabs swarmed out. The men started yelling, cursing the crabs and smashing them with bayonets and entrenching tools. Some character sprayed cigarette lighter fluid on a crab as it ran into the company street and then threw a match at it. The flaming crab moved a couple of feet before being killed by the flames.

"Hey, you guys, did you see that? That crab looked just like a burning Jap tank."

"Good oh," yelled another man as Marines rushed around trying to find more cans of lighter fluid to spray on the hated land crabs. Men started taking orders for cans of lighter fluid and raced off to the 5th Marines PX tent to buy up all they could find. We killed over a hundred crabs from my tent alone.

One evening after chow as I sprawled on my cot wishing I were back home, I noticed one of Company K's two surviving officers carrying some books and papers down the company street in the twilight. He passed my tent and went to the fifty-five-gallon oil drum that served as a trash can. The lieutenant tossed some maps and papers into the can. He held up a thick book and with obvious anger slammed it into the trash can. He then turned and walked slowly back up the street.

Curious, I went out to have a look. The maps were combat maps of Peleliu. I dropped them back into the trash (and have since regretted I didn't salvage them for future historical reference). Then I found the book. It was a large hardback volume of about a thousand pages, bound in dark blue, obviously not a GI field manual or book of regulations.

Always seeking good reading material, I looked at the spine of the book and read its title, *Men At War* by Ernest Hemingway. This is interesting history, I thought, and was puzzled as to why the lieutenant had thrown it so violently into the trash. I opened the cover. In the twilight I saw written in a bold strong hand, *A. A. Haldane.* A lump rose in my throat as I asked myself why I'd want to read about war when Peleliu had cost us our company commander and so many good friends. I, too, slammed the book down into the trash can in a gesture of grief and disgust over the waste of war I had already experienced firsthand.

After we had been back on Pavuvu about a week, I had one of the most heartwarming and rewarding experiences of my entire enlistment in the Marine Corps. It was after taps, all the flambeaus were out, and all of my tent mates were in their sacks with mosquito nets in place. We were all very tired, still trying to unwind from the tension and ordeal of Peleliu.

All was quiet except for someone who had begun snoring softly when one of the men, a Gloucester veteran who had been wounded on Peleliu, said in steady measured tones, "You know something, Sledgehammer?"

"What?" I answered.

"I kinda had my doubts about you," he continued, "and how you'd act when we got into combat, and the stuff hit the fan. I mean, your ole man bein' a doctor and you havin' been to college and bein' sort of a rich kid compared to some guys. But I kept my eye on you on Peleliu, and by God you did OK; you did OK."

"Thanks, ole buddy," I replied, nearly bursting with pride. Many men were decorated with medals they richly earned for their brave actions in combat, medals to wear on their blouses for everyone to see. I was never awarded an individual decoration, but the simple, sincere personal remarks of approval by my veteran comrade that night after Peleliu were like a medal to me. I have carried them in my heart with great pride and satisfaction ever since.

As Christmas approached, rumor had it we were going to have a feast of real turkey. There were several days out of the year when the Marine Corps tried to give us good chow: 10 November (the Marine Corps' birthday), Thanksgiving, Christmas, and New Year's. The rest of the time in the Pacific war, chow was canned or dehydrated. Refrigeration facilities for large quantities of food were not available, at least not to a unit as mobile and as lacking in all luxuries as a combat division in the Fleet Marine Force. But the scuttlebutt was that there were frozen turkeys for us in the big refrigerators on Banika.

We had special Christmas Eve church services in the palm-thatched regimental chapel that had been constructed skillfully by Russell Island natives. That was followed by a special Christmas program at the regimental theater where we sat on coconut logs and sang carols. I enjoyed it a great deal but felt pretty homesick. Then we had our roast turkey, and it was excellent.

New Year's celebration was even more memorable for me. On New Year's Eve after chow, I heard some yelling and other commotion over at the battalion messhall. The messmen had just about finished squaring away the galley for the night when a sentry shouted, "Corporal of the guard, fire at post number three!"

I saw cooks and messmen in the messhall who were cleaning up by lamplight all rush outside to a fire burning in a grove of trees near the galley. I thought one of the gasoline heaters that boiled water in tubs where we cleaned our mess kits had caught fire. By the light of the flames I could see men running around the galley yelling, and I could hear the mess sergeant cursing and shouting orders. I also saw two figures slide through the shadows toward our company street, but paid them little heed. In a few minutes the fire was put out, just a can of gasoline some distance from the messhall that had somehow caught fire, somebody said.

A friend of mine appeared at my tent and said in a low voice, "Hey, you guys, Howard says come on down to his tent; plenty of turkey for everybody!"

We followed him on the double. As I entered the tent, there sat Howard Nease on his cot, a flambeau flickering beside him, and a towel on his lap under a huge, plump roast turkey.

"Happy New Year, you guys," Howard said with his characteristically broad grin.

We filed past him as he deftly sliced off huge slabs of turkey with his razor-sharp kabar, and placed them into our opened hands. Others came in, and we broke out our two cans of warm beer that each had been issued. Someone produced a can of jungle juice that had been "working." A guitar, a fiddle, and a mandolin struck up the "Spanish Fandango" as Howard sliced turkey until the carcass was cleaned. Then he directed the music, using his kabar as a baton. Howard told us the burning can of gasoline had been merely a diversion to distract the mess sergeant while he and a couple of other daredevils entered the galley and made a moonlight requisition of two turkeys.

We, the survivors of that recent bloodbath on Peleliu, forgot our troubles and howled with laughter at the story. Enjoying the comradeship forged by combat, we had the finest New Year's Eve party I've ever attended. The 11th Marines fired an artillery salute at midnight—as a peaceful gesture.

It was typical of Howard that he pulled off his turkey requisition so neatly and just as typical that he shared it with as many of his buddies as he could. He was one of those wonderfully buoyant souls, always friendly and joking, cool-headed in combat, and though much admired, very modest. When Howard was killed by a Japanese machine gun in the early days of the Okinawa battle (his third campaign), every man who knew him was deeply saddened. By his example, he taught me more than anyone else the value of cheerfulness in the face of adversity.

One of my most treasured memories is the mental picture of Howard Nease sitting on his bunk carving a huge turkey on his lap with his kabar by the light of a flambeau in his tent under Pavuvu's palms on New Year's Eve 1944, grinning and saying, "Happy New Year, Sledgehammer." I profited greatly from knowing him.

Our new division commander, Maj. Gen. Pedro del Valle, former commander of the 11th Marines, ordered regular close-order drills, parades, and reviews. This was better than work parties moving rotting coconuts and added a "spit and polish" to our routine that helped morale.

A regular beer ration of two cans a man each week also helped. During close-order drill we dressed in clean khakis which each man pressed under his mattress pad on his canvas bunk. As we marched back and forth on the neat coral-covered parade ground, I thought about home or some book I was reading and wasn't at all bored.

One day we had a 5th Regiment parade. Decorations and medals were awarded to those cited for outstanding service on Peleliu. Many of our wounded had returned from the hospitals by then. When the Purple Heart medal was awarded to those who had been wounded, there weren't many of us who didn't qualify for it.

During those parades we took great pride in seeing our regimental flag carried with us. Like all the regimental flags, it had a large Marine Corps emblem on it with "United States Marine Corps" emblazoned across the top. Below the emblem was "Fifth Marine Regiment."

But the thing that made our flag unique was the number of battle streamers attached at the top of staff. These streamers (ribbons about a foot long with the names of battles printed on them) represented battles the 5th Marines had fought in and decorations the regiment had won, all the way back to Belleau Wood (World War I) and the Banana Wars (in South America). We had just added Peleliu to the World War II collection. Those streamers represented more battles than any other Marine regiment had fought in. One buddy said our flag had so many battle streamers, decorations, and ribbons that it looked like a mop—an unsophisticated yet straight-from-the-shoulder summation of a proud tradition!

After we had been back on Pavuvu several weeks, I was told one day to dress in clean khakis and to report to the company headquarters tent promptly at 0100. There was some vague reference to an interview that might lead to officers' candidate school back in the States.

"Hey, Sledgehammer, you'll have it made, being an officer and all that, wheeling and dealing Stateside," a buddy said as I got ready for the interview.

"If you're lucky maybe you can land a desk job," another said.

Some of my buddies were obviously envious as I left and walked nervously down the street. The thoughts in my head were that I didn't want or intend to leave Company K (unless as a casualty or rotated home for good) and why on earth had I been chosen for an interview regarding OCS.

When I arrived at the company headquarters, I was sent to a tent a short distance away, near the battalion headquarters. I reported to the tent and was greeted cordially by a first lieutenant. He was an extremely handsome man and, I gathered from his composure and modest self-confidence, a combat veteran.

He asked me in detail about my background and education. He was sincere and friendly. I felt he was trying carefully to determine whether the men he interviewed were suitable to be Marine officers. He and I hit it off well, and I was perfectly honest with him. He asked me why I had not succeeded in the V-12 officers' candidate program, and I told him how I felt about joining the Marine Corps and being sent to college.

"How do you feel about it now that you've been in combat?" he asked.

I told him it would be nice to be back in college. I said I had seen enough on Peleliu to satisfy my curiosity and ardor for fighting. "In fact," I said, "I'm ready to go home."

He laughed good-naturedly and knowingly. He asked me how I liked the Marine Corps and my unit. I told him I was proud to be a member. He asked me how I liked being a 60mm mortar crewman, and I said it was my first choice. Then he got very serious and asked, "How would you feel about sending men into a situation where you knew they would be killed?"

Without hesitation I answered, "I couldn't do it, sir."

The lieutenant looked at me long and hard in a friendly, analytical way. He asked me a few more questions, then said, "Would you like to be an officer?"

"Yes, sir, if it meant I could go back to the States," I said. He laughed and with a few more friendly remarks told me that was all.

My buddies asked me for all the details of the interview. When I told them all about it one said, "Sledgehammer, damn if you ain't got to be as Asiatic as Haney. Why the hell didn't you snow that lieutenant so you could go into OCS?"

I replied that the lieutenant was experienced and too wise to fall for a snow job. That was true, of course, but I really had no desire to leave Company K. It was home to me, and I had a strong feeling of belonging to the company no matter how miserable or dangerous conditions might be. Besides, I had found my niche as a mortarman. The weapon and its deployment interested me greatly, and if I had to fight again, I was confident of doing the Japanese far more damage as a mortarman than as a second lieutenant. I had no desire to be an officer or command anybody; I just wanted to be the best mortar crewman I could—and to survive the war.

There was nothing heroic or unique in my attitude. Other men felt the same way. Actually, in combat our officers caught just as much hell as the enlisted men. They also were burdened with responsibility. As one buddy (a private) said, "When the stuff hits the fan, all I have to do is what I'm told, and I can look out for just me and my buddy. Them officers all the time got to be checkin' maps and squarin' people away."

We began to assimilate the new replacements into the company, and we added a third mortar to my section. The battalion ordnance section checked all weapons, and we got new issues for those worn out in the fight for Peleliu.

There were some drafted Marines among the new replacements and also a sprinkling of NCOs who had been in navy yards and other stateside duty stations. The presence of the NCOs caused some bitterness among a few of the Gloucester and Peleliu veterans who were by then senior in their squads because of the heavy casualties on Peleliu. The latter wouldn't get promoted with new NCOs entering the company to take our leadership positions. From what I saw, however, the new NCOs were mostly men with numerous years of service, although not combat veterans. They did a good job of assuming their authority while respecting us combat veterans for our experience.

The drafted Marines took a good bit of kidding about being "hand-cuffed volunteers" from those of us who had enlisted into the Marine Corps. Some of the drafted men insisted vehemently that they were volunteers who had enlisted like most of us. But they were careful to conceal their records and identification, because "SS" (for Selective Service) appeared after the serial number if a man had been drafted.

The draftees sometimes had their laugh on us, though. If we griped and complained, they grinned and said, "What you guys bitchin' about? You asked for it, didn't you?" We just grumbled at them; no one got angry about it. For the most part, the replacements were good men, and the company retained its fighting spirit.

Our training picked up in intensity, and rumors began to fly regarding the next "blitz" (a term commonly used for a campaign). We heard that the 1st Marine Division was to be put into an army to invade the China coast or Formosa (Taiwan). Many of my buddies feared that we would lose our identity as Marines and that the Marine Corps would finally be absorbed into the U.S. Army (a fate that has caused anxiety to U.S. Marines of many generations, as history well documents). Our training emphasized street fighting and cooperation with tanks in open country. But we still didn't know the name of our objective. After we were shown maps (without names) of a long, narrow island, we still didn't know.

One day Tom F. Martin, a friend of mine in Company L, who also had been in the V-12 program and was a Peleliu veteran, came excitedly to my tent and showed me a *National Geographic* map of the Northern Pacific. On it we saw the same oddly shaped island. Located 325 miles south of the southern tip of the Japanese home island of Kyushu, it was called Okinawa Shima. Its closeness to Japan assured us of one thing beyond any doubt: Whatever else happened, the battle for Okinawa was bound to be bitter and bloody. The Japanese never had·sold any island cheaply, and the pattern of the war until then had shown that the battles became more vicious the closer we got to Japan.

We made practice landings, fired various small arms, and underwent intensive mortar training. With a third weapon added to our mortar section, I felt as though we were Company K's artillery battery.

At this time hepatitis broke out among the troops. We called it yellow jaundice, and I got a bad case. We could look at a man and tell whether he had the malady by the yellowing of the whites of his eyes. Even our deeply tanned skins took on a sallow appearance. I felt terrible, was tired, and the smell of food nauseated me. Pavuvu's muggy heat didn't help any either. I went to sick call one morning, as other Marines were doing in increasing numbers. The medical officer gave me a "light duty slip," a piece of paper officially relieving me from the intense exertion of routine training but still making me subject to minor work parties such as picking up trash, straightening tent ropes, and the like. It was the only time during my entire service in the Marine Corps that I got out of regular duties because of illness.

Had we been civilians, I'm confident those of us with hepatitis would have been hospitalized. Instead, we received APC pills from a corpsman.* This medication was the standard remedy for everything except bayonet, gunshot, or shrapnel wounds. After several days I was pronounced recovered enough for resumption of regular duties and surrendered my cherished light duty slip to an officer in sick bay.

Training intensified. During January 1945 the company boarded an LCI† and, in convoy with other such vessels, went to Guadalcanal for maneuvers. After a division-sized field problem, we returned to Pavuvu on 25 January.

Then we listened daily with sympathetic interest to the news reports of the terrible fighting encountered by the 3d, 4th, and 5th Marine divisions during the battle for Iwo Jima that began on 19 February.

"It sounds just like a larger version of Peleliu," a buddy of mine said one day.

He didn't realize how correct he was. The new pattern of defense-in-depth and no *banzai* charges that the Japanese had tried on the 1st Marine Division at Peleliu was repeated on Iwo Jima. When that island was

---

*A nonprescription, all-purpose painkiller containing aspirin and caffeine, among other ingredients.

†Landing Craft, Infantry; a sort of miniature LST which carried about a company of infantry plus a few vehicles.

declared secured on 16 March, the cost to the three Marine divisions which fought there sounded like our Peleliu casualties magnified three times.

During our training we were told that we would have to climb over a seawall or cliff (exact height unknown) to move inland during the coming battle. Several times we practiced scaling a sheer coral cliff (about forty feet high) across the bay from the division's camp on Pavuvu. We had no more than two ropes to get the entire company up and over the cliff. Supposedly we would be furnished rope ladders before D day, but I never saw any.

While we stood at the foot of the cliff during those exercises, waiting our turn and watching other men struggle up the ropes to the top of the cliff with all their combat gear, I heard some choice comments from my buddies regarding the proceedings. The company officers (all new except First Lieutenant Stanley, the CO) were rushing around with great enthusiasm urging the troops up the cliff like it was some sort of college football training routine.

"What a fouled-up bunch of boot lieutenants if I ever saw any. Just what the hell do they think them goddamn Nips are gonna be doin' while we climb up that cliff one at a time?" grumbled a veteran machine gunner.

"Seems pretty stupid to me. If that beach is anything like Peleliu, we'll get picked off before anybody gets up any cliff," I said.

"You said that right, Sledgehammer, and them Nips ain't gonna be sittin' around on their cans; they're gonna bracket that beach with mortars and artillery, and machine guns are gonna sweep the top of that cliff," he said with melancholy resignation.

Our new mortar section leader was a New Englander out of an Ivy League college. Mac was blond, not large, but was well built, energetic, and talkative, with a broad New England accent. He was a conscientious officer, but he irritated the veterans by talking frequently and at great length about what he was going to do to the Japanese when we went into action again. We sometimes heard such big talk from enlisted replacements who were trying to impress someone (mostly themselves) with how brave they would be under fire, but Mac was about the only officer I ever heard indulge in it.

Whenever he got started with, "The first time one of our guys gets hit, its gonna make me so mad that I'm gonna take my kabar between my teeth and my .45 in my hand and charge the Japs," all the veterans would sit back and smirk. We threw knowing glances at each other and rolled our eyes like disgusted schoolboys listening to a coach brag that he could lick the opposing team single-handed.

I felt embarrassed for Mac, because it was so obvious he conceived combat as a mixture of football and a boy scout camp-out. He wouldn't listen to the few words of caution from some of us who suggested he had a shock coming. I agreed with a buddy from Texas who said, "I hope to God that big mouth Yankee lieutenant has to eat every one of them words of his when the stuff hits the fan.'' The Texan's wish came true on Okinawa, and it was one of the funniest things I ever saw under fire.

Before the next campaign, we had to take the usual inoculations plus some additional ones. Our arms were sore, and many men became feverish. The troops hated getting injections, and the large number (someone said it was seven) before Okinawa made us crotchety. The plague shot burned like fire and was the worst.

Most of our corpsmen did a good job of making the shots as painless as possible, and this helped. But we had one arrogant corpsman who was unfeeling about other people's pain. He wasn't popular, to say the least. (I hasten to add that he was the one—and only—U.S. Navy hospital corpsman I knew in the Marine Corps who didn't conduct himself in an exemplary manner. All other corpsmen I saw were probably more highly respected by Marines—as a group, and as individuals—than any other group of people we were involved with.)

Directly in front of me as we lined up for shots was a buddy who was a Peleliu veteran. In front of him were several new replacements. The more new men "Doc Arrogant" stuck with the needle, the worse he became. He was just plain mean by the time he got to my buddy. "Doc Arrogant" was in a hurry and didn't look up to recognize my buddy as the latter stepped up to the table. It nearly cost Doc dearly. He held the needle like a dart, plunged it into my friend's arm, depressed the plunger, and said, "Move out!"

My friend didn't flinch from the painful shot. He turned slowly, shook his fist in the corpsman's face, and said, "You sonofabitch, if you want to do some bayonet practice, I'll meet you out on the bayonet course with fixed bayonets and no scabbards on the blades, and then see what you can do."

"Doc Arrogant" looked shocked. He was speechless when he realized that the arm he had punctured so roughly wasn't attached to a meek replacement but to a seasoned veteran.

Then my friend said, "If you ever give me another shot like that, I'll grab you by the stacking swivel and beat you down to parade rest. I'll whip your ass so bad you won't even be able to make this next blitz, because they'll hafta award you a Purple Heart when I finish with you, wise guy."

"Doc Arrogant" changed instantly into "Doc Meek." When I stepped up for my shot, he administered it with a gentleness that would have done credit to Florence Nightingale.

We started packing up our gear. Soon we got word that we would have more maneuvers on Guadalcanal, then shove off for our next fight— Okinawa.

# CHAPTER EIGHT

# PRELUDE TO INVASION

From the standpoint of personal satisfaction I've always been glad that as long as we had to pull maneuvers somewhere in preparation for Peleliu and Okinawa, this training took place on Guadalcanal. The name of that island was embroidered in white letters down the red number *One* on our division patch of which we were all very proud. Guadalcanal had great symbolic significance. I was glad I got to see some of the areas fought over by the 1st Marine Division during the campaign and got some first-hand accounts on the spot of what had taken place from veterans who had participated in making that history.

During one period of maneuvers on Guadalcanal, we stayed ashore for two or three weeks and bivouacked in an area that had been the camp of the 3d Marine Division before its troops went into the hell of Iwo Jima. We strung our jungle hammocks and made ourselves as comfortable as possible. Each day for several days we went out into the hills, jungles, and *kunai* grass fields for training. And we enjoyed a cool shower each afternoon after coming in from the field.

Guadalcanal was a big base by early 1945 and had many service troops and rear-echelon units on it. Across the road from us was a battalion of "Seabees" (naval construction battalion). Late one afternoon three or four of us went over and eased quietly into the end of their chow line. Their cooks recognized us as Marines but didn't say anything. We loaded up on real ice cream, fresh pork chops, fresh salad, and good bread (all unheard of delicacies on Pavuvu) and sat at a clean table in a spacious messhall. It sure beat C rations in a bivouac area. As intruders, we expected to be thrown out any minute. No one seemed to notice us, though.

Next afternoon we returned along with other Marines who had the same idea and enjoyed another excellent supper. Next day we tried it again, easing quietly and slowly along to the chow line, trying not to attract attention. To my amazement a large neatly painted white sign with blue letters and blue border had been placed above the entrance to the chow line since the previous evening. I don't remember the exact wording, but it went something close to this, "Marines welcomed in this chow line after all CB personnel have been through."

We were as embarrassed as we were delighted. Those Seabees had been fully aware of us all along and knew exactly how many Marines were slipping into their chow line. But they were willing and glad to share their extra chow with us as long as it lasted. The sign was necessary, because the Seabees knew we would spread the word and more hungry Marines would swarm over their chow line each day like ants.

We were elated and went through the chow line grinning and thanking the messmen. They were the friendliest bunch I ever saw and made us feel like adopted orphans. The sign may have been made earlier for 3d Division Marines who liked the Seabees' food as much as we, or it may have been put up for our benefit. In any event we appreciated the good food and good treatment. It strengthened our respect for the Seabees.

The 3d Battalion, 5th Marines had been in the assault waves at Peleliu; therefore, in the Okinawa campaign we were assigned as regimental reserve. For the voyage to the island, consequently, we would be loaded aboard the attack transport ship USS *McCracken* instead of LSTs. Such APA transports sent troops ashore in LCVPs (small, open landing craft known as Higgins boats) rather than amphibious tractors.

One afternoon following landing exercises and field problems, our company returned to the beach to await the return of the Higgins boats that would pick us up and return us to the ship. Late afternoon sunlight danced on the beautiful blue waves, and a large fleet of ships stood offshore in Sealark Channel. Dozens of Higgins boats and other amphibious craft plied from the ships to shore, loading Marines and ferrying them out to the ships. It looked like some sort of boating festival except that all the craft were military.

One by one the Higgins boats picked up men (about twenty-five at a time) from our beach area. We waited as the sun sank low in the west. The ships formed up in convoy and moved past us, parallel to the beach. We had no rations or extra water, were tired from day-long maneuvers, and had no desire to spend the night on a mosquito-infested beach.

Finally, as the last ship showed us its stern, a Higgins boat came ploughing through the spray toward us. We were the only troops left on the beach. The coxswain revved his engine, ran the bow of the shallow-draft boat up on the beach, and dropped the bow ramp with a bang. We clambered aboard and someone yelled the customary, "Shove off, coxswain, you're loaded." We held on to the bulwarks of the boat as he raised the ramp, reversed engines, turned, and headed out at full throttle toward the disappearing ship.

The sea was rough. As usual Snafu started getting seasick, so he lay down on his side on the deck of the boat. We were crowded: two machine-gun squads and two 60mm mortar squads packed the Higgins boat, along with all our combat gear, small arms, mortars, and machine guns.

A Higgins boat, like any powerful motor-driven boat under full throttle, normally settled down at the stern end with bow elevated and moved easily over the water. But our boat was so loaded with men and equipment that, even though we crowded as far back in the stern as possible, the squared-off bow ramp wasn't elevated sufficiently to skip over the waves. It drove straight against some large waves, and water poured in through an open view port. Usually, this three-foot by two-foot panel rode well above water level. The coxswain yelled instructions to close the folding steel shutters on the panel, which we did as quickly as possible. But water still sprayed over the bow ramp and in through the cracks around the panel.

In the gathering twilight we could see the stern of a transport far ahead of us. It was the last ship in the convoy that had passed from view around the end of Guadalcanal. Our coxswain made as much speed as possible to catch the transport, and we shipped more and more water. If we didn't catch up with that transport before dark we didn't know when we would get back to our ship.

Water began filling the bilges below the floor decking, so the coxswain started the pumps to keep us afloat. We stood by to bail with our helmets, but by the time the water rose above the flooring where we could get at it, the boat would probably sink because of its heavy load. The situation was grim, and I dreaded the thought of trying to swim the couple of miles through rough water to the beach. What irony, I thought, if some of us should die after surviving Peleliu by drowning on maneuvers in Iron Bottom Bay.

Slowly we gained on the transport and finally drew alongside. Towering above us, the ship was packed with Marines. We shouted up to them for help. A navy officer leaned over the rail and asked us which ship we were from. We told him we had missed the *McCracken* and requested to come aboard or we might sink. He gave orders to our coxswain to pull in close under a pair of davits. He did so, and two cables with hooks were lowered to us. Just as the hooks were fastened to rings in the floor, our Higgins boat seemed to start sinking. Only the cables held it up. A cargo net was lowered to us, and we scrambled up and aboard the ship. We were all mighty relieved to be out of that small boat.

Several hours after dark, the ship arrived at the fleet anchorage. A signalman on the bridge went to work with his blinker light sending code to other ships. The *McCracken* was located, and we were soon back aboard.

"Where the hell you guys been so long?" asked a man in my troop compartment as we fell into our racks.

"We went to 'Frisco for a beer," someone answered.

"Wise guy," he replied.

After maneuvers were completed, our convoy sailed from the Russell Islands on 15 March 1945. We were bound for Ulithi Atoll where the convoy would join the gathering invasion fleet. We anchored off Ulithi on 21 March and remained there until 27 March.*

We lined the rails of our transport and looked out over the vast fleet in amazement. We saw ships of every description: huge new battleships, cruisers, sleek destroyers, and a host of fast escort craft. Aircraft carriers were there in greater numbers than any of us had ever seen before. Every conceivable type of amphibious vessel was arrayed. It was the biggest invasion fleet ever assembled in the Pacific, and we were awed by the sight of it.

Because of tides and winds, the ships swung about on their anchor chains, and each day the fleet looked new and different. When I came topside each morning, I felt disoriented. It was a strange sensation, as though I were in a different frame of reference and had to learn my surroundings anew.

The first afternoon at Ulithi a fellow mortarman said, "Break out the field glasses, and let's see how many kinds of ships we can identify." We passed the mortar section's field glasses around and whiled away many hours studying the different ships.

Suddenly someone gasped, "Look over there at that hospital ship off our port bow! Look at them nurses! Gimme them field glasses!"

Lining the rail of the hospital ship were about a dozen American nurses looking out over the fleet. A scuffle erupted among us over who would use

---

*Ulithi Atoll lies about 260 miles northeast of Peleliu on the western edge of the Caroline Islands. It was captured by an element of the 81st Infantry Division as a part of the Palau Islands operation. Ulithi consists of about thirty islets surrounding an enormous lagoon some nineteen miles long and five to ten miles wide. It became the major U.S. fleet anchorage in the Central Pacific.

the field glasses first, but we all finally had a look at the girls. We whistled and waved, but we were too far away to be heard.

Aside from the huge new battleships and carriers, we talked most about a terribly scorched and battered aircraft carrier anchored near us. A navy officer told us she was the *Franklin.* * We could see charred and twisted aircraft on her flight deck, where they had been waiting loaded with bombs and rockets to take off when the ship was hit. It must have been a flaming inferno of bursting bombs and rockets and burning aviation gasoline. We looked silently at the battered, listing hulk until one man said, "Ain't she a mess! Boy, them poor swabbies musta' caught hell." Those of us who had lived through the blast and fire of Peleliu's artillery barrages could appreciate well the bravery of the sailors on the *Franklin.*

While we were anchored at Ulithi, we went ashore on the tiny islet of Mog Mog for recreation and physical conditioning. After some calisthenics, and to the delight of all hands, our officers broke out warm beer and Cokes. We had one of the most enjoyable baseball games I ever played. Everybody was laughing and running like a bunch of little boys. It was good to get off the cramped transport, stretch our legs, and relieve the monotony. We hated to board the Higgins boats at sunset to return to the ship and our cramped quarters.

At Ulithi we received briefings on the coming battle for Okinawa. This time there was no promise of a short operation. "This is expected to be the costliest amphibious campaign of the war," a lieutenant said. "We will be hitting an island about 350 miles from the Japs' home islands, so you can expect them to fight with more determination than ever. We can expect 80 to 85 percent casualties on the beach."

A buddy next to me leaned over and whispered, "How's that for boosting the troops' morale?" I only groaned.

The lieutenant continued, "We may have trouble getting over that cliff or seawall in our sector. Also, according to G-2 there is a large Jap gun, maybe 150mm, emplaced just on the right flank of our battalion sector. We hope naval gunfire can knock it out. Be on the alert for a Jap paratrooper attack in our rear, particularly at night. It's pretty certain the Nips will pull off a massive counterattack, probably supported by tanks, sometime during

---

*During carrier raids on Japan (18–21 March), Japanese suicide planes had crashed into the American carriers *Wasp, Yorktown,* and *Franklin.* The *Franklin* was the most heavily damaged of the three; her loss was 724 killed and 265 wounded. That the ship was saved at all and later towed some 12,000 miles to New York for repairs was a tribute to the bravery and the skill of her crew.

our first night ashore or just before dawn. They'll *banzai* and try to push us off the beachhead.''†

On 27 March the loudspeaker came on with, "Now hear this, now hear this. Special sea detail stand by." Sailors assigned to the detail moved to their stations where they weighed anchor.

"Well, Sledgehammer, they're raising the hook, so it won't be long before we're in it again ole buddy," a friend said.

"Yeah," I said, "and I'm not in any hurry, either."

"You can say that again," he sighed.

The huge convoy got under way like clockwork. Just watching that host of different vessels kept my mind off what was ahead. As we proceeded I was conscious of how cool the weather had become. We had our wool-lined field jackets with us, and it was comfortable on deck, particularly at night. To those of us who had lived and fought in the sweltering tropics for months, cooler weather was very significant.

Most of our voyage from Ulithi was uneventful. Each night during the northward trip I had noticed the beautiful Southern Cross constellation slipping lower and lower on the starlit horizon. Finally it disappeared. It was the only thing about the South and Central Pacific I would miss. The Southern Cross formed a part of our 1st Marine Division shoulder patch and was, therefore, especially symbolic.

We had intense pride in the identification with our units and drew considerable strength from the symbolism attached to them. As we drew closer to Okinawa, the knowledge that I was a member of Company K, 3d Battalion, 5th Marine Regiment, 1st Marine Division helped me prepare myself for what I knew was coming.*

*Okinawa is a large island, some sixty miles long and from two to eighteen miles wide. Like most islands in the Pacific, it is surrounded by a*

---

*By this time in the Pacific war, official unit designations recognized the prevailing system of task organization for combat where supporting elements reinforced the infantry. Such units became regimental combat teams (RCT) and battalion landing teams (BLT); hence official designations were 5th RCT or 3d BLT. But the rank and file infantryman never forgot who he was. Throughout the war I never heard a Marine infantryman refer to his unit by other than its base name. We were always "K/3/5," "3d Battalion, 5th," or "5th Marines."

†Our planners still hadn't realized that this costly large-scale suicide charge tactic had been abandoned for good. The Japanese had shifted to the defense-in-depth tactic as the best means of defeating us. This tactical shift had prolonged our fight on Peleliu and had been repeated with the same murderous results against the Marines on Iwo Jima.

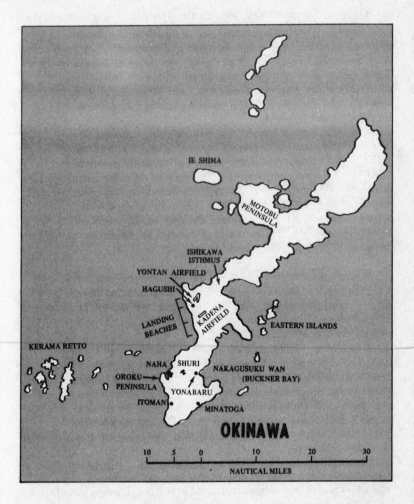

coral reef. But on the west coast that reef lies close to shore, particularly along the invasion beaches at Hagushi.

Through the center of the island runs a ridge rising some 1,500 feet in the wild, mountainous north. South of the Ishikawa Isthmus, the land levels out considerably but is cut by several prominent streams. In 1945, as it remains today, the southern portion of the island contained the bulk of the civilian population.

*Of primary importance to the defense of the island were three east–west ridge systems crossing the southern part of the island. To the north and just below the invasion beaches lay the ridges of Kakazu and Nishibaru. In the middle, running west from Shuri Castle, was the most formidable of the ridges, cut by sheer cliffs and deep draws. Above the extreme southern tip of the island lay Kunishi, Yuza-Dake, and Yaeju-Dake. Together these ridges formed a series of natural defensive barriers to the American forces advancing from the north.*

*Into these natural barriers, Lt. Gen. Mitsuru Ushijima threw the bulk of his 110,000-man Thirty-Second Japanese Army. Natural and man-made barriers were transformed into a network of mutually supporting positions linked by a system of protected tunnels. Each of the ridge lines was held in great strength until it became untenable; then the enemy withdrew to the next defense line. Thus the Japanese drew on their experiences at Peleliu, Saipan, and Iwo Jima to construct a highly sophisticated and powerful defense-in-depth. There they waited and fought to exhaust the will and the resources of the American Tenth Army.*

Tension mounted on the eve of D day. We received final orders to move in off the beach as fast as possible. We were also reminded that although we were in regimental reserve, we would probably "get the hell kicked out of us" coming on the beach. We were advised to hit the sack early; we would need all the rest we could get.*

A predawn reveille ushered in Easter Sunday—April Fool's Day—1945. The ship seethed with activity. We had chow of steak and eggs, the usual feast before the slaughter. I returned to our troop compartment and squared away my ammunition, combat pack, and mortar ammunition bag. The ship's crew manned battle stations and stood by to repel *kamikaze* attacks.† Dawn was breaking, and the preassault bombardment of the beaches had begun. Above it I could hear the drone of enemy aircraft inbound to the attack.

I went into the head to relieve my distressed colon, cramped by fear and apprehension. On the big transport ships the toilet facilities consisted of a row of permanent wooden seats situated over a metal trough through which

---

*Three/Five was scheduled to land after the 1st and 2d battalions of the 5th Marines on the extreme right of the regimental beach. It would form the right flank of the III Marine Amphibious Corps and link with the U.S. Army's XXIV Corps landing to the south.

†Manned suicide planes that dived into American ships. Faith in the *kamikaze's* ("divine wind") ability to cut off the American fleet's support of the landing force ashore was an important element in the Japanese defensive scheme.

ran a constant flow of seawater. There were about twenty seats—no limited facilities here with Haney to delay us as at Peleliu.

Most of the men in my troop compartment had already been to the head and by then had donned their gear and moved out on deck, so I was about the last one in the head. I settled comfortably on a seat. Next to me I noticed a cagelike chute of iron mesh coming through the overhead [ceiling] near one of the 40mm antiaircraft gun tubs. It extended down, through the deck, and into the compartment below.

Startled out of my wits by an incredibly loud sound of clattering, clanking, scraping, and rasping metal, I sprang up with a reflex born of fear and tried to bolt out of the head into the troop compartment. I knew a *kamikaze* had crashed into our ship right above me. My trousers around my ankles hobbled me, and I nearly fell. As I reached to pull them up, the loud clanking and clattering—like a thousand cymbals falling down stone steps— continued. I looked over at the iron mesh chute and saw dozens of empty brass 40mm shell cases cascading down from the guns above. They clattered and clanked through the chute to some collecting bin below decks. My fright subsided into chagrin.

I got on my gear and joined the other men on deck to await orders. We milled around, each man sticking close to his buddy. Higgins boats would take us to rendezvous areas and transfer us to amtracs which previously had delivered the assault waves of infantry across the reef to the beach.

The bombardment of the beach by our warships had grown in intensity, and our planes had joined in with strafing, rockets, and bombing. Japanese planes flew over the fleet at some distance from us. Many of our ships were firing at them.

An order came for all troops to go below (this was to prevent casualties from strafing enemy planes). Loaded with our battle gear, we squeezed our way back through the doorlike hatches into our compartment. Packed like sardines in the aisles between the racks, we waited in the compartment for orders to move back on deck. Sailors on deck dogged our hatches [sealed the doors by turning U-shaped handles positioned all around them]. Like men locked in a closet, we waited and listened to the firing outside. The compartment wasn't large, and the air soon became foul. It was difficult to breathe. Although the weather was cool, we began to sweat.

"Hey, you guys, the blowers [electric ventilating fans] are off. By God, we'll smother in this damn place!" yelled one man. I was next to the hatch, and several of us started yelling at the sailors outside, telling them we needed air. They yelled back from the other side of the steel door that it couldn't be helped, because the electricity was needed to operate the gun mounts. "Then, by God, let us out on deck!"

"Sorry, we've got orders to keep this hatch dogged down."

We all started cursing the sailors, but they were following orders, and I'm sure they didn't want to keep us locked in that stuffy compartment. "Let's get the hell outa here," a buddy said. We all agreed it would be better to get strafed on deck than to suffocate in the compartment. Grasping the levers and moving them to the unlock position, we tried to open the hatch. As fast as we turned each lever, the sailors outside turned it back and kept it dogged down. Other desperate Marines joined us in trying to unclamp the hatch. There were only two sailors outside, so with our combined efforts, we finally got all the clamps open, shoved open the hatch, and burst out into the cool, fresh air.

About that time other Company K men poured out of a hatch on the other side of the compartment. One of the sailors got pushed over and rolled across the deck. In an instant we were all outside breathing in the fresh air.

"All right, you men, return to your quarters. No troops topside. That's an order!" came a voice from a platform slightly aft and above us. We looked up and saw a navy officer, an ensign, standing against the rail glaring at us. He wore khakis, an officer's cap, and insignia bars on his collar, in stark contrast to us dressed in green dungarees, tan canvas leggings, and camouflaged helmet covers, and loaded with battle equipment, weapons, and gear. He wore a web pistol belt with a .45 automatic in the holster.

None of our officers was in the area, so the navy ensign had it all to himself. He swaggered back and forth, ordering us into the foul air of the troop compartment. If he had been a Marine officer, we would have obeyed his order with mutterings and mumblings, but he was so unimposing that we just milled around. Finally, he began threatening us all with courts-martial if we didn't obey him.

A friend of mine spoke up, "Sir, we're goin' to hit that beach in a little while and a lot of us might not be alive an hour from now. We'd rather take a chance on gettin' hit by a Jap plane out here than go back in there and smother to death."

The officer spun around and headed for the bridge—to get help, we assumed. Shortly some of our own officers came up and told us to stand by to go down the nets to the waiting boats. As far as I know, our breakout of the troop compartment for fresh air was never mentioned.

We picked up our gear and moved to assigned areas along the bulwarks of the ship. The weather was mostly clear and incredibly cool (about 75 degrees) after the heat of the South Pacific. The bombardment rumbled and thundered toward the island. Everything from battleships down to rocket and mortar boats were plastering the beaches along with our dive bombers. Japanese planes, their engines droning and whining, came in over the huge convoy, and many ships' antiaircraft fire began bursting in the air. I saw two enemy planes get hit some distance from our ship.

We were all tense, particularly with the intelligence estimate that we could expect 80–85 percent casualties on the beach. Although I was filled with dread about the landing, I wasn't nearly so apprehensive as I had been at Peleliu. Perhaps it was because I was already a combat veteran. I had survived the Peleliu landing and knew what to expect from the Japanese, as well as from myself. Climbing down the cargo net to the Higgins boat, I was still afraid; but it was different from Peleliu.

In addition to the invaluable experience of being a combat veteran, the immensity of our fleet gave me courage. Combat vessels and armed transports ranged as far as we could see. I have no idea how many of our planes were in the air, but it must have been hundreds.

We climbed down the net and settled into the Higgins boat. Someone said, "Shove off, coxswain, you're loaded," as the last Marine climbed into our boat. The coxswain gunned the engine and pulled away from the ship. Other boats loaded with Marines from 3/5 were pulling out all along the side of the ship. I sure hated to leave it. Amphibious craft of every description floated on the water around us. The complexity of the huge invasion was evident everywhere we looked.

Our boat ran some distance from our ship then began circling slowly in company with other boats loaded with men from our battalion. The bombardment of the Hagushi beaches roared on with awesome intensity. Sitting low in the water, we really couldn't see what was going on except in our immediate vicinity. We waited nervously for H hour which was scheduled for 0830.

Some of the ships began releasing thick white smoke as a screen for the convoy's activity. The smoke drifted lazily and mingled in with that of the exploding shells. We continued to circle on the beautiful blue water made choppy by the other boats in our group.

"It's 0830 now," someone said.

"The first wave's goin' in now. Stand by for a ram," Snafu said.

The man next to me sighed. "Yeah, the stuff's gonna' hit the fan now."

CHAPTER NINE

# STAY OF EXECUTION

"The landing is unopposed!"

We looked with amazement at the Marine on the amtrac with which our Higgins boat had just hooked up.

"The hell you say," one of my buddies shot back.

"It's straight dope. I ain't seen no casualties. Most of the Nips musta hauled ass. I just saw a couple of mortar shells fallin' in the water; that's all. The guys went in standin' up. It beats anything I ever saw."

Images of the maelstrom at Peleliu had been flashing through my mind, but on Okinawa there was practically no opposition to the landing. When we overcame our astonishment, everybody started laughing and joking. The release of tension was unforgettable. We sat on the edge of the amtrac's troop compartment singing and commenting on the vast fleet surrounding us. No need to crouch low to avoid the deadly shrapnel and bullets. It was —and still is—the most pleasant surprise of the war.

It suddenly dawned on me, though, that it wasn't at all like the Japanese to let us walk ashore unopposed on an island only 350 miles from their homeland. They were obviously pulling some trick, and I began to wonder what they were up to.

"Hey, Sledgehammer, what's the matter? Why don't you sing like everybody else?"

I grinned and took up a chorus of the "Little Brown Jug."

"That's more like it!"

As our wave moved closer to the island, we got a good view of the hundreds of landing boats and amtracs approaching the beach. Directly ahead of us, we could see the men of our regiment moving about in dispersed combat formations like tiny toy soldiers on the rising landscape. They appeared unhurried and nonchalant, as if on maneuvers. There were no enemy shells bursting among them. The island sloped up gently from the beach, and the many small garden and farm plots of the Okinawans gave it the appearance of a patchwork quilt. It was beautiful, except where the ground cover and vegetation had been blasted by shells. I was overcome with the contrast to D day on Peleliu.

When our wave was about fifty yards from the beach, I saw two enemy mortar shells explode a considerable distance to our left. They spewed up small geysers of water but caused no damage to the amtracs in that area. That was the only enemy fire I saw during the landing on Okinawa. It made the April Fool's Day aspect even more sinister, because all those thousands of first-rate Japanese troops on that island had to be somewhere spoiling for a fight.

We continued to look at the panorama around our amtrac with no thought of immediate danger as we came up out of the water. The tailgate banged down. We calmly picked up our gear and walked onto the beach.

A short distance down the beach on our right, the mouth of Bishi Gawa emptied into the sea. This small river formed the boundary between the army divisions of the XXIV Corps, to the south, and the III Amphibious Corps, to the north of the river. On our side of the mouth of the river, on a promontory jutting out into the sea, I saw the remains of the emplacement containing the big Japanese gun that had concerned us in our briefings. The seawall in our area had been blasted down into a terracelike rise a few feet high over which we moved with ease.

We advanced inland, and I neither heard nor saw any Japanese fire directed against us. As we moved across the small fields and gardens onto higher elevations, I could see troops of the 6th Marine Division heading toward the big Yontan Airfield on our left. Jubilation over the lack of opposition to the landing prevailed, particularly among the Peleliu veterans. Our new replacements began making remarks about amphibious landings being easy.

*Lt. Gen. Simon Bolivar Buckner, Jr., USA commanded the Tenth Army in the assault against Okinawa. Left (north) of the American landing was the III Marine Amphibious Corps led by Maj. Gen. Roy S. Geiger, which consisted of the 1st and 6th Marine divisions with the latter on the left. To the right (south) landed the army's XXIV Corps commanded by Maj. Gen. John R. Hodge and made up of the 7th and 96th Infantry divi-*

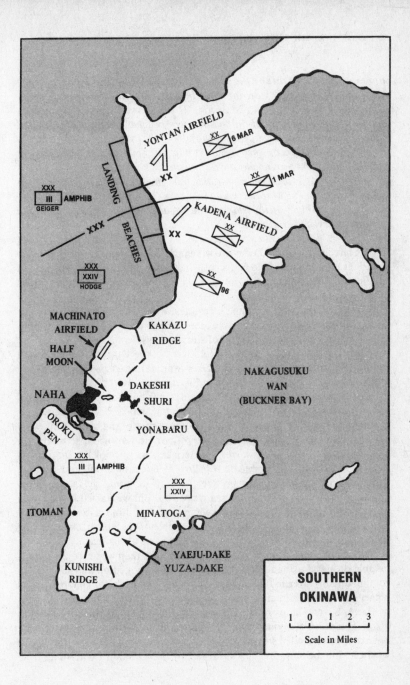

YONTAN AIRFIELD

XX 6 MAR

XX 1 MAR

XXX
III AMPHIB
GEIGER

LANDING

XXX

BEACHES

XX

KADENA AIRFIELD

XX 7

XX

XXX
XXIV
HODGE

XX 96

MACHINATO
AIRFIELD

KAKAZU
RIDGE

HALF
MOON

DAKESHI

NAHA

SHURI

NAKAGUSUKU
WAN
(BUCKNER BAY)

OROKU
PEN

YONABARU

XXX
III AMPHIB

XXX
XXIV

ITOMAN

MINATOGA

KUNISHI
RIDGE

YAEJU-DAKE
YUZA-DAKE

SOUTHERN
OKINAWA

1   0   1   2   3

Scale in Miles

*sions with the latter on the far right. Backing up the XXIV Corps was the 77th Infantry Division with the 27th Infantry Division afloat in reserve. Across the island stood the 2d Marine Division which had conducted an elaborate, full-scale feint at the southeastern beaches. Altogether, Lt. Gen. Buckner had 541,866 men at his disposal.*

*Of the 50,000 troops ashore on D day, the four assault divisions lost only 28 killed, 104 wounded, and 27 missing.*

*The plan of attack called for the four divisions to cross the island, cutting it in two. The Marines would then turn left and move north to secure the upper two-thirds of the island while the army forces wheeled right into line and proceeded south.*

By late afternoon on D day we were ordered to dig in for the night. My squad set up in a small field of recently harvested grain. The clay/loam soil was just right for digging in, so we made a good gun pit. Our company's other two mortars were positioned nearby. We registered in on likely target areas to our front with a couple of rounds of HE, then squared away our ammo for the night. Everybody was expecting a big counterattack with tanks because of the open nature of the countryside.

Once set up, several of us went over to the edge of the field and cautiously explored a neat, clean Okinawan farmhouse. It was a likely hiding place for snipers, but we found it empty.

As we were leaving the house to return to our positions, Jim Dandridge, one of our replacements, stepped on what appeared to be a wooden cover over an underground rainwater cistern at the corner of the house. Jim was a big man, and the wooden planks were rotten. He fell through, sinking in above his waist. The hole wasn't a cistern but a cesspool for the sewage from the house. Jim scrambled out bellowing like a mad bull and smelling worse. We all knew it might be weeks before we could get a change of dungarees, so it was no laughing matter to Jim. But we started kidding him unmercifully about his odd taste in swimming holes. Jim was good-natured, but he quickly had enough and chased a couple of the men back across the field to our positions. They laughed but kept out of his reach.

No sooner had we gotten back to our foxholes than we heard the unmistakable drone of a Japanese aircraft engine. We looked up and saw a Zero coming directly over us. The fighter was high, and the pilot apparently had bigger game than us in mind. He headed out over the beach toward our fleet offshore. Several ships began firing furiously as he circled lazily and then dove. The plane's engine began to whine with increasing intensity as the *kamikaze* pilot headed straight down toward a transport. We saw the smoke where he hit the ship, but it was so far away we couldn't determine what damage had been done. The troops had debarked earlier, but the ship's crew probably had a rough time of it. It was the first *kamikaze* I had seen crash into a ship, but it wasn't the last.

In the gathering dusk we turned our attention to our immediate surroundings and squared away for the night. We each had been issued a small bottle containing a few ounces of brandy to ward off the chill of D day night. Knowing my limited taste, appreciation, and capacity for booze, my buddies began trying to talk me out of my brandy ration. But I was cold after sundown, and thought the brandy might warm me up a bit. I tried a sip, concluding immediately that Indians must have had brandy in mind when they supposedly spoke of "firewater." I traded my brandy for a can of peaches, then broke out my wool-lined field jacket and put it on. It felt good.

We waited in the clear, chilly night for the expected Japanese attack. But all was quiet, with no artillery fire nearby and rarely any rifle or machine-gun fire—stark contrast to the rumbling, crashing chaos of D day night on Peleliu.

When Snafu woke me about midnight for my turn on watch, he handed me our "Tommy" (submachine) gun. (I don't remember how, where, or when we got the Tommy gun, but Snafu and I took turns carrying it and the mortar throughout Peleliu and Okinawa. A pistol was fine but limited at close range, so we valued our Tommy greatly.)

After a few minutes on watch, I noticed what appeared to be a man crouching near me at the edge of a line of shadows cast by some trees. I strained my eyes, averted my vision, and looked in all directions, but I couldn't be sure the dark object was a man. The harder I looked the more convinced I was. I thought I could make out a Japanese fatigue cap. It wasn't a Marine, because none of our people was placed where the figure was. It was probably an enemy infiltrator waiting for his comrades to get in place before acting.

I couldn't be sure in the pale light. Should I fire or take a chance? My teeth began to chatter from the chill and the jitters.

I raised the Tommy slowly, set it on full automatic, flipped off the safety, and took careful aim at the lower part of the figure (I mustn't fire over his head when the Tommy recoiled). I squeezed the trigger for a short burst of several rounds. Flame spurted out of the muzzle, and the rapid explosions of the cartridges shattered the calm. I peered confidently over my sights, expecting to see a Japanese knocked over by the impact of the big .45 caliber slugs. Nothing happened. The enemy didn't move.

Everyone around us began whispering, "What's the dope? What did you see?"

I answered that I thought I had seen a Japanese crouching near the shadows.

There were enemy in the area, for just then we heard shouts in Japanese, a high-pitched yell: "Nippon banzai," then incoherent babbling followed by a burst of firing from one of our machine guns. Quiet fell.

When dawn broke, the first dim light revealed my infiltrator to be a low stack of straw. My buddies kidded me for hours about a Peleliu veteran firing at a straw Japanese.

## Race Across the Island

On 2 April (D + 1) the 1st Marine Division continued its attack across the island. We moved out with our planes overhead but without artillery fire, because no organized body of Japanese had been located ahead of us. Everyone was asking the same question: "Where the hell are the Nips?" Some scattered small groups were encountered and put up a fight, but the main Japanese army had vanished.

During the morning I saw a couple of dead enemy soldiers who apparently had been acting as observers in a large leafless tree when some of the prelanding bombardment killed them. One still hung over a limb. His intestines were strung out among the branches like garland decorations on a Christmas tree. The other man lay beneath the tree. He had lost a leg which rested on the other side of the tree with the leggings and trouser leg still wrapped neatly around it. In addition to their ghoulish condition, I noted that both soldiers wore high-top leather hobnail shoes. That was the first time I had seen that type of Japanese footwear. All the enemy I had seen on Peleliu had worn the rubber-soled canvas split-toed *tabi*.

We encountered some Okinawans—mostly old men, women, and children. The Japanese had conscripted all the young men as laborers and a few as troops, so we saw few of them. We sent the civilians to the rear where they were put into internment camps so they couldn't aid the enemy.

These people were the first civilians I had seen in a combat area. They were pathetic. The most pitiful things about the Okinawan civilians were that they were totally bewildered by the shock of our invasion, and they were scared to death of us. Countless times they passed us on the way to the rear with fear, dismay, and confusion on their faces.

The children were nearly all cute and bright-faced. They had round faces and dark eyes. The little boys usually had close-cropped hair, and the little girls had their shiny jet-black locks bobbed in the Japanese children's style of the period. The children won our hearts. Nearly all of us gave them all the candy and rations we could spare. They were quicker to lose their fear of us than the older people, and we had some good laughs with them.

One of the funnier episodes I witnessed involved two Okinawan women and their small children. We had been ordered to halt and "take ten" (a ten-minute rest) before resuming our rapid advance across the island. My squad stopped near a typical Okinawan well constructed of stone and forming a basin about two feet deep and about four feet by six feet on the sides. Water bubbled out of a rocky hillside. We watched two women and their children getting a drink. They seemed a bit nervous and afraid of us, of course. But life had its demands with children about, so one woman sat on a rock, nonchalantly opened her kimono top, and began breast-feeding her small baby.

While the baby nursed, and we watched, the second child (about four years old) played with his mother's sandals. The little fellow quickly tired of this and kept pestering his mother for attention. The second woman had her hands full with a small child of her own, so she wasn't any help. The mother spoke sharply to her bored child, but he started climbing all over the baby and interfering with the nursing. As we looked on with keen interest, the exasperated mother removed her breast from the mouth of the nursing baby and pointed it at the face of the fractious brother. She squeezed her breast just as you would milk a cow and squirted a jet of milk into the child's face. The startled boy began bawling at the top of his lungs while rubbing the milk out of his eyes.

We all roared with laughter, rolling around on the deck and holding our sides. The women looked up, not realizing why we were laughing, but began to grin because the tension was broken. The little recipient of the milk in the eyes stopped crying and started grinning, too.

"Get your gear on; we're moving out," came the word down the column. As we shouldered our weapons and ammo and moved out amid continued laughter, the story traveled along to the amusement of all. We passed the two smiling mothers and the grinning toddler, his cute face still wet with his mother's milk.

Moving rapidly toward the eastern shore, we crossed terrain often extremely rugged with high, steep ridges and deep gullies. In one area a series of these ridges lay across our line of advance. As we labored up one side and down the other of each ridge, we were tired but glad the Japanese had abandoned the area. It was ideal for defense.

During another halt, we spent our entire break rescuing an Okinawan horse. The animal had become trapped in a narrow flooded drainage ditch about four feet deep. He couldn't climb out or move forward or backward. When we first approached the animal, he plunged up and down in the water rolling his eyes in terror. We calmed him, slipped a couple of empty cartridge belts beneath his belly, and heaved him up out of the ditch.

We had plenty of help, because Texans and horse lovers gravitated to the scene from all over our battalion, which ranged in columns along the valley and surrounding ridges. The city men looked on and gave useless advice. When we got the little horse out of the ditch, he stood on wobbly legs as the water dripped off him, shook himself, and headed for a patch of grass.

No sooner had we washed the mud off the cartridge belts than the word came to move out. We didn't get any rest during that break, and we were tired, but we had the satisfaction of knowing that little horse wouldn't starve to death bogged down in the ditch.

The clear cool weather compensated for our rapid advance over the broken terrain. Those of us with experience in the tropics felt as though we had been delivered from a steam room. The hills and ridges on Okinawa were mostly clay, but it was dry, and we didn't slip or slide with our heavy loads. Pine trees grew everywhere. I had forgotten what a delicious odor the needles gave off. We also saw Easter lilies blooming.

Completing the initial assignment of the 1st Marine Division to cut the island in two, we reached the east coast in an area of marshes and what appeared to be large freshwater reservoirs. Offshore was a bay called Chimu Wan.

We arrived on the afternoon of 4 April, some eight to thirteen days ahead of schedule. Our rapid movement had been possible, of course, only because of the widely scattered opposition. These first four days had been too easy for us. We were confused as to what the Japanese were doing. We knew they weren't about to give up the island without a fierce, drawn-out fight.

And we didn't have to wait long to find out where the enemy was. Later that day rumors began that the army divisions were meeting increasingly stiff opposition as they tried to move south. We knew that sooner or later we'd be down there with them in the thick of it.

We also learned that our namesake company in the 7th Marines had been ambushed to the north of us near the village of Hizaonna and had suffered losses of three killed and twenty-seven wounded. Thus, despite the relative ease with which our division had moved across the center of the island, the Japanese were still there and still hurting the Marines.

*The 1st Marine Division spent the remainder of April mopping up the central portion of Okinawa. Elements of the division, including the 3d Battalion, 5th Marines, conducted a shore-to-shore amphibious operation toward the end of the month to secure the Eastern Islands which lay on the outer edge of Chimu Wan Bay. The purpose was to deny them to the Japanese as an operating base in the rear of the American forces, much the same reason 3/5 had assaulted Ngesebus during the fight for Peleliu.*

*The 6th Marine Division moved north during April and captured the entire upper part of the island. The task wasn't easy. It involved a rough, costly seven-day mountain campaign against strongly fortified Japanese positions in the heights of Motobu Peninsula.*

*Meanwhile three army divisions were coming up short against fierce Japanese resistance in the Kakazu–Nishibaru ridgeline, the first of three main enemy defense lines in the southern portion of the island. Stretched from left to right across Okinawa, the 7th, 96th, and 27th Infantry divisions were getting more than they could handle and were making little progress in their attacks.*

# Patrols

Hardly had we arrived on the shore of Chimu Wan Bay than we received orders to move out. We headed inland and north into an area of small valleys and steep ridges, where we settled into a comfortable bivouac area and erected our two-man pup tents. It was more like maneuvers than combat; we didn't even dig foxholes. We could see Yontan Airfield in the distance to the west. Rain fell for the first time since we had landed five days earlier.

The next day our company began patrolling through the general area around our bivouac site. We didn't need the mortars because of the scattered nature of the enemy opposition. Stowing them out of the weather in our tents, those of us in the mortar section served as riflemen on the patrols.

Mac, our new mortar section leader, led the first patrol I made. Our mission was to check out our assigned area for signs of enemy activity. Burgin was our patrol sergeant. I felt a lot more comfortable with him than with Mac.

On a clear, chilly morning, with the temperature at about 60 degrees, we moved out through open country on a good, rock-surfaced road. The scenery was picturesque and beautiful. I saw little sign of war. We had strict orders not to fire our weapons unless we saw a Japanese soldier or Okinawans we were certain were hostile. No shooting at chickens and no target practice.

"Mac, where we headed?" someone had asked before we left.

"Hizaonna," the lieutenant answered without batting an eye.

"Jesus Christ! That's where K Company, 7th got ambushed the other night," one of the new replacements said.

"Do you mean us few guys are supposed to patrol that place?"

"Yeah, that's right, Hood," Burgin answered. (We had nicknamed a big square-jawed man from Chicago "Hoodlum" because of the notorious gangs of John Dillinger and others in that city during the days of Prohibition.)

My reaction on hearing our destination had been to thrust my Tommy gun toward another new man who wasn't assigned to the patrol and say, "Take this; don't you wanta go in my place?"

"Hell, no!" he replied.

So, off we went with Mac striding along like he was still in OCS back in Quantico, Virginia. The veterans among us looked worried. The new men, like Mac, seemed unconcerned. Because of the strange absence of anything but scattered opposition, some of the new men were beginning to think war wasn't as bad as they had been told it was. Some of them actually chided us about giving them an exaggerated account of the horrors and hardships of Peleliu. Okinawa in April was so easy for the 1st Marine Division that the new men were lulled into a false sense of well-being. We warned them, "When the stuff hits the fan, it's hell," but they grew more and more sure that we veterans were "snowing" them.

Mac didn't help matters either by his loud pronouncements of how he would take his kabar in his teeth and his .45 in hand and charge the Japanese as soon as one of our guys got hit. The April stay of execution tended to lull even the veterans into a state of wishful thinking and false security, although we knew better.

Soon, however, our idyllic stroll on that perfect April morning was broken by an element of the horrid reality of the war that I knew lurked in wait for us somewhere on that beautiful island. Beside a little stream below the road, like a hideous trademark of battle, lay a Japanese corpse in full combat gear.

From our view above, the corpse looked like a gingerbread man in a helmet with his legs still in the flexed position of running. He didn't appear to have been dead many days then, but we passed that same stream many times throughout April and watched the putrid remains decompose gradually into the soil of Okinawa. I was thankful the windswept road with the sweet, fresh smell of pine needles filling our nostrils was too high for us to sense his presence in any way but visually.

As we patrolled in the vicinity of Hizaonna, we moved through some of the area where Company K, 7th Marines had been ambushed a few nights before. The grim evidence of a hard fight lay everywhere. We found numerous dead Japanese where they had fallen. Bloody battle dressings, discarded articles of bloody clothing, and bloodstains on the ground indicated where Marines had been hit. Empty cartridge cases were piled where various Marine weapons had been.

I remember vividly an Okinawan footpath across a low hillock where the Marine column apparently had been attacked from both sides. On the path were empty machine-gun ammo boxes, ammo clips for M1 rifles, and carbine shell cases; discarded dungaree jackets, leggings, and battle dressings; and several large bloodstains, by then dark spots on the soil. Scattered a short distance on both sides of the path were about a score of enemy dead.

The scene was like reading a paragraph from a page of a history book. The Marines had suffered losses, but they had inflicted worse on the attacking Japanese. We saw no Marine dead; all had been removed when the relief troops had come in and aided K/3/7 to withdraw from the ambush.

As I looked at the flotsam of battle scattered along that little path, I was struck with the utter incongruity of it all. There the Okinawans had tilled their soil with ancient and crude farming methods; but the war had come, bringing with it the latest and most refined technology for killing. It seemed so insane, and I realized that the war was like some sort of disease afflicting man. From my experience at Peleliu I had unconsciously come to associate combat with stifling hot, fire-swept beaches, steaming mangrove-choked swamps, and harsh, jagged coral ridges. But there on Okinawa the disease was disrupting a place as pretty as a pastoral painting. I understood then what my grandmother had really meant when she told me as a boy that a blight descended on the land when the South was invaded during the Civil War.

While a buddy and I were looking over the area, Burgin told us to check out a section of sunken roadway nearby. The sunken portion was about thirty yards long and about ten feet deep; the banks were steep and sloping. Heavy bushes grew along their edges at ground level so all we could see was the sky overhead and the sloping road in front and behind us. When we were about halfway along the sunken road, carbine shots rang out from where we had left Burgin and Mac.

"Ambush!" snarled my buddy, a veteran with combat experience stretching back to Cape Gloucester.

We went into a low crouch instinctively, and I put my finger on the safety catch of the Tommy. Hurrying over to the bank toward the sound of the shots, we scrambled up and peered cautiously through the bushes. We both knew we wouldn't have a chance if we got pinned down in that ditch-like road where we could be shot from above. My heart pounded, and I felt awfully lonely as I looked out. There, where we had left him, stood Mac in the farmyard, calmly pointing his carbine straight down toward the ground by his feet at some object we couldn't see. My comrade and I looked at each other in amazement. "What the hell?" my buddy whispered. We climbed out of the sunken road and went toward Mac as he fired his carbine at the ground again. Other members of the patrol were converging cautiously on the area. They looked apprehensive, thinking we were being ambushed.

Burgin stood a short distance behind Mac, shaking his head slowly in disgust. As we came up, I asked Mac what he had fired at. He pointed to the ground and showed us his target: the lower jaw of some long-dead animal. Mac said he just wanted to see if he could shoot any of the teeth loose from the jawbone.

We stared at him in disbelief. There we were, a patrol of about a dozen Marines, miles from our outfit, with orders not to fire unless at the enemy, in an area with dead Japanese scattered all over the place, and our lieutenant was plinking away with his carbine like a kid with a BB gun. If Mac had been a private, the whole patrol would probably have stuck his head in a nearby well. But our discipline was strict, and we just gritted our teeth.

Burgin made some tactful remark to remind Mac he was the officer in charge of a patrol and that the enemy might jump us at any time. Thereupon Mac began spouting off, quoting some training manual about the proper way for troops to conduct themselves on patrol.

Mac wasn't stupid or incompetent. He just didn't seem to realize there was a deadly war going on and that we weren't involved in some sort of college game. Strange as it seemed, he wasn't mature yet. He had enough ability to complete Marine Corps OCS—no simple task—but occasionally he could do some of the strangest things, things only a teenage boy would be expected to do.

Once on another patrol, I saw him taking great pains and effort to position himself and his carbine near a Japanese corpse. After getting just the right angle, Mac took careful aim and squeezed off a couple of rounds. The dead Japanese lay on his back with his trousers pulled down to his knees. Mac was trying very carefully to blast off the head of the corpse's penis. He succeeded. As he exulted over his aim, I turned away in disgust.

Mac was a decent, clean-cut man but one of those who apparently felt no restraints under the brutalizing influence of war—although he had hardly been in combat at that time. He had one ghoulish, obscene tendency that revolted even the most hardened and callous men I knew. When most men felt the urge to urinate, they simply went over to a bush or stopped wherever they happened to be and relieved themselves without ritual or fanfare. Not Mac. If he could, that "gentleman by the act of Congress" would locate a Japanese corpse, stand over it, and urinate in its mouth. It was the most repulsive thing I ever saw an American do in the war. I was ashamed that he was a Marine officer.

During the early part of that beautiful April in our happy little valley —while we veterans talked endlessly in disbelief about the lack of fighting— a few of us had a close view of a Japanese Zero fighter plane. One clear morning after a leisurely breakfast of K rations, several of us sauntered up a ridge bordering our valley to watch an air raid on Yontan Airfield. None of us was scheduled for patrols that day, and none of us was armed. We had violated a fundamental principle of infantrymen: "Carry your weapon on your person at all times."

As we watched the raid, we heard an airplane engine to our right. We turned, looked down a big valley below our ridge, and saw a plane approaching. It was a Zero flying up the valley toward us, parallel to and level with the crest of our ridge. It was moving so slowly it seemed unreal. Unarmed, we gawked like spectators at a passing parade as the plane came across our front. It couldn't have been more than thirty or forty yards away. We could see every detail of the plane and of the pilot seated in the cockpit inside the canopy. He turned his head and looked keenly at our little group watching him. He wore a leather flight helmet, goggles pushed up on his forehead, a jacket, and a scarf around his neck.

The instant the Zero pilot saw us, his face broke into the most fiendish grin I ever saw. He looked like the classic cartoon Japanese portrayed in American newspapers of the war years, with buck teeth, slanted eyes, and a round face. He grinned like a cat, for we were to be his mice. We were a fighter pilot's strafing dream, enemy infantry in the open with no antiair-craft guns and no planes to protect us.

One of my buddies muttered in surprise as the plane went on by to our left, "Did you see that bastard grin at us—that slant-eyed sonofabitch. Where the hell's my rifle?"

It happened so fast, and we were all so astonished at the sight of a plane cruising by at eye level, we almost forgot the war. The Japanese pilot hadn't. He banked, climbed to gain altitude, and headed around another ridge out of sight. It was obvious he was coming back to rake us over. It would be difficult to avoid getting hit. No savior was in sight for us.

As we started to spin around and rush back down the ridge seeking safety, we again heard a plane. This time it wasn't the throb of a cruising engine, but the roar of a plane at full throttle. The Zero streaked past us, going down the valley in the opposite direction from which he had first appeared. He was still flying at eye level and he was in a big hurry, as if the devil were after him. His devil was our savior, a beautiful blue Marine Corsair. That incredible Corsair pilot bore in right behind the Japanese as they roared out of sight over the ridge tops. The planes were moving too fast to see either pilot's face, but I'm confident the emperor's pilot had lost his grin when he saw that Corsair.

On our patrols during April, we investigated many Okinawan villages and farms. We learned a lot about the people's customs and ways of life. Particularly appealing to me were the little Okinawan horses, really shaggy oversized ponies.

The Okinawans used a type of halter on those horses that I had never seen before. It consisted of two pieces of wood held in place by ropes. The wooden pieces on either side of the horse's head were shaped like the letter *F*. They were carved out of fine-grained brown wood and were about as big around as a man's thumb. A short piece of rope or cord held the pieces together across the front, and a rope across the top of the animal's head held the pieces in place on each side of the head just above the opening of the mouth. Two short ropes at the back of the wooden pieces merged into a single rope. When pull was exerted on this single rope, the wooden pieces clamped with gentle pressure against the sides of the animal's face above the mouth, and the animal stopped moving. This apparatus combined the qualities of a halter and a bridle without the need for a bit in the horse's mouth.

I was so intrigued by the Okinawan halter that I took one off a horse we kept with us for several days and replaced it with a rope halter. My intention was to send the wooden halter home—I remember that a bright piece of red cord held the front ends together—so I put it into my pack. After 1 May, however, it seemed increasingly doubtful that I would ever get home myself, and my equipment seemed to get heavier as the mud got deeper. Regretfully, I threw away the halter.

We grew quite attached to the horse our squad had adopted, and he didn't seem to mind when we slung a couple of bags of mortar ammo across his back.

When the time came at the end of April for us to leave our little horse, I removed the rope halter and gave him a lump of ration sugar. I stroked his soft muzzle as he switched flies with his tail. He turned, ambled across a grassy green meadow, and began grazing. He looked up and back at me once. My eyes grew moist. However reluctant I was to leave him, it was for the best. He would be peaceful and safe on the slopes of that green, sunlit hill. Being civilized men, we were duty bound to return soon to the chaotic nether world of shells and bullets and suffering and death.

Ugly rumors began to increase about the difficulties the army troops were having down on southern Okinawa. From high ground on clear nights I could see lights flickering and glowing on the southern skyline. A distant rumble was barely audible sometimes. No one said much about it. I tried unsuccessfully to convince myself it was thunderstorms, but I knew better. It was the flash and the growl of guns.

## A Happy Landing

On 13 April (12 April back in the States) we learned of the death of President Franklin D. Roosevelt. Not the least bit interested in politics while we were fighting for our lives, we were saddened nonetheless by the loss of our president. We were also curious and a bit apprehensive about how FDR's successor, Harry S. Truman, would handle the war. We surely didn't want someone in the White House who would prolong it one day longer than necessary.

Not long after hearing of Roosevelt's death, we were told to prepare to move out. Apprehension grew in the ranks. We thought the order meant the inevitable move into the inferno down south. On the contrary, it was to be a shore-to-shore amphibious operation against one of the Eastern Islands. We learned that Company K was to land on Takabanare Island, and that there might not be any Japanese there. We were highly skeptical. But so far Okinawa had been a strange "battle" for us; anything could happen.

Our battalion boarded trucks and headed for the east coast. We went aboard amtracs and set out into Chimu Wan to make the short voyage to Takabanare. The other companies of our battalion went after other islands of the group.

We landed with no opposition on a narrow, clean, sandy beach with a large rock mass high on our left. The rock hill looked foreboding. It was a vantage point from which flanking fire could have raked the beach. But all went well, and we pushed rapidly over the entire island without seeing a single enemy soldier.

After we moved across the island and found nothing but a few civilians, we recrossed the island to the beach where we set up defensive positions. My squad was situated part way up the slope of the steep rocky hill overlooking the beach. Our mortar was well emplaced among some rocks, so that we could fire on the beach or its approaches in the bay. A small destroyer escort was anchored offshore at the base of the hill. It had been standing by during our landing and remained with us during the several days we stayed on Takabanare. We felt important, as though we had our own private navy.

The weather was pleasant, so sleeping in the open was comfortable. We had few duties other than standing by to prevent a possible enemy move to occupy the island. I wrote letters, read, and explored the area around our positions. Some of the Marines swam the short distance to the ship and went aboard, where the navy people welcomed them and treated them to hot chow and all the hot coffee they wanted. I was content to laze in the sun and the cool air and eat K rations.

We left Takabanare after several days and returned to our bivouac on Okinawa. There we resumed patrolling in the central area of the island. As April wore on, rumors and bad news increased about the situation the army was facing down south. Scuttlebutt ran rampant about our future employment down there. Our fear increased daily, and we finally got the word that we'd be moving south on 1 May to replace the 27th Infantry Division on the right flank of the Tenth Army.

*About mid-April the 11th Marines, the 1st Marine Division's artillery regiment, had moved south to add the weight of its firepower to the army's offensive. On 19 April the 27th Infantry Division launched a disastrous tank-infantry attack against Kakazu Ridge. Thirty army tanks became separated from their infantry support. The Japanese knocked out twenty-two of them in the ensuing fight. The 1st Marine Division's tank battalion offered the closest replacements for the tanks lost by the army.*

*Lt. Gen. Simon B. Buckner, Tenth Army commander, ordered Maj. Gen. Roy S. Geiger, III Amphibious Corps commander, to send the 1st Tank Battalion south to join the 27th Infantry Division. Geiger objected to the piecemeal employment of his Marines, so Buckner changed his orders and sent the entire 1st Marine Division south to relieve the 27th Infantry Division on the extreme right of the line just north of Machinato Airfield.*

During the last days of April, some of our officers and NCOs made a trip down south to examine the positions on the line that we were to move into. They briefed us thoroughly on what they saw, and it didn't sound promising.

"The stuff has hit the fan down there, boys. The Nips are pouring on the artillery and mortars and everything they've got," said a veteran sergeant. "Boys, they're firing knee mortars as thick and fast as we fire M1s."

We were given instructions, issued ammo and rations, and told to square away our gear. We rolled up our shelter halves (I wished I could crawl into mine and hibernate) and packed our gear to be left behind with the battalion quartermaster.

The first of May dawned cloudy and chilly. A few of us mortarmen built a small fire next to a niche in the side of the ridge to warm ourselves.

The dismal weather and our impending move south made us gloomy. We stood around the fire eating our last chow before heading south. The fire crackled cheerily, and the coffee smelled good. I was nervous and hated to leave our little valley. We tossed our last ration cartons and wrappers onto the fire—the area must be left cleaner than when we arrived—and a few of the men drifted away to pick up their gear.

"Grenade!" yelled Mac as we heard the pop of a grenade primer cap.

I saw him toss a fragmentation grenade over the fire into the niche. The grenade exploded with a weak bang. Fragments zipped out past my legs, scattering sparks and sticks from the fire. We all looked astonished, Mac not the least so. No one was hit. I narrowly missed the million-dollar wound (it would have been a blessing in view of what lay ahead of us). The men who had just moved away from the fire undoubtedly would have been hit if they hadn't moved, because they had been standing directly in front of the niche.

All eyes turned on our intrepid lieutenant. He blushed and mumbled awkwardly about making a mistake. Before we moved to board the trucks, Mac had thought it would be funny to play a practical joke on us. So he staged the well-known trick of pouring out the explosive charge from a fragmentation grenade, screwing the detonation mechanism back on the empty "pineapple," and pitching it into the middle of a group of people. When the primer cap went "pop," the perpetrator of the joke could watch with sadistic delight as everyone scrambled for cover expecting the fuse to burn down and the grenade to explode.

By his own admission, however, Mac had been careless. Most of the explosive charge remained in the grenade; he had poured out only part of it. Consequently, the grenade exploded with considerable force and threw out its fragments. Luckily, Mac threw the grenade into the niche in the ridge. If he had thrown it into the open, most of the Company K mortar section would have been put out of action by its own lieutenant before we ever got down south. Fortunately for Mac, the company commander didn't see his foolish joke. We regretted he hadn't.

What a way to start our next fight!

# CHAPTER TEN

# INTO THE ABYSS

We boarded trucks and headed south over dusty roads. In this central portion of Okinawa we first passed many bivouacs of service troops and vast ammunition and supply dumps, all covered with camouflage netting. Next we came to several artillery positions. From the piles of empty brass shell cases, we knew they had fired a lot. And from the numerous shell craters gouged into the fields of grass, we could tell that the Japanese had thrown in plenty of counterbattery fire.

At some unmarked spot, we stopped and got off the trucks. I was filled with dread. We took up a single file on the right side of a narrow coral road and began walking south. Ahead we could hear the crash and thunder of enemy mortar and artillery shells, the rattle of machine guns, and the popping of rifles. Our own artillery shells whistled southbound.

"Keep your five-pace interval," came an order.

We did not talk. Each man was alone with his thoughts.

Shortly a column of men approached us on the other side of the road. They were the army infantry from 106th Regiment, 27th Infantry Division that we were relieving. Their tragic expressions revealed where they had been. They were dead beat, dirty and grisly, hollow-eyed and tight-faced. I hadn't seen such faces since Peleliu.

As they filed past us, one tall, lanky fellow caught my eye and said in a weary voice, "It's hell up there, Marine."

Nervous about what was ahead and a bit irritated that he might think I was a boot, I said with some impatience, "Yeah, I know. I was at Peleliu."

He looked at me blankly and moved on.

We approached a low, gently sloping ridge where Company K would go into the line. The noise grew louder.

"Keep your five-pace interval; don't bunch up," yelled one of our officers.

The mortar section was ordered off the road to the left in dispersed order. I could see shells bursting between us and the ridge. When we left the road, we severed our umbilical connection with the peaceful valley up north and plunged once more into the abyss.

As we raced across an open field, Japanese shells of all types whizzed, screamed, and roared around us with increasing frequency. The crash and thunder of explosions was a nightmare. Rocks and dirt clattered down after each erupting shell blew open a crater.

We ran and dodged as fast as we could to a place on a low gentle slope of the ridge and flung ourselves panting onto the dirt. Marines were running and crawling into position as soldiers streamed past us, trying desperately to get out alive. The yells for corpsmen and stretcher bearers began to be heard. Even though I was occupied with my own safety, I couldn't help but feel sorry for the battle-weary troops being relieved and trying not to get killed during those few critical minutes as they scrambled back out of their positions under fire.

Japanese rifle and machine-gun fire increased into a constant rattle. Bullets snapped and popped overhead. The shelling grew heavier. The enemy gunners were trying to catch men in the open to inflict maximum casualties on our troops running into and out of position—their usual practice when one of our units was relieving another on the line.

It was an appalling chaos. I was terribly afraid. Fear was obvious on the faces of my comrades, too, as we raced to the low slope and began to dig in rapidly. It was such a jolt to leave the quiet, beautiful countryside that morning and plunge into a thunderous, deadly storm of steel that afternoon. Going onto the beach to assault Peleliu and attacking across the airfield there, we had braced ourselves for the blows that fell. But the shock and shells of 1 May at Okinawa, after the reprieve of a pleasant April, caught us off balance.

Fear has many facets, and I do not minimize my fear and terror during that day. But it was different. I was a combat veteran of Peleliu. With terror's first constriction over, I knew what to expect. I felt dreadful fear but not near-panic. Experience had taught me what to expect from the enemy guns. More importantly, I knew I could control my fear. The terrible dread that I might panic was gone. I knew that all anyone could do under shell fire was to hug the deck and pray—and curse the Japanese.

There was the brassy, metallic twang of the small 50mm knee mortar

*A dreaded Japanese 150mm gun in its protected cave emplacement. Okinawa. USMC photo.*

shells as little puffs of dirty smoke appeared thickly around us. The 81mm and 90mm mortar shells crashed and banged all along the ridge. The *whizz-bang* of the high velocity 47mm gun's shells (also an antitank gun), which was on us with its explosion almost as soon as we heard it whizz into the area, gave me the feeling the Japanese were firing them at us like rifles. The slower screaming, whining sound of the 75mm artillery shells seemed the most abundant. Then there was the roar and rumble of the huge enemy 150mm howitzer shell, and the *kaboom* of its explosion. It was what the men called the big stuff. I didn't recall having recognized any of it in my confusion and fear at Peleliu. The bursting radius of these big shells was of awesome proportions. Added to all this noise was the swishing and fluttering overhead of our own supporting artillery fire. Our shells could be heard bursting out across the ridge over enemy positions. The noise of small-arms fire from both sides resulted in a chaotic bedlam of racket and confusion.

We were just below the crest of a low sloping section of the ridge. It was about ten feet high and on the left of our company's zone. Snafu and I began to dig the gun pit, and the ammo carriers dug in with two-man foxholes. Digging in Okinawa's claylike soil was easy, a luxury after the coral rock of Peleliu.

No sooner had we begun to dig in than terrible news arrived about mounting casualties in the company. The biggest blow was the word that Privates Nease and Westbrook had been killed. Both of these men were liked and admired by us all. Westbrook was a new man, a friendly curly-headed blond and one of the youngest married men in the outfit. I believe he wasn't yet twenty. Howard Nease was young in years but an old salt with a combat record that started at Cape Gloucester.

Many men were superstitious about one's chances of surviving a third campaign. By that time one's luck was wearing thin, some thought. I heard this idea voiced by Guadalcanal veterans who also had survived Gloucester and then struggled against the odds on Peleliu.

"Howard's luck just run out, that's all. Ain't no damn way a guy can go on forever without gittin' hit," gloomily remarked a Gloucester veteran who had joined Company K with Nease two campaigns before Okinawa.

We took the news of those deaths hard. Added to the stress of the day, it put us into an angry frame of mind as we dug in. Against whom should we pour out our anger while we were unable to fire at the enemy?

Most of us had finished digging in when we suddenly noticed that our pugnacious lieutenant, Mac, was still digging feverishly. He was excavating a deep one-man foxhole and throwing out a continuous shower of dirt with his entrenching shovel. While shells were still coming in, the fire had slackened a bit in our area. But Mac continued to burrow underground.

I don't know who started it, but I think it was Snafu who reminded Mac of his oft-repeated promise to charge the enemy line as soon as any of our guys got hit. Once the kidding began, several of us veterans chimed in and vigorously encouraged Mac to keep his promise.

"Now that Nease and Westbrook been killed, ain't it about time you took your kabar and .45 and charged them Nips, Mac?" Snafu asked.

Mac never stopped digging; he simply answered that he had to dig in. I told him I would lend him my kabar, but another man said with mock seriousness, "Naw, Sledgehammer, he might not be able to return it to you."

"Boy, when Mac gets over to them Nips, he's gonna clean house, and this blitz gonna be a pushover," someone else said.

But Mac only grunted and showed no inclination to charge the enemy— or to stop digging. He burrowed like a badger. Our jibes didn't seem to phase him. We kept our comments respectful because of his rank, but we gave it to him good for all the bravado and nonsense he had been mouthing off with ever since he joined the company.

"Mac, if you dig that hole much deeper they'll get you for desertion," someone said.

"Yeah, my mom use'ta tell me back home if I dug a hole deep enough I'd come through to China. Maybe if you keep digging you'll get through to the States, and we can all crawl in there and go home, Mac," came one comment accompanied by a grin.

Mac could hear us but was totally oblivious to our comments. It's hard to believe that we actually talked that way to a Marine officer, but it happened, and it was hilarious. He deserved every bit of it.

When he finally got his foxhole deep enough, he began laying wooden boards from ammo boxes over all of the top except for one small opening through which he could squirm. Then he threw about six inches of soil on top of the boards. We sat in our holes, watching him and the shelling to our right rear. When he had completed the cover over his hole, which actually made it a small dugout with limited visibility, Mac got in and proudly surveyed his work. He had been too occupied to pay much heed to us, but now he explained carefully to us how the boards with soil on top would protect him from shell fragments.

George Sarrett, who wasn't interested in the lecture, inched up the little slope several feet and peeped over the crest to see if there were any enemy troops moving around out front. He didn't look long, because a Japanese on the next ridge saw him and fired a burst from a machine gun which narrowly missed him. As the slugs came snapping over, George jerked his head down, lost his balance, slid back down the slope, and landed on top of Mac's dugout, causing the roof to cave in. The startled lieutenant jumped up, pushing boards and soil aside like a turtle rearing up out of a pile of debris.

"You ruined my foxhole!" Mac complained.

George apologized, and I had to bite my lip to keep from laughing. The other men smirked and grinned. We never heard any more from Mac about charging the Japanese line with his kabar and .45 caliber pistol. That enemy shelling had one beneficial result: it dissolved his bravado.

We got our positions squared away for the night and ate some K rations, as well as one could with a stomach tied in knots. More details reached us about the loss of Nease, Westbrook, and others killed and wounded. We regretted any American casualties, but when they were close friends it was terribly depressing. They were just the first of what was to grow into a long tragic list before we would come out of combat fifty hellish days later.*

Before dark we learned there would be a big attack the next morning all along the U.S. line. With the heavy Japanese fire poured onto us as we moved into that line, we dreaded the prospect of making a push. An NCO told us that our objective was to reach the Asato Gawa, a stream about 1,500 yards south of us that stretched inland and eastward to an area near the village of Dakeshi.

Rain ushered in a gloomy dawn. We were apprehensive but hopeful. There was some small-arms fire along the line, and a few shells passed back and forth during early morning. The rain slackened temporarily and we ate some K rations. On the folding pocket-sized tripod issued to us, I heated up a canteen cup of coffee with a sterno tablet. I had to hover over it to keep the rain from drowning it out.

As the seconds ticked slowly toward 0900, our artillery and ships' guns increased their rate of fire. The rain poured down, and the Japanese took up the challenge from our artillery. They started throwing more shells our way, many of which passed over us and exploded far to our rear where our own artillery was emplaced.

Finally we received orders to open fire with our mortars. Our shells exploded along a defilade to our front. Our machine guns opened up in earnest. Our artillery, ships' guns, and 81mm mortars increased the tempo to an awesome rate as the time for the attack approached. The shells whistled, whined, and rumbled overhead, ours bursting out in front of the ridge and the enemy's exploding in our area and to the rear. The noise increased all along the line. Rain fell in torrents, and the soil became muddy and slippery wherever we hurried around the gun pit to break out and stack our ammo.

I looked at my watch. It was 0900. I gulped and prayed for my buddies in the rifle platoons.

"Mortars cease firing and stand by."

We were ready to fire or to take up the mortars at a moment's notice and move forward. Some of our riflemen moved past the crest of the ridge to attack. Noise that had been loud now grew into deafening bedlam. The riflemen hardly got out of their foxholes when a storm of enemy fire from our front and left flank forced them back. The same thing was happening to the battalions on our right and left.

*The 27th Infantry Division had been in action since 15 April. It had suffered heavily in the attacks of 19 April in capturing Kakazu Ridge, Machinato Airfield, and the surrounding area. After the 1st Marine Division relieved it, the 27th Infantry Division went north for patrolling and guard duty.

USS Idaho *firing support for troops ashore. Okinawa. USMC photo.*

The sound of the many machine guns became one incredible rattle against a thundering and booming of artillery. Rifles popped everywhere along the line, while Japanese slugs snapped over the low ridge behind which we lay. We fired some white phosphorous shells to screen our withdrawing troops. Just as we heard "Cease firing," a Marine came running through the mud on the slope to our right, yelling, "The guys pulling back need a stretcher team from mortars!"

Three other mortarmen and I took off on the double after the messenger. With bullets snapping and popping overhead, we ran along for about forty yards, keeping just below the crest of the ridge. We came to a road cut through the ridge about eight feet below the crest; an officer told us to stand behind him until we were ordered to go out and bring in the casualty. This was the exact spot where Nease and Westbrook had been machine-gunned the day before. Japanese bullets were zipping and swishing through the cut like hail pouring through an open window.

A couple of Company K rifle squads were running back toward us from the abortive attack. They rushed along the road in small groups and turned

*1st Lt. Thomas "Stumpy" Stanley, CO of K/3/5, calling for artillery support.*

right and left as soon as they got through the cut to get out of the line of fire. Incredibly, none got hit by the thick fire coming through the cut. I knew most of them well, although some of the new men not as well as the veterans. They all wore wild-eyed, shocked expressions that showed only too vividly they were men who had barely escaped chance's strange arithmetic. They clung to their M1s, BARs, and Tommy guns and slumped to the mud to pant for breath before moving behind the ridge toward their former foxholes. The torrential rain made it all seem so much more unbelievable and terrible.

I hoped fervently that we wouldn't have to step out into that road to pick up a casualty. I felt ashamed for thinking this, because I knew full well that if I were lying out there wounded, my fellow Marines wouldn't leave me. But I didn't see how anyone could go out and get back now that the volume of fire was so intense; since most of our attacking troops had fallen back, the Japanese could concentrate their fire on the stretcher teams as I had seen them do at Peleliu. They showed medical personnel no mercy.

Our company gunnery sergeant, Hank Boyes, was the last man through the cut. He made a quick check of the men and announced—to my immense relief—that everyone had made it back; casualties had been brought back farther down the line where the machine-gun fire hadn't been as heavy.

Boyes was amazing. He had dashed out to the men pinned down in front of the ridge, where he threw smoke grenades to shield them from the Japanese fire. He returned with a hole shot through his dungaree cap (he wasn't wearing his helmet) and another through his pants leg. He had been hit in the leg with fragments from a Japanese knee mortar shell but refused to turn in.*

The officer told us we wouldn't be needed as stretcher bearers and to return to our posts. As we took off on the double to the gun pits, the shells kept up their heavy traffic back and forth, but the bullets began to slacken off somewhat with all our men by then under cover of the ridge. I jumped

*Gy. Sgt. Henry A. Boyes was a former dairy farmer from Trinidad, California. He fought with K/3/5 at Cape Gloucester and landed on Peleliu as a squad leader. He won a Silver Star there and became a platoon sergeant after the assault on Ngesebus. Wounded during the fighting around the Five Sisters, he was evacuated, but returned in time for the landing on Okinawa. Wounded early in May he refused evacuation and became first sergeant of Company K. After the company commander, 1st Lt. Stumpy Stanley was evacuated in late May with malaria, Boyes shared the primary leadership role with 1st Lt. George Loveday. A powerfully built man, Hank Boyes was stern but compassionate. No matter how low morale got, he was always there inspiring like some inexhaustible dynamo. Today he and his family run a successful logging and cattle business in Australia.

*Carrying the wounded. Okinawa. USMC photo.*

into the gun pit, and my temporary replacement hurried back to his hole.*

We crouched in our foxholes in the pouring rain, cursing the Japanese, the shells, and the weather. The enemy gunners poured fire into our company area to discourage another attack. Word came down the line that all attacking Marine units had suffered considerable casualties, so we would remain inactive until the next day. That suited us fine. The Japanese shelling continued viciously for some time. We all felt depressed about the failure of the attack and we still didn't know how many friends we had lost, an uncertainty that always bore down on every man after an attack or fire fight.

From the gun pit, which contained several inches of water, we looked out on a gloomy scene. The rain had settled into a steady pelting that promised much misery. Across the muddy fields we saw our soaked comrades crouching forlornly in their muddy holes and ducking, as we did, each time a shell roared over.

This was my first taste of mud in combat, and it was more detestable

---

*At some time during the attack, Burgin ran out and exposed himself to heavy machine-gun fire from a weapon that no one could locate. He called back a fire mission to the mortars after he spotted the machine gun. Our mortar fire hit on target and knocked out the gun. Burgin won a Bronze Star for his actions.

*Gunnery Sgt. Henry A. Boyes, after the 2 May 1945 attack. Pencil indicates where an enemy bullet went through his cap. Okinawa.*

than I had ever imagined. Mud in camp on Pavuvu was a nuisance. Mud on maneuvers was an inconvenience. But mud on the battlefield was misery beyond description. I had seen photographs of World War I troops in the mud—the men grinning, of course, if the picture was posed. If not posed, the faces always wore a peculiarly forlorn, disgusted expression, an expression I now understood. The air was chilly and clammy, but I thanked God we weren't experiencing this misery in Europe where the foxholes were biting cold as well as wet.

The shelling finally subsided, and things got fairly quiet in our area. We squatted thankfully in our holes and grumbled about the rain. The humid air hung heavily with the chemical odor of exploded shells.

Shortly, to our left rear, we saw a Marine stretcher team bringing a casualty back through the rain. Instead of turning left behind the ridge we were on, or right behind the one farther across the field, the team headed straight back between the two low ridges. This was a mistake, because we knew the Japanese could still fire on that area.

As the stretcher team approached the cover of some trees, Japanese riflemen to our left front opened up on them. We saw bullets kicking up mud and splashing in the puddles of water around the team. The four stretcher bearers hurried across the slippery field. But they couldn't go faster than a rapid walk, or the casualty might fall off the stretcher.

We requested permission to fire 60mm phosphorous shells as a smoke screen (we were too far away to throw smoke grenades to cover the stretcher team). Permission was denied. We weren't allowed to fire across our company front because of the possibility of hitting unseen friendly troops. Thus we watched helplessly as the four stretcher bearers struggled across the muddy field with bullets falling all around them. It was one of those terribly pathetic, heartrending sights that seemed to rule in combat: men struggling to save a wounded comrade, the enemy firing at them as fast as they could, and the rest of us utterly powerless to give any aid. To witness such a scene was worse than personal danger. It was absolute agony.

To lighten their loads, the four carriers had put all of their personal equipment aside except for a rifle or carbine over their shoulders. Each held a handle of the stretcher in one hand and stretched out the other arm for balance. Their shoulders were stooped with the weight of the stretcher. Four helmeted heads hung low like four beasts of burden being flogged. Soaked with rain and spattered with mud, the dark green dungarees hung forlornly on the men. The casualty lay inert on the narrow canvas stretcher, his life in the hands of the struggling four.

To our dismay, the two carriers in the rear got hit by a burst of fire. Each loosened his grip on the stretcher. Their knees buckled, and they fell over backwards onto the muddy ground. The stretcher pitched onto the deck. A gasp went up from the men around me, but it turned almost immediately into roars of relief. The two Marines at the other end of the stretcher threw it down, spun around, and grabbed the stretcher casualty between them. Then each supported a wounded carrier with his other arm. As we cheered, all five assisted one another and limped and hobbled into the cover of the bushes, bullets still kicking up mud all around them. I felt relief and elation over their escape, matched only by a deepened hatred for the Japanese.

Before nightfall we received information that Company K would push again the next day. As the rain slowly diminished and then ceased, we made our grim preparations.

While receiving extra ammo, rations, and water, I saw our company officers and NCOs gathering nearby. They stood or squatted around the CO, talking quietly. Our company commander was obviously in charge, giving orders and answering questions. The senior NCOs and the veteran officers stood by with serious, sometimes worried expressions as they listened. Those of us in the ranks watched their familiar faces carefully for signs of what was in store for us.

The faces of the replacement lieutenants reflected a different mood. They showed enthusiastic, animated expressions with eyebrows raised in eager anticipation of seeing the thing through like a successful field problem at OCS in Quantico. They were very conscientious and determined to do their best or die in the effort. To me, those young officers appeared almost tragic in their naive innocence and ignorance of what lay ahead for us all.

The new officers bore a heavy burden. Not only were they going into combat with all its terrors and unknowns for the first time—conditions even the best of training couldn't possibly duplicate—but they were untried officers. Combat was the acid test. Faced with heavy responsibilities and placed in a position of leadership amid hardened, seasoned Marine combat veterans in a proud, elite division like the First was a difficult situation and a terrific challenge for any young lieutenant. No one I knew in the ranks envied them in the least.

During the course of the long fighting on Okinawa, unlike at Peleliu, we got numerous replacement lieutenants. They were wounded or killed with such regularity that we rarely knew anything about them other than a code name and saw them on their feet only once or twice. We expected heavy losses of enlisted men in combat, but our officers got hit so soon and so often that it seemed to me the position of second lieutenant in a rifle company had been made obsolete by modern warfare.

After the CO dismissed his junior officers, they returned to their respective platoons and briefed the troops about the impending push. Mac was crisp and efficient in his orders to Burgin and the rest of the mortar section NCOs. In turn they told us what to prepare for. (It was good to see Mac divested of his cockiness.) We would get maximum support from heavy artillery and other weapons; casualties would be given swift aid. So we prepared our equipment and waited nervously.

A friend came over from one of the rifle platoons that was to be in the next day's assault. We sat near the gun pit on our helmets in the mud and had a long talk. I lit my pipe and he a cigarette. Things were quiet in the area, so we were undisturbed for some time. He poured out his heart. He had come to me because of our friendship and because I was a veteran. He told me he was terribly afraid about the impending attack. I said everybody was. But I knew he would be in a more vulnerable position than some of us, because his platoon was in the assault. I did my best to cheer him up.

He was so appalled and depressed by the fighting of the previous day that he had concluded he couldn't possibly survive the next day. He confided his innermost thoughts and secrets about his parents and a girl back home whom he was going to marry after the war. The poor guy wasn't just afraid of death or injury—the idea that he might never return to those he loved so much had him in a state of near desperation.

I remembered how Lt. Hillbilly Jones had comforted and helped me through the first shock of Peleliu, and I tried to do the same for my friend. Finally he seemed somewhat relieved, or resigned to his fate, whatever it might be. We got up and shook hands. He thanked me for our friendship, then walked slowly back to his foxhole.

There was nothing unique in the conversation. Thousands like it occurred every day among infantrymen scheduled to enter the chaos and inferno of an attack. But it illustrates the value of camaraderie among men facing constant hardship and frequent danger. Friendship was the only comfort a man had.

It seems strange how men occupied themselves after all weapons and gear had been squared away for an impending attack. We had learned in boot camp that no pack straps should be left with loose ends dangling (any such loose straps on a Marine's pack were called "Irish pennants"—why Irish I never knew—and resulted in disciplinary action or a blast from the drill instructor). So, from pure habit I suppose, we carefully rolled up the loose straps and shaped up our packs. There was always a bit of cleaning and touching up to be done on one's weapon with the toothbrush most of us carried for that purpose. A man could always straighten up his lacings on his leggings, too. With such trivia, doomed men busily occupied themselves, as though when they got up and moved forward out of their foxholes it would be to an inspection rather than to oblivion.

We were partially successful with our attack on 3 May. The knockout of the Japanese heavy machine gun by our mortars the previous day helped our company's advance to the next low ridge line. But we couldn't hold the hills. Heavy enemy machine-gun and mortar fire drove us back about a hundred yards. Thus we gained about three hundred yards for the entire day.

We moved into a quiet area back of the front lines well before dark. Word came that because of heavy casualties over the past two days' fighting, Company K would go into battalion reserve for a while. We dug in around the battalion aid station for its defense.

Our casualties were still coming back from the afternoon's action as we moved into position. Much to my joy I saw the friend with whom I'd had the conversation the night before. He wore a triumphant look of satisfaction, shook hands with me heartily, and grinned as a stretcher team carried him by with a bloody bandage on his foot. God or chance —depending on one's faith—had spared his life and lifted his burden of further fear and terror in combat by awarding him a million-dollar wound. He had done his duty, and the war was over for him. He was in pain, but he was lucky. Many others hadn't been as lucky the last couple of days.

# Counterattack

We settled into our holes for the night, feeling more at ease off the line and in a quiet area. My foxhole partner had the first watch, so I dropped off to sleep, confident that we would have a fairly quiet night. I hadn't slept long before he woke me with, "Sledgehammer, wake up. The Nips are up to something." Startled, I awoke and instinctively unholstered my .45 automatic.

I heard a stern order from an NCO, "Stand by for a ram, you guys. One hundred percent alert!"

I heard heavy artillery and small-arms firing up on the line. It seemed to come mostly from the area beyond our division's left flank where army troops were located. The firing directly forward had increased, too. Our artillery shells swished overhead in incredible numbers. It wasn't just the usual harassing fire against the Japanese; there was too much of it for that.

"What's the dope?" I asked nervously.

"Beats me," said my buddy, "but something sure the hell's going on up on the line. Nips probably pulling a counterattack."

From the increasing fire, enemy as well as friendly, it was obvious something big was happening. As we waited in our holes hoping to get word about what was going on, heavy machine-gun and mortar fire broke out abruptly some distance to our right, to the rear of where the 1st Marines' line reached the sea. From our little mound we saw streams of American machine-gun tracers darting straight out to sea under the eerie light of 60mm mortar flares. That could only mean one thing. The enemy was staging an amphibious attack, trying to come ashore behind the right flank of the 1st Marines, which was the right-hand regiment on the 1st Marine Division's line.

"The Nips must be pullin' a counterlanding, and the 1st Marines' givin' 'em hell," someone said tensely.

Could our comrades in the 1st Marine Regiment stop that attack? That was the question on everyone's mind. But one man said confidently in a low voice, "The 1st Marines'll tear their ass up, betcha." We hoped he was right. With no more than we knew, it was clear that if the Japanese got ashore on our right flank and counterattacked heavily on our left and front, our entire division might be isolated. We sat and listened apprehensively in the darkness.

As if things didn't seem grim enough, the next order came along, "Stand by for possible Jap paratroop attack! All hands turn to. Keep your eyes open."

My blood felt like icewater throughout my body, and I shuddered. We weren't afraid of Japanese paratroopers as such. They couldn't be any tougher to deal with than veteran Japanese infantry. But the fear of being cut off from other U.S. troops by having the enemy land behind us filled us with dread. Most nights on Peleliu we had to keep a sharp lookout to front, rear, right, and left. But that night on Okinawa we had to scan even the dark sky for signs of parachutes.

We lived constantly with the fear of death or maiming from wounds. But the possibility of being surrounded by the enemy and wounded beyond the point of being able to defend myself chilled my soul. They were notorious for their brutality.

A couple of Japanese planes flew over during the night (we recognized the sound of the engines), and I experienced a dread I had never known before. But they passed on without dropping parachutists. They were bombers or fighters on their way to attack our ships lying offshore.

The Japanese and American artillery fire to our left front rumbled and roared on and on with frightening intensity, drowning out the rattle of machine guns and rifles. To our right, elements of the 1st Marine Regiment kept up their small-arms and mortar fire out to sea for quite some time. We heard scattered rifle fire far to our rear. This was disturbing, but some optimist said it was probably nothing more than trigger-happy, rear-echelon guys firing at shadows. Rumors passed that some enemy soldiers had broken through the army's line on our left. It was a long night made worse by the uncertainty and confusion around us. I suffered extremely mixed emotions: glad on the one hand to be out of the fighting, but anxious for those Americans catching the fury of the enemy's attack.

At first light we heard Japanese planes attacking our ships and saw the fleet throwing up antiaircraft fire. Despite the aerial attack, the ships' big guns began heavy firing against the Japanese on land. Toward our right and rear, the firing of our infantry units slackened. We learned that radio messages indicated the 1st Marines had slaughtered hundreds of Japanese in the water when they tried a landing behind our division's flank. The sound of scattered firing told us some enemy had slipped ashore, but the major threat was over.

Our artillery increased its support fire to our front, and we were told that our division would attack during the day. We would remain in position, however—an order we found most agreeable.

Word came that the army troops on our left had held off the main Japanese attack, but things were still grim in that area. Some enemy had gotten through, and others were still attacking. While 3/5 remained in reserve, the 1st Marine Division began its attack to our front, and we heard that the opposition was ferocious. We received orders to be on the lookout for any enemy that might have slipped around the division's flank during the night. There were none.

There was a massive enemy air attack against our fleet at this time. We saw a kamikaze fly through a thick curtain of flak and crash dive into a cruiser. A huge white smoke ring rose thousands of feet into the air. We heard shortly that it was the cruiser USS *Birmingham* that had suffered considerable damage and loss of life among her crew.

*The Japanese counterattack of 3–4 May was a major effort aimed at confusing the American battle plan by isolating and destroying the 1st Marine Division. The Japanese made a night amphibious landing of several hundred men on the east coast behind the 7th Infantry Division. Coordinated with that landing was another on the west coast behind the 1st Marine Division. The Japanese plan called for the two elements to move inland, join up, and create confusion to the rear while the main counterattack hit the American center.*

*The Japanese 24th Infantry Division concentrated its frontal attack on the boundary between the American army's 7th and 77th Infantry divisions. The enemy planned to send a separate brigade through the gap in the American lines created by the 24th Division's attack, swing it to the left behind the 1st Marine Division, and hit the Marines as the Japanese 62d Infantry Division attacked the 1st Marine Division's front.*

*If the plan succeeded, the enemy would isolate and destroy the 1st Marine Division. It failed when the two American army divisions stopped the frontal assault, except for a few minor penetrations, with more than 6,000 Japanese dead counted. At the same time, the 1st Marines (on the right of the 1st Marine Division) discovered the enemy landing on the west coast. They killed over 300 enemy in the water and on the beach.*

# CHAPTER ELEVEN

# OF SHOCK AND SHELLS

Heavy rains began on 6 May and lasted through 8 May, a preview of the nightmare of mud we would endure from the end of the second week of May until the end of the month. Our division had reached the banks of the Asato Gawa at a cost of 1,409 casualties (killed and wounded). I knew losses had been heavy during the first week of May because of the large number of casualties I saw in just the small area we were operating in.

On 8 May Nazi Germany surrendered unconditionally. We were told this momentous news, but considering our own peril and misery, no one cared much. "So what" was typical of the remarks I heard around me. We were resigned only to the fact that the Japanese would fight to total extinction on Okinawa, as they had elsewhere, and that Japan would have to be invaded with the same gruesome prospects. Nazi Germany might as well have been on the moon.

The main thing that impressed us about V-E Day was a terrific, thundering artillery and naval gunfire barrage that went swishing, roaring, and rumbling toward the Japanese. I thought it was in preparation for the next day's attack. Years later I read that the barrage had been fired on enemy targets at noon for its destructive effect on them but also as a salute to V-E Day.

The 6th Marine Division moved into the line on our right, and our division shifted toward the left somewhat. This put us in the center of the American front. As we crouched in our muddy foxholes in the cold rain, the arrival of the 6th Marine Division plus the massive artillery barrage did more for our morale than news about Europe.

The 5th Marines approached the village of Dakeshi and ran into a strong enemy defensive system in an area known as the Awacha Pocket. Talk was that we were approaching the main Japanese defense line, the Shuri Line. But Awacha and Dakeshi confronted us before we reached the main ridges of the Shuri Line.

When our battalion dug in in front of Awacha, our mortars were emplaced on the slope of a little rise about seventy-five yards behind the front line. The torrents of rain were causing us other problems besides chilly misery. Our tanks couldn't move up to support us. Amtracs had to bring a lot of supplies, because the jeeps and trailers bogged down in the soft soil.

Ammunition, boxes of rations, and five-gallon cans of water were brought up as close to us as possible. But because of the mud along a shallow draw that ran to the rear of the mortar section, all the supplies were piled about fifty yards away in a supply dump on the other side of the draw. Working parties went off to carry the supplies from the dump across the draw to the rifle platoons and the mortar section.

Carrying ammo and rations was something the veterans had done plenty of times before. With the others I had struggled up and down Peleliu's unbelievably rugged rocky terrain in the suffocating heat, carrying ammo, rations, and water. Like carrying stretcher cases, it was exhausting work. But this was my first duty on a working party in deep mud, and it surpassed the drudgery of any working party I had ever experienced.

All ammunition was heavy, of course, but some was easier to handle than others. We praised the manufacturers of hand-grenade and belted machine-gun ammunition boxes. The former were wooden with a nice rope handle on each side; the latter were metal and had a collapsible handle on top. But we cursed the dolts who made the wooden cases our .30 caliber rifle ammo came in. Each box contained 1,000 rounds of ammunition. It was heavy and had only a small notch cut into either end. This allowed only a fingertip grip by the two men usually needed to handle a single crate.

We spent a great deal of time in combat carrying this heavy ammunition on our shoulders to places where it was needed—spots often totally inaccessible to all types of vehicles—and breaking it out of the packages and crates. On Okinawa this was often done under enemy fire, in driving rain, and through knee-deep mud for hours on end. Such activity drove the infantryman, weary from the mental and physical stress of combat, almost to the brink of physical collapse.

A great number of books and films about the war ignored this grueling facet of the infantryman's war. They gave the impression that ammunition was always "up there" when needed. Maybe my outfit just happened to get a particularly bad dose of carrying ammo into position on Peleliu because of the heat and rugged terrain and on Okinawa because of the deep mud. But the work was something none of us would forget. It was exhausting, demoralizing, and seemingly unending.

In this first position before Awacha, those of us detailed to the working parties had made a couple of trips across the shallow draw when a Nambu light machine gun opened up from a position to our left. I was about midway across the draw, in no particular hurry, when the Japanese gunner fired his first bursts down the draw. I took off at a run, slipping and sliding on the mud, to the protected area where the supply dump was placed. Slugs snapped viciously around me. The men with me also were lucky as we dove for the protection of a knoll beside the supplies. The enemy machine gunner was well concealed up the draw to our left and had a clear field of fire any-time anyone crossed where we were. We were bound to lose men to that Nambu if we kept moving back and forth. Yet we had to get the ammo distributed for the coming attack.

We looked across the draw toward the mortar section and saw Redifer throw out a phosphorous grenade to give us smoke-screen protection when we came back across. He threw several more grenades which went off with a muffled *bump* and a flash. Thick clouds of white smoke billowed forth and hung almost immobile in the heavy, misty air. I grabbed a metal box of 60mm mortar ammo in each hand. Each of the other men also picked up a load. We prepared to cross. The Nambu kept firing down the smoke-covered draw. I was reluctant to go, as were the others, but we could see Redifer standing out in the draw, throwing more phosphorous grenades to hide us. I felt like a coward. My buddies must have felt the same way as we glanced anxiously at each other. Someone said resignedly, "Let's go, on the double, and keep your five-pace interval."

We dashed into the smoky, murky air. I lowered my head and gritted my teeth as the machine-gun slugs snapped and zipped around us. I expect-ed to get hit. So did the others. I wasn't being brave, but Redifer was, and I would rather take my chances than be yellow in the face of his risks to screen us. If he got hit while I was cringing in safety, I knew it would haunt me the rest of my life—that is, if I lived much longer, which seemed more unlikely every day.

The smoke hid us from the gunner, but he kept firing intermittent bursts down the draw to prevent our crossing. Slugs popped and snapped, but we made it across. We rushed behind the knoll and flung the heavy ammo boxes down on the mud. We thanked Redifer, but he seemed more concerned with solving the problem at hand than talking.

"Boy, that Nip's got the best-trained trigger finger I ever heard. Listen to them short bursts he gets off," a buddy said. We panted and listened to the machine gun half in terror and half in admiration of the Japanese gunner's skill. He continued to fire across the rear of our position. Each burst was two or three rounds and spaced: *tat,tat . . . tat,tat,tat . . . tat,tat.*

Just then we heard the engine of a tank some distance across the draw. Without a word, Redifer sped across the draw toward the sound. He got across safely. We could see him dimly through the drifting smoke as he contacted the tankers. Shortly we saw him backing toward us slowly, giving the tankers hand signals as he directed the big Sherman across the draw. The Nambu kept firing blindly through the smoke as we watched Redifer anxiously. He seemed unhurried and reached us safely with the tank.

The tankers had agreed to act as a shield for us in our hazardous crossing. With several of us crouching in the welcome protection it afforded us, the tank moved back and forth across the draw, always between us and the enemy machine gun. We loaded up on ammo and moved slowly across the machine-gun-swept draw, hugging the side of the tank like chicks beside a mother hen. We kept this up until all the ammo was brought safely across.

The troops often expressed the opinion that whether an enlisted man was or wasn't recommended for a decoration for outstanding conduct in combat depended primarily on who saw him perform the deed. This certainly was true in the case of Redifer and what he had done to get the ammunition across the draw. I had seen other men awarded decorations for less, but Redifer was not so fortunate as to receive the official praise he deserved. Just the opposite happened.

As we finished the chore of moving the ammo across the draw, a certain first lieutenant, who by some unlucky chance had been assigned to Company K after Peleliu, came up. We called him simply "Shadow." A tall, skinny man, he was the sloppiest Marine—officer or enlisted—I ever saw.

His dungarees hung on him like old, discarded clothes on a scarecrow: his web pistol belt was wrapped around his waist like a loose sash on a dressing gown; his map case flopped around; and every packstrap dangled more "Irish pennants" than any new recruit had in boot camp. Shadow never wore canvas leggings when I saw him. His trouser legs were rolled up unevenly above his skinny ankles. He didn't fit his camouflaged cloth helmet cover tightly over his helmet like most Marines. It sagged to one side like some big stocking cap. For some reason, he frequently carried his helmet upside down in his left hand clutched against his side like a football. On his head he wore a green cloth fatigue cap like the rest of us wore under our helmets. But his cap was torn across the top so that his dark hair protruded like straw through a scarecrow's hat.

Shadow's disposition was worse than his appearance. Moody, ill-tempered, and highly excitable, he cursed the veteran enlisted men worse than most DIs did recruits in boot camp. When he was displeased with a Marine about something, he didn't reprimand the man the way our other officers did. He threw a tantrum. He would grab his cap by the bill, fling it onto the muddy deck, stamp his feet, and curse everyone in sight. The veteran sergeant who accompanied Shadow would stand silently by during these temper displays, torn between a compulsion to reprimand us, if it seemed his duty to do so, and embarrassment and disapproval over his officer's childish behavior.

In all fairness, I don't know how competent an officer Shadow was considered to be by his superiors. Needless to say, he wasn't highly regarded in the ranks, simply on the basis of his lack of self-control. But he was brave. I'll give him that.

Shadow "pitched a fit" in reaction to what Redifer had done in facilitating our ammo transportation across the draw. It was just the first of many such performances I was to witness, and they never ceased to amaze as well as disgust me.

He went to Redifer and unleashed such a verbal assault against him that anyone who didn't know better would have assumed that Redifer was a coward who had deserted his post in the face of the enemy instead of having just performed a brave act. Shadow yelled, gesticulated, and cursed Redifer for "exposing himself unnecessarily to enemy fire" when he was throwing the smoke grenades into the draw and when he went to contact the tank.

Redifer took it quietly, but he was obviously dismayed. We looked on in disbelief, having expected Shadow to praise the man for showing bravery and initiative under fire. But here was this ranting, raving officer actually cursing and berating a man for doing something any other officer would have considered a meritorious act. It was so incredibly illogical that we couldn't believe it.

Finally, having vented his rage on a Marine who rightfully deserved praise, Shadow strode off grumbling and cursing the individual and collective stupidity of enlisted men. Redifer didn't say anything. He just looked off into the distance. We growled mightily, though.

As midday approached on 9 May, everyone was tense about the coming attack. Ammunition had been issued, men had squared away their gear and had done their last-minute duties: adjusting cartridge belts, packstraps, leggings, and leather rifle slings—all those forlorn little gestures of no value that released tension in the face of impending terror. We had previously

*Marines wait to attack as a barrage of white phosphorous shells explodes on enemy positions. USMC photo.*

registered our mortars on selected targets and had stacked HE and phosphorous shells off the mud on pieces of boxes for quick access.

The ground having dried sufficiently for our tanks to maneuver, several stood by with engines idling, hatches open, and the tankers waiting— waiting like everyone else. War is mostly waiting. The men around me sat silently with drawn faces. Some replacements had come into the company to make up for our earlier losses. These new men looked more confused than afraid.

The big guns had fired periodically during the morning, but then had died away. There wasn't much noise as we waited for the preattack bombardment to begin.

Then the preassault bombardment commenced. The big shells swished overhead as each battery of our artillery and each ship's guns began to shell the Japanese Awacha defenses ahead of us. At first we could identify each type of shell—75mm, 105mm, and 155mm artillery, along with the 5-inch ship's guns—as it added to the storm of steel.

We saw our planes overhead, Corsairs and dive bombers. Air strikes began as the planes dove firing rockets, dropping bombs, and strafing to our front. The firing thundered and rumbled until finally even the experienced ears of the veterans could distinguish nothing, only that we were glad that all that stuff was ours.

Enemy artillery and mortar shells began coming in as the Japanese tried to disrupt the attack. The replacements looked utterly bewildered amid the bedlam. I remembered my first day in combat and sympathized with them. The sheer massiveness of the preattack bombardment was an awesome and frightening thing to witness as a veteran, let alone as a new replacement.

Soon the order came, "Mortar section, stand by." We took directions from Burgin, who was up on the observation post to spot targets and direct our fire. Although our 60mm shells were small compared to the huge shells rushing overhead, we could fire close-in to the company front where bigger mortars and the artillery couldn't shoot without endangering our own people. This closeness made it doubly critical that we fire skillfully and avoid short rounds.

We had fired only a few rounds when Snafu began cursing the mud. With each round, the recoil pushed the mortar's base plate against the soft soil in the gun pit, and he had trouble resighting the leveling bubbles to retain proper alignment of the gun on the aiming stake.

After we completed the first fire mission, we quickly moved the gun a little to one side of the pit onto a harder surface and resighted it. At Peleliu we often had to hold the base plate as well as the bipod feet onto the coral rock to prevent the recoil from making the base plate bounce aside, knocking the mortar's alignment out too far. On Okinawa's wet clay soil, just the opposite happened. The recoil drove the base plate into the ground with each round we fired. This problem got worse as the rains increased during May, and the ground became softer and softer.

The order came to secure the guns and to stand by. The air strike ended, and the artillery and ships' guns slacked off. The tanks and our riflemen moved out as tank-infantry teams, and we waited tensely. Things went well for a couple of hundred yards during this attack made by 3/5 and 3/7 before heavy fire from Japanese on the left flank stopped the attack. Our OP (observation post) ordered us to fire smoke because heavy enemy fire was coming from our left. We fired phosphorous rapidly to screen the men from the enemy observers.

Our position got a heavy dose of Japanese 90mm mortar counter-battery fire. We had a difficult time keeping up our firing with those big

*Marines throwing smoke grenades to screen stretcher bearers. Okinawa. USMC photo.*

*The survivor grieves. Okinawa. USMC photo.*

90mm shells crashing around us. Shell fragments whined through the air, and the big shells slung mud around. But we had to keep up our fire. The riflemen were catching hell from the flank and had to be supported. Our artillery began firing again at the enemy positions to our left to aid the harassed riflemen.

We always knew when we were inflicting losses on the Japanese with our 60mm mortars by the amount of counterbattery mortar and artillery fire they threw back at us. If we weren't doing them any damage, they usually ignored us unless they thought they could inflict a lot of casualties. If the Japanese counterbattery fire was a real indicator of our effectiveness in causing them casualties, we were satisfyingly effective during the Okinawa campaign.

During the attack of 9 May against Awacha, Company K suffered heavy losses. It was the same tragic sight of bloody, dazed, and wounded men benumbed with shock, being carried or walking to the aid station in the rear. There also were the dead, and the usual anxious inquiries about friends. We were all glad when the word came that 3/5 would move into reserve for the 7th Marines—for a couple of days, it turned out. The 7th Marines were fighting to our right against Dakeshi Ridge.

*In the path of the 1st Marine Division, from north to south, lay Awacha, Dakeshi Ridge, Dakeshi Village, Wana Ridge, Wana Village, and Wana Draw. South of the latter lay the defenses and the heights of Shuri itself. All these ridges and villages were defended heavily by well-prepared, mutually supporting fortifications built into a skillful system of defense-in-depth. Similarly powerful defensive positions faced the 6th Marine Division on the right and the army infantry divisions on the left. The Japanese ferociously defended every yard of ground and conserved their strength to inflict maximum losses on the American forces. The tactics turned Okinawa into a bloodbath.*

The battle against Awacha raged on to our left. We dug in for the night in the wet ground. Our mortars weren't set up. We were to act as riflemen and to keep watch across an open, sloping valley. Above us the other two mortar squads dug in in two parallel lines about twenty feet apart and perpendicular to the line of the crest of the embankment above us. Water and rations were issued and mail brought to us.

Mail usually was a big morale booster, but not for me that time. There was a chilly drizzling rain off and on. We were weary and my spirits weren't the best. I sat on my helmet in the mud and read a letter from my parents. It brought news that Deacon, my beloved spaniel, had been hit by an automobile, had dragged himself home, and had died in my father's arms. He had been my constant companion during the several years before I had left home for college. There, with the sound of heavy firing up ahead and the sufferings and deaths of thousands of men going on nearby, big tears rolled down my cheeks, because Deacon was dead.

During the remainder of the night, the sound of firing toward Dakeshi Ridge indicated that the 7th Marines were having a lot of trouble trying to push the Japanese off the ridge. Just before dawn we could hear heavy firing off to our left front where 1/5 and 2/5 were fighting around the Awacha Pocket.

"Stand by, you guys, and be prepared to move out," came the order from an NCO on the embankment above us.

"What's the hot dope?" a mortarman asked.

"Don't know, except the Nips are counterattacking on the 5th Marines' front and the battalion [3/5] is on standby to go up and help stop 'em."

We greeted the news with an understandable lack of enthusiasm. We were still tired and tense from the punishment the battalion took at Awacha the day before. What's more, we didn't relish moving anywhere in the darkness. But we squared away our gear, chewing gum nervously or gnawing on ration biscuits. The sound of firing rose and fell to our left front as we waited and wondered.

Finally, during the misty gray light of early morning, the order came, "OK, you guys, let's go." We picked up our loads and moved toward the front lines.

Other than occasional shells whining over in both directions, things were rather calm. Our column moved along a ridge just below the crest to the emplacements of the Marines who had been under attack. We found them assessing the damage they had done to the Japanese and caring for their own wounded. Some of the men told us the enemy had come into bayonet range before being repulsed. "But we tore their ass up, by God," one man said to me as he pointed out at about forty Japanese corpses sprawled beyond the Marine foxholes.

In the pale dawn, the air was misty and still smoky from phosphorous shells the enemy had fired to hide their approach. There was a big discussion in the ranks. Comments passed along to us from the Marines in place had it that somebody had seen a woman advancing with the attacking Japanese and that she was probably among the dead out there. We couldn't see her from our positions.

Then word came, "About face; we're moving back." In short, our help wasn't needed, so we were to be deployed somewhere else. Back through the rain and the mud we went.

All movements during most of May and early June were physically exhausting and utterly exasperating because of the mud. Typically, we moved in single file, five paces apart, slipping and sliding up and down muddy slopes and through boggy fields. When the column slowed or stopped, we tended to bunch up, and the NCOs and officers ordered sternly, "Keep your five-pace interval; don't bunch up." The everpresent danger of shells even far behind the lines made it necessary that we stay strung out. However, sometimes it was so dark that in order not to get separated and lost, each man was ordered to hold onto the cartridge belt of the man in front of him. This made the going difficult over rough and muddy terrain. Often if a man lost his footing and fell, several others went down with him, sprawling over each other in the mud. There were muffled curses and exasperated groans as they wearily disentangled themselves and regained their footing, groping about in the inky darkness to reform the column.

As soon as we stopped, the order came, "Move out." So the column always moved forward but like an accordion or an inchworm: compressed, then strung out, stopping and starting. If a man put down his load for a brief respite, he was sure to hear, "Pick up your gear; we're moving out!" So the load had to be hoisted onto shoulders again. But if you didn't put it down, chances were you missed an opportunity to rest for a few seconds, or even up to an hour, while the column halted up ahead for reasons usually unknown. To sit down on a rock or on a helmet when drunk with fatigue was like pressing a button to signal some NCO to shout, "On your feet; pick up your gear; we're moving out again." So the big decision in every man's mind at each pause in the column's forward progress was whether to drop his load and hope for a lengthy pause or to stand there and support all the weight rather than putting it down and having to pick it up again right away.

The column wound around and up and down the contours of terrain which in May and early June was covered nearly always with slippery mud varying in depth from a few inches to knee deep. The rain was frequent and chilly. It varied from drizzles to wind-driven, slashing deluges that flooded our muddy footprints almost as soon as we made them. The helmet, of course, kept one's head dry, but a poncho was the only body protection we had. It was floppy and restricted movement greatly. We had no raincoats. So, rather than struggle over slippery terrain with our loads, encumbered further by a loose-fitting poncho, we just got soaking wet and shivered in misery.

We tried to wisecrack and joke from time to time, but that always faded away as we grew more weary or closer to the front lines. That kind of movement over normal terrain or on roads would try any man's patience, but in Okinawa's mud it drove us to a state of frustration and exasperation bordering on rage. It can be appreciated only by someone who has experienced it.

Most men finally came to the state where they just stood stoically immobile with a resigned expression when halted and waited to move out. The cursing and outbursts of rage didn't seem to help, although no one was above it when goaded to the point of desperation and fatigue with halting and moving, slipping and sliding, and falling in the mud. Mud didn't just interfere with vehicles. It exhausted the man on foot who was expected to keep on where wheels or treaded vehicles couldn't move.

At some point during our moves, our mortar section completely wiped out an enemy force that had held an elongated ridge for three days against repeated Marine infantry attacks supported by heavy artillery fire. Burgin was observing. He reasoned that there must have been a narrow gully running along the ridge that sheltered the Japanese from the artillery fire. He registered our three mortars so that one fired from right to left, another from left to right, and the third along the crest of the ridge. Thus the Japanese in the gully couldn't escape.

Lieutenant Mac ordered Burgin not to carry out the fire mission. He said we couldn't spare the ammo. Burgin, a three-campaign veteran and a skillful observer, called the company CP and asked if they could get us the ammo. The CP told him yes.

Over the sound-powered phone, Burgin said, "On my command, fire."

Mac was with us at the gun pits and ordered us not to fire. He told Burgin the same over the phone.

Burgin told him to go to hell and yelled, "Mortar section, fire on my command; commence firing!"

We fired as Mac ranted and raved.

When we finished firing, the company moved against the ridge. Not a shot was fired at our men. Burgin checked the target area and saw more than fifty freshly killed Japanese soldiers in a narrow ravine, all dead from wounds obviously caused by our mortar fire. The artillery shells had exploded in front of or to the rear of the Japanese who were protected from them. Our 60mm mortar shells fell right into the ravine, however, because of their steeper trajectory.

We had scored a significant success with the teamwork of our mortar section. The event illustrated the value of experience in a veteran like Burgin compared with the poor judgment of a "green" lieutenant.

The short period of rest in May helped us physically and mentally. Such periodic rests off the lines, lasting from a day to several days, enabled us to keep going. The rations were better. We could shave and clean up a bit using our helmets for a basin. Although we had to dig in because of long-range artillery or air raids, two men could make a simple shelter with their ponchos over their hole and be relatively (but not completely) dry on rainy nights. We could relax a little.

I'm convinced we would have collapsed from the strain and exertion without such respites. But I found it more difficult to go back each time we squared away our gear to move forward into the zone of terror. My buddies' joking ceased as we trudged grim-faced back into that chasm where time had no meaning and one's chances of emerging unhurt dwindled with each encounter. With each step toward the distant rattle and rumble of that hellish region where fear and horror tortured us like a cat tormenting a mouse, I experienced greater and greater dread. And it wasn't just dread of death or pain, because most men felt somehow they wouldn't be killed. But each time we went up, I felt the sickening dread of fear itself and the revulsion at the ghastly scenes of pain and suffering among comrades that a survivor must witness.

Some of my close friends told me they felt the same way. Significantly, those who felt it most acutely were the more battle-wise veterans for whom Okinawa was their third campaign. The bravest wearied of the suffering and waste, even though they showed little fear for their own personal safety. They simply had seen too much horror.

The increasing dread of going back into action obsessed me. It became the subject of the most tortuous and persistent of all the ghastly war nightmares that have haunted me for many, many years. The dream is always the same, going back up to the lines during the bloody, muddy month of May on Okinawa. It remains blurred and vague, but occasionally still comes, even after the nightmares about the shock and violence of Peleliu have faded and been lifted from me like a curse.

The 7th Marines secured Dakeshi Ridge on 13 May after a bitter fight. Some of the Peleliu veterans in that regiment noted that the vicious battle resembled the fighting on Bloody Nose Ridge. We could see the ridge clearly. It certainly looked like Bloody Nose. The crest was rugged and jagged on the skyline and had an ugly thin line of blackened, shattered trees and stumps.

Our company moved into a smashed, ruined village that an officer told me was Dakeshi. Some of us moved up to a stout stone wall where we were ordered to hold our fire while we watched a strange scene about one hundred yards to our front. We had to stand there inactive and watch as

*Passing through a small village. Note split-toe tabi on dead Japanese soldier. April 1945, Okinawa. USMC photo.*

about forty or fifty Japanese soldiers retreated through the ruins and rubble. They had been flushed by men of the 7th Marines. But we were in support of the 7th Marines, some elements of which were forward of us on the right and left, out of our field of vision. We couldn't risk firing for fear of hitting those Marines. We could only watch the enemy trotting along holding their rifles. They wore no packs, only crossed shoulder straps supporting their cartridge belts.

As they moved through the rubble with helmets bobbing up and down, a man next to me fingered the safety catch on his M1 rifle and said in disgust, "Look at them bastards out there in the open, and we can't even fire at 'em."

"Don't worry, the 7th Marines will catch them in a cross fire farther on," an NCO said.

"That's the word," said an officer confidently.

Just then a swishing, rushing sound of shells passing low overhead made us all duck reflexively, even though we recognized the sound as our own artillery. Large, black, sausage-shaped clouds of thick smoke erupted in the air over the Japanese as each of those deadly 155mm bursts exploded with a flash and a *karump*. The artillerymen were zeroed in on target. The Japanese broke into a dead run, looking very bowlegged to me (as they always did when running). Even as they ran away under that deadly hail of steel, showing us their backs, I felt there was an air of confident arrogance about them. They didn't move like men in panic. We knew they simply had been ordered to fall back to other strongly prepared defensive positions to prolong the campaign. Otherwise they would have stayed put or attacked us, and in either case fought to the death.

More of our 155s swished over, erupting above the Japanese. We stood in silence and watched as the artillery fire took its toll of them. It was a grim sight, still vivid in my mind. The survivors moved out of sight through drifting smoke as we heard the rattle of Marine machine guns on our right and left front.

We received orders to move out along a little road bordered by stone walls. We passed through the ruins of what had been a quaint village. What had been picturesque little homes with straw-thatched or tiled roofs were piles of smoldering rubble.

After bitter fighting, the Awacha defenses and then those around Dakeshi fell to our division. Yet, between us and Shuri, there remained another system of heavy Japanese defenses: Wana. The costly battle against them would become known as the battle for Wana Draw.

# Chapter Twelve

# OF MUD AND MAGGOTS

*T*he boundary between the III Amphibious Corps (Marines) and the XXIV Corps (Army) ran through the middle of the main Japanese defensive position on the heights of Shuri. As the Marines moved southward, the 1st Marine Division remained on the left in the III Amphib-. ious Corps' zone of action with the 6th Marine Division on the right. Within the 1st Marine Division's zone of action, the 7th Marines occupied the left flank and the 5th Marines the right. The 1st Marines was in reserve.

Beyond Awacha–Dakeshi, the Marines next faced Wana Ridge. On the other side of Wana Ridge lay Wana Draw, through which meandered the Asato Gawa. Forming the southern high ground above Wana Draw was yet another ridge, this one extending eastward from the city of Naha and rising to the Shuri Heights. This second ridge formed a part of the main Japanese defensive positions, the Shuri Line.

Wana Draw aimed like an arrow from the northwest directly into the heart of the Japanese defenses at Shuri. Within this natural avenue of approach, the Japanese took advantage of every difficult feature of terrain; it couldn't have provided a better opportunity for their defense if they had designed it. The longest and bloodiest ordeal of the battle for Okinawa now faced the men of the 1st Marine Division.

For the attack against Wana on 15 May 1945, the 5th Marines sent 2/5 forward with 3/5 in close support. The 1st Battalion came behind in reserve.

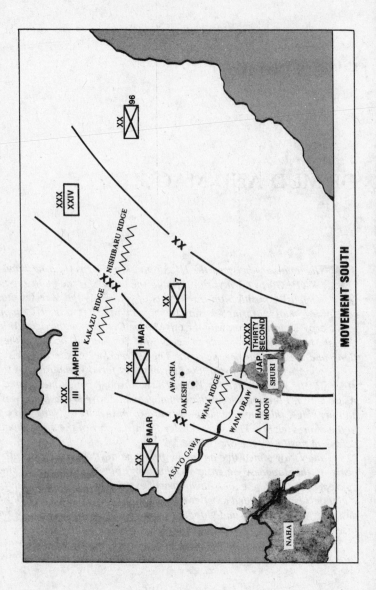

*Shell-blasted Wana Ridge. Okinawa. USMC photo.*

Before 2/5's attack began, we moved into a position behind that battalion. We watched tanks firing 75s and M7s firing 105s thoroughly shell the draw. The tanks received such heavy Japanese fire in return that the riflemen of 2/5 assigned to attack with the tanks had to seek any protection they could in ditches and holes while they covered the tanks from a distance; no man on his feet could have survived the hail of shells the enemy fired at the tanks. And the tanks couldn't move safely beyond the cover the riflemen provided because of Japanese suicide tank-destroyer teams. Finally, we saw the tanks pull back after suffering some hits. Our artillery and naval gunfire threw a terrific barrage at the Japanese positions around the draw. Shortly after that the tanks withdrew. Then an air strike was made against the draw. The bombardment of the draw seemed very heavy to us, but it wasn't anything compared to what was to become necessary before the draw was taken.

We moved from one position to another behind 2/5 until I was so confused I had no idea where we were. Late in the afternoon, we halted temporarily along a muddy trail running along the treeless slope of a muddy ridge. Marines of 2/5 moved past us going the other direction. Japanese shells whistled across the ridge and burst to the rear. Our artillery roared and swished overhead, the explosions booming and thundering out in the draw across the ridge.

Nearby our regimental Protestant chaplain had set up a little altar made out of a box from which he was administering Holy Communion to a small group of dirty Marines. I glanced at the face of a Marine opposite me as the file halted. He was filthy like all of us, but even through a thickly mud-caked dark beard I could see he had fine features. His eyes were bloodshot and weary. He slowly lowered his light machine gun from his shoulder, set the handle on his toe to keep it off the mud, and steadied the barrel with his hand. He watched the chaplain with an expression of skepticism that seemed to ask, "What's the use of all that? Is it gonna keep them guys from gettin' hit?" That face was so weary but so expressive that I knew he, like all of us, couldn't help but have doubts about his God in the presence of constant shock and suffering. Why did it go on and on? The machine gunner's buddy held the gun's tripod on his shoulder, glanced briefly at the muddy little communion service, and then stared blankly off toward a clump of pines to our rear—as though he hoped to see home back there somewhere.

"Move out," came along their file.

The machine gunner hoisted the heavy weapon onto his shoulder as they went slipping and sliding around a bend in the trail into the gathering dusk.

We were told to spread out, take cover, and await further orders. Some of us found holes. Others scooped out what they could. Soon several Japanese shells exploded not far from me. I heard a shout for a corpsman and then, "Hey, you guys, Doc Caswell got hit!"

I forgot about the shells and felt sick. I ran in the direction of the shout to look for Kent Caswell, praying with every step that he wasn't hurt badly. Several other Marines were already with Doc, and a fellow corpsman was bandaging his neck. Doc Caswell lay back in the foxhole and looked up at me as I bent over him and asked him how he was doing (no doubt a stupid question, but my throat was constricted with grief). He opened his lips to speak, and blood trickled out from between them. I was heartbroken, because I didn't see how he could possibly survive. I feared that vital blood vessels in his neck had been severed by the shell fragments.

"Don't talk Doc, they'll get you outa here, and you'll be OK," I managed to stammer.

"OK you guys, let's get him outa here," the corpsman said as he finished his aid.

*Flamethrower tank cleaning out enemy. Okinawa. USMC photo.*

As I said so long to Doc and got up to leave, I noticed a cloverleaf of 60mm mortar shells lying on the side of the foxhole. A shell fragment had sliced a gash through the thick black metal endplate. I shuddered as I wondered whether it had passed first through Doc's neck.*

Our massive artillery, mortar, naval gunfire, and aerial bombardment continued against Wana Draw on our front and Wana Ridge on our left. The Japanese continued to shell everything and everybody in the area, meeting each tank-infantry attack with a storm of fire. A total of thirty tanks, including four flamethrowers, blasted and burned Wana Draw. Our artillery, heavy mortars, ships' guns, and planes then plastered the enemy positions all over again until the noise and shock made me wonder what it was like to be in a quiet place. We had been under and around plenty of

---

*Some time later we learned that Doc had survived the trip to the aid station with the stretcher team and that he would live. He returned to his native Texas where he remains one of my most faithful friends from our days in K/3/5.

*Pfc. Paul Isen of the 5th Marines dashing across through Japanese machine-gun fire as he crosses "death valley." Okinawa. USMC photo.*

"heavy stuff" at Peleliu, but not on nearly so massive a scale or for such unending periods of time as at Wana. The thunderous American barrages went on and on for hours and then days. In return, the Japanese threw plenty of shells our way. I had a continuous headache I'll never forget. Those thunderous, prolonged barrages imposed on me a sense of stupefaction and dullness far beyond anything I ever had experienced before.

It didn't seem possible for any human being to be under such thunderous chaos for days and nights on end and be unaffected by it—even when most of it was our own supporting weapons, and we were in a good foxhole. How did the Japanese stand up under it? They simply remained deep in their caves until it stopped and then swarmed up to repulse each attack, just as they had done at Peleliu. So our heavy guns and air strikes had to knock down, cave in, or otherwise destroy the enemy's well-constructed defensive positions.

At some time during the fight for Wana Draw, we crossed what I supposed was the draw itself, somewhere near its mouth. To get to that point, we fought for days. I had lost count of how many. Marines of 2/5 had just gone across under fire, while we waited in an open field to move across. We eased up to the edge of the draw to cross in dispersed order. An NCO ordered three men and me to cross at a particular point and to stay close behind the 2/5 troops directly across the draw from us. The other side looked mighty far away. Japanese machine guns were firing down the draw from our left, and our artillery was swishing overhead.

"Haul ass, and don't stop for anything til you get across," said our NCO. (We could see other Marines of our battalion starting across on our right.) He told me to leave my mortar ammo bag and that someone else would bring it. I had the Thompson (submachine gun) slung over my shoulder.

We left the field and slid down a ten-foot embankment to the sloping floor of the draw. My feet hit the deck running. The man ahead of me was a Company K veteran whom I knew well, but the other two were replacements. One I knew by name, but the other not at all. I ran as fast as I could, and was glad I was carrying only my Tommy, pistol, and combat pack.

The valley sloped downward toward a little stream and then upward to the ridge beyond. The Japanese machine guns rattled away. Bullets zipped and snapped around my head, the tracers like long white streaks. I looked neither right nor left, but with my heart in my throat raced out, splashed across the little stream, and dashed up the slope to the shelter of a spur of ridge projecting out into the draw to our left. We must have run about three hundred yards or more to get across.

Once behind the spur I was out of the line of machine-gun fire, so I slowed to a trot. The veteran ahead of me and a little to my right slowed up, too. We glanced back to see where the two new men were. Neither one of them had made more than a few strides out into the draw from the other side. One was sprawled in a heap, obviously killed instantly. The other was wounded and crawling back. Some Marines ran out, crouching low, to drag him to safety.

"Jesus, that was close, Sledgehammer," said the man with me.

"Yeah," I gasped. That was all I could say.

We went up the slope and contacted a couple of riflemen from 2/5.

"We got a kid right over there just got hit. Can you guys get him out?" one of them said. "There's some corpsmen set up in a ravine along the ridge there." He pointed out the location of the casualty and then the dressing station.

We hailed two Company K men coming along the ridge, and they said they would help. One ran back along the ridge to get a stretcher. We other three moved up the ridge and into some brush where we found the wounded Marine. He lay on his back still clutching his rifle. As we came up he said, "Boy, am I glad to see you guys."

"You hit bad?" I asked as I knelt beside him.

"Look out you guys! Nips right over there in the bushes."

I unslung my Tommy and, watching where he indicated the Japanese were, I talked to him. My two buddies knelt beside us with their weapons ready, watching for enemy soldiers through the brush while we waited for the stretcher.

"Where you hit?" I asked the wounded Marine.

"Right here," he said, pointing to the lower right portion of his abdomen.

He was talkative and seemed in no pain—obviously still shocked and dazed from his wound. I knew he would hurt badly soon, because he was hit in a painful area. I saw a smear of blood around a tear in his dungaree trousers, so I unhooked his cartridge belt and then his belt and his trousers to see how serious the wound was. It wasn't the round, neat hole of a bullet, but the gash characteristic of a shell fragment. About two inches long, it oozed a small amount of blood.

"What hit you?" I asked.

"Our company sixty mortars," answered the wounded Marine.

I felt a sharp twinge of conscience and thought some 60mm mortarman in the poor guy's own company fouled up and dropped some short rounds.

Almost as though he had read my thoughts, he continued, "It was my own damn fault I got hit, though. We were ordered to halt back there a way and wait while the mortars shelled this area. But I saw a damn Nip and figured if I got a little closer I could get a clear shot at the sonofabitch. When I got here the mortars came in, and I got hit. Guess I'm lucky it wasn't worse. I guess the Nip slipped away."

"You better take it easy now," I said as the stretcher came up.

We got the young Marine on the stretcher, put his rifle and helmet alongside him, and moved back down the ridge a little way to a corpsman. Several corpsmen were at work in a deep ravine cut into the ridge by erosion. It had sheer walls and a level floor and was perfectly protected. About a dozen wounded, stretcher cases, and walking wounded were there already.

As we set our casualty onto the floor of the ravine, he said, "Thanks a lot you guys; good luck." We wished him luck and a quick trip to the States.

Before we left, I paused and watched the corpsmen a moment. It was admirable how efficiently they handled the wounded, with more coming in

*Wana Ridge. Marine on left has Thompson submachine gun; his buddy has a BAR. Okinawa. USMC photo.*

continuously as stretcher teams left for evacuation centers with those already given field first-aid.

We split up, moved apart a little, and sought shelter along the slope to await orders. I found a commodius two-man standing foxhole commanding a perfect wide view of the draw for a long distance right and left. It obviously had been used as a defensive position against any movement in the draw and probably had sheltered a couple of Japanese riflemen or perhaps a light machine gunner. The hole was well dug in dry clay soil; the ridge sloped up steeply behind it. But the hole and its surroundings were devoid of any enemy equipment or trash of any kind. There wasn't so much as an empty cartridge case or ammo carton to be seen. But there were enemy tracks in the soft soil thrown out of the hole, tracks of tabi sneakers and hobnail-sole field shoes.

The Japanese had become so security conscious they not only removed their dead when possible but sometimes even picked up their expended ''brass'' just as we did on a rifle range. Sometimes all we found were bloodstains on the ground where one had been killed or wounded. They removed everything they could when possible to conceal their casualties. But when they removed even empty cartridge cases, and we found only tracks, we got an eerie feeling—as though we were fighting a phantom enemy.

During their battle on the Motobu Peninsula in April, Marines of the 6th Division had seen evidence of increased security consciousness on the part of the Japanese. But we had seen nothing like it on Peleliu, and Guadalcanal veterans had told me nearly every Japanese they "field stripped" had a diary on him. The same was said about Gloucester.

After sitting out another thunderous barrage of friendly artillery fire, the three of us shouldered our weapons and moved along the ridge to rejoin Company K. Once together, our company formed into extended file and headed westward toward the regimental right flank. (I lost track of the date, as we moved about for several days.) The shell-blasted terrain was treeless and increasingly low and flat. We dug in, were shelled off and on, and were thoroughly bewildered as to where we were, other than we were said to be still somewhere in Wana Draw. Shuri loomed to our left front.

About that time Burgin was wounded. He was hit in the back of the neck by a shell fragment. Fortunately, he wasn't killed. Burgin was a Texan and as fine a sergeant as I ever saw. He was a Gloucester veteran whose luck had run out. We would miss him from the mortar section, and were delighted when he returned later after eighteen days of convalescence.

The weather turned cloudy on 21 May, and the rains began. By midnight the drizzle became a deluge. It was the beginning of a ten-day period of torrential rains. The weather was chilly and mud, mud, mud was everywhere. We slipped and slid along the trails with every step we took.

*While the 1st Marine Division was fighting the costly, heartbreaking battle against the Wana positions, the 6th Marine Division (on the right and slightly forward) had been fighting a terrible battle for Sugar Loaf Hill. Sugar Loaf and the surrounding pieces of prominent terrain—the Horse Shoe and Half Moon—were located on the main ridge running from Naha to Shuri. Like Wana, they were key Japanese defensive positions in the complex that guarded the Shuri Heights.*

*During the morning of 23 May, the boundary between the 1st Marine Division and the 6th Marine Division shifted to the right (west) so the latter could rearrange its lines. The 3d Battalion, 5th Marines went into line on the right to take over the extended front.*

I remember the move vividly, because we entered the worst area I ever saw on a battlefield. And we stayed there more than a week. I shudder at the memory of it.

We shouldered our weapons and gear and the column telescoped its way circuitously through muddy draws, slipping and sliding along the slopes of barren hills to avoid observation and consequent shelling by the enemy. It rained off and on. The mud got worse the farther we went. As we approached our destination, the Japanese dead, scattered about in most areas since 1 May, became more numerous.

When we had dug in near enemy dead and conditions permitted, we always shoveled soil over them in a vain effort to cut down the stench and to control the swarming flies. But the desperate fighting for ten days against and around Sugar Loaf Hill and the continued, prolonged Japanese artillery and mortar fire had made it impossible for the Marine units there to bury the enemy dead.

We soon saw that it also had been impossible to remove many Marine dead. They lay where they had fallen—an uncommon sight even to the veterans in our ranks. It was a strong Marine tradition to move our dead, sometimes even at considerable risk, to an area where they could be covered with a poncho and later collected by the graves registration people. But efforts to remove many Marines killed in the area we entered had been in vain, even after Sugar Loaf Hill had been captured following days of terrible fighting.

The rains had begun 21 May, almost as soon as Sugar Loaf Hill had been secured by men of the 6th Marine Division. Because of the deep mud, the able-bodied could scarcely rescue and evacuate their wounded and bring up vital ammo and rations. Regrettably, the dead had to wait. It couldn't have been otherwise.

We slogged along through a muddy draw around the base of a knoll. On our left we saw six Marine corpses. They were lying face down against a gentle muddy slope where they apparently had hugged the deck to escape Japanese shells. They were "bunched up"—in a row, side by side, scarcely a foot apart. They were so close together that they probably had all been killed by the same shell. Their browning faces lay against the mud in an even row. One could imagine the words of fear or reassurance that had been passed among them as they lay under the terror of the shelling. Each clutched a rusting rifle, and every sign indicated that those tragic figures were new replacements, fresh to the shock of combat.

The first man's left hand was extended forward, palm down. His fingers clutched the mud in a death grip. A beautiful, shiny gold watch was held in place around the decaying wrist by an elaborate gold metal stretch band. (Most of the men I knew—and myself—wore plain, simple luminous-dial, waterproof, shockproof wristwatches with a plain green cloth wristband.) How strange, I thought, for a Marine to wear a flashy,

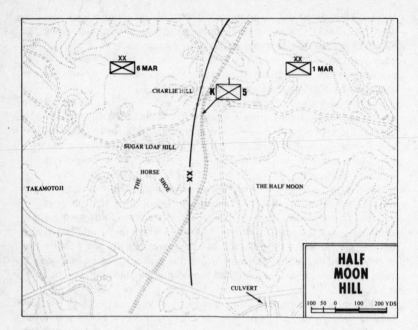

conspicuous watch while on the front lines, stranger still that some Japanese hadn't slipped out during a dark night and taken it.

As we filed past the dead Marines, each of my buddies turned his head and gazed at the horrible spectacle with an expression that revealed how much the scene inwardly sickened us all.

I had heard and read that combat troops in many wars became hardened and insensitive to the sight of their own dead. I didn't find that to be the case at all with my comrades. The sight of dead Japanese didn't bother us in the least, but the sight of Marine dead brought forth regret, never indifference.

## Half Moon Hill

While the artillery swished and whined overhead in both directions, we moved to our new positions in the westernmost extension of Wana Draw. By twos and threes, the Company K men forming the front line eased onto a barren, muddy, shell-torn ridge named Half Moon Hill and into the foxholes of the company we were relieving. Our mortar section went into place behind a low rise of ground below the ridge and about a hundred yards back of the front lines. The terrain between us and Half Moon was nearly flat. The little elevation behind which we emplaced our guns was so low that when we stood up beside the gun pit, we could see clearly up to the company's forward lines on the ridge.

Readily visible beyond that, to the left front, were the still higher, smoke-shrouded Shuri Heights, the heart of the Japanese defensive system. That ominous and formidable terrain feature was constantly under bombardment of varying intensity from our artillery, heavy mortars, and gunfire support ships. No matter, though. It didn't seem to deter the enemy observers from directing their artillery and heavy mortars in shelling our whole area frequently, every day and every night.

We faced south on Half Moon. A narrow-gauge railroad track lay a short distance to our right and ran south through a flat area between Half Moon and a ridge to our right known as the Horse Shoe. Beyond that it swung westward toward Naha. An officer told us that the ridge to our right (west) and slightly to our rear across the railroad was Sugar Loaf Hill.

Company K was on the right flank of 3/5 and moved up onto the western part of the base of Half Moon. The Japanese still occupied caves in both of the southward-pointing tips of the crescent. The right-flank foxhole of our company was dug on the crest at the western edge of the end of the base of Half Moon. Below it to the right the ridge dropped away to low flat ground.

Our company CP was situated in the sunken railroad bed to the right of our mortar section's position. A nice tarpaulin was stretched over the CP from one side of the railroad embankment to the other. This kept the post snug and dry while torrents of chilly rain kept shivering riflemen, machine gunners, and mortarmen soaked, cold, and miserable day and night in open foxholes. The rain greeted us as we moved into our assigned area.

*The almost continuous downpour that started on 21 May turned Wana Draw into a sea of mud and water that resembled a lake. Tanks bogged down and even amtracs could not negotiate the morass. Living conditions on the front lines were pitiful. Supply and evacuation problems were severe. Food, water, and ammunition were scarce. Foxholes had to be bailed out constantly. The men's clothing, shoes, feet, and bodies remained constantly wet. Sleep was nearly impossible. The mental and physical strain took a mounting toll on the Marines.*

*Making an almost impossible situation worse were the deteriorating bodies of Marines and Japanese that lay just outside the foxholes where they had fallen during the five days of ferocious fighting that preceded Company K's arrival on Half Moon. Each day's fighting saw the number of corpses increase. Flies multiplied, and amoebic dysentery broke out. The men of Company K, together with the rest of the 1st Marine Division, would live and fight in that hell for ten days.*

We dispersed our guns and dug gun pits as best we could in the mud. Snafu and I took compass readings and set aiming stakes based on the readings from our observer. As soon as we fired a couple of rounds of HE to register in my gun, it was obvious we had a bad problem with the base plate of our mortar being driven farther into the soft soil with the recoil of each shell. We reasoned the rain would soon stop, however, or if it didn't, a couple of pieces of ammo box under the base plate would hold it firm. What a mistake!

After digging in the gun, registering in on the aiming stakes, and preparing ammo for future use, I had my first opportunity to look around our position. It was the most ghastly corner of hell I had ever witnessed. As far as I could see, an area that previously had been a low grassy valley with a picturesque stream meandering through it was a muddy, repulsive, open sore on the land. The place was choked with the putrefaction of death, decay, and destruction. In a shallow defilade to our right, between my gun pit and the railroad, lay about twenty dead Marines, each on a stretcher and covered to his ankles with a poncho—a commonplace, albeit tragic, scene to every veteran. Those bodies had been placed there to await transport to the rear for burial. At least those dead were covered from the torrents of rain that had made them miserable in life and from the swarms of flies that sought to hasten their decay. But as I looked about, I saw that other Marine dead couldn't be tended properly. The whole area was pocked with shell craters and churned up by explosions. Every crater was half full of water, and many of them held a Marine corpse. The bodies lay pathetically just as they had been killed, half submerged in muck and water, rusting weapons still in hand. Swarms of big flies hovered about them.

"Why ain't them poor guys been covered with ponchos?" mumbled my foxhole buddy as he glanced grimly about with a distraught expression on his grizzled face. His answer came the moment he spoke. Japanese 75mm shells came whining and whistling into the area. We cowered in our hole as they crashed and thundered around us. The enemy gunners on the commanding Shuri Heights were registering their artillery and mortars on our positions. We realized quickly that anytime any of us moved out of our holes, the shelling began immediately. We had a terrible time getting our wounded evacuated through the shell fire and mud without the casualty- and stretcher-bearers getting hit. Thus it was perfectly clear why the Marine dead were left where they had fallen.

Everywhere lay Japanese corpses killed in the heavy fighting. Infantry equipment of every type, U.S. and Japanese, was scattered about. Helmets, rifles, BARs, packs, cartridge belts, canteens, shoes, ammo boxes, shell cases, machine-gun ammo belts, all were strewn around us up to and all over Half Moon.

The mud was knee deep in some places, probably deeper in others if one dared venture there. For several feet around every corpse, maggots crawled about in the muck and then were washed away by the runoff of the rain. There wasn't a tree or bush left. All was open country. Shells had torn up the turf so completely that ground cover was nonexistent. The rain poured down on us as evening approached. The scene was nothing but mud; shell fire; flooded craters with their silent, pathetic, rotting occupants; knocked-out tanks and amtracs; and discarded equipment—utter desolation.

The stench of death was overpowering. The only way I could bear the monstrous horror of it all was to look upward away from the earthly reality surrounding us, watch the leaden gray clouds go skudding over, and repeat over and over to myself that the situation was unreal—just a nightmare— that I would soon awake and find myself somewhere else. But the ever-present smell of death saturated my nostrils. It was there with every breath I took.

I existed from moment to moment, sometimes thinking death would have been preferable. We were in the depths of the abyss, the ultimate horror of war. During the fighting around the Umurbrogol Pocket on Peleliu, I had been depressed by the wastage of human lives. But in the mud and driving rain before Shuri, we were surrounded by maggots and decay. Men struggled and fought and bled in an environment so degrading I believed we had been flung into hell's own cesspool.

Not long after 3/5 took over Half Moon, several of us were on a work party, struggling through knee-deep mud to bring ammo from the rear up to the mortar positions. We passed near the company CP in the railroad bed.

"Hey, you guys, looka there; Stumpy's in bad shape!" said a Marine in an excited low voice. We all stopped and looked toward the CP. There was our CO, Stumpy Stanley, just outside the edge of the tarpaulin, trying to stand by himself. But he had to be supported by a man on each side. He looked haggard and weary and was shaking violently with malarial chills. He could barely hold up his head. The men supporting him seemed to be arguing with him. He was objecting as best he could. But it was a feeble effort, because he was so sick.

"Po' Stumpy got that goddamn bug so bad he can't hardly stand up. But looka there; he's all man, by God. He don't wanna be 'vacuated," said Snafu gravely.

"He's a damn good Joe," someone else said.

We thought highly of Stumpy and respected him greatly. He was a good skipper, and we had confidence in him. But malaria made him too ill to stay on his feet. The chilly rain, the emotional stress, and the physical exertion and strain of those days were enough to make a well man collapse. Obviously those who had malarial infections couldn't possibly keep going. So, for the second time in May, we lost our commanding officer. Stumpy was the last of our Peleliu officers, and his evacuation ended an era for me. He was the last tie to Capt. Andy Haldane. For me, Company K was never the same after that day.

As we feared, Shadow became the CO. It's best that I don't record what we said about that.

At daybreak the morning after we took over the line on Half Moon, George Sarrett and I went up onto the ridge to our observation post. Half Moon was shaped like a crescent, with the arms pointing southward. Our battalion line stretched along the crest of the ridge as it formed the base of the crescent. The arms extended outward beyond our front lines, and Japanese occupied caves in the reverse slopes of those arms, particularly the one on the left (east). They made our line a hot spot.

To our front, the ridge sloped down sharply from the crest then more gently all the way to a big road embankment approximately three hundred yards out and running parallel to our lines. A large culvert opened toward us through the embankment. The area to our front was well drained and as bare as the back of one's hand. It wasn't heavily cratered. Two shallow ditches about fifty yards apart ran across the area between the southern tips of the Half Moon. These ditches were closer to the road embankment than to our lines. The sloping area leading to the culvert resembled an amphitheater bordered by the base of the crescent (where we were) to the north, the arms of the crescent extending southward, and the high road embankment running east and west at the southern end. Our visibility within the amphitheater was perfect (except for the reverse slopes of the arms of the crescent).

Marines of 2/4 had warned us as they departed that the Japanese came out of the caves in the reverse slopes of the crescent's arms at night and generally raised hell. To combat that, our ships kept star shells aloft, and our 60mm mortars kept flares burning in the wet sky above the ridge all night every night we were there.

As the dawn light grew brighter, we could see the lay of the land through the drizzle and thin fog. So we registered the mortar section's three guns with an aiming stake on one of each of three important terrain features. We had one gun register in on the reverse slope of the left-hand extension of the Half Moon. A second mortar we registered on the reverse slope of the road embankment. We registered the third gun to cover the area around the mouth of the culvert.

No sooner had we registered the guns than we got a reaction. Big 90mm Japanese mortar shells began crashing along the crest of the ridge. They came so thick and so fast we knew an entire enemy mortar section was firing on us, not an isolated gun. They were zeroed in on the ridge and traversed along the crest from my left to the far right end of the company's line. It was an awful pounding. Each big shell fluttered and swished down and went off with a flash and an ear-splitting crash. Shrapnel growled through the air, and several men were wounded badly. Each shell threw stinking mud around when it exploded. The wounded were moved down behind the ridge with great difficulty because of the slippery, muddy slopes. A corpsman gave them aid, and they were carried to the rear—shocked, torn, and bleeding.

An uneasy quiet then settled along the line. Suddenly, someone yelled, "There goes one." A single Japanese soldier dashed out of the blackness of the culvert. He carried his bayoneted rifle and wore a full pack. He ran into the open, turned, and headed for shelter behind the tip of the southern end of the crescent arm on our left front. It looked as though he had about a thirty-yard dash to make. Several of our riflemen and BARmen opened up, and the soldier was bowled over by their bullets before he reached the shelter of the ridge. Our men cheered and yelled when he went down.

As the day wore on, more Japanese ran out of the culvert in ones and twos and dashed for the shelter of the same ridge extension. It was obvious they wanted to concentrate on the reverse slope there from where they could launch counterattacks, raids, and infiltration attempts on our front line. Obviously, it was to our best interest to stop them as quickly as possible. Any enemy soldier who made it in behind that slope might become one's unwelcome foxhole companion some night.

When the Japanese ran out of the culvert, our men fired on them and nearly always knocked them down. The riflemen, BARmen, and machine gunners looked on it as fine target practice, because we received no return small-arms fire, and the Japanese mortars were quiet.

I kept busy with the field glasses, observing, adjusting range, and calling fire orders onto the slope and the road embankment. I had the Tommy with me, but it wasn't as steady and accurate at the two- to three-hundred-yard range as an M1 Garand rifle. We had an M1 and an ammo belt in our OP, though, and I wanted to throw down that phone and the field glasses and grab up that M1 every time an enemy popped into view. As long as our mortar section was firing a mission, I had no choice but to continue observing.

The Japanese kept up their efforts to move behind the slope. Some made it, because our men missed them. Our 60mm mortar shells crashed away steadily on the target areas. We could see Japanese emerge from the culvert and be killed by our shells.

The longer this action continued without our receiving any return fire, the more relaxed my buddies became. The situation began to take on certain aspects of a rifle range, or more likely, an old-fashioned turkey shoot. My buddies started making bets about who had hit which Japanese. Lively arguments developed, but with rifles, BARs and several machine guns firing simultaneously, no one could tell for sure who hit which enemy soldier.

The men yelled and joked more and more in one of their few releases from weeks of tension under the pounding of heavy weapons. So they began to get careless and to miss some of the Japanese scurrying for the slope. Shadow saw this. He ran up and down our firing line cursing and yelling at everybody. Then the men settled down and took more careful aim. Finally the enemy stopped coming, and I received orders to call "cease firing" to our mortars. We sat and waited.

During the lull, I moved over into the machine-gun emplacement next to our mortar OP to visit with the gunner. It contained a Browning .30 caliber water-cooled heavy machine gun manned by a gunner who had joined Company K as a replacement after Peleliu. On Pavuvu, he and I had become good friends. We called him "Kathy" after a chorus girl he knew in California. He was married and very much in love with his wife, so he bore a heavy burden of guilt because he had had an affair with Kathy on his way overseas and couldn't get her out of his mind.

As we sat alone in the machine-gun pit, he asked me whether I wanted to see a picture of Kathy. I said yes. He carefully and secretively picked up his rain-soaked combat pack and took out a waterproof plastic map holder. Folding back the canvas cover, he said, "Here she is."

My eyes nearly popped out of my head. The eight- by ten-inch photo was a full-length portrait of one of the most beautiful girls I ever saw. She was dressed, or undressed, in a scanty costume which exposed a good portion of her impressive physical endowments.

I gasped audibly, and "Kathy" said, "Isn't she a beauty?"

"She really is!" I told him, and added, "You've got a problem on your hands with a girl like that chorus girl and a wife you love." I kidded him about the possible danger of getting the letters to his wife and his girl crossed up and in the wrong envelopes. He just laughed and shook his head as he looked at the photo of the beautiful girl.

The scene was so unreal I could barely believe it: two tired, frightened young men sitting in a hole beside a machine gun in the rain on a ridge, surrounded with mud—nothing but stinking mud, with so much decaying human flesh buried or half buried in it that there were big patches of wriggling fat maggots marking the spots where Japanese corpses lay—looking at the picture of a beautiful seminude girl. She was a pearl in a mudhole.

Viewing that picture made me realize with a shock that I had gradually come to doubt that there really was a place in the world where there were no explosions and people weren't bleeding, suffering, dying, or rotting in the mud. I felt a sense of desperation that my mind was being affected by what we were experiencing. Men cracked up frequently in such places as that. I had seen it happen many times by then. In World War I they had called it shell shock or, more technically, *neuresthenia*. In World War II the term used was combat fatigue.

Strange that such a picture provoked such thoughts, but I vividly recall grimly making a pledge to myself. The Japanese might kill or wound me, but they wouldn't make me crack up. A peaceful civilian back home who sat around worrying about losing his mind probably didn't have much to occupy him, but in our situation there was plenty of reason for the strongest-willed individuals to crack up.

My secret resolve helped me through the long days and nights we remained in the worst of the abyss. But there were times at night during that period when I felt I was slipping. More than once my imagination ran wild during the brief periods of darkness when the flares and star shells burned out.

"There comes another one," somebody yelled. "Kathy" quickly stowed his picture in his pack, spun around, gripped the machine-gun handle in his left hand, poised his trigger finger, and grabbed the aiming knob with his right hand. His assistant gunner appeared from out of nowhere and jumped to his post to feed the ammo belt into the gun. I started back to the OP hole but saw that George had phone in hand, and the mortars were still "secured." So I grabbed up an M1 rifle "Kathy" had in the machine-gun emplacement.

I saw enemy soldiers rushing out of the culvert. Our line started firing as I counted the tenth Japanese to emerge. Those incredibly brave soldiers formed a skirmish line abreast, with a few yards between each other, and started trotting silently toward us across open ground about three hundred yards away. Their effort was admirable but so hopeless. They had no supporting fire of any kind to pin us down or even to make us cautious. They looked as though they were on maneuvers. They had no chance of getting close to us.

I stood up beside the machine gun, took aim, and started squeezing off shots. The Japanese held their rifles at port arms and didn't even fire at us. Everybody along our line was yelling and firing. The enemy soldiers wore full battle gear with packs, which meant they had rations and extra ammo, so this might be the beginning of a counterattack of some size.

Within seconds, eight of the ten enemy soldiers pitched forward, spun around, or slumped to the deck, dead where they fell. The remaining two must have realized the futility of it all, because they turned around and started back toward the culvert. Most of us slackened our fire and just watched. Several men kept firing at the two retreating enemy soldiers but missed, and it looked as though they might get away. Finally one Japanese fell forward near one of the shallow ditches. The surviving soldier kept going.

Just as "Kathy" got his machine-gun sights zeroed in on him, the order "cease firing" came along the line. But the machine gun was making so much noise we didn't hear the order. "Kathy" had his ammo belts loaded so that about every fifth cartridge was a tracer. He squeezed off a long burst of about eight shots. The bullets struck the fleeing Japanese soldier in the middle of his pack and tore into him between his shoulders.

I was standing directly behind "Kathy," looking along his machine-gun barrel. The tracers must have struck the man's vertebrae or other bones and been deflected, because I clearly saw one tracer flash up into the air out of the soldier's right shoulder and another tracer come out of the top of his left shoulder. The Japanese dropped his rifle as the slugs knocked him face down into the mud. He didn't move.

"I got him; I got the bastard," Kathy yelled, jumping around slapping me on the back, and shaking hands with his assistant gunner. He had reason to be proud. He had made a good shot.

The enemy soldier who fell near the ditch began crawling and flopped into it. Some of the men started firing at him again. The bullets kicked up mud all around the soldier as he slithered desperately along in the shallow ditch which didn't quite hide him. Machine-gun tracers ricocheted off the ground like vicious red arrows as the Japanese struggled along the shallow ditch.

Then, on one of the rare occasions I ever saw compassion expressed for the Japanese by a Marine who had to fight them, one of our men yelled, "Knock it off, you guys. The poor bastard's already hit and ain't got a snowball's chance in hell."

Someone else yelled angrily, "You stupid jerk; he's a goddamn Nip ain't he? You gone Asiatic or something?"

The firing continued, and bullets hit the mark. The wounded Japanese subsided into the muddy little ditch. He and his comrades had done their best. "They died gloriously on the field of honor for the emperor," is what their families would be told. In reality, their lives were wasted on a muddy, stinking slope for no good reason.

Our men were in high spirits over the affair, especially after being pounded for so long. But Shadow was yelling, "Cease firing, you dumb bastards." He came slipping and sliding along the line, cursing and stopping at intervals to pour out storms of invective on some smiling, muddy Marine. He carried his helmet in his left hand and periodically took off his cap and flung it down into the mud until it was caked. Each man looked glum and sat or stood motionless until Shadow had finished insulting him and moved on.

As Shadow passed the machine-gun pit, he stopped and screamed at "Kathy," who was still jumping around in jubilation over his kill. "Knock it off, you goddamn fool!" Then he glared at me and said, "You're supposed to be observing for the mortars; put that goddamn rifle down, you bastard."

I wasn't impetuous, but, had I thought I could get away with it, I would certainly have clubbed him over the head with that M1 rifle.

I didn't, but Shadow's asinine conduct and comment did make me rash enough to say, "The guns are secured, sir. We were all sent out here to kill Nips, weren't we? So what difference does it make what weapon we use when we get the chance?"

His menacing expression turned into surprise and then doubt. With a quizzical look on his face, he cocked his head to one side as he pondered my remark, while I stood silently with the realization that I should have kept my mouth shut. The fine sergeant accompanying Shadow half glared and half smiled at me. Suddenly, without another glance, Shadow strode off along the ridge crest, cursing and yelling at the Marines in each foxhole as he passed them. I resolved to keep my mouth shut in the future.

As daylight waned, I looked out to our front through the drizzling rain falling through the still, foul air. A wisp of smoke rose straight up from the pack of the Japanese soldier "Kathy" had shot. The tracers had set something on fire. The thin finger of smoke rose high and then spread out abruptly to form a disc that appeared to rest on the column. So delicate and unreal, the smoke stood in the stagnant, fetid air like a marker over the corpse. Everything out there was motionless, only death and desolation among the enemy bodies.

George and I got orders to return to our mortar gun pits. Someone else would man the OP for the night. Getting back to the mortar emplacements from the company's front line was a major effort and an extremely dangerous one. From the moment we stepped to the rear of the crest of the ridge to descend the muddy slope, it was like trying to walk down a greased slide.

A large and unknown number of Japanese all over the ridge had been killed during the early counterattacks. They had been covered with soil as soon as possible. And Japanese were still being killed out front. Infiltrators also were being killed all along the ridge at night. Our men could only spade mud over them.

The situation was bad enough, but when enemy artillery shells exploded in the area, the eruptions of soil and mud uncovered previously buried Japanese dead and scattered chunks of corpses. Like the area around our gun pits, the ridge was a stinking compost pile.

If a Marine slipped and slid down the back slope of the muddy ridge, he was apt to reach the bottom vomiting. I saw more than one man lose his footing and slip and slide all the way to the bottom only to stand up horror-stricken as he watched in disbelief while fat maggots tumbled out of his muddy dungaree pockets, cartridge belt, legging lacings, and the like. Then he and a buddy would shake or scrape them away with a piece of ammo box or a knife blade.

We didn't talk about such things. They were too horrible and obscene even for hardened veterans. The conditions taxed the toughest I knew almost to the point of screaming. Nor do authors normally write about such vileness; unless they have seen it with their own eyes, it is too preposterous to think that men could actually live and fight for days and nights on end under such terrible conditions and not be driven insane. But I saw much of it there on Okinawa and to me the war was insanity.

# CHAPTER THIRTEEN

# BREAKTHROUGH

The rains became so heavy that at times we could barely see our buddies in the neighboring foxhole. We had to bail out our gun pit and foxholes during and after each downpour or they filled with water.

Snafu and I dug a deep foxhole close to the gun pit and placed pieces of wooden ammo crates across braces set on the muddy clay at the bottom. At one end of this foxhole, beyond the extension of the boards, we dug a sump. As the surface water poured into our foxhole and down under the boards, we bailed out the sump with a C ration can for a day or two. But the soil became so saturated by continued downpours that water poured in through the four sides of the foxhole as though it were a colander. We then had to use a discarded helmet to bail out the sump, because the ration can couldn't take out water fast enough to keep up with that pouring in.

The board "floor" kept us out of the water and mud, provided we worked diligently enough at the bailing detail. Necessity being the mother of invention, we had "reinvented" the equivalent of duckboards commonly used in flooded World War I trenches. The duckboards pictured and described in 1914–18 in Flanders were, of course, often prefabricated in long sections and then placed in the trenches by infantrymen. But the small board floor we placed in our foxhole served the same function.

Continued firing finally caused my mortar's base plate to drive the pieces of wood supporting it deep into the mud in the bottom of the gun pit. We couldn't sight the gun properly. We tugged and pulled the gun up out of the mud, then it was a choice of emplacing it either on some firmer base in the gun pit or on the surface outside. The latter prospect would have meant sure death from the enemy shelling, so we had to come up with something better in a hurry.

Somebody got the bright idea of building a "footing" on which to rest the base plate. So in the bottom of the gun pit, we dug out a deep square hole larger than the base plate and lined it with boards. We next placed several helmets full of coral gravel we found in the side of the railroad bed into the footing. We set the mortar's base plate on the firm coral footing, resighted the gun, and had no more trouble with recoil driving the base plate into the mud. I suppose the other two squads in our mortar section fixed their guns' base plates in the same manner.

The Japanese infantry kept up their activity to our front and tried to infiltrate our lines every night, sometimes with success. Snafu made good about then on the threat he had made to the CP on Peleliu about any enemy headed toward the Company K CP. On Peleliu one night after we came off the lines Snafu shot two Japanese with his Thompson. He had killed one and fatally wounded the other. A sergeant made Snafu bury the dead soldier. Snafu objected strenuously because he said, and rightly so, if he hadn't shot the Japanese they would have kept on going right into the company CP. Sarge said maybe so, but the corpse had to be buried, and since Snafu had shot it, he must bury it. Snafu promised he would never shoot another enemy soldier headed for the CP.

One day as dawn broke with a thin fog and a pelting rain, Snafu woke me out of the nearest thing to sleep that could be attained in that miserable place with, "Halt who goes there? What's the password?"

Jolted out of my fatigue stupor, I saw Snafu's face silhouetted against the gray sky. Rain poured off his helmet, and drops of moisture on the end of each whisker of the thick stubbly beard on his jutting square jaw caught the dim light like glass beads. I snatched the Tommy up off my lap as he raised his .45 pistol and aimed it toward two dim figures striding along about twenty yards away. Visibility was so poor in the dim light, mist, and rain that I could tell little about the shadowy figures other than they wore U.S. helmets. At the sound of Snafu's challenge, the two men speeded up instead of halting and identifying themselves.

"Halt or I'll fire!" he yelled.

The two took off for the railroad bed as fast as they could on the slippery ground. Snafu fired several shots with his .45 but missed. Shortly we heard a couple of American grenades explode in the railroad bed. Then a buddy yelled that the Japanese had been killed by his grenades. Daylight came rapidly, so we went over to the railroad embankment to ask what had happened.

When Snafu and I got to the foxhole by the railroad embankment, we found two Marine snipers grinning and laughing. The grenade explosions had scared awake the Marines in the dryness under the tarpaulin in the company CP and had chased them out into the rain. They were drifting back to the shelter as we arrived. We waved, but got only glares in return.

We took a look at the dead enemy before returning to our foxhole. They had been wearing Marine helmets but otherwise were dressed in Japanese uniforms. A grenade had exploded in the face of one. There was no face and little head remaining. The other wasn't as badly mangled.

Snafu and I returned to our hole and got settled just in time to see Hank come stalking along from the CP. He was stopping at every foxhole along the way to find out who had been so negligent as to let the Japanese soldiers get past them and almost to the CP. Hank arrived at our foxhole and asked us why we hadn't seen the two soldiers pass if one of us was on watch as we were supposed to be.

Snafu spoke up immediately and said, "Hell, I saw 'em go right by here, but I reckoned they was headed for the company CP." (He didn't mention his challenging the Japanese or firing at them.)

Hank looked astonished and said, "What do you mean, Snafu?"

Snafu swelled with indignation and answered, "You remember when they made me bury that Nip I shot on Peleliu when them two was headed for the CP?"

"Yeah, so what?" answered Hank in a low, menacing voice.

"Well, I told them then if they made me bury 'im, then by God, next time I seen a Nip headin' for the CP I wasn't gonna' stop 'im!"

I groaned in a low voice, "Oooh, shut up, Snafu."

One didn't talk like that to a senior NCO and get away with it. Hank was a very formidable person and merited the tremendous respect we felt for him, but woe be unto the Marine who didn't do a task properly and incurred his wrath. Hank treated us with respect and compassion—if we followed orders and did our best. I had no desire to see what he would do to someone who didn't, but I thought I was about to. So I turned my head and half closed my eyes, as did all the awestruck men in the foxholes within earshot who had been watching Snafu and Hank.

Nothing happened. I glanced at Snafu and Hank as they stood there glaring at each other, a bantam rooster glaring up at a mighty eagle.

Finally Hank said, "You'd better not let that happen again!" He turned and stalked back to the CP.

Snafu mumbled and grumbled. The rest of us sighed with relief. I fully expected Hank at least to order Snafu to bury the two Japanese down there on the railroad, and then Snafu, as my corporal, would order me onto the burial detail as had happened on Peleliu. But he didn't, and someone else spaded mud over the two corpses.

Much later, when Hank was leaving Company K for home after an outstanding record in three campaigns, I asked him what he had thought about that incident. He just looked at me and grinned, but wouldn't say anything about it. His grin revealed, however, that he respected Snafu and knew he wasn't lax in any way, and probably that he himself had been ordered by some officer to look into the affair.

Because of the surroundings, our casualties during the stalemate on Half Moon were some of the most pathetic I ever had seen. Certainly a beautiful landscape didn't make a wound less painful or a death less tragic. But our situation before Shuri was the most awful place conceivable for a man to be hurt or to die.

Most of the wounds resulted from enemy shell fragments, but it seemed to me we had more than the usual number of cases of blast concussion from exploding shells. That was understandable because of the frequent heavy shellings we were subjected to. All the casualties were muddy and soaking wet like the rest of us. That seemed to accentuate the bloody battle dressings on their wounds and their dull expressions of shock and pain which made the horror and hopelessness of it all more vivid as we struggled through the chilly driving rain and deep mud to evacuate them.

Some of the concussion cases could walk and were helped and led (some seemed to have no sure sense of direction) to the rear like men walking in their sleep. Some wore wild-eyed expressions of shock and fear. Others whom I knew well, though could barely recognize, wore expressions of idiots or simpletons knocked too witless to be afraid anymore. The blast of a shell had literally jolted them into a different state of awareness from the rest of us. Some of those who didn't return probably never recovered but were doomed to remain in mental limbo and spend their futures in a veteran's hospital as "living dead."

The combat fatigue cases were distressing. They ranged in their reactions from a state of dull detachment seemingly unaware of their surroundings, to quiet sobbing, or all the way to wild screaming and shouting. Stress was the essential factor we had to cope with in combat, under small-arms fire, and in warding off infiltrators and raiders during sleepless, rainy nights for prolonged periods; but being shelled so frequently during the prolonged Shuri stalemate seemed to increase the strain beyond that which many otherwise stable and hardened Marines could endure without mental or physical collapse. From my experience, of all the hardships and hazards the troops had to suffer, prolonged shell fire was more apt to break a man psychologically than anything else.

In addition to the wounded, quite a number of men were evacuated and described in the muster rolls simply as "sick." Some of them suffered attacks of malaria. Others had fever, respiratory problems, or were just exhausted and seemed to have succumbed to the rigors of exposure and the chilly rains. There were numerous cases of pneumonia. Many men weren't evacuated, although they suffered serious ailments resulting from the cold rains and being soaking wet for more than a week.

Most of us had serious trouble with our feet. An infantryman with sore feet was in miserable shape under the best of living conditions. During a period of about fourteen or fifteen days, as near as I can calculate the time (from 21 May to 5 June), my feet and those of my buddies were soaking wet, and our boondockers were caked with sticky mud. Being up on the line and frequently shelled prevented a man from taking off his boondockers to put on a pair of dry socks. And even if he had dry socks, there was no way to clean and dry the leather boondockers. Most of us removed our mud-caked canvas leggings and tucked our trouser cuffs into our sock tops, but it didn't help our feet much. Consequently most men's feet were in bad condition.

My feet were sore, and it hurt to walk or run. The insides of my boondockers gave me the sensation of being slimy when I wiggled my toes to try to warm my feet with increased circulation. The repulsive sensation of slippery, slimy feet grew worse each day. My sore feet slid back and forth inside my soaked boondockers when I walked or ran. Fortunately they never became infected, a miracle in itself.

Sore feet caused by prolonged exposure to mud and water was called immersion foot, I learned later. In World War I they called the same condition trench foot. To me it was an unforgettable sensation of extreme personal filth and painful discomfort. It was the kind of experience that would make a man sincerely grateful for the rest of his life for clean, dry socks. As simple a condition as dry socks seemed a luxury.

The almost constant rain also caused the skin on my fingers to develop a strange shrunken and wrinkled appearance. My nails softened. Sores developed on the knuckles and backs of both hands. These grew a little larger each day and hurt whenever I moved my fingers. I was always knocking the scabs off against ammo boxes and the like. Similar sores had tormented combat troops in the South Pacific campaigns and were called jungle rot or jungle sores.*

Our own mail came up to us in canvas bags, usually with the ammo and rations. It was of tremendous value in boosting sagging morale. On several occasions I actually had to bend over my letters and read as rapidly as possible to shield them from the torrents of rain before the ink was smeared across the soggy paper and the writing became illegible.

Most of us received letters from family and civilian friends. But occasionally we received letters from old Company K buddies who had returned to the States. Their early letters expressed relief over being back with family or with "wine, women, and song." But later the letters often became disturbingly bitter and filled with disillusionment. Some expressed a desire to return if they could get back into the old battalion. Considering the dangers and hardships those men had been through before they were sent home, and considering our situation in front of Shuri, the attitudes of our buddies who had returned Stateside puzzled us.

They expressed themselves in various ways, but the gist of their disillusionment was a feeling of alienation from everyone but their old comrades. Although there was gasoline and meat rationing back in the States, life was safe and easy. Plenty of people were ready to buy a Marine combat veteran wearing campaign ribbons and battle stars a drink or a beer anytime. But all the good life and luxury didn't seem to take the place of old friendships forged in combat.

There was talk of war profiteers and able-bodied men who got easy duty at the expense of others. Some letters said simply that folks back in the States "just don't understand what the hell it's all about, because they have had it so easy." I heard more than one buddy express the opinion, as we sat in the mud, that civilians would "understand" if the Japanese or the Germans bombed an American city. Some men thought that would have been a good idea *if* no American civilians got killed, just scared. But nobody wanted it to be *his* hometown.

It was hard to believe that some of our old friends who had wanted so much to return home actually were writing us that they thought of volunteering again for overseas duty. (Some actually did.) They had had enough of war, but they had greater difficulty adjusting to civilians or to comfort-

*After the campaign on Okinawa ended, a battalion surgeon told me the sores on my hands were probably caused by malnutrition, the filth we lived in, or both. The festering sores that developed on my hands in late May didn't heal until nearly five months after we came out of combat.

able Stateside military posts. We were unable to understand their attitudes until we ourselves returned home and tried to comprehend people who griped because America wasn't perfect, or their coffee wasn't hot enough, or they had to stand in line and wait for a train or bus.

Our buddies who had gone back had been greeted enthusiastically—as those of us who survived were received later on. But the folks back home didn't, and in retrospect couldn't have been expected to, understand what we had experienced, what in our minds seemed to set us apart forever from anyone who hadn't been in combat. We didn't want to indulge in self-pity. We just wished that people back home could understand how lucky they were and stop complaining about trivial inconveniences.

Siegfried Sassoon, an English combat infantry officer and poet in World War I, experienced the same feeling when he returned home. He summed it up in the following verse:

> You smug-faced crowds with kindling eye
> Who cheer when soldier lads march by,
> Sneak home and pray you'll never know
> The hell where youth and laughter go.*

The poet might just as well have been referring to Peleliu or to the mudfields in front of Shuri as to France in World War I.

Some of the younger replacements who came to us then had trouble adjusting, and not just to the shelling. That was enough to shake up the strongest veteran, but they were utterly dismayed by our horrible surroundings. Numerous Marine replacements for combat units on Okinawa never had their names added to their units' muster rolls, because they got hit before notice of their transfer from their replacement draft to the combat unit ever reached Headquarters, U.S. Marine Corps. So they were listed on the casualty rolls as members of various replacement drafts.

It was also common throughout the campaign for replacements to get hit before we even knew their names. They came up confused, frightened, and hopeful, got wounded or killed, and went right back to the rear on the route by which they had come, shocked, bleeding, or stiff. They were forlorn figures coming up to the meat grinder and going right back out of it like homeless waifs, unknown and faceless to us, like unread books on a shelf. They never "belonged" to the company or made any friends before they got hit.

---

*Sassoon, Siegfried, "Suicide in Trenches" in *Collected Poems,* Viking Press, N.Y. 1949.

Of course, those replacements who got hit right away with the "million-dollar wound" were actually fortunate.*

Our food usually consisted of a cold can of C rations and, rarely, a canteen cup of hot coffee. When we could brew it up, it was a treat. It was difficult to warm anything with our little heat tablets because of the almost constant rain. Sometimes I had to hunch over and shield a can of C-ration stew from the rain, because the can would fill up with rainwater as fast as I spooned the cold stew into my mouth.

We ate only because hunger forced us to do so. No other stimulus could have forced me to eat when my nostrils were so saturated with the odor of decay that I frequently felt sick. I ate little during that period, but drank hot coffee or bouillon at every opportunity.

The constant rain caused our weapons to rust. Most of us lined the holsters for our .45 automatic pistols with the green plastic covers we were issued. These came in long sleevelike pieces and could be placed over carbines, rifles, and Tommy guns. We kept a plastic hood draped over our mortar when it wasn't in use. This plastic cover was issued to be placed over ourselves while crouching down to avoid being sprayed with mustard gas, should that weapon have been used by the Japanese. We kept our weapons heavily oiled and actually had little trouble with them considering the battlefield conditions.

Field sanitation was nonexistent because of the shelling and the mud. Each man simply used a grenade canister or ammo carton and threw his own waste out into the already foul mud around his foxhole.

By day the battlefield was a horrible scene, but by night it became the most terrible of nightmares. Star shells and flares illuminated the area throughout the nights but were interspersed with moments of chilling, frightening blackness.

Sleep was almost impossible in the mud and cold rain, but sometimes I wrapped my wet poncho around me and dozed off for brief periods while my foxhole mate was on watch and bailing out the hole. One usually had to attempt sleep while sitting or crouching in the foxhole.

As usual, we rarely ventured out of our foxholes at night unless to care for wounded or to get ammunition. When a flare or star shell lighted the area, everyone froze just as he was, then moved during the brief periods of darkness. When the area lighted up with that eerie greenish light, the big

---

*K/3/5 landed at full strength of 235 officers and men on 1 April 1945. The company joined 250 replacements during the campaign for a total of 485 serving. Of the fifty men left at the end of the campaign, only twenty-six had made the landing.

rain drops sparkled like silver shafts as they slanted downward. During a strong wind they looked as though they were being driven along almost horizontal to the deck. The light reflected off the dirty water in the craters and off the helmets and weapons of the living and the dead.

I catalogued in my mind the position of every feature on the surrounding terrain. There was no vegetation, so my list consisted of mounds and dips in the terrain, foxholes of my comrades, craters, corpses, and knocked-out tanks and amtracs. We had to know where everyone, living and dead, was located. If one of us fired at an enemy infiltrating or on a raid, he needed to know where his comrades were so as not to hit them. The position and posture of every corpse was important, because infiltrating Japanese also would freeze when illuminating shells lit up. So they might go unnoticed among the dead.

The longer we stayed in the area, the more unending the nights seemed to become. I reached the state where I would awake abruptly from my semi-sleep, and if the area was lit up, note with confidence my buddy scanning the terrain for any hostile sign. I would glance about, particularly behind us, for trouble. Finally, before we left the area, I frequently jerked myself up into a state in which I was semiawake during periods between star shells.

I imagined Marine dead had risen up and were moving silently about the area. I suppose these were nightmares, and I must have been more asleep than awake, or just dumbfounded by fatigue. Possibly they were hallucinations, but they were strange and horrible. The pattern was always the same. The dead got up slowly out of their waterlogged craters or off the mud and, with stooped shoulders and dragging feet, wandered around aimlessly, their lips moving as though trying to tell me something. I struggled to hear what they were saying. They seemed agonized by pain and despair. I felt they were asking me for help. The most horrible thing was that I felt unable to aid them.

At that point I invariably became wide awake and felt sick and half-crazed by the horror of my dream. I would gaze out intently to see if the silent figures were still there, but saw nothing. When a flare lit up, all was stillness and desolation, each corpse in its usual place.

Among the craters off the ridge to the west was a scattering of Marine corpses. Just beyond the right edge of the end foxhole, the ridge fell away steeply to the flat, muddy ground.* Next to the base of the ridge, almost directly below me, was a partially flooded crater about three feet in diameter

---

*The flat, muddy, cratered landscape to the west of Half Moon Hill was a no-man's-land to the railroad and beyond to the Horse Shoe and Sugar Loaf Hill, where the left flank of the 6th Marine Division was located. At no time did I see any Americans in that low, flooded ground

and probably three feet deep. In this crater was the body of a Marine whose grisly visage has remained disturbingly clear in my memory. If I close my eyes, he is as vivid as though I had seen him only yesterday.

The pathetic figure sat with his back toward the enemy and leaned against the south edge of the crater. His head was cocked, and his helmet rested against the side of the crater so that his face, or what remained of it, looked straight up at me. His knees were flexed and spread apart. Across his thighs, still clutched in his skeletal hands, was his rusting BAR. Canvas leggings were laced neatly along the sides of his calves and over his boondockers. His ankles were covered with muddy water, but the toes of his boondockers were visible above the surface. His dungarees, helmet, cover, and 782 gear appeared new. They were neither mud-spattered nor faded.

I was confident that he had been a new replacement. Every aspect of that big man looked much like a Marine "taking ten" on maneuvers before the order to move out again. He apparently had been killed early in the attacks against the Half Moon, before the rains began. Beneath his helmet brim I could see the visor of a green cotton fatigue cap. Under that cap were the most ghastly skeletal remains I had ever seen—and I had already seen too many.

Every time I looked over the edge of that foxhole down into that crater, that half-gone face leered up at me with a sardonic grin. It was as though he was mocking our pitiful efforts to hang on to life in the face of the constant violent death that had cut him down. Or maybe he was mocking the folly of the war itself: "I am the harvest of man's stupidity. I am the fruit of the holocaust. I prayed like you to survive, but look at me now. It is over for us who are dead, but you must struggle, and will carry the memories all your life. People back home will wonder why you can't forget."

During the day I sometimes watched big rain drops splashing into the crater around that corpse and remembered how as a child I had been fascinated by rain drops splashing around a large green frog as he sat in a ditch near home. My grandmother had told me that elves made little splashes like that, and they were called water babies. So I sat in my foxhole and watched the water babies splashing around the green-dungaree-clad corpse. What an

---

astride the railroad. Thus a gap of considerable size existed between the 1st and 6th Marine Divisions.

An officer told me that machine guns and strong points to the right rear covered the area. He said the low flat terrain was so vulnerable to Japanese fire from the heights of Shuri that extending the lines to meet on that flooded ground would have sentenced the men involved to sure death. At night star shells illuminated the area so that the enemy couldn't infiltrate across it.

unlikely combination. The war had turned the water babies into little ghouls that danced around the dead instead of little elves dancing around a peaceful bullfrog. A man had little to occupy his mind at Shuri—just sit in muddy misery and fear, tremble through the shellings, and let his imagination go where it would.

One of the very few humorous incidents I saw during those terrible days before Shuri occurred toward the end of the awful stalemate. Two Marines from the other mortar squad were dug in to the left of my gun pit. One morning at the first pale light of dawn I heard a commotion in their foxhole. I could hear a poncho being flung aside as someone began thrashing around. There were grunts and swearing. I strained my eyes through the steaming rain and brought the Tommy gun up to my shoulder. From all indications, one or more Japanese had slipped up on the weary occupants of the foxhole, and they were locked in a life and death struggle. But I could do nothing but wait and alert other men around us.

The commotion grew louder, and I could barely make out two dark figures struggling in the foxhole. I was utterly helpless to aid a buddy in distress, because I couldn't identify who was Marine and who was Japanese. None of us dared leave his own foxhole and approach the two. The enemy soldier must have already knifed one of the Marines and was grappling with the other, I thought.

The dark figures rose up. Standing toe to toe, they leaned into each other and exchanged blows with their fists. Everyone's eyes were fixed on the struggling figures but could see little in the semidarkness and pouring rain. The mumblings and swearing became louder and understandable, and we heard, "You dumb jerk; gimme that range card. It's mine." I recognized the voice of a man who had come into Company K before Okinawa.

"No it's not; it's mine. You betta gimme it. I don't take no crap from nobody." The latter was the familiar voice of Santos, a Peleliu veteran. We all started in surprise.

"Hey, you guys, what the hell's goin' on over there?" growled an NCO.

The two struggling figures recognized his voice and immediately stopped hitting each other.

"You two eightballs," the NCO said as he went over to them. "It woulda served ya right if we hada shot you both. We figured a Nip had got in your foxhole."

Each of the two battlers protested that the other was the cause of all the trouble. The light was good by then, and some of us went over to their foxhole to investigate.

"What's all the row about?" I asked.

"This, by God; nothin' but this!" snarled the NCO as he glared at the two sheepish occupants of the foxhole and handed me a range card.

I was puzzled why two Marines would squabble over a range card.* But when I looked at the card, I saw it was special and unique. Impressed on it in lipstick was the ruby red imprint of a woman's lips. The men had found the unique card in a canister while breaking out ammo for the guns the previous afternoon and had argued all night about who would keep it. Toward dawn they came to blows over it.

The NCO continued to chew them out, as I handed the card back to him and returned to my foxhole. We all got a good laugh out of the episode. I often wondered what that woman back in that ammunition factory in the States would have thought about the results of her efforts to add a little morale booster for us in a canister of mortar ammo.

During the last few days of May we received several small but vicious counterattacks from the Japanese soldiers who had been occupying the caves in the reverse slope of Half Moon's left-hand arm. One morning we got a message that a large number of enemy was massing behind the crescent. I was ordered to leave the OP and return to the gun pit in preparation for a big fire mission. I moved down the ridge and across the reeking, shell-pocked wasteland to the gun pits without mishap. Once there, we squared away the three 60mm mortars to fire on the reverse slope of the left crescent arm.

The firing pattern of the mortars was arranged to box in the Japanese and prevent their escape while our three guns shelled the area heavily in an attempt to wipe them out. Consequently, we had to fire rapid-fire, searching and traversing the target area. The ammo carriers were kept busy breaking out more HE shells, but I was so busy on my mortar I didn't have time to notice them. The tube (barrel) became intensely hot. We wrapped a dungaree jacket around the lower half of it, and one of the ammo carriers poured helmets full of water taken from a shell crater over the cloth to cool the steaming barrel, while we continued rapid-fire.†

*A five- by seven-inch range card came in each canister of 60mm mortar ammunition. It contained printed columns of numbers denoting range, sight setting, and number of powder increments to be attached to each mortar shell for a given range. Thus the cards were as common as ammo canisters.

†I've read accounts of "mortars glowing red" when firing rapidly for long periods. They sound dramatic and impressive. But from my experience I'm skeptical that a mortar can be fired safely and accurately when its barrel is glowing red. My experience was that if a barrel got

We fired I don't know how many hundreds of shells before the order came to cease firing. My ears rang. I was exhausted, and had a roaring headache. Beside each of the three gun pits was a huge stack of empty HE canisters and ammo crates from the large number of shells we had fired. We were anxious to know the results of our firing. But our observers couldn't see the target area, because it was on the reverse slope of the ridge.

A few days later when our regiment went forward in the attack, we didn't move through the target area, so we still didn't see the effects of the fire mission. But one Company K NCO who did see the area told us that he had counted more than two hundred enemy dead who apparently had been trapped and killed by our fire. I assume he was right, because after our barrage, the Japanese ceased activity along the ridge.

## Shuri

The rain began to slacken, and rumors spread that we would attack soon. We also heard that the main enemy force had withdrawn from the Shuri line. But the Japanese had left a strong rear guard to fight to the death. So we could expect no signs of weakness. The Japanese had been spotted retreating from Shuri under cover of the bad weather. Our naval guns, artillery, heavy mortars, and even a few airplanes had thrown a terrific bombardment into them. But withdrawal or not, Shuri wasn't going to fall easily. We anticipated a hard fight once the weather cleared.

On a quiet day or two before the 5th Marines moved out for the big push against Shuri, several Marines from the graves registration section came into our area to collect the dead. Those dead already on stretchers presented no problem, but the corpses rotting in shell craters and in the mud were another matter.

We sat on our helmets and gloomily watched the graves registration people trying to do their macabre duty. They each were equipped with large rubber gloves and a long pole with a stiff flap attached to the end (like some huge spatula). They would lay a poncho next to a corpse, then place the

---

very hot from rapid fire—so hot that the surrounding air had insufficient cooling effect—it was dangerous to drop a round down the tube. The one time I did, the heat ignited the increments, then the propellant cartridge ignited before the shell slid all the way down the barrel. Consequently, the shell wobbled out of the barrel and fell short after having slid down only about half its length.

Thus, to avoid short rounds, we either had to wait for the air to cool our barrel, fire at a slower rate, or, as in this fire mission, which was an emergency, cool the barrel with water.

poles under the body, and roll it over onto the poncho. It sometimes took several tries, and we winced when a corpse fell apart. The limbs or head had to be shoved onto the poncho like bits of garbage. We felt sympathy for the graves registration men. With the corpses being moved, the stench of rotting flesh became worse (if possible) than ever before.

Apparently the enemy had withdrawn guns and troops from Shuri to the extent that their shelling of our area had all but stopped. A miserable drizzling rain commenced again. Almost out on my feet with fatigue, I decided to take advantage of the quiet. I unfolded an unused stretcher, set it on some boards, lay down on my back, and covered my head and body with my poncho. It was the first time in two months—since leaving my canvas rack aboard ship on 1 April (D day)—that I had been able to lie down on anything but hard ground or mud. The canvas stretcher felt like a deluxe bed, and my poncho shielded all but my mud-caked boondockers and ankles from the rain. For the first time in about ten days I fell into a deep sleep.

How long I slept I don't know, but after a while I became aware of being lifted upward. At first I thought I was dreaming, but then I awoke fully and realized someone had picked up the stretcher. Throwing the poncho away from me, I sprang off the stretcher, spun around, and saw two clean, neatly shaven Marines looking at me in utter astonishment.

Several of my grimy buddies squatting on their muddy helmets nearby began to laugh. The two strangers were graves registration men. They had picked up the stretcher thinking I was just another poncho-covered corpse. It never occured to them that instead, I was just a weary Marine trying to catch a nap on a comfortable stretcher who had covered himself to keep off the rain. They grinned when they realized what had happened. I accused my buddies of telling the two men to pick up my stretcher, but they only laughed and asked why my nap had ended so abruptly. I was left with an eerie feeling from the incident, but my buddies enjoyed the joke thoroughly.

Dawn broke clearly without rain on 28 May, and we prepared to attack later in the morning. About 1015 we attacked southward against long-range mortar and machine-gun fire. We were elated that the opposition was so light and that the sun was shining. We actually advanced several hundred yards that day, quite an accomplishment in that sector.

Moving through the mud was still difficult, but we were all glad to get out of the stinking, half-flooded garbage pit around the Half Moon. That night we learned that we would continue the attack the next day by moving directly against the Shuri Ridge.

About midmorning on 29 May, 3/5 attacked Shuri with Company L in the lead and Companies K and I following closely. Earlier in the morning Company A, 1st Battalion, 5th Marines had attacked eastward into the

*Collecting supplies air-dropped on Shuri Ridge after mud halted land movement to the front. USMC photo.*

ruins of Shuri Castle and had raised the Confederate flag. When we learned that the flag of the Confederacy had been hoisted over the very heart and soul of Japanese resistance, all of us Southerners cheered loudly. The Yankees among us grumbled, and the Westerners didn't know what to do. Later we learned that the Stars and Stripes that had flown over Guadalcanal were raised over Shuri Castle, a fitting tribute to the men of the 1st Marine Division who had the honor of being first into the Japanese citadel.*

We all were filled with a sense of accomplishment that night as we dug in somewhere around Shuri Castle. We in the ranks were well aware of its strategic importance to the progress of the campaign.

*For the assault against Shuri Castle, 1/5 and 3/5 actually attacked eastward, turning approximately ninety degrees to the left of the southward-facing front. The 5th Marines thus crossed over into the zone of the 77th Infantry Division to reach Shuri Castle. The 77th Infantry Division was located north of Shuri, and a large number of Japanese were still entrenched between the army division and the 5th Marines as the latter moved eastward behind the Japanese who were blocking the 77th Division's advance.

Although the whole place was in ruins, we could still see that the area around Shuri Castle had been impressive and picturesque before its destruction by the incessant U.S. bombardment. Shuri Castle itself was a mess, and I couldn't tell much about its former appearance. It had been an ancient stone building surrounded by a moat and what appeared to have been terraces and gardens. As we picked our way through the rubble, I looked at the terraced stonework and shattered blackened tree stumps. I thought it must have been a pretty place once.

We dug in that night with the knowledge that even though we were at last in Shuri Castle, there were strongly entrenched Japanese still north of us in Wana Draw, east of us, and south of us. The lines were terribly confused to many of us in the ranks, and we assumed that the enemy could come at us from almost any direction. But they remained quiet during the night, except for the usual raiders.

We attacked again the next day, and got shelled badly. I was totally confused as to where we were for several days and can't clarify it now in my mind even after careful study of the notes and references at my disposal.

At dusk on one of those last few days of May, we moved onto a muddy, slippery ridge and were told to dig in along the crest. One of the three 60mm mortar squads was to set up its gun down behind the ridge, but my squad and the remaining squad were ordered to dig in along the ridge crest and to function as riflemen during the night. The weather turned bad again, and it started raining.

Mac, our mortar section leader, was nowhere to be seen. But Duke, who had been our section leader on Peleliu and who was by then leading the battalion's 81mm mortar platoon, came up to take charge. He ordered an NCO to have us dig two-man foxholes five yards apart along the crest of the ridge. My buddy went off down the ridge to draw ammo and chow while I prepared to dig.

The ridge was about a hundred feet high, quite steep, and we were on a narrow crest. Several discarded Japanese packs, helmets, and other gear lay scattered along the crest. From the looks of the muddy soil, the place had been shelled heavily for a long time. The ridge was a putrid place. Our artillery must have killed Japanese there earlier, because the air was foul with the odor of rotting flesh. It was just like being back at Half Moon Hill. Off toward our front, to the south, I had only a dim view through the gathering gloom and curtain of rain of the muddy valley below.

The men digging in on both sides of me cursed the stench and the mud. I began moving the heavy, sticky clay mud with my entrenching shovel to shape out the extent of the foxhole before digging deeper. Each shovelful had to be knocked off the spade, because it stuck like glue. I was thoroughly

*Rubble of the walls of Shuri Castle. Okinawa. USMC photo.*

exhausted and thought my strength wouldn't last from one sticky shovelful to the next.

Kneeling on the mud, I had dug the hole no more than six or eight inches deep when the odor of rotting flesh got worse. There was nothing to do but continue to dig, so I closed my mouth and inhaled with short shallow breaths. Another spadeful of soil out of the hole released a mass of wriggling maggots that came welling up as though those beneath were pushing them out. I cursed, and told the NCO as he came by what a mess I was digging into.

"You heard him, he said put the holes five yards apart."

In disgust, I drove the spade into the soil, scooped out the insects, and threw them down the front of the ridge. The next stroke of the spade unearthed buttons and scraps of cloth from a Japanese army jacket buried in the mud—and another mass of maggots. I kept on doggedly. With the next thrust, metal hit the breastbone of a rotting Japanese corpse. I gazed down in horror and disbelief as the metal scraped a clean track through the mud along the dirty whitish bone and cartilage with ribs attached. The shovel skidded into the rotting abdomen with a squishing sound. The odor nearly overwhelmed me as I rocked back on my heels.

I began choking and gagging as I yelled in desperation, "I can't dig in here! There's a dead Nip here!"

The NCO came over, looked down at my problem and at me, and growled, "You heard him; he said put the holes five yards apart."

"How the hell can I dig a foxhole through a dead Nip?" I protested.

Just then Duke came along the ridge and said, "What's the matter, Sledgehammer?"

I pointed to the partially exhumed corpse. Duke immediately told the NCO to have me dig in a little to the side away from the rotting remains. I thanked Duke and glared at the NCO. How I managed not to vomit during that vile experience I don't know. Perhaps my senses and nerves had been so dulled by constant foulness for so long that nothing could evoke any other response but to cry out and move back.

I soon had a proper foxhole dug to one side of the site of my first attempt. (A few spades full of mud thrown back into that excavation did little to reduce the horrid odor.) My buddy returned, and we began to square away our gear for the coming night. There was some small-arms fire to our left, but all was quiet around us. Duke was down at the foot of the ridge behind us with a map in his hand. He called us to come down for a critique and a briefing on the next day's attack.

Glad to leave the stinking foxhole, I got up and carefully started down the slippery ridge. My buddy rose, took one step down the ridge, slipped, and fell. He slid on his belly all the way to the bottom, like a turtle sliding off a log. I reached the bottom to see him stand erect with his arms partially extended and look down at his chest and belt with a mixed expression of horror, revulsion, and disbelief. He was, of course, muddy from the slide. But that was the least of it. White, fat maggots tumbled and rolled off his cartridge belt, pockets, and folds of his dungaree jacket and trousers. I picked up a stick and handed him another. Together we scraped the vile insect larvae off his reeking dungarees.

That Marine was a Gloucester veteran with whom I had often shared a hole on Peleliu and Okinawa. He was as tough and as hard as any man I ever knew. But that slide was almost too much for him. I thought he was going to scream or crack up. Having to wallow in war's putrefaction was almost more than the toughest of us could bear. He shook himself like a wet dog, however, cursed, and threw down the stick when we got him scraped free of maggots.

Duke's group of eight to ten Marines showed their sympathy for my buddy and their appreciation of the vileness of his accident. Muddy, bearded, and red-eyed with fatigue, Duke called our attention to the map, and that helped us focus on other subjects. He showed us where we were and told us some of the plans for the next day's attack, which was supposed to break completely through the Shuri line.

I was so revolted and sickened by what had just happened and so weary that I didn't remember much of what he told us. It is a pity in retrospect, because that briefing was the only time in my combat experience that an officer ever showed a group of privates a map of the battlefield and explained recent events and future attack plans. Usually an NCO simply relayed the word to us. We then followed orders as they were given, rarely knowing what was going on.

We never knew why Duke held the little critique that night, whether he was ordered to do so or not. I suspect he did it on his own. He realized we wanted to know and understand our role in the overall plan.

It was a historic time, and we were participating in events of key importance to the American effort on Okinawa. All eyes were on Shuri. My buddies and I were key participants at a critical juncture in one of the epic land battles of World War II, and we were having our tiny role in that battle explained. Duke asked if there were any questions. A few were asked, which he answered clearly. I maintained my condition of near stupefaction through it all. Then we slowly climbed back up the filthy ridge after he dismissed us.

That night the rain came down in torrents. It was without exaggeration the most terrific deluge I've ever seen. The wind blew fiercely, slashing the rain horizontally across the crest of the ridge and stinging our faces and hands. The star shells burst but gave little illumination because they were snatched away immediately by the unseen hand of the gale. Visibility was limited to about six feet. We couldn't see our buddies in their foxholes on either side of us. What a terrible night to grapple with Japanese infiltrators or a counterattack, I thought to myself all night long.

Considerable machine-gun fire, bursts of rifle fire, and grenade explosions erupted throughout the night a short way down the line to our left. But all was mercifully quiet, albeit tense, in our immediate area. Next morning I realized why we weren't molested by the enemy as the men to our left had been. For a considerable distance to our right and left, the ridge fell away almost perpendicularly to the valley below. The Japanese simply couldn't crawl up the slick surface.

*In the latter days of May while the Japanese held on to the center of their line around Shuri, the U.S. Army divisions to the east and the 6th Marine Division to the west (around Naha) finally made progress to the* south. *Their combined movements threatened to envelop the main Japanese defense forces in the center. Thus the enemy had to withdraw. By dawn on 30 May, most of the Japanese Thirty-Second Army had departed the Shuri line, leaving only rear guards to cover their retreat.*

*In the sixty-one days of fighting on Okinawa after D day, an estimated 62,548 Japanese soldiers had lost their lives and 465 had been captured. American dead numbered 5,309; 23,909 had been wounded; and 346 were missing in action. It wasn't over yet.*

# CHAPTER FOURTEEN

# BEYOND SHURI

We pushed past Shuri over some muddy hills in the army's zone of action and came across a group of about twenty Japanese prisoners. Each man was stripped except for a G-string. They stood barefooted in the mud alongside a trail winding along the slope of a barren hill. Several dirty and battle-weary army infantrymen guarded them. The captured enemy had been ordered by an interpreter (army lieutenant) to stand off the trail so Company K's column could pass.

We slipped and slid wearily toward the sound of firing up ahead. A grizzled rifleman in front of me and I had been cursing the mud and exchanging remarks about how glad we were to be past Shuri. Suddenly a Japanese prisoner stepped in front of my friend, blocking his way.

"Get outa the way, you crazy bastard," growled the Marine.

The soldier folded his arms calmly, raised his chin, and displayed a picture of arrogance. My buddy and I heated up fast. He pushed the Japanese backward and sent him sprawling into the mud. The enemy soldier sprang up quickly and assumed his former position.

"What's that crazy bastard doin'?" I yelled as I dropped my mortar ammo bag and reached for my .45 pistol.

My buddy unslung his rifle, grasped it by the stock with his left hand and by the pistol grip with his right hand. He planted his muddy feet firmly on the trail, flexed his knees, and growled, "Git outa my way, you bastard."

Other Marines behind us had halted when we did. Seeing what was happening, they started cursing the Japanese.

"What's the hold up? Move out," someone behind us yelled.

The army first lieutenant (he was actually wearing his silver bars on his collars), clean-shaven and spotless except for muddy combat boots, came along the column to ascertain the problem. Seeing my buddy's stance and realizing he might soon have one less prisoner, he said, "You can't mistreat these men. They are prisoners of war. According to the Geneva Code, POWs must be treated humanely." He looked desperate; the whole column of muddy, raggedy-ass Marines glared at and cursed the prisoners strung out alongside us on the trail.

"Screw the Geneva Code. If that slant-eyed sonofabitch don't move outa my way, I'll give him a vertical butt stroke in his big mouth and knock out every one of them goddamn buck teeth." My buddy slowly moved his rifle back and forth, and the enemy soldier's arrogant expression began to fade. The army lieutenant knew he had a bad problem on his hands, and he obviously didn't know how to solve it. (It was commonly said that Marines rarely took prisoners.) A couple of GI riflemen of the prisoner-guard detail stood by relaxed and grinned their endorsement of our sentiments. They obviously had been in the "meat grinder" long enough to have no more love for the Japanese than we did. The lieutenant obviously wasn't one of their officers but from some rear-echelon outfit.

Just then, one of our officers hurried up from the rear of the column. The army lieutenant was mighty relieved to see him and explained the situation. Our officers went over and quietly told my buddy to get back into ranks. He then told the army language officer that if he didn't get his prisoners out of the way, he (our officer) couldn't guarantee that some of them wouldn't get hurt. The army officer spoke kindly in Japanese to the POWs, and they all stepped farther back away from the trail, giving us plenty of room. The language officer acted and sounded more like an elementary school teacher giving little children directions than an officer giving orders to a bunch of tough Japanese soldiers.

During the whole episode, most of the Japanese never appeared afraid, merely chagrined or ashamed because they had acted disgracefully by surrendering. Perhaps the one who acted so arrogantly thought that one last act of defiance would soothe his conscience somewhat. Most Americans at the time couldn't comprehend the Japanese determination to win or fight to the death. To the Japanese, surrender was the ultimate disgrace.

We didn't feel that POWs should be mistreated or handled roughly, but neither did we feel that one should be allowed to block our path and get away with the act. My view that some language officers were often overly solitous about the comfort of prisoners and unduly courteous to them was shared by other infantrymen in the "meat grinder." We were too familiar with the sight of helpless wounded Americans lying flat on their backs on stretchers getting shot by Japanese snipers while we struggled to evacuate them.

After the breakthrough, we moved rapidly through areas where the opposition was light or absent. Our supply lines, communications, and casualty evacuation had a difficult time keeping up with us because the mud was still such a serious problem. Although the rain fell less frequently, it hadn't ceased.

As our column moved along the base of a road embankment on one occasion, a Marine walking along the road above us carrying a field telephone and a small roll of wire shouted down and asked for the identity of our unit. His buddy followed him along the road at a little distance carrying a roll of wire. These men were clean-shaven and neat. They looked suspiciously like rear-echelon people to us.

"Hey, what outfit you guys in?" shouted the first man up on the road. "K/3/5," I yelled.

His buddy behind him asked him, "What outfit did he say?"

"K/3/5, whatever the hell that means."

The effect on us was instant and dramatic. Men who had paid little attention to what seemed a routine inquiry looked angrily up at the man. I flushed with anger. My unit and I had been insulted. The mortarman next to me threw down his ammo bag and started up the embankment. "I'll show you what the hell it means, you rear-echelon sonofabitch! I'm gonna whip your ass."

I wasn't given to brawling. The Japanese provided me with all the excitement and fighting I wanted. But I lost my head completely. I threw down my ammo bag and started up the embankment. Other mortarmen started up, too.

"What's the dope?" I heard a man back along the column shout.

"That rear-echelon bastard up there cussed K Company," someone answered.

Immediately other Company K men started up the bank. The two men up on the road looked utterly bewildered as they saw bearded, muddy Marine infantrymen cursing, grounding their weapons, dropping their loads, and surging angrily up the embankment. One of our officers and a couple of NCOs saw what had happened and rushed up ahead of us.

The officer turned and yelled, "You people get back in ranks on the double! Move! Move!"

We stopped, each of us knowing that to disobey orders invited severe disciplinary action. The two men on the road had become frightened, and we saw them hustling along the road to the rear. They looked back anxiously several times to see whether they were being followed. We must have been an angry, menacing-looking bunch from their viewpoint. I suspect those two Marines knew the real meaning and essence of esprit de corps after that experience.

We picked up our weapons and gear and moved out again below the road only to halt shortly. The officers consulted their maps, held a critique, and decided that place was as good as any for the company to leave the muddy low ground, go up the bank, and take advantage of the coral-surfaced road (probably the east–west Naha–Yonabaru highway, a segment of which our regiment captured about then). We moved up onto the road, took off our gear, and settled onto the side of a large ridge with a wide grass- and tree-covered crest. Okinawan burial vaults and emplacements lay all along the slope of the ridge, but the Japanese hadn't left many men to defend it. However, they gave a good account of themselves before being wiped out.

Toward dusk, I was examining a Japanese 75mm dual-purpose gun which they had abandoned in perfect condition. Several of us had a lot of fun turning its cranks and wheels, which we didn't understand but which moved the big barrel up and down, right and left. Our play was interrupted by the shriek of several enemy artillery shells that exploded up on the ridge crest near a group of Company K men.

"Corpsman!"

We raced up onto the ridge, hoping no more shells came in but wondering who was hit and knowing we might be needed to help with the casualties. We could see the smoke from the shells and the Marines scurrying around to aid the casualties and to disperse.

In the gathering twilight, I ran up to a little knot of Marines bending over a casualty. To my dismay, the wounded Marine was good-natured, cigar-chewing Joe Lambert, a demolitions expert I had known so long. I knelt beside him and was distressed to see that he had multiple wounds from shell fragments in his body.

The men had eased a poncho under Lambert and were preparing to carry him down the ridge for evacuation. I wished him luck, made the usual jokes about not being too romantic with the nurses on the hospital ship, and asked him to drink a beer and think of me when he got Stateside—the usual comments one made to a badly wounded friend who had little chance.

Lambert looked up at me in the gathering darkness. With the stump of an unlighted cigar clenched in his teeth, he said with irony in his voice, "Sledgehammer, ain't this a helluva' thing—a man been in the company as long as me, and hafta get carried out on a poncho?"

I made some feeble attempts to comfort him. I knew he was going to die, and I wanted to cry.

"Wish I could light that cigar for you, Cobber, but the smokin' lamp is out."

"That's OK, Sledgehammer."

"One of those good-lookin' nurses'll light it for you," I said as they picked up the poncho and started off down the slope of the ridge with him.

I stood up and looked at a nearby group of beautiful pines silhouetted against the darkening sky. The wind blew their fresh scent into my face, and I thought how much like Southern pine it smelled. But poor, brave Lambert would never get back home again. I was thankful that when his luck finally ran out and he was fatally wounded, it happened on a high, clear, grassy ridge crest near a clump of fragrant pines and not back in the stinking muck of the quagmire around Shuri.

Corporal Lambert was a great favorite in Company K. Any of us who had fought on Peleliu's Bloody Nose Ridge had seen him numerous times standing above some Japanese cave, swinging a satchel charge of explosives on a rope until he got it just right, then releasing the rope and yelling, "Fire in the hole"—just before the muffled explosion. He would grin, then climb down and rejoin us wringing wet with sweat from his face to his boondockers. He would relight his cigar (which served in turn as a lighter for his satchel-charge fuses) and discuss the damage done to the cave. He was big, round-faced, and jovial. Rumor said that he had been scheduled to return to the States after Peleliu but refused because he wanted to remain with Company K. Not long after he was carried out, we learned that Lambert had died. It's one of the war's many personal tragedies that he was killed after having served so long and so bravely.

Next day we moved out into a wide valley below the ridge. We saw Japanese equipment and dead on several roads destroyed by the big U.S. bombardment the last week of May when the enemy had evacuated Shuri. We also encountered numerous Japanese supply dumps. Most of the food and rations didn't suit our tastes. The Japanese iron rations, which I had seen first in gauze sacs on Peleliu, tasted like dog biscuits. But I found several cans of preserved Japanese deep-sea scallops which were delicious. Several cans of these stored in my pack were a welcome change from C and K rations.

We made one rapid advance across a wide grassy valley only to be halted by snipers in some rocks on the crest of the opposite ridge. We set up the guns, registered in on the areas where snipers were, and began firing. Stretcher teams came and went up and down the slope of the open ridge. Four of us were ordered off for a stretcher team to pick up a corpsman who had been hit by sniper fire.

We went up the gently sloping, grass-covered ridge and came to the "doc." Another stretcher team passed us carrying the Marine whom the doc had been tending when he himself was wounded. The Marine had been shot by a sniper, and the corpsman had come to administer medical aid. While he was working over the wounded Marine, a Japanese shot him in the thigh. Although wounded painfully, he continued to work on his patient. Then the sniper had shot Doc in the other thigh. As we arrived, he cautioned us to be careful or we would get hit, too.

We quickly got him on a stretcher and took off as fast as possible. Doc was a fairly tall, well-built man, larger than any of us. We carried him a long distance: down the ridge and across the wide valley to a steep-sided ditch spanned by a footbridge. An ambulance jeep was waiting on the other side of the footbridge. We were all nearly exhausted from the exertions and lack of sleep of the past two weeks, and it was quite a struggle. Twice wounded though he was, he kept insisting we stop and rest for a while. But we four felt obligated to get him to the jeep and evacuated as soon as possible.

Finally, we agreed to stop for a breather. Setting the stretcher down, we fell out flat on the grass, panting for breath. Doc talked to us calmly, admonishing us to take it easy and not to overexert ourselves. I felt ashamed. That unselfish, dedicated corpsman was more concerned because we were so tired from carrying him out than he was with his own wounds.

We picked up the stretcher and got to the ditch. There on the bank I saw a bush with several small red tomatoes. I managed to grab three or four tomatoes and put them on the stretcher as we got Doc across the narrow footbridge. I told him to eat them, that they'd make him feel better. He thanked me, but said we should eat them, because he would get good chow in the hospital.

Who should walk around the jeep just as we were loading our corpsman but Doc Arrogant, notorious for painful shots on Pavuvu. "I'll take those," he said, reaching for the tomatoes.

"The hell you say!" I exclaimed, snatching them out of his hand.

One of my buddies went up to him and said, "You bastard, you'd take candy from a baby, wouldn't ya?"

Arrogant looked surly, turned around, and went back around the jeep. Our Doc handed me the tomatoes and insisted we eat them. We said we would and wished him luck as the jeep bumped off to the rear.

We recrossed the footbridge and fell exhausted onto the grass. We had a smoke, divided up the juicy little tomatoes, cussed Doc Arrogant, and voiced our admiration for all other corpsmen.

On 4 June we moved rapidly southward through open country in a torrential rain. Although the opposition was sporadic, we still had to check out all houses, huts, and former Japanese emplacements. While searching a small hut, I came across an old Okinawan woman seated on the floor just inside the doorway. Taking no chances, I held my Thompson ready and motioned to her to get up and come out. She remained on the floor but bowed her old gray head and held her gnarled hands toward me, palms down, to show the tattoos on the backs of her hands indicating she was Okinawan.

"No Nippon," she said slowly, shaking her head as she looked up at me with a weary expression that bespoke of much physical pain. She then opened her ragged blue kimono and pointed to a wound in the lower left side of her abdomen. It was an old wound, probably caused by shell or bomb fragments. It was an awful sight. A large area around the scabbed-over gash was discolored and terribly infected with gangrene. I gasped in dismay. I guessed that such a severe infection in the abdominal region was surely fatal.

The old woman closed her kimono. She reached up gently, took the muzzle of my Tommy, and slowly moved it so as to direct it between her eyes. She then released the weapon's barrel and motioned vigorously for me to pull the trigger. Oh no, I thought, this old soul is in such agony she actually wants me to put her out of her misery. I lifted my Tommy, slung it over my shoulder, shook my head, and said "no" to her. Then I stepped back and yelled for a corpsman.

"What's up, Sledgehammer?"

"There's an old gook woman in there that's been hit in the side real bad."

"I'll see what I can do for her," he said as we met about fifty yards from the hut.

At that moment, a shot rang out from the hut. I spun around. The corpsman and I went down into a crouching position.

"That was an M1," I said.

"Sure was. What the hell?" he said.

Just then a Marine emerged nonchalantly from the hut, checking the safety on his rifle. I knew the man well. He was attached at that time to company headquarters. I called to him by name and said, "Was there a Nip in that hut? I just checked it out."

"No," he said as we approached him, "just an old gook woman who wanted me to put her out of her misery; so I obliged her!"

The doc and I stared at each other, and then at the Marine. That quiet, neat, mild-mannered young man just wasn't the type to kill a civilian in cold blood.

When I saw the crumpled form under the faded blue kimono in the hut door, I blew up. "You dumb bastard! She tried to get me to shoot her, and I called Doc to come help her."

The executioner looked at me with a puzzled expression.

"You sonofabitch," I yelled. "If you want to shoot at somebody so damn bad, why don't you trade places with a BARman or a machine gunner and get outa that damn CP and shoot at Nips? They shoot back!"

He stammered apologies, and Doc cursed him.

I said, "We're supposed to kill Nips, not *old women!*"

The executioner's face flushed. An NCO came up and asked what happened. Doc and I told him. The NCO glared and said, "You dirty bastard."

Somebody yelled, "Let's go Sledgehammer, we're movin' out."

"You guys shove off, I'll take care of this," said the NCO to Doc and me. We ran off to catch up with the mortar section while the NCO continued to chew out the executioner. I never knew whether or not he was disciplined for his cold-blooded act.

*On the right of the 1st Marine Division, the 7th Marines extended its lines to the west coast and sealed off the Oroku Peninsula. Then the 6th Marine Division came in and fought a ten-day battle of attrition to annihilate the Japanese defenders there. The division killed nearly 5,000 Japanese, taking only 200 prisoners, at a loss of 1,608 Marines killed and wounded.*

*On 4 June, the 1st Marines relieved the 5th Marines as the assault regiment for the 1st Marine Division's drive to the south. The 5th Marines went into reserve for III Marine Amphibious Force, a stance that still involved much danger for its weary Marines because of a mission to aggressively patrol and mop up behind the forward elements.*

We dug in as a secondary line along a low ridge with some ruins of Okinawan houses behind us and a broad open valley stretching south to our front as far as we could see. The rain ended the night of 5–6 June. I'll never forget the sensation of profound physical relief when I removed my soaked, muddy boondockers for the first time in approximately two weeks. As I pulled off my slimy, stinking socks, bits and shreds of dead flesh sloughed off the soles of my feet. A buddy, Myron Tesreau, commented on the overpowering odor, only to discover that his feet were just as bad. My socks, a pair of khaki-colored, woolen army socks (thicker and heavier than our white Marine Corps issue) were so slimy and putrid I couldn't bear to wash them in my helmet. I had traded a candy bar to a soldier for them back in April. They were my prized possession because of their comfort when wet.

With regret, I threw my prize socks aside and spaded dirt over them as though covering up a foul corpse.

It was great to wash my feet, holding them up on an ammo box to let the sun shine on them while I wiggled my toes. Everybody got his feet clean and dry as soon as possible. Mine were extremely sore and red over the entire soles, almost to the point of bleeding. All of the normal friction ridges of the skin had sloughed off, and the soles were furrowed with deep, reddish grooves. But after drying them in the sun and putting on dry socks and boondockers, they soon felt better. Months passed, however, before the soles appeared normal again.

We had our mortars set up in pits at the base of the low ridge along which the Company K line was dug in. George Sarrett and I had a regular two-man foxhole on the ridge next to a road cut that came through at right angles to the ridge. During the nights we were there, we mortarmen took turns on the guns and fired flares periodically over our company area.

Between patrols and nightly vigils we began to get rested and dried out. We had air drops of supplies, food, water, and ammo. During the day we could build campfires and heat rations, which all enjoyed. We had ten-in-one rations there, always a welcome change from C and K rations. The method of air drop used to supply water had not been perfected then. The water was contained in long plastic bags, four of which were stored in a metal cylinder attached to the parachute. Quite often the impact of the cylinder hitting the deck caused one or more of the bags to break, and some or all of the water in it was lost.

We always had a lot of fun when supplies were air-dropped to us, even though it was hard work running through the mud collecting up the ammo, rations, and other supplies attached to the brightly colored chutes. Most of the time Marine torpedo bombers made the drops while flying low over us. Their accuracy was remarkable. During the periods when deep mud covered much of the battlefield we always welcomed a clear day, not only because we hated the rain, but because it meant our planes could be up and supply us with air drops. Otherwise supplies had to be manhandled miles through the mud.

While we were in reserve, another mortarman and I were sent on a routine mission to carry a message to the west coast regarding supplies. It was the kind of ordinary thing every infantryman was called on to do many times. Typically, it was good duty, because we were temporarily out from under the eagle eye of the company gunny sergeant, could move at our own pace, and do a little sightseeing along the way through areas already fought over and secured. It wasn't considered hazardous.

Our instructions were straightforward. Our company gunny, Hank

Boyes, told us to keep on the main east–west road all the way to the beach and back. He told us who to contact and what to ask for. Then he warned us against screwing around souvenir hunting and cautioned us about the possibility of bypassed enemy.

We started off in high spirits for what we thought would be an interesting jaunt into the area south of the Oroku Peninsula. We had gotten cleaned up by then. Our dungarees had been washed, and our leggings and boondockers were dry and scraped clean of mud. We carried the usual two canteens of water. We also had ration chocolate bars because we would be gone several hours and could eat those on the move. My buddy was armed with a carbine. I carried the Tommy and my .45 pistol. The weather had dried out, and it was an ideal day for a little harmless diversion from the patrols we had been making.

After we moved out of our battalion area and onto the road, we saw almost no one. As we walked along the silent road, the only sounds in our immediate surroundings were our own voices, the crunching of our boondockers on the road, the muffled sloshing of the water in our canteens, and the occasional thump of our weapons' stocks against our canteens or kabar scabbards. We moved in that silent world that characterized the backwash of battle.

The area was replete with the flotsam of war. The storm front had passed, but its wreckage was left behind. Our experienced eyes read the silent signs and reconstructed the drama and pathos of various life-and-death struggles that had occurred. We encountered numerous enemy corpses, which we always passed on the windward side. We saw no Marine dead. But a bloody dungaree jacket here, a torn boondocker there, a helmet with the camouflage cloth cover and steel beneath ripped by bullets, discarded plasma bottles, and bloody battle dressings gave mute testimony of the fate of their former owners.

We passed through an embankment for a railroad track and entered the outskirts of a town. All buildings were badly damaged, but some were still standing. We stopped briefly to explore a quaint little store. Displayed in its window were various cosmetics. In the street in front of the store lay a corpse clad in a blue kimono. Someone had placed a broken door over the pathetic body. We speculated he had been the proprietor of the little shop. We passed a burned-out bus station with the ticket booth still standing in front. To our right and distant the battle rumbled and rattled as the 6th Marine Division fought the enemy on the Oroku Peninsula.

Without incident we continued through the ruins toward the beach when an amtrac came rattling toward us. The driver was the first living soul we had seen. We hailed him, and it turned out he was expecting us at the beach but had started along the road hoping to locate us. After receiving the information about our unit, he spun his amtrac around and headed back toward the beach. With our mission completed, my buddy and I started back along the road through the ruins.

We passed the little cosmetic shop and the dead Okinawan covered by the door and approached the bus station on our left. A gentle breeze was blowing. Only the clanking of a piece of loose tin on the ruined bus station roof broke the silence. If I blotted out the distant rumble of battle, our surroundings reminded me of walking past some deserted farm building on a peaceful spring afternoon back home. It seemed like an interesting place to take ten, explore the bus station, and eat our ration bars. We had saved time by meeting the amtrac, so we could stop for a while.

The harsh snapping and cracking of a long burst of Japanese machine-gun bullets zipping chest high in front of us sent my buddy and me scrambling for cover. We dove behind the concrete ticket booth and lay on the rubble-strewn concrete, breathing hard.

"God, that was close, Sledgehammer!"

"Too damned close!"

The enemy gunner had been zeroed in perfectly on his elevation, but he had led us too much. The bullets ricocheted and whined around inside the burned-out bus station. We heard the tinkle of glass as the slugs broke windows among the burned-out buses.

"Where the hell is that bastard?" asked my buddy.

"I don't know, but he's probably a couple of hundred yards away from the sound of the gun."

We lay motionless for a moment, the silence interrupted only by the peaceful, lazy clanking of the tin in the breeze. Cautiously I peered out from behind the base of the ticket booth. Another burst of slugs narrowly missed my head and went clattering through the building after striking the concrete alongside us.

"That bastard's zeroed in on us for sure," groaned my buddy.

The ticket booth in front of the building was surrounded by an open expanse of concrete in all directions. The gunner had us pinned down tightly. My buddy peeped around his side of the narrow booth and got the same reception as I had. The enemy machine gunner then fired a burst across the top of the concrete portion of the booth, shattering what was left of the windows in the upper part of the booth. We were sure that the Nambu gunner was up on the south side of the railroad embankment.

"Maybe we can get back among them buses and out of sight and then slip out of the rear of the building," my buddy said. He moved slightly to one side to look behind us, but another burst of fire proved his plan faulty.

"I guess we'll hafta wait it out till dark and then slip out of here," I said.

"Guess you're right. We sure as hell ain't gonna get outa here during the daylight without gettin' hit. He's got us pinned down tight. Sledgehammer, after all the crap we've been through, damned if we ain't between a rock and the hard place. Goddamit to hell!"

The minutes grew into lonely hours as time dragged by. We kept a sharp lookout in all directions in case other Japanese might slip in behind us while we were occupied by the machine gun.

Toward late afternoon we heard a burst of M1 rifle fire over in the direction where the enemy gunner was located. After a few minutes we peeped out. To our delight we saw a group of four or five Company K Marines striding along the road from the direction of the road cut.

"Look out for that Nambu!" we yelled, pointing back toward where the fire had been coming from.

A grinning Marine held up the machine gun and yelled, "Rack 'em up. You guys OK? The gunny figured you'd run into trouble when you didn't come back and sent us out to look for you."

*By mid-June familiar faces were scarce in Company K and in all the infantry units of the 1st Marine Division. On 1 June the company lost thirty-six men to enemy action. Ten days later, twenty-two men left with immersion foot and other severe illnesses. Despite midmonth replacements, Company K moved toward its final major fight with about one hundred men and two or three officers—only half of whom had landed at Hagushi two and a half months earlier.*

## Carnage on Kunishi Ridge

Toward the middle of June we began to hear disturbing rumors about a place south of us called Kunishi Ridge. Rumors circulated that our division's other infantry regiments, the 7th Marines and later the 1st Marines, were involved in bitter fighting there and would need our help. Our hopes began to fade that the 5th Marines wouldn't be committed to the front lines again.

We continued our patrols. I enjoyed my canned Japanese scallops and hoped there was no such place as Kunishi Ridge. But, the inevitable day came with the order, "Square away your gear; we're movin' out again."

The weather turned dry and warm as we moved south. The farther we proceeded, the louder the sound of firing became: the bumping of artillery, the thudding of mortars, the incessant rattle of machine guns, the popping of rifles. It was a familiar combination of noise that engendered the old feelings of dread about one's own chances as well as the horrible images of the wounded, the shocked, and the dead—the inevitable harvest.

*Following the retreat from Shuri, the Japanese defenders of Okinawa withdrew into their final defensive lines along a string of ridges near the southern end of the island. The western anchor was Kunishi Ridge. In the middle was Yuza-Dake. Farther east was Yaeju-Dake.* \*

*Kunishi Ridge was about 1,500 yards long, a sheer coral escarpment. The Japanese dug into caves and emplacements on its forward and reverse slopes. The northern frontal approaches to Kunishi lay wide open: flat grasslands and rice paddies across which the Japanese had perfect fields of fire.*

*On 12 June the 7th Marines made a predawn attack and captured a portion of Kunishi. The Marines were on the ridge, but the enemy was in it. For four days, the Marines of the 7th Regiment were isolated atop the ridge. Air drops and tanks supplied them, and tanks removed their dead and wounded.*

*On 14 June the 1st Marines attacked portions of Kunishi and suffered heavy losses for their efforts. On the same day, the 1st Battalion—led by Lt. Col. Austin Shofner (former CO of 3/5 on Peleliu)—attacked and captured Yuza-Dake but suffered terrible casualties from the Japanese defenders there and from intense fire sent over from Yaeju-Dake.*

Into the hellish confusion we went on 14 June with the words still ringing in our ears, "The 5th Marines may not be committed again." We plodded along the sides of a dusty road, next to tanks and amtracs moving forward and a steady stream of ambulance jeeps returning loaded with the youthful human wreckage of the battle for Kunishi Ridge.

That afternoon our company deployed along a row of trees and bushes on the south side of the road. We saw and heard heavy firing on Kunishi Ridge across the open ground ahead. My mortar section dug in near the road with our guns adjusted to fire flares over a picturesque bridge that remained intact over a high stream bank.

A couple of us went to look at the bridge before dark. We walked down to the stream on a trail leading from the road. The water was crystal clear and made a peaceful gurgling sound over a clean pebbly bottom. Ferns grew from the overhanging mossy banks and between rocks on both sides. I had

---

\**Dake* means "hill" in Japanese.

the urge to look for salamanders and crayfish. It was a beautiful place, cool and peaceful, so out of context with the screaming hell close above it.

The next morning we relieved 1/1 on Yuza-Dake. As we moved up along a road, we passed a small tree with all the limbs blasted off. So many communication wires hung from it at all angles that it looked like a big inverted mop. A ricocheting bullet whined between me and the man in front of me. It raised a little dust cloud as it smashed into a pile of dry brush by the roadside. Back into the meat grinder again, I thought, as we moved up toward the sound of heavy firing.

Yuza-Dake looked terrible to me. It resembled one of the hellish coral ridges on Peleliu. We could see Kunishi Ridge on our right and the Yaeju-Dake escarpment on our left. Army tanks were moving against the latter while machine guns and 75mm cannons hammered away.

For the first time in combat I heard the wailing of sirens. We were told that the army had put sirens on their tanks for the psychological effect it might have on the Japanese. To me the sirens just made the whole bloody struggle more bizarre and unnerving. The Japanese rarely surrendered in the face of flamethrowers, artillery, bombs, or anything else, so I didn't understand how harmless sirens would bother them. We got mighty tired of hearing them wailing against the constant rattle of small arms and the crash of shell fire.

While we were on Yuza-Dake under sporadic enemy fire, 2/5 joined the 7th Marines in the bitter fighting to capture the rest of Kunishi Ridge. The Japanese emplacements and caves received terrific bombardment by mortars, artillery, heavy naval gunfire, and air strikes consisting of twenty-five to thirty planes. It reminded me more and more of Bloody Nose Ridge on Peleliu.

The 2d Battalion, 5th Marines gained some ground on Kunishi but needed help. Company K was attached to 2/5 and arrived just in time to help that battalion fight off a company-sized night counterattack on 17 June. Later that night we heard that our company would attack the next morning to seize the remainder of Kunishi Ridge in the 5th Marines' zone of action. Once again we would enter the abyss of close combat.

We learned that we would move out well before daylight and deploy for the attack, because we had to move across a wide open area to get to the ridge. An officer came along giving us what sounded like a pep talk about how the 5th Marines could finish the job on Kunishi Ridge. (We all knew that the 1st Marines and the 7th Marines had already been terribly shot up taking most of the ridge.)

Moving in the darkness was something the old salts of Gloucester and

Peleliu didn't like at all. We were stubborn in our belief that nobody but the Japanese, or damned fools, moved around at night. The new replacements who had come into the company a few days before seemed so pitifully confused they didn't know the difference. But moving up under cover of darkness was the only sane way to approach Kunishi Ridge. The 1st Marines and the 7th Marines had already found it necessary to move that way to get across the open ground without being slaughtered.

We moved slowly and cautiously across dry rice paddies and cane fields. Up ahead we saw shells exploding on and around the ridge as our artillery swished overhead. We heard the familiar popping of rifles, rattle of machine guns, and banging of grenades. Enemy shells also exploded on the ridge. We all knew that this was probably the last big fight before the Japanese were wiped out and the campaign ended. While I plodded along through the darkness, my heart pounding, my throat dry and almost too tight to swallow, near-panic seized me. Having made it that far in the war, I knew my luck would run out. I began to sweat and pray that when I got hit it wouldn't result in death or maiming. I wanted to turn and run away.

We came closer to the ridge silhouetted against the skyline. Its crest looked so much like Bloody Nose that my knees nearly buckled. I felt as though I were on Peleliu and had it all to go through again.

The riflemen moved up onto the ridge. We mortarmen were positioned to watch out for Japanese infiltrating from the left rear. We didn't set up our weapons: the fighting was so close-in with the enemy on the reverse slope and in the ridge that we couldn't fire high explosives.

Our 105mm artillery was firing over Kunishi Ridge while we moved into position in the dark. To our dismay, a shell exploded short in our company's line. The company CP alerted the artillery observers that we had received short rounds. Another 105 went off with a terrible flash and explosion.

"Corpsman!" someone yelled.

"Goddamit, we're getting casualties from short rounds!" an officer yelled into his walkie-talkie.

"What's the word on those short rounds?" the company executive officer asked.

"Says they'll check it out."

Our artillery was firing across the ridge into and around the town of Kunishi to prevent the enemy from moving more troops onto the ridge. But each time they shot, it seemed that one gun fired its shells in a traversing pattern right along the ridge in Company K's lines. It was enough to drive anyone into a state of desperation.

The Japanese were throwing grenades all along the line, and there was some rifle and machine-gun fire. On the right we began to hear American grenades exploding well within our lines.

"Hey you guys; Nips musta gotten hold of a box of our grenades. Listen to that, wouldja?"

"Yeah, them bastards'll use anything they can get their hands on."

During the next flurry of grenades, we heard no more U.S. models explode within our area. Then the word came along in the dark to be sure all the new replacements knew exactly how to use grenades properly. One of our new men had been discovered removing each grenade canister from a box of grenades, pulling the sealing tape from the canister, and then throwing the unopened canister at the enemy. The Japanese opened each canister, took out the grenade, pulled the pin, and threw the deadly "pineapple" back at us. The veterans around me were amazed to find out what had happened. The incident, however, was just one of many examples of the poor state of combat readiness of the latest group of new replacements.

With daylight I got a good look at our surroundings. Only then could I appreciate fully what a desperate, bitter battle the fight for Kunishi Ridge had been—and was continuing to be. The ridge was coral rock, painfully similar to Peleliu's ridges. But Kunishi was not so high nor were the coral formations so jagged and angular as those on Peleliu. Our immediate area was littered with the usual debris of battle including about thirty poncho-covered dead Marines on stretchers.

Some of our riflemen moved eastward along the ridge, while others moved up the slopes. We still didn't set up our mortars: it was strictly a riflemen's fight. We mortarmen stood by to act as stretcher bearers or riflemen.

Snipers were all over the ridge and almost impossible to locate. Men began getting shot one right after another, and the stretcher teams kept on the run. We brought the casualties down to the base of the ridge, to a point where tanks could back in out of the view of snipers on the ridge crest. We tied the wounded onto the stretchers and then tied the stretchers onto the rear deck of the tanks. Walking wounded went inside. Then the tanks took off in a cloud of dust along a coral road to the aid station. As many men as possible fired along the ridge to pin down the snipers, so they couldn't shoot the wounded on the tanks.

Shortly before the company reached the east end of the ridge, we watched a stretcher team make its way up to bring down a casualty. Suddenly four or five mortar shells exploded in quick succession near the team, wounding slightly three of the four bearers. They helped each other back down the ridge, and another stretcher team, of which I was a member, started up to get the casualty. To avoid the enemy mortar observer, we moved up by a slightly different route. We got up the ridge and found the casualty lying above a sheer coral ledge about five feet high. The Marine, Leonard E. Vargo, told us he couldn't move much because he had been shot in both feet. Thus he couldn't lower himself down off the ledge. "You guys be careful. The Nip that shot me twice is still hiding right over there in those rocks." He motioned toward a jumble of boulders not more than twenty yards away.

We reasoned that if the sniper had been able to shoot Vargo in both feet, immobilizing him, he was probably waiting to snipe at anyone who came to the rescue. That meant that anyone who climbed up to help Vargo down would get shot instantly. We stood against the coral rock with our heads about level with Vargo, but out of the line of fire of the sniper, and looked at each other. I found the silence embarrassing. Vargo lay patiently, confident of our aid.

"Somebody's got to get up there and hand him down," I said. My three buddies nodded solemnly and made quiet comments in agreement. I thought to myself that if we fooled around much longer, the sniper might shoot and kill the already painfully wounded and helpless Marine. Then we heard the crash of another 105mm short round farther along the ridge —then another. I was seized with a grim fatalism—it was either be shot by the sniper or have all of us get blown to bits by our own artillery. Feeling ashamed for hesitating so long, I scrambled up beside Vargo.

"Watch out for that Nip," he said again.

As I placed my hands under his shoulders, I glanced over and saw the entrance of the sniper's small cave. It was a black space about three feet in diameter. I expected to see a muzzle flash spurt forth. Strangely, I felt at peace with myself and, oddly, wasn't particularly afraid. But there was no sound or sight of the sniper.

My buddies had Vargo well in hand by then, so for a brief instant I stood up and looked south. I felt a sensation of wild exhilaration. Beyond the smoke of our artillery to the south lay the end of the island and the end of the agony.

"Come on Sledgehammer. Let's move out!"

With another quick glance at the mouth of the small cave—puzzled over where the sniper was and why he hadn't fired at me—I scrambled back down the rock to the stretcher team. We carried Vargo down Kunishi Ridge without further incident.

After bringing down another casualty, I passed our company CP among some rocks at the foot of the ridge and overheard one of our officers talking confidentially to Hank Boyes. The officer said his nerves were almost shattered by the constant strain, and he didn't think he could carry on much longer. The veteran Boyes talked quietly, trying to calm the officer. The officer sat on his helmet, frantically running his hands through his hair. He was almost sobbing.

I felt compassion for the officer. I'd been in the same forlorn frame of mind more than once, when horror piled on horror seemed too much to bear. The officer also carried a heavy responsibility, which I didn't have.

As I walked past, the officer blurted out in desperation, "What's the matter with those guys up on the ridge? Why the hell don't they move out faster and get this thing over with?"

Compassion aside, my own emotional and physical state was far from good by then. Completely forgetting my lowly rank, I walked right into the CP and said to the officer, "I'll tell you what's the matter with those guys on the ridge. They're gettin' shot right and left, and they can't move any faster!"

He looked up with a dazed expression. Boyes turned around, probably expecting to see the battalion or regimental commander. When he saw me instead, he looked surprised. Then he glared at me the way he did the time I had too much to say to Shadow back on Half Moon. Coming quickly to my senses and remembering that a private's advice to first lieutenants and gunny sergeants wasn't considered standard operating procedure in the Marine Corps, I backed away quietly and got out of there.

Toward afternoon, several of us were resting among some rocks near the crest of the ridge. We had been passing ammo and water up to some men just below the crest. A Japanese machine gun still covered the crest there, and no one dared raise his head. Bullets snapped over the crest and ricochets whined off into the air after striking rocks. The man next to me was a rifleman and a fine Peleliu veteran whom I knew well. He had become unusually quiet and moody during the past hour, but I just assumed he was as tired and as weary with fear and fatigue as I was. Suddenly he began babbling incoherently, grabbed his rifle, and shouted, "Those slant-eyed yellow bastards, they've killed enougha my buddies. I'm goin' after 'em." He jumped up and started for the crest of the ridge.

"Stop!" I yelled and grabbed at his trouser leg. He pulled away.

A sergeant next to him yelled, "Stop, you fool!" The sergeant also grabbed for the frantic man's legs, but his hands slipped. He managed to clutch the toe of one boondocker, however, and gave a jerk. That threw the man off balance, and he sprawled on his back, sobbing like a baby. The front of his trousers was darkened where he had urinated when he lost control of himself. The sergeant and I tried to calm him but also made sure he couldn't get back onto his feet. "Take it easy Cobber. We'll get you outa' here," the NCO said.

We called a corpsman who took the sobbing, trembling man out of the meat grinder to an aid station.

"He's a damn good Marine, Sledgehammer. I'll lower the boom on anybody says he ain't. But he's just had all he can take. That's it. He's just had all he can take."

The sergeant's voice trailed away sadly. We had just seen a brave man crack up completely and lose all control of himself, even to the point of losing his desire to live.

"If you hadn't grabbed his foot and jerked him down before he got to the crest, he'd be dead now, for sure," I said.

"Yeah, the poor guy woulda gotten hit by that goddamn machine gun; no doubt about it," the sergeant said.

By the end of the day, Company K reached the eastern end of Kunishi Ridge and established contact with army units that had gained the high ground on Yuza-Dake and Yaeju-Dake. Mail came up to us along with rations, water, and ammo. Among my letters was one from a Mobile acquaintance of many years. He had joined the Marine Corps and was a member of some rear-echelon unit of service troops stationed on northern Okinawa. He insisted that I write him immediately about the location of my unit. He wrote that when he found out where I was, he would visit me at once. I read his words to some of my buddies, and they got a good laugh out of it.

"Don't that guy know there's a war on? What the hell does he think the First Marine Division is doin' down here anyway?"

Someone else suggested I insist not only that he come to see me at once, but that he stay and be my replacement if he wanted to be a true friend. I never answered the letter.

A small patrol from the 7th Marines came by, and we talked with an old buddy. He said his regiment had been in terrible fighting for the several days it had been on Kunishi Ridge. Then we sat silently, ruefully watching a group of Marines far over to the right get shelled by large-caliber Japanese artillery. Word came along the line about the death earlier in the day of the U.S. Tenth commander, General Buckner.*

---

*Gen. Simon Bolivar Buckner, USA, had come up to the front lines to watch the 8th Marine Regiment, 2d Marine Division, in its first combat action on Okinawa. He was observing from between two coral boulders when six Japanese 47mm artillery rounds struck the base of the rocks. Hit in the chest, he died shortly thereafter. Lt. Gen. Roy S. Geiger, USMC, III Amphibious Corps commander, took command of the Tenth Army and carried through to the end of

Not long after we were relieved on Kunishi Ridge (in the afternoon of 18 June), I asked Gy. Sgt. Hank Boyes how many men we had lost fighting on Yuza-Dake and Kunishi. He told me Company K had lost forty-nine enlisted men and one officer, half of our number of the previous day. Almost all the newly arrived replacements were among the casualties. Now the company consisted of a mere remnant, twenty-one percent of its normal strength of two hundred and thirty-five men. We had been attached to 2/5 for only twenty-two hours and had been on Kunishi Ridge for less time than that.

---

the fighting a few days later. To this date in 1981, Geiger remains the only Marine officer to command a force of army size.

CHAPTER FIFTEEN

# END OF THE AGONY

*F**rom 11 to 18 June the fierce battle for the Kunishi–Yuza–Yaeju escarpment cost the 1st Marine Division 1,150 casualties. The fight marked the end of organized Japanese resistance on Okinawa.*

The battle for the Kunishi escarpment was unforgettable. It reminded many of us of Peleliu's ridges, and we still weren't used to the fact that night attacks by Marines had played a significant role in capturing the difficult objective. Among my friends in the ranks, the biggest surprise was the poor state of readiness and training of our newest Marine replacements, as compared to the more efficient replacements who had come into the company earlier in the campaign (they had received some combat training in the rear areas before joining us). But most of the new men who joined us just before Kunishi Ridge had come straight from the States. Some of them told us they had had only a few weeks training or less after boot camp.

It's no wonder they were so confused and ineffective when first exposed to intense enemy fire. When we had to evacuate a casualty under fire, some of the new men were reluctant to take the chances necessary to save the wounded Marine. This reticence infuriated the veterans, who made such threats against them that the new men finally did their share. They were motivated by greater fear of the veteran Marines than of the Japanese. This isn't to reflect on their bravery; they simply weren't trained and conditioned properly to cope with the shock, violence, and hellish conditions into which they were thrown. The rank and file, usually sympathetic toward new replacements, simply referred to them "as fouled up as Hogan's goat," or some other more profound but profane description.

With a feeling of intense relief, we came down off Kunishi Ridge late in the day of 18 June. After rejoining the other companies of 3/5, we moved in column on a road cut through the ridge. As we wound south, we talked with men of the 8th Marines who were moving along the road with us. We were glad to see a veteran Marine regiment come in to spearhead the final push south. We were exhausted.

The veterans in our ranks scrutinized the men of the 8th Marines with that hard professional stare of old salts sizing up another outfit. Everything we saw brought forth remarks of approval: they looked squared away, and many of them were combat veterans themselves.*

I talked to a 60mm mortarman who was carrying almost an entire cloverleaf of HE shells on a backpack rig. Asking why he was so overloaded, I was told his battalion commander wanted the mortarmen to try the arrangement because they could carry more ammo than in a regular ammo bag. I hoped fervently that none of our officers saw that rig.

I also saw a machine-gun squad with "Nip Nemesis" stenciled neatly on the water jacket of their .30 caliber heavy machine gun. They were a sharp looking crew.

We passed a large muddy area in the road cut. In it lay the body of a dead Japanese soldier in full uniform and equipment. It was a bizzare sight. He had been mashed down into the mud by tank treads and looked like a giant squashed insect.

Our column moved down into a valley at five-pace intervals, one file on each side of the road. An amtrac came clattering slowly along, headed toward the front farther south. It passed me as I was daydreaming about the delightful possibility that we might not get shelled or shot at anymore. But my reverie was terminated rudely and abruptly by *whiz . . . bang! whiz . . . bang!*

"Disperse!" someone yelled. We scattered like a covey of quail. About ten of us jumped into a shallow ditch. The first enemy antitank shell had passed over the top of the amtrac and exploded in a field beyond. But the second shell scored a direct hit on the left side of the amtrac. The machine jolted to a stop and began smoking. We peeped out of the ditch as the driver tried to start the engine. His crewman peered back into the cargo compartment to assess the damage. Two more shells slammed into the side of the

---

*The 8th Marines came up from Saipan to reinforce the 1st Marine Division in the final drive on Okinawa. Among the many streamers on its regimental battle color flew one for Tarawa.

disabled amtrac. The two Marines in the cab jumped out, ran over, and flopped down, panting, into the ditch near us.

"What kinda cargo is in there?" I asked.

"We got a full unit of fire for a rifle company—'thirty' ball, grenades, mortar ammo—the works. Boy, she is gonna blow like hell when that fire gets to that ammo. The gas tanks are hit so bad there's no way to put it out." The driver crawled off along the ditch to find a radioman to report that his load of ammo couldn't get through to the front.

Just then a man crawled over next to me and stood upright. I looked up at him in surprise. Every Marine in the area was hugging the deck waiting for the inevitable explosion from the amtrac. The man was clad in clean dungarees with the new sheen still on the cloth, and he displayed the relaxed appearance of a person who could wash up and drink hot coffee at a CP whenever he was in the mood to do so. He carried a portable movie camera with which he began avidly filming the pillow of thick black smoke boiling up from the amtrac. Rifle cartridges began popping in the amtrac as the heat got to them.

"Hey mate," I said. "You'd better get down! That thing is gonna blow sky high any minute. It's loaded with ammo!"

The man held his camera steady but stopped filming. He turned and looked down at me with a contemptuous stare of utter disdain and disgust. He didn't demean himself to speak to me as I cringed in the ditch, but turned back to his camera eyepiece and continued filming.

At that moment came a flash accompanied by a loud explosion and terrific concussion as the amtrac blew up. The concussion knocked the cameraman completely off his feet. He was uninjured but badly shaken and terribly frightened. He peered wide-eyed and cautious over the ditch bank at the twisted amtrac burning on the road.

I leaned over to him and said pleasantly, "I told you so."

He turned his no longer arrogant face toward me. I grinned at him with the broadest smile I could conjure, "like a mule eatin' briars through a barbed wire fence," as the Texans would say. Speechless, the cameraman turned quickly and crawled off along the ditch toward the rear.

Four or five Marine tanks were parked close together in the valley downhill from us about one hundred yards away. Their heavily armored fronts faced up the valley to our left. The crewmen had been alerted by the first enemy round fired at the amtrac; we saw them swinging their 75s toward our left and closing their turret hatches. Not a moment too soon. The entire Japanese 47mm gun battery opened rapid fire on the tanks. Too bad the movie cameraman had felt the call of duty summon him to the rear after the amtrac exploded, because he missed a dramatic scene. The enemy guns fired with admirable accuracy. Several of their tracer-like armor piercing shells hit the turrets of the tanks and ricocheted into the air. The tanks returned fire. In a few minutes, the Japanese guns were knocked out or ceased firing, and everything got quiet. The tanks sustained only minor damage. We went back onto the road and moved on south without further incident.

Until the island was secured on 21 June, we made a series of rapid moves southward, stopping only to fight groups of diehard Japanese in caves, pillboxes, and ruined villages. The fresh 8th Marines pushed south rapidly. "The Eighth Marines goin' like a bat outa hell," a man said as news drifted back to us.

We were fortunate in not suffering many casualties in the company. The Japanese were beaten, and the hope uppermost in every weary veteran's mind was that his luck would hold out a little longer, until the end of the battle.

We used loudspeakers, captured Japanese soldiers, and Okinawan civilians to persuade the remaining enemy to surrender. One sergeant and a Japanese lieutenant who had graduated from an Ivy League college and spoke perfect English gave themselves up in a road cut. Just after they came out and surrendered, a sniper opened fire on us. We eight or ten Marines took cover next to the embankment, but the Japanese officer and NCO stood in the middle of the road with the bullets kicking up dirt all around them. The sniper obviously was trying to kill them because they had surrendered.

We looked at the two Japanese standing calmly, and one of our NCOs said, "Get over here under cover, you dumb bastards."

The enemy officer grinned affably and spoke to his NCO. They walked calmly over and got down as ordered.

Some Company K men shot the gun crew of a 150mm howitzer emplaced in the mouth of a well-camouflaged cave. The Japanese defended their big artillery piece with their rifles and died to the last man. Farther on we tried to get a group of enemy in a burial vault to surrender, but they refused. Our lieutenant, Mac, jumped in front of the door and shouted in Japanese, "Do not be afraid. Come out. I will not harm you." Then he fired a complete twenty-round magazine from his submachine gun into the door. We all just shook our heads and moved on. About a half hour later, the five or six Japanese rushed out fighting. Some of our Marines behind us killed them.

Our battalion was one of the first American units to reach the end of the island. It was a beautiful sight even though there were still snipers around. We stood on a high hill overlooking the sea. Below to our left we saw army infantry advancing toward us, flushing out and shooting down enemy soldiers singly and in small groups. Army 81mm mortar fire kept pace ahead of the troops, and some of our weapons joined in coordination. We got a bit edgy when the army mortar fire kept getting closer and closer to our positions even after the unit had been apprised of our location. One of our battalion officers became furious as the big shells came dangerously close. He ordered a radioman to tell the army officer in charge that if they didn't cease fire immediately, our 81s would open fire on his troops. The army mortars stopped shooting.

The night of 20 June we made a defensive line on the high ground overlooking the sea. My mortar was dug in near a coral road and was to illuminate or fire HE on the area. Other guns of the section covered the seaward part of the company's sector.

Earlier we had seen and heard some sort of strange-looking rocket fired by the Japanese from over in our army's sector. The projectiles were clearly visible as they went up with a terrible screaming sound. Most of them exploded in the 8th Marines area. The things sounded like bombs exploding. A call came for every available corpsman to help with casualties resulting from those explosions.

The Japanese on Okinawa had a 320mm-spigot-mortar unit equipped to fire a 675-pound shell. Americans first encountered this awesome weapon on Iwo Jima. I don't know whether what we saw fired several times during the last day or two on Okinawa was a spigot mortar, but whatever it was, it was a frightful-sounding weapon that caused great damage.

The night turned into a long series of shooting scrapes with Japanese who prowled all over the place. We heard someone coming along the road, the coral crunching beneath his feet. In the pitch dark, a new replacement fired his carbine twice in that direction and yelled for the password. Somebody laughed, and several enemy started firing in our direction as they ran past us along the road. A bullet zipped by me and hit the hydrogen cylinder of a flamethrower placed on the side of the adjacent foxhole. The punctured cylinder emitted a sharp hissing sound.

"Is that thing gonna blow up?" I asked anxiously.

"Naw, just hit the hydrogen tank. It won't ignite," the flamethrower gunner said.

We could hear the enemy soldiers' hobnailed shoes pounding on the road until a fatal burst of fire from some other Company K Marines sent them sprawling. As we fieldstripped them the next morning, I noted that each carried cooked rice in his double-boiler mess gear—all bullet-riddled then.

Other Japanese swam or walked along in the sea just offshore. We saw them in the flarelight. A line of Marines behind a stone wall on the beach fired at them. One of our men ran up from the wall to get more carbine ammo.

"Come on Sledgehammer. It's just like Lexington and Concord."

"No thanks. I'm too comfortable in my hole."

He went back down to the wall, and they continued firing throughout the night.

Just before daylight, we heard a couple of enemy grenades explode. Japanese yelled and shouted wildly where one of our 37mm guns was dug in across the road, covering the valley out front. Shots rang out, then desperate shouts and cursing.

"Corspman!"

Then silence. A new corpsman who had joined us recently started toward the call for help, but I said, "Hold it Doc. I'll go with you."

I wasn't being heroic. I was quite afraid. But knowing the enemy's propensity for treachery, I thought somebody should accompany him.

"As you were, Sledgehammer. Ya might be needed on the gun. Take off, Doc, and be careful," an NCO said. A few minutes later he said, "OK, Sledgehammer, take off if ya wanta."

I grabbed the Tommy and followed the corpsman. He was just finishing bandaging one of the wounded Marines of the 37mm gun crew when I got there. Other Marines were coming over to see if they could help. Several men had been wounded by the firing when two enemy officers crept up the steep slope, threw grenades into the gun emplacement, and jumped in swinging their samurai sabers. One Marine had parried a saber blow with his carbine. His buddy then had shot the Japanese officer who fell backwards a short distance down the slope. The saber blow had severed a finger and sliced through the mahogany carbine forestock to the metal barrel.

The second Japanese officer lay dead on his back next to the wheel of the 37mm gun. He was in full-dress uniform with white gloves, shiny leather leggings, Sam Browne belt, and campaign ribbons on his chest. Nothing remained of his head from the nose up—just a mass of crushed skull, brains, and bloody pulp. A grimy Marine with a dazed expression stood over the Japanese. With a foot planted firmly on the ground on each side of the enemy officer's body, the Marine held his rifle by the forestock with both hands and slowly and mechanically moved it up and down like a plunger. I winced each time it came down with a sickening sound into the gory mass. Brains and blood were splattered all over the Marine's rifle, boondockers, and canvas leggings, as well as the wheel of the 37mm gun.

The Marine was obviously in a complete state of shock. We gently took him by the arms. One of his uninjured buddies set aside the gore-smeared rifle. "Let's get you outa here, Cobber."

The poor guy responded like a sleepwalker as he was led off with the wounded, who were by then on stretchers. The man who had lost the finger clutched the Japanese saber in his other hand. "I'm gonna keep this bastard for a souvenir."

We dragged the battered enemy officer to the edge of the gun emplacement and rolled him down the hill. Replete with violence, shock, blood, gore, and suffering, this was the type of incident that should be witnessed by anyone who has any delusions about the glory of war. It was as savage and as brutal as though the enemy and we were primitive barbarians rather than civilized men.

Later in the day of 21 June 1945, we learned the high command had declared the island secured. We each received two fresh oranges with the compliments of Admiral Nimitz. So I ate mine, smoked my pipe, and looked out over the beautiful blue sea. The sun danced on the water. After eighty-two days and nights, I couldn't believe Okinawa had finally ended. I was tempted to relax and think that we would board ship immediately for rest and rehabilitation in Hawaii.

"That's what the scuttlebutt is, you guys. Straight dope. We're headed for Waikiki," a grinning buddy said. But long conditioning by the hardships that were our everyday diet in a rifle company made me skeptical. My intuition was borne out shortly.

"Get your gear on; check your weapons. We're moving back north in skirmish line. You people will mop up the area for any Nips still holding out. You will bury all enemy dead. You will salvage U.S. and enemy equipment. All brass above .50 caliber in size will be collected and placed in neat piles. Stand by to move out."

## A Final Chore

If this were a novel about war, or if I were a dramatic storyteller, I would find a romantic way to end this account while looking at that fine sunset off the cliffs at the southern end of Okinawa. But that wasn't the reality of what we faced. Company K had one more nasty job to do.

To the battle-weary troops, exhausted after an eighty-two-day campaign, mopping up was grim news. It was a nerve-wracking business at best. The enemy we encountered were the toughest of the diehards, selling their lives as expensively as possible. Fugitives from the law of averages, we were nervous and jittery. A man could survive Gloucester, Peleliu, and Okinawa only to be shot by some fanatical, bypassed Japanese holed up in a cave. It was hard for us to accept the order. But we did—grimly. Burying enemy dead and salvaging brass and equipment on the battlefield, however, was the last straw to our sagging morale.

"By lawd, why the hell we gotta bury them stinkin' bastards after we killed 'em? Let them goddamn rear-echelon people git a whiff of 'em. They didn't hafta fight 'em.''

"Jeez, picking up brass; that's the most stupid, dumb jerk of a order I ever did hear of.''

Fighting was our duty, but burying enemy dead and cleaning up the battlefield wasn't for infantry troops as we saw it. We complained and griped bitterly. It was the ultimate indignity to men who had fought so hard and so long and had won. We were infuriated and frustrated. For the first time, I saw several of my veteran comrades flatly refuse to obey an order. If some of us hadn't prevailed on them to knock off arguing hotly with an NCO, they would have been severely punished for insubordination.

I'll never forget cajoling, arguing with, and begging two veteran buddies to be quiet and follow orders as I unstrapped my entrenching shovel from my pack. We stood wearily in a trampled cane field beside a bloated Jap corpse. Both buddies were three-campaign men who were outstanding in combat but had reached the end of their ropes. They weren't about to bury any stinking Japanese, no sirree. I prevailed, however, just as Hank Boyes came over grim-faced and yelling at them to turn to.

So we dragged ourselves back north in skirmish line. We cursed every dead enemy we had to bury. (We just spaded dirt over them with our entrenching shovels.) We cursed every cartridge case "above .50 caliber in size" we collected to "place in neat piles.'' Never before were we more thankful to have the support of our tanks. The flame tanks were particularly effective in burning out troublesome Japanese in caves.* Fortunately, we had few casualties.

In a few days we assembled in an open field and fell out to await further orders. The weather was hot, so we all took off our packs, sat on our helmets, drank some water, and had a smoke. We were to be there for several hours, an NCO said, so we got the order to chow down.

A friend and I went over to a little wooded area near the field to eat our K rations in the shade. We walked into a completely untouched scene that resembled a natural park in a botanical garden: low graceful pines cast dense shade, and ferns and moss grew on the rocks and banks. It was cool,

---

*The total number of Japanese killed by the five American divisions during the mop up was 8,975, a large enough number of enemy to have waged intense guerrilla warfare if they hadn't en annihilated.

*At battle's end, three weary K Company mortarmen: L to R, John Redifer, Vincent Santos, Gene Farrar. Photo by Gene Farrar.*

and the odor of fresh pine filled the air. Miraculously, it bore not a single sign of war.

"Boy, this is beautiful, isn't it, Sledgehammer?"

"It looks unreal," I said as I took off my pack and sat down on the soft green moss beside a clump of graceful ferns. We each started heating a canteen cup of water for our instant coffee. I took out the prized can of cured ham I had obtained by trade from a man in the company CP. (He had stolen it from an officer.) We settled back in the cool silence. The war, military discipline, and other unpleasant realities seemed a million miles away. For the first time in months, we began to relax.

"OK, you guys. Move out. Move! Move! Outa here," an NCO said with authority ringing out in every word.

"Is the company moving out already?" my friend asked in surprise.

"No, it isn't, but you guys are."

"Why?"

"Because this is off limits to enlisted men," the NCO said, turning and pointing to a group of officers munching their rations as they strolled into our new-found sanctuary.

"But we aren't in the way," I said.

"Move out and follow orders."

To his credit, the NCO appeared in sympathy with us and seemed to feel the burden of his distasteful task. We sullenly picked up our half-cooked rations and our gear, went back out into the hot sun, and flopped down in the dusty field.

"Some crap, eh?"

"Yeah," I said, "we weren't even near those officers. The fighting on this goddamn island is over. The officers have started getting chicken again and throwing the crap around. Yesterday while the shootin' was still goin' on, it was all buddy-buddy with the enlisted men."

Our grumblings were interrupted by the sound of a rifle shot. A Marine I knew very well reeled backward and fell to the ground. His buddy dropped his rifle and rushed to him, followed by several others. The boy was dead, shot in the head by his buddy. The other man had thought his rifle was unloaded when his young friend had stood over him and placed his thumb playfully over the muzzle.

"Pull the trigger. I bet it's not loaded."

He pulled the trigger. The loaded rifle fired and set a bullet tearing up through the head of his best friend. Both had violated the cardinal rule: "Don't point a weapon at anything you don't intend to shoot."

Shock and dismay showed on the man's face from that moment until he ft the company a few weeks later. He went, we heard, to stand a general rt-martial and a probable prison term. But his worst punishment was living with the horror of having killed his best friend by playing with a loaded weapon.

While the company was still sitting in the field, five or six men and I were told to get our gear and follow an NCO to waiting trucks. We were to go north to a site where our division would make a tent camp after the mop-up in the south was completed. Our job was to unload and guard some company gear.

We were apprehensive about leaving the company, but it turned out to be good duty. During the long and dusty truck ride to the Motobu Peninsula, we rode past some areas we had fought through. By then we could barely recognize them—they were transformed with roads, tent camps, and supply dumps. The number of service troops and the amount of equipment was beyond our belief. Roads that had been muddy tracks or coral-covered paths were highways with vehicles going to and fro and MPs in neat khaki directing traffic. Tent camps, quonset huts, and huge parks of vehicles lay along our route.

We had come back to civilization. We had climbed up out of the abyss once more. It was exhilarating. We sang and whistled like little boys until our sides were sore. As we went north, the countryside became beautiful. Most of it seemed untouched by the war. Finally our truck turned off into a potato field not far from high rocky cliffs overlooking the sea and a small island which our driver said was Ie Shima.

The land around our future campsite was undamaged. We unloaded the company gear from the truck. The driver had picked up five-gallon cans of water for us. Plenty of K rations had been issued. We set up a bivouac. Corporal Vincent was in charge, and we were glad of it. He was a great guy and a Company K veteran.

Our little guard detail spent several quiet, carefree days basking in the sun by day and mounting one-sentry guard duty at night. We were like boys on a camp-out. The fear and terror were behind us.

Our battalion came north a few days later. All hands went to work in earnest to complete the tent camp. Pyramidal tents were set up, drainage ditches were dug, folding cots and bed rolls were brought to us, and a canvas-roofed messhall was built. Every day old friends returned from the hospitals, some hale and hearty but others showing the effects of only partial recovery from severe wounds. To our disgust, rumors of rehabilitation in Hawaii faded. But our relief that the long Okinawa ordeal was over at last was indescribable.

Very few familiar faces were left. Only twenty-six Peleliu veterans who had landed with the company on 1 April remained. And I doubt there were even ten of the old hands who had escaped being wounded at one time or another on Peleliu or Okinawa. Total American casualties were 7,613 killed and missing and 31,807 wounded in action. Neuropsychiatric, "non-battle," casualties amounted to 26,221—probably higher than in any other previous Pacific Theater battle. This latter high figure is attributed to two causes: The Japanese poured onto U.S. troops the heaviest concentrations of artillery and mortar fire experienced in the Pacific, and the prolonged, close-in fighting with a fanatical enemy.

Marines and attached Naval medical personnel suffered total casualties of 20,020 killed, wounded and missing.

Japanese casualty figures are hazy. However, 107,539 enemy dead were counted on Okinawa. Approximately 10,000 enemy troops surrendered, and about 20,000 were either sealed in caves or buried by the Japanese themselves. Even lacking an exact accounting, in the final analysis the enemy garrison was, with rare exceptions, annihilated. Unfortunately, approximately 42,000 Okinawan civilians, caught between the two opposing armies, perished from artillery fire and bombing.

The 1st Marine Division suffered heavy casualties on Okinawa. Officially, it lost 7,665 men killed, wounded, and missing. There were also an undetermined number of casualties among the replacements whose names never got on a muster roll. Considering that most of the casualties were in the division's three infantry regiments (about 3,000 strength in each), it's obvious that the rifle companies took the bulk of the beating, just as they had on Peleliu. The division's losses of 6,526 on Peleliu and 7,665 on Okinawa total 14,191. Statistically, the infantry units had suffered over 150 percent losses through the two campaigns. The few men like me who never got hit can claim with justification that we survived the abyss of war as fugitives from the law of averages.*

## It Was Over

As we finished building our tent camp, we began trying to unwind from the grueling campaign. Some of the Cape Gloucester veterans rotated home almost immediately, and replacements arrived. Ugly rumors circulated that we would hit Japan next, with an expected casualty figure of one million Americans. No one wanted to talk about that.

On 8 August we heard that the first atomic bomb had been dropped on Japan. Reports abounded for a week about a possible surrender. Then on 15 August 1945 the war ended.

We received the news with quiet disbelief coupled with an indescribable

---

*The 1st Marine Division received the Presidential Units Citation for its part in the Okinawa ʌpaign.

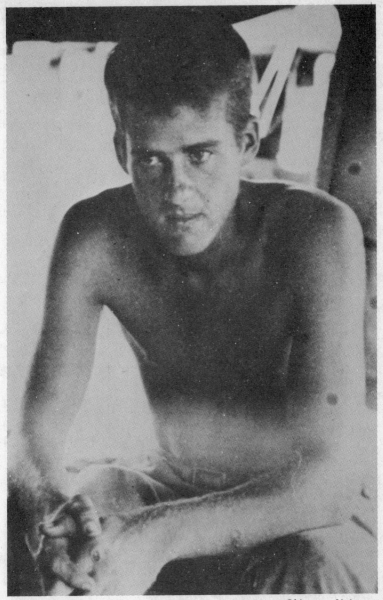

*Author at the end of the campaign. Tent camp on Okinawa. Unknown photographer.*

*Eugene B. Sledge after return from Peking in 1946.*

sense of relief. We thought the Japanese would never surrender. Many refused to believe it. Sitting in stunned silence, we remembered our dead. So many dead. So many maimed. So many bright futures consigned to the ashes of the past. So many dreams lost in the madness that had engulfed us. Except for a few widely scattered shouts of joy, the survivors of the abyss sat hollow-eyed and silent, trying to comprehend a world without war.

In September, the 1st Marine Division went to North China on occupation duty, the 5th Marines to the fascinating ancient city of Peking. After about four and a half months there, I rotated Stateside.

My happiness knew no bounds when I learned I was slated to ship home. It was time to say goodbye to old buddies in K/3/5. Severing the ties formed in two campaigns was painful. One of America's finest and most famous elite fighting divisions had been my home during a period of the most extreme adversity. Up there on the line, with nothing between us and the enemy but space (and precious little of that), we'd forged a bond that time would never erase. We were brothers. I left with a sense of loss and sadness, but K/3/5 will always be a part of me.

It's ironic that the record of our company was so outstanding but that so few individuals were decorated for bravery. Uncommon valor was displayed so often it went largely unnoticed. It was expected. But nearly every man in the company was awarded the Purple Heart. My good fortune in being one of the few exceptions continues to amaze me.

War is brutish, inglorious, and a terrible waste. Combat leaves an indelible mark on those who are forced to endure it. The only redeeming factors were my comrades' incredible bravery and their devotion to each other. Marine Corps training taught us to kill efficiently and to try to survive. But it also taught us loyalty to each other—and love. That esprit de corps sustained us.

Until the millenium arrives and countries cease trying to enslave others, it will be necessary to accept one's responsibilities and to be willing to make sacrifices for one's country—as my comrades did. As the troops used to say, "If the country is good enough to live in, it's good enough to fight for." With privilege goes responsibility.

# A ROLL OF HONOR
## Peleliu Veterans with K / 3 / 5 at the End of Okinawa

1. James Allen
2. Charles Anderson
3. James C. F. Anderson
4. Franklin Batchelor
5. Henry (Hank) Boyes   W/NE
6. R. V. Burgin   W/R
7. J. T. Burke
8. Guy E. Farrar
9. Peter Fouts
10. G. C. Gear
11. Anton Haas
12. Julius (Frenchy) Labeeuw
13. Les Land
14. Thorkil (Toby) Paulsen
15. Les Porter
16. Bobby Ragan
17. John Redifer
18. D. B. A. Salsby   W/R
19. Vincent Santos
20. George Sarrett
21. Henry K. Schaeffer
22. Merriel (Snafu) Shelton   S/R
23. E. B. Sledge
24. Myron Tesreau
25. Orly C. Uhls
26. W. F. Vincent

Note: W/R—wounded returned to duty; W/NE—wounded not evacuated; S/R—sick returned to duty.

Of the approximately 65 Peleliu veterans who landed with the company on Okinawa, only the above survived death, injury or illness, and were present at the end of the battle. Many of the above had been wounded on Cape Gloucester or Peleliu.

# BIBLIOGRAPHY

The books and documents listed here are not the only accounts and references to the battles of Peleliu and Okinawa, nor should the reader construe them to be suggestions for further reading. My story is personal. It relates what I saw and knew. I used the following references to check my facts for the few pieces of connecting tissue I've included to orient the reader to the larger war that raged around me and to be sure I had the names and places right.

Appleman, Roy E., *et al. Okinawa: The Last Battle.* Washington: Historical Division, Department of the Army, 1948.

Davis, Burke. *Marine! The Life of Lieutenant General Lewis B. (Chesty) Puller.* Boston: Little, Brown and Company, 1962.

Davis, Russell. *Marine At War.* Scholastic Book Services, N.Y., 1961.

Falk, Stanley. *Bloodiest Victory: Palaus.* New York: Ballantine Books, 1974.

Frank, Benis M. *Okinawa: Touchstone to Victory.* New York: Ballantine Books, 1974.

Frank, Benis M. and Henry I. Shaw, Jr. *Victory and Occupation: History of Marine Corps Operations in World War II,* Vol. V. Washington: Historical Branch, G-3 Division, Headquarters, U.S. Marine Corps (hereinafter HQMC), 1968.

Garand, George W. and Truman R. Strobridge. *Western Pacific Operations: History of U.S. Marine Corps Operations in World War II,* Vol. IV. Washington: Historical Division, HQMC, 1971.

Heinl, Robert D., Jr. *Soldiers of the Sea: The United States Marine Corps, 1775–1962.* Annapolis: United States Naval Institute, 1962.

Hough, Maj. Frank O. *The Assault on Peleliu.* Washington: Historical Division, HQMC, 1950.

Hunt, George P. *Coral Comes High.* New York: Harper and Brothers, 1946.

Isley, Jeter A. and Philip Crowl. *The U.S. Marines and Amphibious War.* Princeton, NJ: Princeton University Press, 1951.

James, D. Clayton. *The Years of MacArthur,* Vol. II, 1941–45. Boston: Houghton Mifflin, 1975.

Leckie, Robert. *Strong Men Armed: The United States Marines Against Japan.* New York: Random House, 1962.

Mayer, S. L., ed. *The Japanese War Machine.* Secaucus, NJ: Chartwell Books, 1976.

McMillan, George. *The Old Breed: A History of the First Marine Division in World War II.* Washington: Infantry Journal Press, 1949.

Moran, John A. *Creating a Legend.* Chicago: Publishing Division, Moran/Andrews, Inc., 1973.

Morison, Samuel Eliot. *The Two-Ocean War.* Boston: Little, Brown and Company, 1963.

Moskin, J. Robert. *The U.S. Marine Corps Story.* New York: McGraw-Hill Book Company, 1977.

Muster Roll of Officers and Enlisted Men of the U.S. Marine Corps: Third Battalion, Fifth Marines, First Marine Division, Fleet Marine Force. From 1 September to 30 September, 1944, inclusive; from 1 October to 31 October, 1944, inclusive; from 1 April to 30 April, 1945, inclusive; from 1 May to 31 May, 1945, inclusive; from 1 June to 30 June, 1945, inclusive. Washington: History and Museums Division, HQMC.

Nichols, Charles S., Jr., and Henry I. Shaw, Jr. *Okinawa: Victory in the Pacific.* Rutland, VT: Charles E. Tuttle Company, 1966. Originally published in 1955 by the Historical Branch, G-3 Division, HQMC.

Paige, Mitchell. *A Marine Named Mitch.* New York: Vantage Press, 1975.

Shaw, Henry I., Jr., Bernard C. Nalty, and Edwin T. Turnbladh. *Central Pacific Drive: History of U.S. Marine Corps Operations in World War II,* Vol. III. Washington: Historical Branch, G-3 Division, HQMC, 1966.

Smith, S. E., ed. and comp. *The United States Marine Corps in World War II.* New York: Random House, 1969.

Steinberg, Rafael. *Island Fighting.* Morristown, NJ: Time-Life Books, 1978.

Stockman, James R. *The First Marine Division on Okinawa: 1 April–30 June 1945.* Washington: Historical Division, HQMC, 1946.

*Time* Magazine, 9 October 1944, p. 29; and 16 October 1944, p. 38.

Toland, John. *The Rising Sun.* New York: Random House, 1970.

United States 1st Marine Division. Operation Plan 1-44. Annex A, B Serial 0003 over 1990-5-80 over 458/332; dated 15 Aug 1944.

———— Palau Operation, Special Action Report, Serial 0775 over 1990-5-80 over 458/390; dated 13 Sept 1944.

———— Field Order No. 1-44 through 9-44. Serial 1990-5-80 over 458/332; dated 20 Sept, 21 Sept, 22 Sept, 25 Sept, 2 Oct, 5 Oct, 8 Oct, 10 Oct, and 13 Oct 1944.

# INDEX*

*This Index has been prepared as an aid to the general reader. For the sake of brevity the names of comrades have been omitted except for those directly involved in the chain of command.